INTRODUCTION TO FINANCIAL ACCOUNTING

Pearson

At Pearson, we have a simple mission: to help people make more of their lives through learning.

We combine innovative learning technology with trusted content and educational expertise to provide engaging and effective learning experience that serve people wherever and whenever they are learning.

We enable our customers to access a wide and expanding range of market-leading content from world-renowned authors and develop their own tailor-made book. From classroom to boardroom, our curriculum materials, digital learning tools and testing programmes help to educate millions of people worldwide — more than any other private enterprise.

Every day our work helps learning flourish, and wherever learning flourishes, so do people.

To learn more, please visit us at: www.pearson.com/uk

INTRODUCTION TO FINANCIAL ACCOUNTING

A customised edition of

Accounting and Finance: An Introduction
Tenth Edition
Eddie McLaney and Peter Atrill

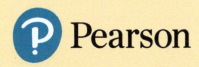

Harlow, England • London • New York • Boston • San Francisco • Toronto • Sydney • Dubai • Singapore • Hong Kong
Tokyo • Seoul • Taipei • New Dehli • Cape Town • São Paulo • Mexico City • Madrid • Amsterdam • Munich • Paris • Milan

Pearson
KAO Two
KAO Park
Harlow
Essex CM17 9NA

And associated companies throughout the world

Visit us on the World Wide Web at:
www.pearson.com/uk

Compiled from:

Accounting and Finance: An Introduction
Tenth Edition
Eddie McLaney and Peter Atrill
ISBN 978-1-292-31226-2
© Prentice Hall Europe 1999 (print)
© Pearson Education Limited 2002, 2005, 2008, 2010, 2012 (print)
© Pearson Education Limited 2014, 2016, 2018, 2020 (print and electronic)

ISBN 978-1-83961-745-4

Printed and bound in Great Britain by CPI Group.

Contents

CHAPTER 1

Introduction to accounting and finance

Introduction

We begin this opening chapter by considering the roles of accounting and finance. We shall then go on to identify the main users of financial information and discuss their information needs. We shall see how both accounting and finance can be valuable tools in helping users improve the quality of their decisions. In subsequent chapters, we develop this decision-making theme by examining in some detail the kinds of financial reports and methods used to aid decision making.

Since this book is mainly concerned with accounting and financial decision making for private-sector businesses, we shall devote some time to examining the business environment. We shall consider the purpose of a private-sector business, the main forms of business enterprise and the ways in which a business may be structured. We shall also consider what the key financial objective of a business is likely to be. These are all important considerations as they help to shape the kind of accounting and financial information that is produced.

Learning outcomes

When you have completed this chapter, you should be able to:

- explain the nature and roles of accounting and finance;

- identify the main users of financial information and discuss their needs;

- identify and discuss the characteristics that make accounting information useful; and

- explain the purpose of a business and describe how businesses are organised and structured.

What are accounting and finance?

Let us start by trying to understand the purpose of each. **Accounting** is concerned with *collecting, analysing* and *communicating* financial information. The ultimate aim is to help those using this information to make more informed decisions. Unless the financial information being communicated can improve the quality of decisions made by users, there is really no point in producing it. We shall see who the main users are, and why they use financial information, a little later in the chapter.

Sometimes the impression is given that the purpose of accounting is simply to prepare financial (accounting) reports on a regular basis. While it is true that accountants undertake this kind of work, it does not represent an end in itself. As already mentioned, the ultimate aim of the accountant's work is to give users better financial information on which to base their decisions. This decision-making perspective of accounting fits in with the theme of this book and shapes the way in which we deal with each topic.

Finance (or financial management), like accounting, exists to help decision makers. It is concerned with the ways in which funds for a business are raised and invested. This lies at the very heart of what business is about. In essence, a business exists to raise funds from investors (owners and lenders) and then to use those funds to make investments (in equipment, premises, inventories and so on) in order to create wealth. As businesses often raise and invest large amounts over long periods, the quality of the financing and investment decisions can have a profound impact on their fortunes.

The way in which funds are raised must fit with the particular needs of the business. An understanding of finance should help in identifying:

- the main forms of finance available;
- the costs, benefits and risks of each form of finance;
- the risks associated with each form of finance; and
- the role of financial markets in supplying finance.

Once funds are raised, they must be invested in a way that will provide the business with a worthwhile return. An understanding of finance should also help in evaluating the risks and returns associated with an investment.

There is little point in trying to make a sharp distinction between accounting and finance. We have seen that both are concerned with the financial aspects of decision making. Furthermore, there are many overlaps and interconnections between the two areas. For example, accounting reports are a major source of information for financing and investment decisions.

Who are the users of accounting information?

For accounting information to be useful, the accountant must be clear *for whom* the information is being prepared and *for what purpose* the information will be used. There are likely to be various groups of people (known as 'user groups') with an interest in a particular organisation, in the sense of needing to make decisions about it. For the typical private-sector business, the more important of these groups are shown in Figure 1.1. Take a look at this figure and then try Activity 1.1.

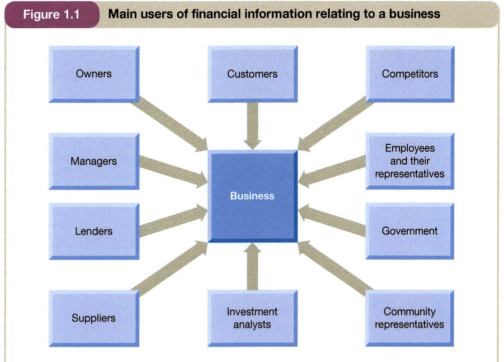

Figure 1.1   **Main users of financial information relating to a business**

Several user groups have an interest in accounting information relating to a business. The majority of these are outside the business but, nevertheless, have a stake in it. This is not meant to be an exhaustive list of potential users; however, the groups identified are normally the most important.

Activity 1.1

Ptarmigan Insurance plc (PI) is a large motor insurance business. Taking the user groups identified in Figure 1.1, suggest, for each group, the sorts of decisions likely to be made about PI and the factors to be taken into account when making these decisions.

Your answer may be along the following lines:

User group	Decision
Customers	Whether to take further motor policies with PI. This might involve an assessment of PI's ability to continue in business and to meet customers' needs, particularly in respect of any insurance claims made.
Competitors	How best to compete against PI or, perhaps, whether to leave the market on the grounds that it is not possible to compete profitably with PI. This might involve competitors using PI's performance in various respects as a 'benchmark' when evaluating their own performance. They might also try to assess PI's financial strength and to identify significant changes that may signal PI's future actions (for example, raising funds as a prelude to market expansion).

Activity 1.1 *continued*

User group	Decision
Employees	Whether to continue working for PI and, if so, whether to demand higher rewards for doing so. The future plans, profits and financial strength of the business are likely to be of particular interest when making these decisions.
Government	Whether PI should pay tax and, if so, how much, whether it complies with agreed pricing policies, whether financial support is needed and so on. In making these decisions an assessment of PI's profits, sales revenues and financial strength would be made.
Community representatives	Whether to allow PI to expand its premises and/or whether to provide economic support for the business. When making such decisions, PI's ability to continue to provide employment for the community, its use of community resources, and its likely willingness to fund environmental improvements are likely to be important considerations.
Investment analysts	Whether to advise clients to invest in PI. This would involve an assessment of the likely risks and future returns associated with PI.
Suppliers	Whether to continue to supply PI with goods and services and, if so, whether to supply these on credit. This would require an assessment of PI's ability to pay for any goods and services supplied at the due dates.
Lenders	Whether to lend money to PI and/or whether to require repayment of any existing loans. PI's ability to pay the interest and to repay the principal sum on time would be important factors in such decisions.
Managers	Whether the performance of the business needs to be improved. Performance to date would be compared with earlier plans or some other 'benchmark' to decide whether action needs to be taken. Managers may also wish to consider a change in PI's future direction. This may involve determining whether the business has the financial flexibility and resources to take on new challenges.
Owners	Whether to invest more in PI or to sell all, or part, of the investment currently held. This would involve an assessment of the likely risks and returns associated with PI. Owners may also be involved with decisions on the rewards offers to senior managers. When doing so, the financial performance of the business would normally be taken into account.

Although this answer covers many of the key points, you may have identified other decisions and/or other factors to be taken into account by each group.

The conflicting interests of users

We have just seen that each user group will have its own particular interests. There is always a risk, however, that the interests of the various user groups will collide. The distribution of a particular business's wealth provides the most likely area for collisions to take place. Take, for example, the position of owners and managers. Although managers are appointed to act in the best interests of the owners, they may not always do so. Instead, they may use the wealth of the business to award themselves large pay rises, to furnish large offices or to buy expensive cars for their own use. Accounting can play an important role in monitoring and reporting how various groups benefit from the business. Owners may, therefore, rely on accounting information to see whether pay and benefits received by managers are appropriate and are in line with agreed policies.

There is also a potential collision of interest between lenders and owners. Funds loaned to a business, for example, may not be used for their intended purpose. They may be withdrawn by the owners for their own use rather than used to expand the business as agreed. Thus, lenders may rely on accounting information to see whether the owners have kept to the terms of the loan agreement.

Activity 1.2

Can you think of other examples where accounting information may be relied on by a user group to see whether the distribution of business wealth is appropriate and/or in line with particular agreements? Try to think of at least one example.

Two possible examples that spring to mind are:

- employees wishing to check that they are receiving a 'fair share' of the wealth created by the business and that managers are complying with agreed profit-sharing schemes; and
- governments wishing to check that the owners of a monopoly do not benefit from excessive profits and that any pricing rules concerning the monopoly's goods or services have not been broken.

You may have thought of other examples.

How useful is accounting information?

No one would seriously claim that accounting information fully meets all of the needs of each of the various user groups. Accounting is still a developing subject and we still have much to learn about user needs and the ways in which these needs should be met. Nevertheless, the information contained in accounting reports should help users make decisions relating to the business. It should reduce uncertainty about the financial position and performance of the business. It should also help to answer questions concerning the availability of funds to pay owners a return, to repay loans, to reward employees and so on.

Typically, there is no close substitute for the information provided by the financial statements. Thus, if users cannot glean the required information from the financial statements, it is often unavailable to them. Other sources of information concerning the financial health of a business are normally much less useful.

Activity 1.3

What other sources of information might, say, an investment analyst use in an attempt to gain an impression of the financial position and performance of a business? (Try to think of at least four.) What kind of information might be gleaned from these sources?

Activity 1.3 *continued*

Other sources of information available include:

- meetings with managers of the business;
- public announcements made by the business;
- newspaper and magazine articles;
- websites, including the website of the business;
- radio and TV reports;
- information-gathering agencies (for example, agencies that assess businesses' credit-worthiness or credit ratings);
- industry reports; and
- economy-wide reports.

These sources can provide information on various aspects of the business, such as new products or services being offered, management changes, new contracts offered or awarded, the competitive environment within which the business operates, the impact of new technology, changes in legislation, changes in interest rates and future levels of inflation.

The kind of information identified in Activity 1.3 is not really a substitute for accounting information. Rather, it is best used in conjunction with accounting information to provide a clearer picture of the financial health of a business.

Evidence on the usefulness of accounting

There are arguments and convincing evidence that accounting information is at least *perceived* as being useful to users. Numerous research surveys have asked users to rank the importance of accounting reports, in relation to other sources of information, for decision-making purposes. Generally, these studies have found that users rank accounting information very highly. There is also considerable evidence that businesses choose to produce accounting information that exceeds the minimum requirements imposed by accounting regulations. (For example, businesses often produce a considerable amount of accounting information for managers, which is not required by any regulations.) Presumably, the cost of producing this additional accounting information is justified on the grounds that users find it useful. Such arguments and evidence, however, leave unanswered the question of whether the information produced is actually used for decision-making purposes, that is: does it affect people's behaviour?

It is normally very difficult to assess the impact of accounting on decision making. One situation arises, however, where the impact of accounting information can be observed and measured. This is where the **shares** (portions of ownership of a business) are traded on a stock exchange. The evidence shows that, when a business makes an announcement concerning its accounting profits, the prices at which shares are traded and the volume of shares traded often change significantly. This suggests that investors are changing their views about the future prospects of the business as a result of this new information becoming available to them. This, in turn, leads some of them to make a decision either to buy or to sell shares in the business.

While there is evidence that accounting reports are seen as useful and are used for decision-making purposes, it is impossible to measure just how useful they really are to users.

Activity 1.4

Can you figure out why it is impossible to measure this?

Accounting reports will usually represent only one input to a particular decision. The weight attached to them by the decision maker, and the resulting benefits, cannot normally be accurately assessed.

We cannot say with certainty, therefore, whether the cost of producing these reports represents value for money.

It is possible, however, to identify the kinds of qualities which accounting information must possess in order to be useful. Where these qualities are lacking, the usefulness of the information will be diminished. Let us now consider this point in more detail.

Providing a service

One way of viewing accounting is as a form of service. The user groups identified in Figure 1.1 can be seen as 'clients' and the accounting (financial) information produced can be seen as the service provided. The value of this service to these 'clients' can be judged according to whether the accounting information meets their needs.

To be useful to users, particularly investors and lenders, the information provided should possess certain qualities, or characteristics. In particular, it must be relevant and it must faithfully represent what it is supposed to represent. These two qualities, **relevance** and **faithful representation**, are regarded as fundamental qualities and require further explanation.

- *Relevance.* Accounting information should make a difference. That is, it should be capable of influencing decisions made. To do this, it must help to predict future events (such as predicting the next year's profit), or help to confirm past events (such as establishing the previous year's profit), or do both. By confirming past events, users can check on the accuracy of their earlier predictions. This may, in turn, help them to improve the ways in which they make predictions in the future.

  To be relevant, accounting information must cross a threshold of **materiality**. An item of information should be considered material, or significant, if its omission or misstatement would change the decisions that users make.

Activity 1.5

Do you think that information that is material for one business will also be material for all other businesses?

No. It will often vary from one business to the next. What is material will normally depend on factors such as the size of the business, the nature of the information and the amounts involved.

Ultimately, what is considered material is a matter of judgement. When making this kind of judgement, managers should consider how this information is likely to be used. If a piece of information is not considered material, it should not be included within the accounting reports. It will merely clutter them up and, perhaps, interfere with the users' ability to interpret them.

● *Faithful representation.* Accounting information should portray what it is supposed to portray. To do so, the information provided must reflect the substance of what has occurred rather than simply its legal form. Take, for example, a manufacturer that provides goods to a retailer on a sale-or-return basis. The manufacturer may wish to treat this arrangement as two separate transactions. Thus, a contract may be agreed for the sale of the goods and a separate contract agreed for the return of the goods, if unsold by the retailer. This may result in a sale being reported when the goods are delivered to the retailer even though they are returned at a later date. The economic substance, however, is that the manufacturer made no sale as the goods were subsequently returned. They were simply moved from the manufacturer's business to the retailer's business and then back again. Accounting reports should reflect this economic substance. To do otherwise would be misleading.

To provide a perfectly faithful portrayal, the information provided should be complete. In other words, it should incorporate everything needed to understand what is being portrayed. This will normally include a description of its nature, some suitable numerical measurement and, where necessary, explanations of important facts. Information should also be neutral, which means that the information should be presented and selected without bias. No attempt should be made to manipulate the information is such a way as to influence user attitudes and behaviour. Finally, it should be free from error. This is not the same as saying that it must be perfectly accurate; this may not be possible. Accounting information often contains estimates, such as future costs and sales, which may turn out to be inaccurate. Nevertheless, estimates can still be faithfully represented providing they are accurately described and properly prepared.

Activity 1.6

In practice, do you think that each piece of accounting information produced will be perfectly complete, neutral and free from error?

Probably not – however, each piece of information should be produced with these aims in mind.

Accounting information must contain both fundamental qualities if it is to be useful. There is little point in producing information that is relevant, but which lacks faithful representation, or producing information that is irrelevant, even if it is faithfully represented.

Further qualities

Where accounting information is both relevant and faithfully represented, there are other qualities that, if present, can *enhance* its usefulness. These are **comparability, verifiability, timeliness** and **understandability**. Each of these qualities is now considered.

- *Comparability.* When making choices, users of accounting information often seek to make comparisons. They may want to compare performance of the business over time (for example, profit this year compared to last year). They may also want to compare certain aspects of business performance (such as the level of sales achieved during the year) to those of similar businesses. Better comparisons can be made where the accounting system treats items that are alike in the same way. Items that are not alike, on the other hand, should not be treated as though they are. Users must be able to detect both similarities and differences in items being compared.

- *Verifiability.* This quality provides assurance to users that the accounting information provided faithfully portrays what it is supposed to portray. Accounting information is verifiable where different, independent experts could reach broad agreement that it provides a faithful portrayal. Verification can be direct, such as checking a bank account balance, or indirect, such as checking the underlying assumptions and methods used to derive an estimate of a future cost.

- *Timeliness.* Accounting information should be made available in time for users to make their decisions. A lack of timeliness will undermine the usefulness of the information. Broadly speaking, the later accounting information is produced, the less useful it becomes.

- *Understandability.* Accounting information should be set out in as clear and as concise a form as possible. Nevertheless, some accounting information may be too complex to be presented in an easily digestible form. This does not mean, however, that it should be ignored. To do so would result in reporting only a partial view of financial matters. (See Reference 1 at the end of the chapter.)

Activity 1.7

Accounting reports are aimed at users with a reasonable knowledge of accounting and business and who are prepared to invest time in studying them. Do you think, however, that accounting reports should be understandable to users without any knowledge of accounting or business?

It would be very helpful if everyone could understand accounting reports. This, however, is unrealistic as complex financial events and transactions cannot normally be expressed in simple terms. Any attempts to do so are likely to produce a very distorted picture of reality.

It is probably best that we regard accounting reports in the same way that we regard a report written in a foreign language. To understand either of these, we need to have had some preparation. When producing accounting reports, it is normally assumed that the user not only has a reasonable knowledge of business and accounting but is also prepared to invest some time in studying the reports. Nevertheless, the onus is clearly on accountants to provide information in a way that makes it as understandable as possible to non-accountants.

It is worth emphasising that the four qualities just discussed cannot make accounting information useful. They can only enhance the usefulness of information that is already relevant and faithfully represented.

Weighing up the costs and benefits

Even though an item of accounting information may have all the qualities described, this does not automatically mean that it should be collected and reported to users. There is still one more hurdle to jump. Consider Activity 1.8.

Activity 1.8

Suppose an item of information is capable of being provided. It is relevant to a particular decision and can be faithfully represented. It is also comparable, verifiable and timely, and can be understood by the decision maker.

Can you think of the reason why, in practice, you might choose not to produce the information?

The reason is that you judge the cost of doing so to be greater than the potential benefit of having the information. This cost–benefit issue will limit the amount of accounting information provided.

In theory, a particular item of accounting information should only be produced if the costs of providing it are less than the benefits, or value, to be derived from its use. Figure 1.2 shows the relationship between the costs and value of providing additional accounting information.

Figure 1.2 | **Relationship between costs and the value of providing additional accounting information**

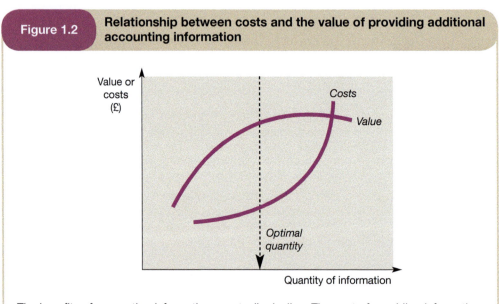

The benefits of accounting information eventually decline. The cost of providing information, however, will rise with each additional piece of information. The optimal level of information provision is where the gap between the value of the information and the cost of providing it is at its greatest.

The figure shows how the value of information received by the decision maker eventually begins to decline. This is, perhaps, because additional information becomes less relevant, or because of the problems that a decision maker may have in processing the sheer quantity of information provided. The costs of providing the information, however, will increase with each additional piece of information. The broken line indicates the point at which the gap between the value of information and the cost of providing that information is at its greatest. This represents the optimal amount of information that can be provided. This theoretical model, however, poses a number of problems in practice.

To illustrate the practical problems of establishing the value of information, let us assume that we accidentally reversed our car into a wall in a car park. This resulted in a dented boot and scraped paintwork. We want to have the dent taken out and the paintwork resprayed at a local garage. We know that the nearest garage would charge £450 but we believe that other local garages may offer to do the job for a lower price. The only way of finding out the prices at other garages is to visit them, so that they can see the extent of the damage. Visiting the garages will involve using some fuel and will take up some of our time. Is it worth the cost of finding out the price for the job at the various local garages? The answer, as we have seen, is that if the cost of discovering the price is less than the potential benefit, it is worth having that information.

To identify the various prices for the job, there are several points to be considered, including:

- How many garages shall we visit?
- What is the cost of fuel to visit each garage?
- How long will it take to make all the garage visits?
- At what price do we value our time?

The economic benefit of having the information on the price of the job is probably even harder to assess. The following points need to be considered:

- What is the cheapest price that we might be quoted for the job?
- How likely is it that we shall be quoted a price cheaper than £450?

As we can imagine, the answers to these questions may be far from clear – remember that we have only contacted the local garage so far. When assessing the value of accounting information, we are confronted with similar problems.

Producing accounting information can be very costly. Furthermore, these costs can be difficult to quantify. Direct, out-of-pocket costs, such as salaries of accounting staff, are not usually a problem, but these are only part of the total costs involved. There are other costs such as the cost of users' time spent on analysing and interpreting the information provided. These costs are much more difficult to quantify and may well vary between users.

Activity 1.9

What about the economic benefits of producing accounting information? Do you think it is easier, or harder, to assess the economic benefits of accounting information than to assess the costs of producing it?

It is normally much harder to assess the benefits. We saw earlier that, even if we could accurately measure the economic benefits arising from a particular decision, we must bear in mind that accounting information will be only one factor influencing that decision. Furthermore, the benefits of accounting information, like the associated costs, can vary between users.

There are no easy answers to the problem of weighing costs and benefits. Although it is possible to apply some 'science' to the problem, a lot of subjective judgement is normally involved.

The qualities, or characteristics, influencing the usefulness of accounting information, which we have just discussed, are summarised in Figure 1.3.

Figure 1.3 **The qualities that influence the usefulness of accounting information**

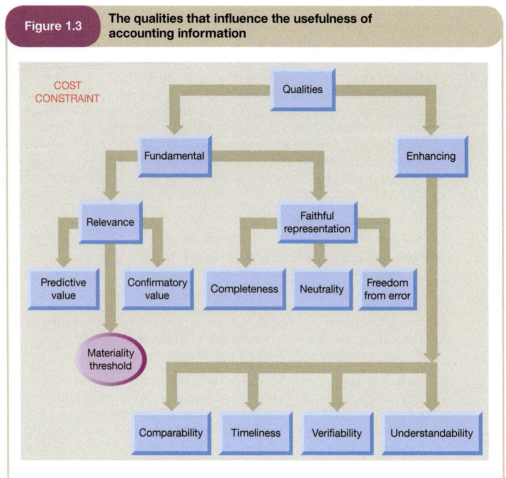

There are two fundamental qualities that determine the usefulness of accounting information. In addition, there are four qualities that enhance the usefulness of accounting information. The benefits of providing the information, however, should outweigh the costs.

Accounting as an information system

We have already seen that accounting can be seen as the provision of a service to 'clients'. Another way of viewing accounting is as a part of the business's total information system. Users, both inside and outside the business, have to make decisions concerning the allocation of scarce resources. To ensure that these resources are efficiently allocated, users often need financial information on which to base decisions. It is the role of the accounting system to provide this information.

The **accounting information system** should have certain features that are common to all information systems within a business. These are:

- identifying and capturing relevant information (in this case financial information);
- recording, in a systematic way, the information collected;
- analysing and interpreting the information collected; and
- reporting the information in a manner that suits the needs of users.

The relationship between these features is set out in Figure 1.4.

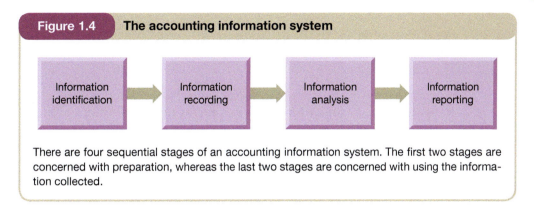

Figure 1.4   The accounting information system

There are four sequential stages of an accounting information system. The first two stages are concerned with preparation, whereas the last two stages are concerned with using the information collected.

Given the decision-making emphasis of this book, we shall be concerned primarily with the final two elements of the process: the analysis and reporting of financial information. We shall place much more emphasis on the way in which information is used by, and is useful to, users rather than the way in which it is identified and recorded.

Effective accounting information systems are an essential ingredient of an efficient business. When they fail, the results can be disastrous. **Real World 1.1** describes how spreadsheets, which are widely used to prepare accounting and financial information, may introduce errors that can lead to poor financial decisions.

Real World 1.1

Systems error!

Almost one in five large businesses have suffered financial losses as a result of errors in spreadsheets, according to F1F9, which provides financial modelling and business forecasting to large businesses. It warns of looming financial disasters as 71 per cent of large British business always use spreadsheets for key financial decisions.

The company's new white paper entitled *Capitalism's Dirty Secret* showed that the abuse of humble spreadsheet could have far-reaching consequences. Spreadsheets are used in the preparation of British company accounts worth up to £1.9 trillion and the UK manufacturing sector uses spreadsheets to make pricing decisions for up to £170 billion worth of business.

In total, spreadsheet calculations represent up to £38 billion of British private sector investment decisions per year, data harvested through YouGov found. Yet 16 per cent of large companies have admitted finding inaccurate information in spreadsheets more than 10 times in 2014.

Grenville Croll, a spreadsheet risk expert, said of the findings: 'Spreadsheets have been shown to be fallible yet they underpin the operation of the financial system. If the uncontrolled use of spreadsheets continues to occur in highly leveraged markets and companies, it is only a matter of time before another "Black Swan" event occurs causing catastrophic loss.'

The report warns that while 33 per cent of large businesses report poor decision-making as a result of spreadsheet problems, a third of the financial decision-makers using spreadsheets in large UK businesses are still given zero training.

Source: Adapted extract from Burn-Callander, R. (2015) Stupid errors in spreadsheets could lead to Britain's next corporate disaster, www.telegraph.co.uk, 7 April.

Management accounting and financial accounting

Accounting is usually seen as having two distinct strands. These are:

- **management accounting**, which seeks to meet the accounting needs of managers; and
- **financial accounting**, which seeks to meet the needs of owners and lenders. It should also, however, be useful to other users that were identified earlier in the chapter (see Figure 1.1).

The difference in their targeted user groups has led to each strand of accounting developing along different lines. The main areas of difference are as follows:

- *Nature of the reports produced.* Financial accounting reports tend to be general purpose. As mentioned above, they are aimed primarily at providers of finance (owners and lenders) but contain financial information that should also be useful for a broad range of external users. Management accounting reports, on the other hand, are often specific-purpose reports. They are designed with a particular decision in mind and/or for a particular manager.
- *Level of detail.* Financial accounting reports provide users with a broad overview of the performance and position of the business for a period. As a result, information is aggregated (that is, added together) and detail is often lost. Management accounting reports, however, often provide managers with considerable detail to help them with a particular operational decision.
- *Regulations.* Financial accounting reports, for many businesses, are subject to accounting regulations imposed by the law and accounting rule makers. These regulations often require a standard content and, perhaps, a standard format to be adopted. Management accounting reports, on the other hand, are not subject to regulation and can be designed to meet the needs of particular managers.

Activity 1.10

Why are financial accounting reports subject to regulation, whereas management accounting reports are not?

Financial accounting reports are for external publication. To protect external users, who depend on the quality of information provided by managers, they are subject to regulation. Management accounting reports, on the other hand, are produced exclusively for managers and so are for internal use only.

- *Reporting interval.* For most businesses, financial accounting reports are produced on an annual basis, though some large businesses produce half-yearly reports and a few produce quarterly ones. Management accounting reports will be produced as frequently as needed by managers. A sales manager, for example, may require routine sales reports on a daily, weekly or monthly basis, so as to monitor performance closely. Special-purpose reports can also be prepared when the occasion demands: for example, where an evaluation is required of a proposed investment in new equipment.
- *Time orientation.* Financial accounting reports reflect the performance and position of the business for the past period. In essence, they are backward looking. Management accounting reports, on the other hand, often provide information concerning future performance as well as past performance. It is an oversimplification, however, to suggest that financial accounting reports never incorporate expectations concerning the future. Occasionally, businesses will release projected information to other users in an

attempt to raise capital or to fight off unwanted takeover bids. Even preparation of the routine financial accounting reports typically requires making some judgements about the future (as we shall see in Chapter 3).

- *Range and quality of information.* Two key points are worth mentioning. First, financial accounting reports concentrate on information that can be quantified in monetary terms. Management accounting also produces such reports, but is also more likely to produce reports that contain information of a non-financial nature, such as physical volume of inventories, number of sales orders received, number of new products launched, physical output per employee and so on. Second, financial accounting places greater emphasis on the use of objective, verifiable evidence when preparing reports. Management accounting reports may use information that is less objective and verifiable, but nevertheless provide managers with the information they need.

We can see from this that management accounting is less constrained than financial accounting. It may draw from a variety of sources and use information that has varying degrees of reliability. The only real test to be applied when assessing the value of the information produced for managers is whether or not it improves the quality of the decisions made.

The main differences between financial accounting and management accounting are summarised in Figure 1.5.

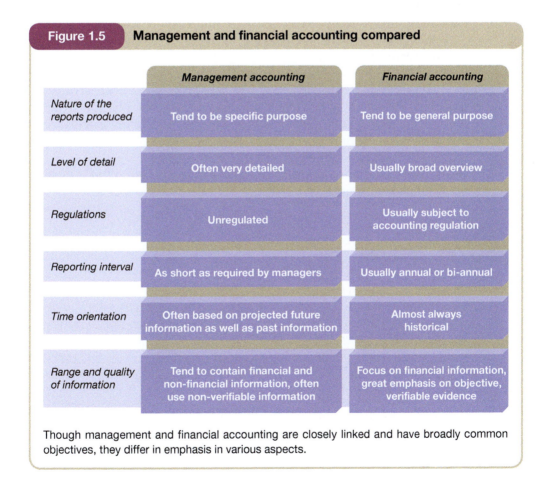

Figure 1.5 **Management and financial accounting compared**

	Management accounting	Financial accounting
Nature of the reports produced	Tend to be specific purpose	Tend to be general purpose
Level of detail	Often very detailed	Usually broad overview
Regulations	Unregulated	Usually subject to accounting regulation
Reporting interval	As short as required by managers	Usually annual or bi-annual
Time orientation	Often based on projected future information as well as past information	Almost always historical
Range and quality of information	Tend to contain financial and non-financial information, often use non-verifiable information	Focus on financial information, great emphasis on objective, verifiable evidence

Though management and financial accounting are closely linked and have broadly common objectives, they differ in emphasis in various aspects.

The differences between management accounting and financial accounting suggest that there are differences in the information needs of managers and those of other users. While differences undoubtedly exist, there is also a good deal of overlap between these needs.

Activity 1.11

Can you think of any areas of overlap between the information needs of managers and those of other users? (*Hint*: Think about the time orientation and the level of detail of accounting information.)

Two points that spring to mind are:

● Managers will, at times, be interested in receiving a historical overview of business operations of the sort provided to other users.
● Other users would be interested in receiving detailed information relating to the future, such as the planned level of profits and non-financial information, such as the state of the sales order book and the extent of product innovations.

To some extent, differences between the two strands of accounting reflect differences in access to financial information. Managers have much more control over the form and content of the information that they receive. Other users have to rely on what managers are prepared to provide or what financial reporting regulations insist must be provided. Although the scope of financial accounting reports has increased over time, fears concerning loss of competitive advantage and user ignorance about the reliability of forecast data have resulted in other users not receiving the same detailed and wide-ranging information as that available to managers.

In the past, accounting systems were biased in favour of providing information for external users. Financial accounting requirements were the main priority and management accounting suffered as it tended to be an offshoot of financial accounting. Survey evidence suggests, however, that this is no longer the case. Modern management accounting systems usually provide managers with information that is relevant to their needs rather than that determined by external reporting requirements. External reporting cycles, however, retain some influence over management accounting. Managers tend to be aware of external users' expectations. (See Reference 2 at the end of the chapter.)

Scope of this book

This book covers both financial accounting and management accounting topics. The next six chapters (Part 1, Chapters 2 to 7) are broadly concerned with financial accounting, and the following six (Part 2, Chapters 8 to 13) with management accounting. The final chapters of the book (Part 3, Chapters 14 to 16) is concerned with the financial management of the business, that is, with issues relating to the financing and investing activities of the business. As we have seen, accounting information is usually vitally important for financial management decisions.

The changing face of accounting

Over the past fifty years, the environment within which businesses operate has become increasingly turbulent and competitive. Various reasons have been identified to explain these changes, including:

- the increasing sophistication of customers;
- the availability of rapid and sophisticated forms of information and communication (such as the internet);
- the development of a global economy where national frontiers become less important;
- rapid changes in technology;
- the deregulation of domestic markets (for example, electricity, water and gas);
- increasing pressure from owners (shareholders) for competitive economic returns; and
- the increasing volatility of financial markets.

This new, more complex, environment has brought new challenges for managers and other users of accounting information. Their needs have changed and both financial accounting and management accounting have had to respond. To meet the changing needs of users, there has been a radical review of the kind of information to be reported.

The changing business environment has given added impetus to the search for a clear conceptual framework, or framework of principles, upon which to base financial accounting reports. Various attempts have been made to clarify their purpose and to provide a more solid foundation for the development of accounting rules. Work on developing a conceptual framework tries to address such fundamental questions as:

- Who are the users of financial accounting information?
- What kinds of financial accounting reports should be prepared and what should they contain?
- How should items such as profit and asset values be identified and measured?

The internationalisation of businesses has created a need for accounting rules to have an international reach. This has led to an increasing harmonisation of accounting rules across national frontiers. It can no longer be assumed that users of accounting information relating to a particular business are based in the country in which the business operates. Neither can it be assumed that the users are familiar with the accounting rules of that country.

Activity (1.12)

How should the harmonisation of accounting rules benefit:

(a) an international investor?
(b) an international business?

To answer this activity, you may have thought of the following:

(a) An international investor should benefit because accounting definitions and policies used in preparing financial accounting reports will not vary between countries. This should make comparisons of performance between businesses operating in different countries much easier.

(b) An international business should benefit because the cost of producing accounting reports to comply with the rules of different countries can be expensive. Harmonisation can, therefore, lead to significant cost savings. It may also broaden the appeal of the business among international investors. Where there are common accounting rules, they may have greater confidence to invest.

In response to criticisms that the financial reports of some businesses are opaque and difficult for users to interpret, great efforts have been made to improve reporting rules. Accounting rule makers have tried to ensure that the accounting policies of businesses are more comparable and transparent and that the financial reports provide a more faithful portrayal of economic reality.

Management accounting has also changed by becoming more outward looking in its focus. In the past, information provided to managers has been largely restricted to that collected within the business. However, the attitude and behaviour of customers and rival businesses have now become the object of much information gathering. Increasingly, successful businesses are those that are able to secure and maintain competitive advantage over their rivals.

To obtain this advantage, businesses have become more 'customer driven' (that is, concerned with satisfying customer needs). This has led to the production of management accounting information that provides details of customers and the market, such as customer evaluation of services provided and market share. In addition, information about the costs and profits of rival businesses, which can be used as 'benchmarks' by which to gauge competitiveness, is gathered and reported.

To compete successfully, businesses must also find ways of managing costs. The cost base of modern businesses is under continual review and this, in turn, has led to the development of more sophisticated methods of measuring and controlling costs.

Why do I need to know anything about accounting and finance?

At this point you may be asking yourself, 'Why do I need to study accounting and finance? I don't intend to become an accountant!' Well, from the explanation of what accounting and finance is about, which has broadly been the subject of this chapter so far, it should be clear that the accounting/finance function within a business is a central part of its management information system. On the basis of information provided by the system, managers make decisions concerning the allocation of resources. As we have seen, these decisions may concern whether to:

- continue with certain business operations;
- invest in particular projects; and
- sell particular products.

These decisions can have a profound effect on all those connected with the business. It is important, therefore, that *all* those who intend to work in a business should have a fairly clear idea of certain key aspects of accounting and finance. These aspects include:

- how financial reports should be read and interpreted;
- how financial plans are made;
- how investment decisions are made; and
- how businesses are financed.

Many, if not most, students have a career goal of being a manager within a business – perhaps a human resources manager, production manager, marketing manager or IT manager. If you are one of these students, an understanding of accounting and finance is very important. When you become a manager, even a junior one, it is almost certain that you will have to use financial reports to help you to carry out your role. It is equally certain that it is largely on the basis of financial information and reports that your performance as a manager will be judged.

As part of your management role, you will be expected to help in plotting the future path of the business. This can often involve the preparation of forward-looking financial reports and setting financial targets. If you do not understand what the financial reports really mean and the extent to which the financial information is reliable, you will find yourself at a distinct disadvantage to those who do. Along with other managers, you will also be expected to help decide how the limited resources available to the business should be allocated between competing options. This will require an ability to evaluate the costs and benefits of the different options available. Once again, an understanding of accounting and finance is important when carrying out this management task.

This is not to say that you cannot be an effective and successful human resources, production, marketing or IT manager unless you are also a qualified accountant. It does mean, however, that you need to become a bit 'streetwise' in accounting and finance if you are to succeed. The aim of the book is to help you to achieve this.

Accounting for business

We have seen that the needs of the various user groups will determine the kind of accounting information to be provided. The forms of business ownership and the ways in which a business is organised and structured, however, will partly shape those needs. In the sections that follow, we consider the business environment within which accounting information is produced. This should help our understanding of points that crop up in later chapters.

What is the purpose of a business?

Peter Drucker, an eminent management thinker, has argued that 'the purpose of business is to create and keep a customer'. (See Reference 3 at the end of the chapter.) Drucker defined the purpose of a business in this way in 1967, at a time when few businesses adopted this strong customer focus. His view, therefore, represented a radical challenge to the accepted view of what businesses should do. More than fifty years on, however, his approach has become part of the conventional wisdom. It is now widely recognised that, in order to succeed, businesses must focus on satisfying the needs of the customer.

Although the customer has always provided the main source of revenue for a business, this has often been taken for granted. In the past, too many businesses have assumed that the customer would readily accept whatever services or products were on offer. When competition was weak and customers were passive, businesses could operate under this assumption and still make a profit. However, the era of weak competition has passed. Now, customers have much greater choice and are much more assertive concerning their needs. They now demand higher quality services and goods at cheaper prices. They also require that services and goods be delivered faster with an increasing emphasis on the product being tailored to their individual needs. If a particular business cannot meet these needs, a competitor often can. Thus, the business mantra for the current era is '*the customer is king*'. Most businesses now recognise this fact and organise themselves accordingly.

Real World 1.2 describes how the internet and social media have given added weight to this mantra. It points out that dissatisfied customers now have a powerful medium for broadcasting their complaints.

Real World 1.2

The customer is king

The mantra that the 'customer is king' has gained even greater significance among businesses in recent years because of the rise of the internet and social media. In the past, a dissatisfied customer might tell only a few friends about a bad buying experience. As a result, the damage to the reputation of the business concerned would normally be fairly limited. However, nowadays, through the magic of the internet, several hundred people, or more, can be very speedily informed of a bad buying experience.

Businesses are understandably concerned about the potential of the internet to damage reputations, but are their concerns justified? Do customer complaints, which wing their way through cyberspace, have any real effect on the businesses concerned? A Harris Poll survey of 2,000 adults in the UK and US suggests they do and so businesses should sit up and take note. It seems that social media can exert a big influence on customer buying decisions.

The Harris Poll survey, which was conducted online, found that around 20 per cent of those surveyed use social media when making buying decisions. For those in the 18 to 34 age range, the figure rises to almost 40 per cent. Furthermore, 60 per cent of those surveyed indicated that they would avoid buying from a business that receives poor customer reviews for its products or services.

The moral of this tale appears to be that, in this internet age, businesses must work even harder to keep their customers happy if they are to survive and prosper.

Source: Based on information in Miesbach, A. (2015) Yes, the customer is still king, www.icmi.com, 30 October.

What kinds of business ownership exist?

The particular form of business ownership has certain implications for financial accounting and so we need to be clear about the main forms of ownership that can arise. There are basically three arrangements for private-sector businesses:

- sole proprietorship;
- partnership; and
- limited company.

Let us now consider these in turn.

Sole proprietorship

Sole proprietorship, as the name suggests, is where an individual is the sole owner of a business. This type of business is often quite small (as measured, for example, by sales revenue generated or number of staff employed); however, the number of such businesses is very large indeed. Examples of sole-proprietor businesses can be found in most business sectors but particularly within the service sector. Hence, services such as electrical repairs, picture framing, photography, driving instruction, retail shops and hotels have a large proportion of sole-proprietor businesses.

The sole-proprietor business is very easy to set up. No formal procedures are required and operations can often commence immediately (unless special permission is required because of the nature of the trade or service, such as running licensed premises (a pub)).

The owner can decide the way in which the business is to be conducted and has the flexibility to restructure or dissolve the business whenever it suits. The law does not recognise the sole-proprietor business as being separate from the owner, so the business will cease on the death of the owner.

Although the owner must produce accounting information about the business to satisfy the taxation authorities, there is no legal requirement to provide it to other user groups. Some user groups, however, may demand accounting information about the business and may be in a position to enforce their demands (for example, a bank requiring accounting information on a regular basis as a condition of a loan). A sole proprietor has unlimited liability which means that no distinction is made between the proprietor's personal wealth and that of the business if there are business debts to be paid.

Partnership

A **partnership** exists where two or more individuals carry on a business together with the intention of making a profit. Partnerships have much in common with sole-proprietor businesses. They are usually quite small in size (although some, such as partnerships of accountants and solicitors, can be very large). They are also easy to set up, as no formal procedures are required (and it is not even necessary to have a written agreement between the partners). The partners can agree whatever arrangements suit them concerning the financial and management aspects of the business. Similarly, the partnership can be restructured or dissolved by agreement between the partners.

Partnerships are not recognised in law as separate entities and so contracts with third parties must be entered into in the name of individual partners. The partners of a business usually have unlimited liability.

Activity 1.13

What are the main advantages and disadvantages that should be considered when deciding between a sole proprietorship and a partnership? Try to think of at least two of each.

The main advantages of a partnership over a sole-proprietor business are:

- sharing the burden of ownership;
- the opportunity to specialise rather than cover the whole range of services (for example, in a solicitors' practice each partner may specialise in a different aspect of the law); and
- the ability to raise capital where this is beyond the capacity of a single individual.

The main disadvantages of a partnership compared with a sole proprietorship are:

- the risks of sharing ownership of a business with unsuitable individuals; and
- the limits placed on individual decision making that a partnership will impose.

Limited company

A **limited company** can range in size from quite small to very large. The number of individuals who subscribe capital and become the owners may be unlimited, which provides the opportunity to create a very large-scale business. The liability of owners, however, is limited (hence 'limited' company), which means that those individuals investing in the company's shares are liable only for debts incurred by the company up to the amount that they have invested or agreed to invest. This cap on the liability of the owners is designed to limit risk and to produce greater confidence to invest. Without such limits on owner liability, it is difficult to see how a modern capitalist economy could operate. In many cases, the owners of a limited company are not involved in the day-to-day running of the business and will, therefore, invest in a business only if there is a clear limit set on the level of investment risk.

Note that this 'limited liability' does not apply to sole proprietors and partners. These people have a legal obligation to meet all of their business debts, if necessary using, what they may have thought of as, private assets (for example, their private houses). This ability of the owners of limited companies to limit their liability can make limited companies a more attractive way of setting up a business, compared with sole proprietorships and partnerships.

The benefit of limited liability, however, imposes certain obligations on such limited companies. To create a limited company, documents of incorporation must be prepared that set out, among other things, the objectives of the business. Furthermore, a framework of regulations exists that places obligations on limited companies concerning the way in which they conduct their affairs. Part of this regulatory framework requires annual financial reports to be made available to owners and lenders and, usually, an annual general meeting of the owners has to be held to approve the reports. In addition, a copy of the annual financial reports must be lodged with the Registrar of Companies for public inspection. In this way, the financial affairs of a limited company enter the public domain.

With the exception of small companies, there is also a requirement for the annual financial reports to be subject to an audit. This involves an independent firm of accountants examining the annual reports and underlying records to see whether the reports provide a true and fair view of the financial health of the company and whether they comply with the relevant accounting rules established by law and by accounting rule makers. Limited companies are considered in more detail later in Chapters 4 and 5.

All of the large household-name UK businesses (Marks and Spencer, Tesco, Shell, Sky, Rolls-Royce, BT, easyJet and so on) are limited companies.

Activity 1.14

What are the main advantages of forming a partnership business rather than a limited liability company? Try to think of at least three.

The main advantages are:

- the ease of setting up the business;
- the degree of flexibility concerning the way in which the business is conducted;
- the degree of flexibility concerning restructuring and dissolution of the business; and
- freedom from administrative burdens imposed by law (for example, the annual general meeting and the need for an independent audit).

As we have just seen, a major disadvantage of a partnership compared with a limited company is that it is not normally possible to limit the liability of all of the partners. There is, however, a hybrid form of business ownership that is referred to as a limited liability partnership (LLP). This has many of the attributes of a normal partnership but differs insofar that the LLP, rather than the individual partners, is responsible for any debts incurred. Accountants and solicitors often use this type of partnership.

This book concentrates on the accounting aspects of limited liability companies because they are, by far, the most important in economic terms. The early chapters will introduce accounting concepts through examples that do not draw a distinction between the different types of business. Once we have dealt with the basic accounting principles, which are the same for all three types of business, we can then go on to see how they are applied to limited companies.

How are businesses organised?

Most businesses that involve more than a few owners and/or employees are set up as limited companies. Finance will come from the owners (shareholders) both in the form of a direct cash investment to buy shares (in the ownership of the business) and through the shareholders allowing past profits, which belong to them, to be reinvested in the business. Finance will also come from lenders (banks, for example), who earn interest on their loans. Further finance will be provided through suppliers of goods and services being prepared to supply on credit.

In larger limited companies, the owners (shareholders) tend not to be involved in the daily running of the business; instead they appoint a board of directors to manage the business on their behalf. The board is charged with three major tasks:

1 setting the overall direction and strategy for the business;
2 monitoring and controlling the activities of the business; and
3 communicating with shareholders and others connected with the business.

Each board has a chair, elected by the directors, who is responsible for running the board in an efficient manner. In addition, each board has a chief executive officer (CEO) who is responsible for running the business on a day-to-day basis. Occasionally, the roles of chair and CEO are combined, although it is usually considered to be a good idea to separate them in order to prevent a single individual having excessive power.

The board of directors represents the most senior level of management. Below this level, managers are employed, with each manager being given responsibility for a particular part of the business's operations.

Activity 1.15

Why are most larger businesses *not* managed as a single unit by just one manager?

Three common reasons are:

- The sheer volume of activity or number of staff employed makes it impossible for one person to manage them.
- Certain business operations may require specialised knowledge or expertise.
- Geographical remoteness of part of the business operations may make it more practical to manage each location as a separate part, or set of separate parts.

The operations of a business may be divided for management purposes in different ways. For smaller businesses offering a single product or service, separate departments are often created, with each department responsible for a particular function (such as marketing, production, human resources and finance). The managers of each department will then be accountable to the board of directors. In some cases, individual board members may also be departmental managers.

A typical departmental structure, organised along functional lines, is shown in Figure 1.6.

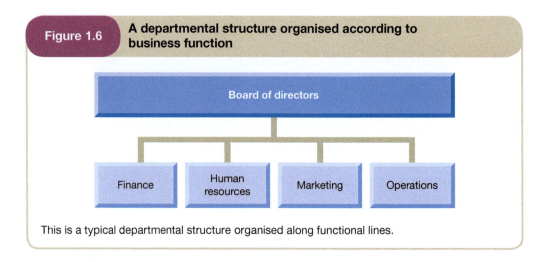

Figure 1.6 **A departmental structure organised according to business function**

This is a typical departmental structure organised along functional lines.

The structure set out in Figure 1.6 may be adapted according to the particular needs of the business. Where, for example, a business has few employees, the human resources function may not form a separate department but may form part of another department. Where business operations are specialised, separate departments may be formed to deal with each specialist area. Example 1.1 illustrates how Figure 1.6 may be modified to meet the needs of a particular business.

Example 1.1

Supercoach Ltd owns a small fleet of coaches that it hires out with drivers for private group travel. The business employs about 50 people. It might be departmentalised as follows:

- *marketing department*, dealing with advertising, dealing with enquiries from potential customers, maintaining good relationships with existing customers and entering into contracts with customers;
- *routing and human resources department*, responsible for the coach drivers' routes, schedules, staff duties and rotas, and problems that arise during a particular job or contract;
- *coach maintenance department*, looking after repair and maintenance of the coaches, buying spares, giving advice on the need to replace old or inefficient coaches;
- *finance department*, responsible for managing the cash flows, costing business activities, pricing new proposals, paying wages and salaries, billing and collecting amounts due from customers, processing and paying invoices from suppliers.

For large businesses that have a diverse geographical spread and/or a wide product range, the simple departmental structure set out in Figure 1.6 will usually have to be adapted. Separate divisions are often created for each geographical area and/or major product group. Each division will be managed separately and will usually enjoy a degree of autonomy. Within each division, however, departments will often be created and organised along functional lines. Some functions providing support across the various divisions, such as human resources, may be undertaken at head office to avoid duplication. The managers of each division will be accountable to the board of directors. In some cases, individual board members may also be divisional managers.

A typical divisional organisational structure is set out in Figure 1.7. Here the main basis of the structure is geographical. North division deals with production and sales in the north and so on.

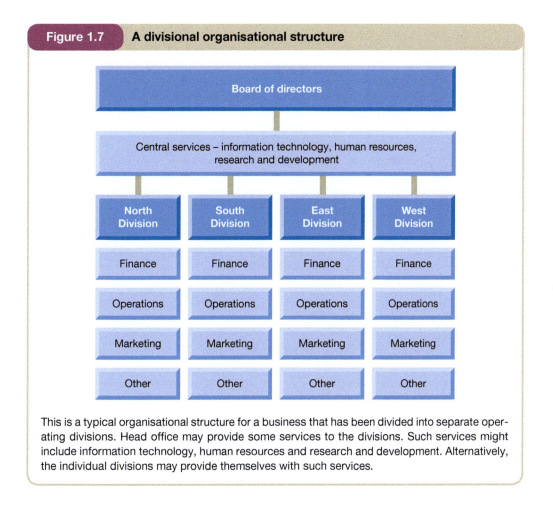

Figure 1.7   **A divisional organisational structure**

This is a typical organisational structure for a business that has been divided into separate operating divisions. Head office may provide some services to the divisions. Such services might include information technology, human resources and research and development. Alternatively, the individual divisions may provide themselves with such services.

Once a particular divisional structure has been established, it need not be permanent. Successful businesses constantly strive to improve their operational efficiency. This could well result in revising their divisional structure. **Real World 1.3** comprises extracts from an article that describes how one well-known business has reorganised in order to simplify operations and to reduce costs.

Real World 1.3

Engineering change

The chief executive of Rolls-Royce has shaken up its senior management team and scrapped two divisions as part of his attempt to turnaround the struggling engineer. Warren East . . . will scrap the aerospace and land & sea divisions that split Rolls into two parts . . . .

The move means that Rolls will operate with five smaller businesses all reporting directly to East. The Rolls chief executive plans to bring in a chief operating officer to assist him in running the company.

Rolls said the revamp will 'simplify the organisation, drive operational excellence and reduce cost'.

The Rolls boss is overhauling the company after it issued five profit warnings in less than two years. East wants to cut costs by between £150 million and £200 million a year. The level of concern about the future of Rolls was underlined earlier this week when it emerged the government has drawn up contingency plans to nationalise its nuclear submarine business or force it to merge with defence manufacturer BAE Systems in the event that the company's performance worsens.

East said: 'The changes we are announcing today are the first important steps in driving operational excellence and returning Rolls-Royce to its long-term trend of profitable growth. This is a company with world-class engineering capability, strong market positions and exceptional long-term prospects.'

Under the new structure Rolls will operate with five divisions from 1 January 2016 – civil aerospace, defence aerospace, marine, nuclear, and power systems.

Source: Extracts from Ruddick G. (2016) Rolls-Royce to scrap two divisions amid restructuring, www.theguardian.com, 16 December.

While both divisional and departmental structures are very popular in practice, it should be noted that other organisational structures are found.

How are businesses managed?

We have already seen that the environment in which businesses operate has become increasingly turbulent and competitive. The effect of these environmental changes has been to make the role of managers more complex and demanding. It has meant that managers have had to find new ways to manage their business. This has increasingly led to the introduction of **strategic management**.

Strategic management is concerned with setting the long-term direction of the business. It involves setting long-term goals and then ensuring that they are implemented effectively. To enable the business to develop a competitive edge, strategic management focuses on doing things differently rather than simply doing things better. It should provide a business with a clear sense of purpose, along with a series of steps to achieve that purpose. The steps taken should link the internal resources of the business to the external environment (competitors, suppliers, customers and so on). This should be done in such a way that any business strengths, such as having a skilled workforce, are exploited and any weaknesses, such as being short of investment finance, are not exposed. To achieve this requires the development of strategies and plans that take account of the business's strengths and weaknesses, as well as the opportunities offered and threats posed by the external environment. Access to a new, expanding market is an example of an opportunity; the decision of a major competitor to reduce prices would normally be a threat. This topic will be considered in more depth in Chapter 12 when we consider business planning and budgeting.

Real World 1.4 provides an indication of the extent to which strategic planning is carried out in practice.

Real World 1.4

Strategic planning high on the list

A survey, carried out in 2017, investigated the use of various management tools throughout the world. It found that strategic planning was used by 48 per cent of those businesses that took part. This made it the most popular of the 25 management tools surveyed. The survey, which has been conducted 16 times in the past 25 years, has placed strategic planning consistently among the top ten management tools employed by businesses. As well as being in widespread use, strategic planning scored highly in terms of user satisfaction, with a mean score of 4.03 out of 5.

The results were based on a survey of 1,268 senior executives throughout the world.

Source: Rigby, D. and Bilodeau, B. (2018) *Management Tools and Trends 2017*, Bain and Company.

The quest for wealth creation

A business is normally formed to enhance the wealth of its owners. Throughout this book, we shall assume that this is its main objective. This may come as a surprise, as other objectives may be pursued that relate to the needs of others with a stake in the business.

Activity 1.16

What other objectives might a business pursue? Try to think of at least two.

A business may seek:

- to provide well-paid jobs and good working conditions for its employees;
- to conserve the environment for the local community;
- to produce products or services that will benefit its customers; and/or
- to support local suppliers.

You may have thought of others.

Although a business may pursue other such objectives, it is normally set up primarily with a view to increasing the wealth of its owners. In practice, the behaviour of businesses over time appears to be consistent with this objective.

Within a market economy there are strong competitive forces at work that ensure that failure to enhance owners' wealth will not be tolerated for long. Competition for the funds provided by the owners and competition for managers' jobs will normally mean that the owners' interests will prevail. If the managers do not provide the expected increase in ownership wealth, the owners have the power to replace the existing management team with a new team that is more responsive to owners' needs.

Meeting the needs of other stakeholders

The points made above do not mean that the needs of other groups with a stake in the business, such as employees, customers, suppliers and the community, are unimportant. In fact, the opposite is true if the business wishes to survive and prosper over the longer term. For example, a business with disaffected customers may well find that they turn to another supplier, resulting in a loss of owners' wealth. **Real World 1.5** provides examples of businesses that acknowledge the vital link between satisfying customers' needs and creating wealth (value) for their owners (shareholders).

Real World 1.5

Keeping it clean

Unilever plc, a leading provider of household cleaning and food products, states its approach as follows:

> We create value for our shareholders by placing consumers and their interests at the heart of what we do to generate growth that is consistent, competitive, profitable and responsible.

Check this out

J. Sainsbury plc, a supermarket chain, states:

> Since we first opened our doors in 1869 we've helped our customers live well for less. It's the lifeblood of our business. It shapes our strategy, which delivers value to customers and shareholders.

Sources: www.unilever.com, accessed 3 November 2018; www.about.sainsburys.co.uk, accessed 3 November 2018.

Other stakeholders that contribute towards the wealth creation process must also be considered. A dissatisfied workforce can result in low productivity and strikes while dissatisfied suppliers can withhold vital supplies or give lower priority to orders received. A discontented local community can withdraw access to community resources. In each case, the owners' wealth will suffer.

Real World 1.6 describes how one well-known business came to recognise that future success depended on the continuing support of one important stakeholder group – its customers.

Real World 1.6

The price of clothes

Nike is a highly successful business with a globally-recognised brand. However, it was not so long ago that the business was mired in controversy. It had become a focal point for protesters who regarded the business as a byword for 'sweatshop' labour practices. In 1992, an article was published that exposed the low wages and poor working conditions of those producing Nike products in Indonesia. Subsequent protests and further revelations resulted in unwanted media attention to which the business was, at first, slow to respond properly. However, by 1998, weakening demand for its products meant that the issue could no longer be lightly dismissed. Nike publicly acknowledged the reputation it had gained for 'sweat-shop' labour practices and the adverse effect this was having on customer attitudes.

Its management realised that, if nothing else, it was good business to improve the working lives of those producing Nike products in third world countries. This resulted in a commitment to better working conditions, higher wages and a minimum working age. A code of conduct for Nike suppliers concerning the treatment of their workforce was established and independent audits were implemented to monitor adherence to the code. The business also committed to greater transparency: it now publishes reports on its responsibilities and the ways in which these have been fulfilled.

Although Nike was not the only large business engaged in sweatshop practices, it took a lead in trying to eradicate them and, by doing so, removed the stain from its reputation. This has been rewarded by a continuing demand for its products.

Sources: Based on information in Nisen, M. (2013) How Nike solved its sweatshop problem, *Business Insider,* 9 May; Allarey, R. (2015) This is how Nike managed to clean up its sweatshop reputation, www.complex.com, 8 June.

It is clear from what we have seen that generating wealth for the owners is not the same as seeking to maximise the current year's profit. Wealth creation is concerned with the longer term. It relates not only to this year's profit but to that of future years as well. In the short term, corners can be cut and risks taken that improve current profit at the expense of future profit. **Real World 1.7** provides some examples of how emphasis on short-term profit can be very damaging.

Real World 1.7

Short-term gains, long-term problems

For many years, under the guise of defending capitalism, we have been allowing ourselves to degrade it. We have been poisoning the well from which we have drawn wealth. We have misunderstood the importance of values to capitalism. We have surrendered to the idea that success is pursued by making as much money as the law allowed without regard to how it was made.

Thirty years ago, retailers would be quite content to source the shoes they wanted to sell as cheaply as possible. The working conditions of those who produced them was not their concern. Then headlines and protests developed. Society started to hold them responsible for previously invisible working conditions. Companies like Nike went through a transformation. They realised they were polluting their brand. Global sourcing became visible. It was no longer viable to define success simply in terms of buying at the lowest price and selling at the highest.

Financial services and investment are today where footwear was thirty years ago. Public anger at the crisis will make visible what was previously hidden. Take the building up of huge portfolios of loans to poor people on US trailer parks. These loans were authorised without proper scrutiny of the circumstances of the borrowers. Somebody else then deemed them fit to be securitised and so on through credit default swaps and the rest without anyone seeing the transaction in terms of its ultimate human origin.

Each of the decision makers thought it okay to act like the thoughtless footwear buyer of the 1970s. The price was attractive. There was money to make on the deal. Was it responsible? Irrelevant. It was legal, and others were making money that way. And the consequences for the banking system if everybody did it? Not our problem.

The consumer has had a profound shock. Surely, we could have expected the clever and wise people who invested our money to be better at risk management than they have shown themselves to be in the present crisis? How could they have been so gullible in not challenging the bankers whose lending proved so flaky? How could they have believed that the levels of bonuses that were, at least in part, coming out of their savings could have been justified in 'incentivising' a better performance? How could they have believed that a 'better' performance would be one that is achieved for one bank without regard to its effect on the whole banking system? Where was the stewardship from those exercising investment on their behalf?

The answer has been that very few of them do exercise that stewardship. Most have stood back and said it doesn't really pay them to do so. The failure of stewardship comes from the same mindset that created the irresponsible lending in the first place. We are back to the mindset that has allowed us to poison the well: never mind the health of the system as a whole, I'm making money out of it at the moment. Responsibility means awareness for the system consequences of our actions. It is not a luxury. It is the cornerstone of prudence.

FT *Source:* Extracts from Goyder, M. (2009) How we've poisoned the well of wealth, *Financial Times,* 15 February.
© The Financial Times Limited 2012. All Rights Reserved.

Balancing risk and return

All decision making involves the future. Financial decision making is no exception. The only thing certain about the future, however, is that we cannot be sure what will happen. Things may not turn out as planned and this risk should be carefully considered when making financial decisions.

As in other aspects of life, risk and return tend to be related. Evidence shows that returns relate to risk in something like the way shown in Figure 1.8.

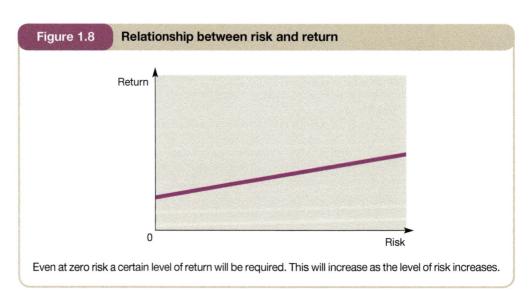

Figure 1.8 **Relationship between risk and return**

Even at zero risk a certain level of return will be required. This will increase as the level of risk increases.

Activity 1.17

Look at Figure 1.8 and state, in broad terms, where an investment in

(a) a UK government savings account, and
(b) shares in an oil exploration business

should be placed on the risk–return line.

A UK government savings account is normally a very safe investment. Even if the government is in financial difficulties, it may well be able to print more money to repay investors. Returns from this form of investment, however, are normally very low.

Investing in shares in a commercial business runs a risk of losing part or, possibly, the entire amount invested. On the other hand, such an investment can produce very high positive returns. Thus, the government savings account should be placed towards the far left of the risk–return line and the oil exploration business shares, which can be a very risky investment, towards the far right.

This relationship between risk and return has important implications for setting financial objectives for a business. The owners will require a minimum return to induce them to invest at all, but will require an additional return to compensate for taking risks; the higher the risk, the higher the required return. Managers must be aware of this and must strike the appropriate balance between risk and return when setting objectives and pursuing particular courses of action.

Turmoil in the banking sector during the early 2000s showed, however, that the right balance is not always struck. Some banks took on excessive risks in pursuit of higher returns and, as a consequence, incurred massive losses. They are now being kept afloat with taxpayers' money. **Real World 1.8** discusses the collapse of one leading bank, in which the UK government took a majority stake, and points out that the risk appetite of banks had to change.

Real World 1.8

Banking on change

The taxpayer has become the majority shareholder in the Royal Bank of Scotland (RBS). This change in ownership, resulting from the huge losses sustained by the bank, will shape the future decisions made by its managers. This does not simply mean that it will affect the amount that the bank lends to homeowners and businesses. Rather it is about the amount of risk that it will be prepared to take in pursuit of higher returns.

In the past, those managing banks such as RBS saw themselves as producers of financial products that enabled banks to grow faster than the economy as a whole. They did not want to be seen as simply part of the infrastructure of the economy. It was too dull. It was far more exciting to be seen as creators of financial products that created huge profits and, at the same time, benefited us all through unlimited credit at low rates of interest. These financial products, with exotic names such as 'collateralised debt obligations' and 'credit default swaps', ultimately led to huge losses that taxpayers had to absorb in order to prevent the banks from collapse.

Now that many banks throughout the world are in taxpayers' hands, they are destined to lead a much quieter life. They will have to focus more on the basics such as taking deposits, transferring funds and making simple loans to customers. Is that such a bad thing?

Real World 1.8 *continued*

The history of banking has reflected a tension between carrying out their core functions and the quest for high returns through high risk strategies. It seems, however, that for some time to come they will have to concentrate on the former and will be unable to speculate with depositors' cash.

Source: Based on information in Peston, R. (2008) We own Royal Bank, *BBC News,* www.bbc.co.uk, 28 November.

Reasons to be ethical

The way in which individual businesses operate in terms of the honesty, fairness and transparency with which they treat their stakeholders (customers, employees, suppliers, the community, the shareholders and so on) has become a key issue. There have been many examples of businesses, some of them very well known, acting in ways that most people would regard as unethical and unacceptable. Examples of such actions include:

- paying bribes to encourage employees of other businesses to reveal information about the employee's business that could be useful;
- oppressive treatment of suppliers, for example making suppliers wait excessive periods before payment; and
- manipulating the financial statements to mislead users of them, for example to over-state profit so that senior managers become eligible for performance bonuses (known as 'creative accounting').

Despite the many examples of unethical acts that have attracted publicity over recent years, it would be very unfair to conclude that most businesses are involved in unethical activities. Nevertheless, revelations of unethical practice can be damaging to the entire business community. Lying, stealing and fraudulent behaviour can lead to a loss of confidence in business and the imposition of tighter regulatory burdens. In response to this threat, businesses often seek to demonstrate their commitment to acting in an honest and ethical way. One way in which this can be done is to produce, and adhere to, a code of ethics concerning business behaviour.

Accountants are likely to find themselves at the forefront with issues relating to business ethics. In the three examples of unethical business activity listed above, an accountant would probably have to be involved either in helping to commit the unethical act or in covering it up. Accountants are, therefore, particularly vulnerable to being put under pressure to engage in unethical acts. Some businesses recognise this risk and produce an ethical code for their accounting staff. **Real World 1.9** provides an example of one such code.

Real World 1.9

The only way is ethics

Vodafone plc, the telecommunications business, has a code of ethics for its chief executive and senior finance and accounting staff. The code states that they have a duty to:

. . . act with integrity. Integrity requires, among other things, being honest and candid. Deceit, dishonesty and subordination of principle are inconsistent with integrity. Service to the Company should never be subordinated to personal gain and advantage.

The code specifically states that they must:

- act with integrity, including being honest and candid while still maintaining the confidentiality of Company information where required or in the Company's interests;
- observe, fully, applicable governmental laws, rules and regulations;
- comply with the requirements of applicable accounting and auditing standards and Company policies in the maintenance of a high standard of accuracy and completeness in the Company's financial records;
- adhere to a high standard of business ethics and not seek competitive advantage through unlawful or unethical business practices; and
- avoid conflicts of interest wherever possible. Anything that would be a conflict for a Relevant Officer will also be a conflict if it is related to a member of his or her family or a close relative.

Source: Vodafone plc, Code of Ethics, www.vodafone.com, accessed 13 February 2019.

Not-for-profit organisations

Although the focus of this book is accounting as it relates to private-sector businesses, there are many organisations that do not exist mainly for the pursuit of profit.

Activity 1.18

Can you think of at least four types of organisation that are not primarily concerned with making profits?

We thought of the following:

- charities;
- clubs and associations;
- universities;
- local government authorities;
- national government departments;
- churches; and
- trade unions.

All of these organisations need to produce accounting information for decision-making purposes. Once again, various user groups need this information to help them to make better decisions. These user groups are often the same as, or similar to, those identified for private sector businesses. They usually have a stake in the future viability of the organisation and may use accounting information to check that the wealth of the organisation is properly managed and used in a way consistent with its objectives.

Some not-for-profit organisations, such as charities, however, often suffer from a lack of financial skills among its trustees and managers. **Real World 1.10** contains extracts from the *Guardian* newspaper, which describes how one high-profile UK charity collapsed amid claims of weak accounting controls and financial mismanagement.

Real World 1.10

No kidding?

Senior directors at the charity Kids Company repeatedly warned trustees of the need to build up financial reserves or face going to the wall, the Guardian can reveal, as an analysis of the accounts show that its funding increased by more than 75% in five years.

Two finance directors at Kids Company left in less than three years because of their frustrations that no one – from the board of trustees, led by the BBC's Alan Yentob, to the chief executive, Camila Batmanghelidjh – heeded warnings of the need to build a financial cushion to protect the charity from catastrophe, the Guardian understands.

'If you keep building an organisation without building reserves, then it's a house of cards and it will fall down,' said one source who worked in a senior role at the charity for several years.

A Guardian analysis of five years of accounts show how the charity got itself into dire financial straits. Despite receiving millions of pounds in government funding, it lived hand to mouth, never built up any reserves, and spent almost all its income each year.

Analysis of the charity's accounts from 2009 to 2013 shows the organisation was receiving huge injections of funding, which included millions of pounds in government grants. Between 2009 and 2013, its income increased by 77% from £13m to £23m, but the charity was spending almost every penny it brought in. In the same period, its outgoings increased by 72%.

Despite repeated warnings on the accounts seen by trustees and presented to the Charity Commission, no consistent reserve was built up.

In March 2014, an audit of the charity was commissioned by the Cabinet Office and carried out by accountancy firm PKF Littlejohn. It noted that the charity was facing a 'serious cashflow' issue.

Historical note: The charity collapsed in August 2015.

Source: Laville, S. Barr, C. and Slawson, N. (2015) Kids Company trustees accused of ignoring finance warnings, www.theguardian.com, 6 August.

Summary

The main points of this chapter may be summarised as follows:

What are accounting and finance?

- Accounting provides financial information to help various user groups make better judgements and decisions.
- Finance also helps users to make better decisions and is concerned with the financing and investing activities of the business.

Accounting and user needs

- For accounting to be useful it must be clear for whom and for what purpose the information will be used.
- Owners, managers and lenders are important user groups but there are several others.
- Conflicts of interest between users may arise over the ways in which business wealth is generated or distributed.
- The evidence suggests that accounting is both used and useful for decision-making purposes.

Providing a service

- Accounting can be viewed as a form of service as it involves providing financial information to various users.

- To provide a useful service, accounting information must possess certain qualities, or characteristics.

- The fundamental qualities required are relevance and faithful representation. Other qualities that enhance the usefulness of accounting information are comparability, verifiability, timeliness and understandability.

- Providing a service to users can be costly and, in theory, financial information should be produced only if the cost of providing the information is less than the benefits gained.

Accounting information

- Accounting is part of the total information system within a business. It shares the features that are common to all information systems within a business, which are the identification, recording, analysis and reporting of information.

Management accounting and financial accounting

- Accounting has two main strands – management accounting and financial accounting.

- Management accounting seeks to meet the needs of the business's managers, and financial accounting seeks to meet the needs of providers of owners and lenders but will also be of use to other user groups.

- These two strands differ in terms of the types of reports produced, the level of reporting detail, the time orientation, the degree of regulation and the range and quality of information provided.

The changing face of accounting

- Changes in the economic environment have led to changes in the nature and scope of accounting.

- Financial accounting has improved its framework of rules and there has been greater international harmonisation of accounting rules.

- Management accounting has become more outward looking, and new methods for managing costs have emerged to help a business gain competitive advantage.

Why study accounting?

- Accounting and finance exert an enormous influence over the ways in which a business operates. As a result, everyone connected with business should be a little 'streetwise' about these areas.

What is the purpose of a business?

- According to Drucker, the purpose of a business is to create and keep customers.

What kinds of business ownership exist?

There are three main forms of business unit:

- sole proprietorship – easy to set up and flexible to operate but the owner has unlimited liability;

- partnership – easy to set up and spreads the burdens of ownership, but partners usually have unlimited liability and there are ownership risks if the partners are unsuitable; and
- limited company – limited liability for owners but obligations imposed on the way a company conducts its affairs.

How are businesses organised and managed?

- Most businesses of any size are set up as limited companies.
- A board of directors is appointed by owners (shareholders) to oversee the running of the business.
- Businesses are often divided into departments and organised along functional lines; however, larger businesses may be divisionalised along geographical and/or product lines.
- The move to strategic management has been caused by the changing and more competitive nature of business.

The quest for wealth creation

- The key financial objective of a business is to enhance the wealth of the owners.
- To achieve this objective, the needs of other groups connected with the business, such as employees, suppliers and the local community, cannot be ignored.
- When setting financial objectives, the right balance must be struck between risk and return.

Ethical behaviour

- Accounting staff may be put under pressure to commit unethical acts.
- Businesses may produce a code of ethical conduct to help protect accounting staff from this risk.

Not-for-profit organisations

- They produce accounting information for decision making purposes in much the manner as do commercial businesses.
- They have user groups that are similar to, or the same as, those of commercial businesses.

Key terms

For definitions of these terms, see Appendix B.

accounting *p. 2*

finance *p. 2*

shares *p. 6*

relevance *p. 7*

faithful representation *p. 7*

materiality *p. 7*

comparability *p. 8*

verifiability *p. 8*

timeliness *p. 8*

understandability *p. 8*

accounting information system *p. 12*

management accounting *p. 14*

financial accounting *p. 14*

sole proprietorship *p. 20*

partnership *p. 21*

limited company *p. 21*

strategic management *p. 26*

References

1 International Accounting Standards Board (2018) *Conceptual Framework for Financial Reporting,* pages 14 to 20.

2 Dugdale, D., Jones, C. and Green, S. (2006) *Contemporary Management Accounting Practices in UK Manufacturing,* CIMA/Elsevier.

3 Drucker, P. (1967) *The Effective Executive,* Heinemann.

Further reading

If you would like to explore the topics covered in this chapter in more depth, we recommend the following:

Drury, C. (2018) *Management and Cost Accounting,* 10th edn, Cengage Learning EMEA, Chapter 1.

Elliott, B. and Elliott, J. (2017) *Financial Accounting and Reporting,* 18th edn, Pearson, Chapters 6 and 7.

McLaney, E. (2017) *Business Finance: Theory and Practice,* 11th edn, Pearson, Chapters 1 and 2.

Scott, W. (2014) *Financial Accounting Theory,* 7th edn, Pearson, Chapters 1 to 3.

Critical review questions

Solutions to these questions can be found at the back of the book on pages 770–771

1.1 What, in economic principle, should determine what accounting information is produced? Should economics be the only issue here? (Consider who the users of accounting information are.)

1.2 Identify the main users of accounting information for a university. For what purposes would different user groups need information? Is there a major difference in the ways in which accounting information for a university would be used compared with that of a private-sector business?

1.3 Accounting is sometimes described as 'the language of business'. Why do you think this is the case? Is this an apt description of what accounting is?

1.4 Financial accounting statements tend to reflect past events. In view of this, how can they be of any assistance to a user in making a decision when decisions, by their very nature, can only be made about future actions?

PART 1

Financial accounting

We saw in Chapter 1 that accounting has two distinct strands: financial accounting and management accounting. Part 1 of this book deals with the former. Here, we introduce the three major financial statements:

- the statement of financial position;
- the income statement; and
- the statement of cash flows.

In Chapter 2, we provide an overview of these three statements and then go on to examine the first of them, the statement of financial position, in some detail. This examination will include an explanation of the main accounting conventions used when preparing the statement. These accounting 'conventions' are generally accepted rules that have evolved to help deal with practical problems experienced by preparers and users of the statement.

In Chapter 3, we examine the second of the major financial statements, the income statement. Here we discuss important issues such as how profit is measured and the point at which it should be recognised. Once again, we consider the main accounting conventions used when preparing this financial statement.

In the UK, the limited company is the most important form of business unit. Chapters 4 and 5 are devoted to an examination of its main features and financing arrangements. From an accounting viewpoint, there is no essential difference between a limited company and any other type of business unit. There are, however, points of detail that must be understood. Chapter 4 examines the nature of limited companies, the way in which they are financed and the accounting issues that relate specifically to this form of business. Chapter 5 considers the duty of directors of a limited company to account to its owners and to others, and the regulatory framework imposed on limited companies. Some additional financial statements, which are prepared by large limited companies, are also considered.

Chapter 6 deals with the last of the three financial statements, the statement of cash flows. This sets out the inflows and outflows of cash during a reporting period. In this chapter, we shall see that making profit is not enough. A business must also be able to generate sufficient cash to pay its obligations when they become due. The statement of cash flows helps users to assess its ability to do this.

When taken together, the three financial statements provide useful information about a business's performance and position for a particular period. We may, however, gain even greater insights by using financial ratios and other techniques based on these financial statements. By combining two figures from the financial statements in the form of a ratio, and then comparing the result with a similar ratio for, say, another business, we have a basis for assessing financial health. In Chapter 7, we consider various financial ratios and other techniques that can be used for assessing financial strengths and weaknesses.

CHAPTER 2

Measuring and reporting financial position

Introduction

We begin this chapter by taking an overview of the three major financial statements that form the core of financial accounting. We shall see how each contributes towards an assessment of the overall financial position and performance of a business. We shall also examine how these three statements are linked.

Following this overview, we shall undertake a more detailed examination of one of these financial statements: the statement of financial position. We shall identify its key elements and consider the interrelationships between them. We also consider the main accounting conventions, or rules, to be followed when preparing the statement of financial position.

We saw in Chapter 1 that accounting information should be useful to those seeking to make decisions about a business. Thus, we end the chapter by considering the value of the statement of financial position for decision-making purposes.

Learning outcomes

When you have completed this chapter, you should be able to:

● explain the nature and purpose of the three major financial statements;

● prepare a simple statement of financial position and interpret the information that it contains;

● discuss the accounting conventions underpinning the statement of financial position; and

● discuss the uses and limitations of the statement of financial position for decision-making purposes.

The major financial statements – an overview

The major financial accounting statements aim to provide a picture of the financial position and performance of a business. To achieve this, a business's accounting system will normally produce three financial statements on a regular, recurring basis. These three statements are concerned with answering the following questions relating to a particular period:

- What cash movements took place?
- How much wealth was generated?
- What is the accumulated wealth of the business at the end of the period and what form does it take?

To address each of these questions, there is a separate financial statement. The financial statements are:

- the **statement of cash flows**;
- the **income statement** (also known as the profit and loss account); and
- the **statement of financial position** (also known as the balance sheet).

Together they provide an overall picture of the financial health of the business.

Perhaps the best way to introduce these financial statements is to look at an example of a very simple business. From this we shall be able to see the sort of information that each of the statements can usefully provide. It is, however, worth pointing out that, while a simple business is our starting point, the principles for preparing the financial statements apply equally to the largest and most complex businesses. This means that we shall frequently encounter these principles again in later chapters.

Example 2.1

Paul was unemployed and unable to find a job. He therefore decided to embark on a business venture. With Christmas approaching, he decided to buy gift wrapping paper from a local supplier and to sell it on the corner of his local high street. He felt that the price of wrapping paper in the high street shops was unreasonably high. This provided him with a useful business opportunity.

He began the venture with £40 of his own money, in cash. On Monday, Paul's first day of trading, he bought wrapping paper for £40 and sold three-quarters of it for £45 cash.

- **What cash movements took place in Paul's business during Monday?**
  For Monday, a *statement of cash flows* showing the cash movements (that is, cash in and cash out) for the day can be prepared as follows:

Statement of cash flows for Monday

	£
Cash introduced (by Paul)	40
Cash from sales of wrapping paper	45
Cash paid to buy wrapping paper	(40)
Closing balance of cash	45

The statement shows that Paul placed £40 cash into the business. The business received £45 cash from customers, but paid £40 cash to buy the wrapping paper. This left £45 of cash by Monday evening. Note that we are taking the standard approach found in financial statements of showing figures to be deducted (in this case the £40 paid out) in brackets. We shall take this approach consistently throughout the chapters dealing with financial statements.

- **How much wealth (that is, profit) was generated by the business during Monday?**

An *income statement* can be prepared to show the wealth generated (profit) on Monday. The wealth generated arises from trading and will be the difference between the value of the sales made and the cost of the goods (that is, wrapping paper) sold.

Income statement for Monday

	£
Sales revenue	45
Cost of goods sold ($^3/_4$ of £40)	(30)
Profit	15

Note that it is only the cost of the wrapping paper *sold* that is matched against (and deducted from) the sales revenue in order to find the profit, not the whole of the cost of wrapping paper acquired. Any unsold inventories (also known as *stock*) will be charged against the future sales revenue that it generates. In this case, the cost of the unsold inventories is $^1/_4$ of £40 = £10.

- **What is the accumulated wealth on Monday evening and what form does it take?**

To establish the accumulated wealth at the end of Monday's trading, we can draw up a *statement of financial position* for Paul's business. This statement will also list the forms of wealth held at the end of that day.

Statement of financial position as at Monday evening

	£
Cash (closing balance)	45
Inventories of goods for resale ($^1/_4$ of £40)	10
Total assets	55
Equity	55

Note the terms 'assets' and 'equity' that appear in this statement. 'Assets' are business resources (things of value to the business) and include cash and inventories. 'Equity' is the word used in accounting to describe the investment, or stake, of the owner(s) – in this case Paul – in the business. Both of these terms will be discussed in detail a little later in this chapter. Note that the equity on Monday evening was £55. This represented the £40 that Paul put in to start the business, plus Monday's profit (£15) – profits belong to the owner(s).

Let us now continue by looking at what happens on the following day.

On Tuesday, Paul bought more wrapping paper for £20 cash. He managed to sell all of the new inventories and what remained of the earlier inventories, for a total of £48.

Example 2.1 *continued*

The statement of cash flows for Tuesday will be as follows:

Statement of cash flows for Tuesday

	£
Opening balance (from Monday evening)	45
Cash from sales of wrapping paper	48
Cash paid to buy wrapping paper	(20)
Closing balance	73

The income statement for Tuesday will be as follows:

Income statement for Tuesday

	£
Sales revenue	48
Cost of goods sold (£20 + £10)	(30)
Profit	18

The statement of financial position as at Tuesday evening will be:

Statement of financial position as at Tuesday evening

	£
Cash (closing balance)	73
Inventories	–
Total assets	73
Equity	73

We can see that the total business wealth has increased to £73 by Tuesday evening. This represents an increase of £18 (that is, £73 − £55) over Monday's figure – which, of course, is the amount of profit made during Tuesday, as shown in the income statement.

We can see from the financial statements in Example 2.1 that each statement provides part of a picture of the financial performance and position of the business. We begin by showing the cash movements. Cash is a vital resource that is necessary for any business to function effectively. It is used to meet debts that become due and to acquire other resources (such as inventories). Cash has been described as the 'lifeblood' of a business.

Reporting cash movements alone, however, is not enough to portray the financial health of the business. To find out how much profit was generated, we need an income statement. It is important to recognise that cash and profits rarely move in unison. During Monday, for example, the cash balance increased by £5, but the profit generated, as shown in the income statement, was £15. The cash balance did not increase in line with profit because part of the wealth (£10) was held in the form of inventories.

The statement of financial position that was drawn up as at the end of Monday's trading provides an insight into the total wealth of the business. This wealth can be held in various forms. For Paul's business, wealth is held in the form of cash and inventories. This means that, when drawing up the statement of financial position, both forms will be listed. For a large business, many other forms of wealth may be held, such as property, equipment, motor vehicles and so on.

Activity 2.1

On Wednesday, Paul bought more wrapping paper for £46 cash. However, it was raining hard for much of the day and sales were slow. After Paul had sold half of his total inventories for £32, he decided to stop trading until Thursday morning.

Have a go at drawing up the three financial statements for Paul's business for Wednesday.

Statement of cash flows for Wednesday

	£
Opening balance (from the Tuesday evening)	73
Cash from sales of wrapping paper	32
Cash paid to buy wrapping paper	(46)
Closing balance	59

Income statement for Wednesday

	£
Sales revenue	32
Cost of goods sold ($\frac{1}{2}$ of £46)	(23)
Profit	9

Statement of financial position as at Wednesday evening

	£
Cash (closing balance)	59
Inventories ($\frac{1}{2}$ of £46)	23
Total assets	82
Equity	82

Note that the total business wealth has increased by £9 (that is, the amount of Wednesday's profit) even though the cash balance has declined. This is because the business is holding more of its wealth in the form of inventories rather than cash, compared with the position on Tuesday evening.

By Wednesday evening, the equity stood at £82. This arose from Paul's initial investment of £40, plus his profits for Monday (£15), Tuesday (£18) and Wednesday (£9). This represents Paul's total investment in his business at that time. The equity of most businesses will similarly arise from injections of funds by the owner, plus any accumulated profits.

We can see that the income statement and statement of cash flows are both concerned with measuring flows (of wealth and cash respectively) during a particular period. The statement of financial position, however, is concerned with the financial position at a particular moment in time. Figure 2.1 illustrates this point.

The three financial statements discussed are often referred to as the **final accounts** of the business.

For external users of the financial statements (that is, virtually all users except the managers of the business concerned), these statements are normally backward-looking because they are based on information concerning past events and transactions. This can be useful in providing feedback on past performance and in identifying trends that provide clues to future performance. However, the statements can also be prepared using projected data

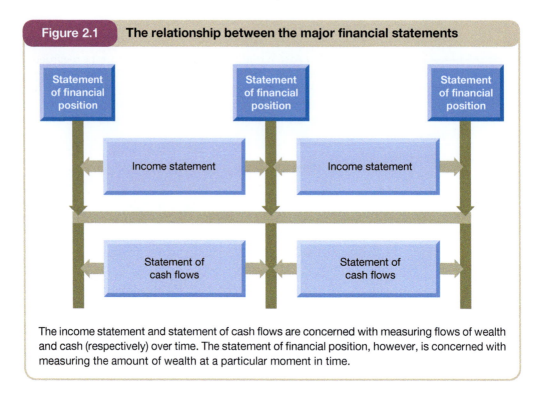

Figure 2.1   The relationship between the major financial statements

The income statement and statement of cash flows are concerned with measuring flows of wealth and cash (respectively) over time. The statement of financial position, however, is concerned with measuring the amount of wealth at a particular moment in time.

to help assess likely future profits, cash flows and so on. Normally, this is done only for management decision-making purposes.

Now that we have an overview of the financial statements, we shall consider each one in detail. The remainder of this chapter is devoted to the statement of financial position.

The statement of financial position

We saw a little earlier that this statement shows the forms in which the wealth of a business is held and how much wealth is held in each form. It also shows the sources of funding for that wealth. We can, however, be more specific about the nature of this statement by saying that it sets out the **assets** of a business, on the one hand, and the **claims** against the business, on the other. Before looking at the statement of financial position in more detail, we need to be clear about what these terms mean.

Assets

As asset is essentially a resource held by a business. To qualify as an asset for inclusion in the statement of financial position, however, a resource must possess the following three characteristics:

● *It must be an economic resource.* This type of resource provides the right to potential economic benefits. These benefits must not, however, be equally available to others. Take, for example, what economists refer to as *public goods*. These include resources such as the road system, GPS satellites or official statistics. Although these may provide economic benefits to a business, perhaps considerable economic benefits, others can receive the same benefits at no great cost. A public good cannot, therefore, be regarded as an asset of a business.

Economic benefits flowing from a resource can take various forms depending on how it is used by a business.

Activity 2.2

What forms might these benefits take? Try to think of at least two.

Benefits flowing from an economic resource may take the following forms:

- cash generated by using it to produce goods or services;
- cash received from the proceeds of its sale;
- the value received when exchanged for another economic resource;
- the value received when used to satisfy debts incurred by the business;
- cash generated from renting or leasing it.

You may have thought of others.

Note that an economic resource need only have the potential to generate benefits. These benefits need not be certain, or even probable.

● *The economic resource must be under the control of the business.* This gives a business the exclusive right to decide how the resource is used as well as the right to any benefits that flow. Control is usually acquired by a business through legal ownership or through a contractual agreement (for example, leasing equipment).

Activity 2.3

Assume a business owns a 20 per cent stake in a gold mine. As this ownership stake will not give control over the whole of the gold mine, can this resource be regarded as an asset of the business?

In this case, the asset of the business will be the 20 per cent share of the mine that is under its control, rather than the whole of the gold mine.

The event, or transaction, leading to control of the resource must have occurred in the past. In other words, the business must already exercise control over it. (See Reference 1 at the end of the chapter.)

● *The economic resource must be capable of measurement in monetary terms.* Often, an economic resource cannot be measured with a great deal of certainty. Estimates may be used that ultimately prove to be inaccurate. Nevertheless, it can still be reported as an asset for inclusion in the statement of financial position as long as a sufficiently faithful representation of its measurement can be produced. There are cases, however, where uncertainty regarding measurement is so great that this cannot be done. Take for example, the title of a magazine (such as *Hello!* or *Vogue*) that was created by its publisher.

While it may be extremely valuable to the publishing business, any attempt to measure this resource would be extremely difficult: it would have to rely on arbitrary assumptions. As a result, any measurement produced is unlikely to be useful. The publishing title will not, therefore, appear as an asset in the statement of financial position.

Note that *all* the characteristics identified must exist if a resource is to qualify for recognition. This will strictly limit the resources that are regarded as assets for inclusion in the statement of financial position. Once included, an asset will continue to be recognised until the economic benefits are exhausted, or the business disposes of it.

Figure 2.2 summarises the above discussion in the form of a decision chart.

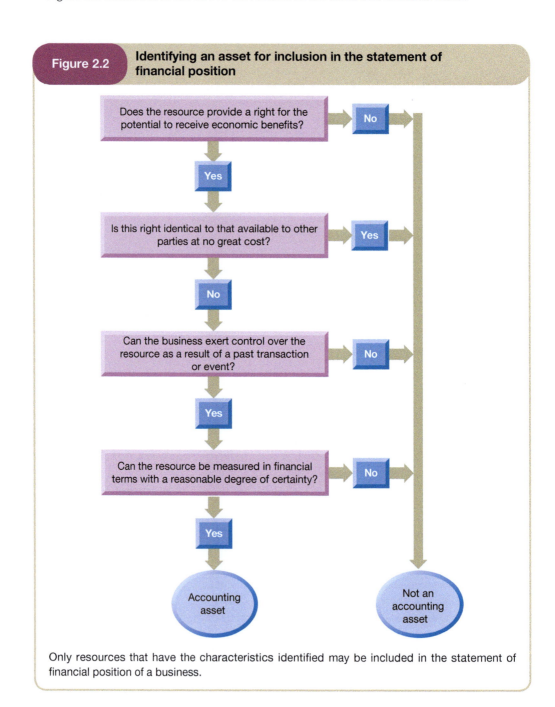

Figure 2.2 — Identifying an asset for inclusion in the statement of financial position

Only resources that have the characteristics identified may be included in the statement of financial position of a business.

Activity 2.4

Indicate which of the following items could appear as an asset on the statement of financial position of a business. Explain your reasoning in each case.

1 £1,000 owed to the business by a credit customer who is unable to pay.
2 A patent, bought from an inventor, that gives the business the right to produce a new product. Production of the new product is expected to increase profits over the period during which the patent is held.
3 A recently hired new marketing director who is confidently expected to increase profits by over 30 per cent during the next three years.
4 A recently purchased machine that will save the business £10,000 each year. It is already being used by the business but it has been acquired on credit and is not yet paid for.

Your answer should be along the following lines:

1 Under normal circumstances, a business would expect a customer to pay the amount owed. Such an amount is therefore typically shown as an asset under the heading '**trade receivables**' (or 'trade debtors'). However, in this particular case, the customer is unable to pay. As a result, this not an economic resource and the £1,000 owing would not be regarded as an asset. Debts that are not paid are referred to as *bad debts.*
2 The patent has all the characteristics identified and would, therefore, be regarded as an asset.
3 The new marketing director would not be considered as an asset. One argument in support of this position is that the business does not have rights of control over the director. Nevertheless, it may have control over the services that the director provides. Even if these services provide the focus of attention, however, it is usually impossible to measure them in monetary terms with any degree of certainty.
4 The machine has the characteristics identified and so would be considered an asset even though it is not yet paid for. Once the business has contracted to buy the machine, and has accepted it, it gains ownership even though payment is still outstanding. (The amount outstanding would be shown as a claim, as we shall see shortly.)

The sorts of items that often appear as assets in the statement of financial position of a business include:

- property (land and buildings);
- plant and equipment;
- fixtures and fittings;
- patents and trademarks;
- trade receivables (debtors); and
- investments outside the business.

Activity 2.5

Can you think of two additional items that might appear as assets in the statement of financial position of a typical business?

You may be able to think of a number of other items. Two that we have met so far, because they were held by Paul's wrapping paper business (in Example 2.1), are inventories and cash.

Note that an asset does not have to be a physical item – it may be a non-physical one that gives a right to potential benefits. Assets that have a physical substance and can be touched (such as inventories) are referred to as **tangible assets**. Assets that have no physical substance but which, nevertheless, provide future benefits (such as patents) are referred to as **intangible assets**.

Claims

A claim is an obligation of the business to provide cash, or some other form of benefit, to an outside party. It will normally arise as a result of the outside party providing assets for use by the business. There are essentially two types of claim against a business:

- **Equity**. This represents the claim of the owner(s) against the business. This claim is sometimes referred to as the *owner's capital*. Some find it hard to understand how the owner can have a claim against the business, particularly when we consider the example of a sole-proprietor-type business, like Paul's, where the owner is, in effect, the business. For accounting purposes, however, a clear distinction is made between the business and the owner(s). The business is viewed as being quite separate from the owner. It is seen as a separate entity with its own separate existence. This means that, when financial statements are prepared, they relate to the business rather than to the owner(s). Viewed from this perspective, any funds contributed by the owner will be seen as coming from outside the business and will appear as a claim against the business in its statement of financial position.
- **Liabilities**. Liabilities represent the claims of other parties, apart from the owner(s). They involve an obligation to transfer economic resources (usually cash) as a result of past transactions or events. A liability incurred by a business cannot be avoided and so will remain a liability until it is settled.

Most liabilities arise for legal or contractual reasons, such as from acquiring goods or services or from borrowing funds. They can, however, arise from the policies and practices adopted by the business, such as 'no quibble' refunds.

Now that the meanings of the terms *assets, equity* and *liabilities* have been established, we can consider the relationship between them. This relationship is quite straightforward. If a business wishes to acquire assets, it must raise the necessary funds from somewhere. It may raise them from the owner(s), or from other outside parties, or from both. Example 2.2 illustrates this relationship.

Example 2.2

Jerry and Company is a new business that was created by depositing £20,000 in a bank account on 1 March. This amount was raised partly from the owner (£6,000) and partly from borrowing (£14,000). Raising funds in this way will give rise to a claim on the business by both the owner (equity) and the lender (liability). If a statement of financial position of Jerry and Company is prepared following these transactions, it will appear as follows:

Jerry and Company
Statement of financial position as at 1 March

	£
ASSETS	
Cash at bank	20,000
Total assets	20,000
EQUITY AND LIABILITIES	
Equity	6,000
Liabilities – borrowing	14,000
Total equity and liabilities	20,000

We can see from the statement of financial position that the total claims (equity and liabilities) are the same as the total assets. Thus:

$$\text{Assets} = \text{Equity} + \text{Liabilities}$$

This equation – which we shall refer to as the *accounting equation* – will always hold true. Whatever changes may occur to the assets of the business or the claims against it, there will be compensating changes elsewhere that will ensure that the statement of financial position always 'balances'. By way of illustration, consider the following transactions for Jerry and Company:

2 March	Bought a motor van for £5,000, paying by cheque.
3 March	Bought inventories (that is, goods to be sold) on one month's credit for £3,000. (This means that the inventories were bought on 3 March, but payment will not be due to be made to the supplier until 3 April.)
4 March	Repaid £2,000 of the amount borrowed, to the lender, by a bank transfer.
6 March	Owner introduced another £4,000 into the business bank account.

A statement of financial position may be drawn up after each day in which transactions have taken place. In this way, we can see the effect of each transaction on the assets and claims of the business. The statement of financial position as at 2 March will be:

Jerry and Company
Statement of financial position as at 2 March

	£
ASSETS	
Cash at bank (20,000 − 5,000)	15,000
Motor van	5,000
Total assets	20,000
EQUITY AND LIABILITIES	
Equity	6,000
Liabilities – borrowing	14,000
Total equity and liabilities	20,000

→

Example 2.2 *continued*

As we can see, the effect of buying the motor van is to decrease the balance at the bank by £5,000 and to introduce a new asset – a motor van – to the statement of financial position. The total assets remain unchanged. It is only the 'mix' of assets that has changed.

The claims against the business remain the same because there has been no change in the way in which the business has been funded.

The statement of financial position as at 3 March, following the purchase of inventories, will be:

Jerry and Company
Statement of Financial Position as at 3 March

	£
ASSETS	
Cash at bank	15,000
Motor van	5,000
Inventories	3,000
Total assets	23,000
EQUITY AND LIABILITIES	
Equity	6,000
Liabilities – borrowing	14,000
Liabilities – trade payable	3,000
Total equity and liabilities	23,000

The effect of buying inventories has been to introduce another new asset (inventories) to the statement of financial position. Furthermore, the fact that the goods have not yet been paid for means that the claims against the business will be increased by the £3,000 owed to the supplier, who is referred to as a **trade payable** (or 'trade creditor') on the statement of financial position.

Activity 2.6

Try drawing up a statement of financial position for Jerry and Company as at 4 March.

The statement of financial position as at 4 March, following the repayment of part of the borrowing, will be:

Jerry and Company
Statement of financial position as at 4 March

	£
ASSETS	
Cash at bank (15,000 – 2,000)	13,000
Motor van	5,000
Inventories	3,000
Total assets	21,000
EQUITY AND LIABILITIES	
Equity	6,000
Liabilities – borrowing (14,000 – 2,000)	12,000
Liabilities – trade payable	3,000
Total equity and liabilities	21,000

The repayment of £2,000 of the borrowing will result in a decrease in the balance at the bank of £2,000 and a decrease in the lender's claim against the business by the same amount.

Activity 2.7

Try drawing up a statement of financial position as at 6 March for Jerry and Company.

The statement of financial position as at 6 March, following the introduction of more funds, will be:

Jerry and Company
Statement of financial position as at 6 March

	£
ASSETS	
Cash at bank (13,000 + 4,000)	17,000
Motor van	5,000
Inventories	3,000
Total assets	25,000
EQUITY AND LIABILITIES	
Equity (6,000 + 4,000)	10,000
Liabilities – borrowing	12,000
Liabilities – trade payable	3,000
Total equity and liabilities	25,000

The introduction of more funds by the owner will result in an increase in the equity of £4,000 and an increase in the cash at bank by the same amount.

This example (Jerry and Company) illustrates the point that the accounting equation (assets equals equity plus liabilities) will always hold true. It reflects the fact that, if a business wishes to acquire more assets, it must raise funds equal to the cost of those assets. The funds raised must be provided by the owners (equity), or by others (liabilities), or by a combination of the two. This means that the total cost of assets acquired should equal the total equity plus liabilities.

It is worth pointing out that businesses do not normally draw up a statement of financial position after each day, as shown in the example. We have done this to illustrate the effect on the statement of financial position of each transaction separately. In practice, a statement of financial position for a business is usually prepared at the end of a defined period. The period over which businesses measure their financial results is usually known as the reporting period, but it is sometimes called the 'accounting period' or 'financial period'.

Determining the length of the reporting period will involve weighing up the costs of producing the information against the perceived benefits of having that information for decision-making purposes. In practice, the reporting period will vary between businesses; it could be monthly, quarterly, half-yearly or annually. For external reporting purposes, an annual reporting period is the norm (although certain businesses, typically larger ones, report more frequently than this). For internal reporting purposes to managers, however, more frequent (perhaps monthly) financial statements are likely to be prepared.

The effect of trading transactions

In the example (Jerry and Company), we showed how various types of transactions affected the statement of financial position. However, one very important type of transaction – trading transactions – has yet to be considered. To show how this type of transaction affects the statement of financial position, let us return to Jerry and Company.

Example 2.2 *continued*

The statement of financial position that we drew up for Jerry and Company as at 6 March was as follows:

Jerry and Company
Statement of financial position as at 6 March

	£
ASSETS	
Cash at bank	17,000
Motor van	5,000
Inventories	3,000
Total assets	25,000
EQUITY AND LIABILITIES	
Equity	10,000
Liabilities – borrowing	12,000
Liabilities – trade payable	3,000
Total equity and liabilities	25,000

On 7 March, the business managed to sell all of the inventories for £5,000 and received a cheque immediately from the customer for this amount. The statement of financial position on 7 March, after this transaction has taken place, will be:

Jerry and Company
Statement of financial position as at 7 March

	£
ASSETS	
Cash at bank (17,000 + 5,000)	22,000
Motor van	5,000
Inventories (3,000 − 3000)	−
Total assets	27,000
EQUITY AND LIABILITIES	
Equity (10,000 + (5,000 − 3,000))	12,000
Liabilities – borrowing	12,000
Liabilities – trade payable	3,000
Total equity and liabilities	27,000

We can see that the inventories (£3,000) have now disappeared from the statement of financial position, but the cash at bank has increased by the selling price of the inventories (£5,000). The net effect has therefore been to increase assets by £2,000 (that is, £5,000 less £3,000). This increase represents the net increase in wealth (the profit) that has arisen from trading. Also note that the equity of the business has increased by £2,000, in line with the increase in assets. This increase in equity reflects the fact that wealth generated, as a result of trading or other operations, will be to the benefit of the owners and will increase their stake in the business.

Activity 2.8

What would have been the effect on the statement of financial position if the inventories had been sold on 7 March for £1,000 rather than £5,000?

The statement of financial position on 7 March would then have been:

Jerry and Company
Statement of financial position as at 7 March

	£
ASSETS	
Cash at bank (17,000 + 1,000)	18,000
Motor van	5,000
Inventories (3,000 − 3000)	–
Total assets	23,000
EQUITY AND LIABILITIES	
Equity (10,000 + (1,000 − 3,000))	8,000
Liabilities – borrowing	12,000
Liabilities – trade payable	3,000
Total equity and liabilities	23,000

As we can see, the inventories (£3,000) will disappear from the statement of financial position but the cash at bank will rise by only £1,000. This will mean a net reduction in assets of £2,000. This reduction represents a loss arising from trading and will be reflected in a reduction in the equity of the owners.

What we have just seen means that the accounting equation can be extended as follows:

> Assets (at the end   = Equity (amount at the start of the period
> of the period)   + Profit (or − Loss) for the period)
>   + Liabilities (at the end of the period)

(This is assuming that the owner makes no injections or withdrawals of equity during the period.)

Any funds introduced or withdrawn by the owners also affect equity. If the owners withdrew £1,500 for their own use, the equity of the owners would be reduced by £1,500. If these drawings were in cash, the cash balance would decrease by £1,500 in the statement of financial position.

Like all items in the statement of financial position, the amount of equity is cumulative. This means that any profit not taken out as drawings by the owner(s) remains in the business. These retained (or 'ploughed-back') earnings have the effect of expanding the business.

Classifying assets

In the statement of financial position, assets and claims are usually grouped into categories. This is designed to help users, as a haphazard listing of these items could be confusing. Assets are usually categorised as being either *current* or *non-current.*

Current assets

Current assets are basically assets that are held for the short term. To be more precise, they are assets that meet any of the following conditions:

- they are held for sale or consumption during the business's normal operating cycle;
- they are expected to be sold within a year after the date of the relevant statement of financial position;
- they are held principally for trading; and/or
- they are cash, or near cash such as easily marketable, short-term investments.

The operating cycle of a business, mentioned above, is the time between buying and/or creating a product or service and receiving the cash on its sale. For most businesses, this will be less than a year. (It is worth mentioning that sales made by most businesses, retailers being the exception, are made on credit. The customer pays some time after the goods are received or the service is provided.)

The most common current assets are inventories, trade receivables (amounts owed by customers for goods or services supplied on credit) and cash. For businesses that sell goods, rather than provide a service, the current assets of inventories, trade receivables and cash are interrelated. They circulate within a business as shown in Figure 2.3. We can see that cash can be used to buy inventories, which are then sold on credit. When the credit customers (trade receivables) pay, the business receives an injection of cash and so on.

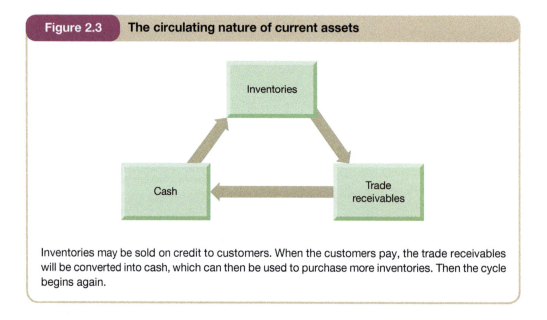

| Figure 2.3 | The circulating nature of current assets |

Inventories may be sold on credit to customers. When the customers pay, the trade receivables will be converted into cash, which can then be used to purchase more inventories. Then the cycle begins again.

For purely service businesses, the situation is similar, except that inventories are not involved.

Non-current assets

Non-current assets (also called *fixed assets*) are simply assets that do not meet the definition of current assets. They tend to be held for long-term operations. Non-current assets may be either tangible or intangible. Tangible non-current assets normally consist of **property, plant and equipment**. We shall refer to them in this way from now on. This is a rather broad term that includes items such as land and buildings, machinery, motor vehicles and fixtures and fittings.

The distinction between those assets continuously circulating (current) and those used for long-term operations (non-current) may help in assessing the mix of assets held. Most businesses need a certain amount of both types of asset to operate effectively.

Activity 2.9

Can you think of two examples of assets that may be classified as non-current assets for an insurance business?

Examples of assets that may be defined as being non-current are:

- property;
- furniture;
- motor vehicles;
- computers;
- computer software; and
- reference books.

This is not an exhaustive list. You may have thought of others.

The way in which a particular asset is classified (that is, between current and non-current) may vary according to the nature of the business. This is because the *purpose* for which the asset is held may vary. For example, a motor van retailer will normally hold inventories of the motor vans for sale; it would, therefore, classify them as part of the current assets. On the other hand, a business that buys one of these vans to use for delivering its goods to customers (that is, as part of its long-term operations) would classify it as a non-current asset.

Activity 2.10

The assets of Kunalun and Co., a large advertising agency, are as follows:

- cash at bank;
- fixtures and fittings;
- office equipment;
- motor vehicles;
- property;
- computers; and
- work in progress (that is, partly completed work for clients).

Which of these do you think should be defined as non-current assets and which as current assets?

Your answer should be as follows:

Non-current assets	*Current assets*
Fixtures and fittings	Cash at bank
Office equipment	Work in progress
Motor vehicles	
Property	
Computers	

Classifying claims

As we have already seen, claims are normally classified into equity (owner's claim) and liabilities (claims of outsiders). Liabilities are further classified as either current or non-current.

Current liabilities

Current liabilities are basically amounts due for settlement in the short term. To be more precise, they are liabilities that meet any of the following conditions:

- they are expected to be settled within the business's normal operating cycle;
- they exist principally as a result of trading;
- they are due to be settled within a year after the date of the relevant statement of financial position; and
- there is no right to defer settlement beyond a year after the date of the relevant statement of financial position.

Non-current liabilities

Non-current liabilities represent amounts due that do not meet the definition of current liabilities and so represent longer-term liabilities.

Activity 2.11

Can you think of one example of a current liability and one of a non-current liability?

An example of a current liability would be amounts owing to suppliers for goods supplied on credit (trade payables) or a bank overdraft (a form of short-term bank borrowing that is repayable on demand). An example of a non-current liability would be long-term borrowings.

It is quite common for non-current liabilities to become current liabilities. For example, borrowings to be repaid 18 months after the date of a particular statement of financial position will normally appear as a non-current liability. Those same borrowings will, however, appear as a current liability in the statement of financial position as at the end of the following year, by which time they would be due for repayment after six months.

This classification of liabilities between current and non-current helps to highlight those financial obligations that must soon be met. It may be useful to compare the amount of current liabilities with the amount of current assets (that is, the assets that either are cash or will turn into cash within the normal operating cycle). This should reveal whether the business is able to cover its maturing obligations.

The classification of liabilities between current and non-current also helps to highlight the proportion of total long-term finance that is raised through borrowings rather than equity. Where a business relies on long-term borrowings, rather than relying solely on funds provided by the owner(s), the financial risks increase. This is because borrowing usually brings a commitment to make periodic interest payments and capital repayments.

The business may be forced to stop trading if this commitment cannot be fulfilled. Thus, when raising long-term finance, the right balance must be struck between long-term borrowings and owner's equity. We shall consider this issue in more detail later in Chapter 7.

Statement layouts

Having looked at the classification of assets and liabilities, we shall now consider the layout of the statement of financial position. Although there is an almost infinite number of ways in which the same information on assets and claims could be presented, we shall consider two basic layouts. The first of these follows the style that we adopted with Jerry and Company earlier (see pages 50–54). A more comprehensive example of this style is shown in Example 2.3.

Example 2.3

Brie Manufacturing
Statement of financial position as at 31 December 2018

	£000
ASSETS	
Non-current assets	
Property	45
Plant and equipment	30
Motor vans	19
	94
Current assets	
Inventories	23
Trade receivables	18
Cash at bank	12
	53
Total assets	147
EQUITY AND LIABILITIES	
Equity	60
Non-current liabilities	
Long-term borrowings	50
Current liabilities	
Trade payables	37
Total equity and liabilities	147

The non-current assets have a total of £94,000 which, together with the current assets total of £53,000, gives a total of £147,000 for assets. Similarly, the equity totals £60,000 which, together with the £50,000 for non-current liabilities and £37,000 for current liabilities, gives a total for equity and liabilities of £147,000.

Within each category of asset (non-current and current) shown in Example 2.3, the items are listed in reverse order of liquidity (nearness to cash). Thus, the assets that are furthest from cash come first and the assets that are closest to cash come last. In the case of non-current assets, property is listed first as this asset is usually the most difficult to turn into cash and motor vans are listed last as there is usually a ready market for them. In the case of current assets, we have already seen that inventories are converted to trade receivables and then trade receivables are converted to cash. As a result, under the heading of current assets, inventories are listed first, followed by trade receivables and finally cash itself. This ordering of assets will occur irrespective of the layout used.

Note that, in addition to a grand total for assets held, subtotals for non-current assets and current assets are shown. Subtotals are also used for non-current liabilities and current liabilities when more than one item appears within these categories.

A slight variation from the layout illustrated in Example 2.3 is as shown in Example 2.4.

Example 2.4

Brie Manufacturing
Statement of financial position as at 31 December 2018

	£000
ASSETS	
Non-current assets	
Property	45
Plant and equipment	30
Motor vans	19
	94
Current assets	
Inventories	23
Trade receivables	18
Cash at bank	12
	53
Total assets	147
LIABILITIES	
Non-current liabilities	
Long-term borrowings	(50)
Current liabilities	
Trade payables	(37)
Total liabilities	(87)
Net assets	60
EQUITY	60

We can see that the total liabilities are deducted from the total assets. This derives a figure for net assets – which is equal to equity. Using this format, the basic accounting equation is rearranged so that:

$$\textbf{Assets} - \textbf{Liabilities} = \textbf{Equity}$$

This rearranged equation highlights the fact that equity represents the residual interest of the owner(s) in the assets of the business, after deducting all liabilities.

Figure 2.4 summarises the two types of layout discussed in this section.

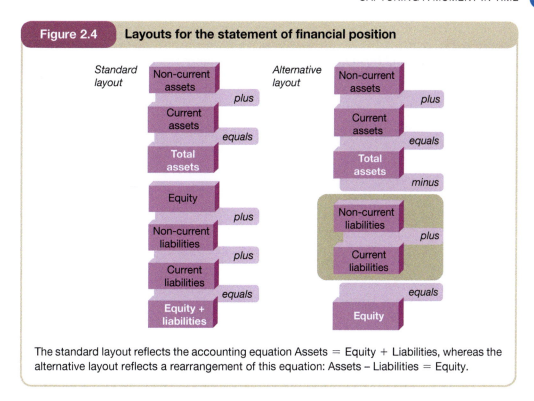

Figure 2.4   Layouts for the statement of financial position

The standard layout reflects the accounting equation Assets = Equity + Liabilities, whereas the alternative layout reflects a rearrangement of this equation: Assets – Liabilities = Equity.

The layout shown in Example 2.3 is very popular in practice and will be used throughout the book.

Capturing a moment in time

As we have already seen, the statement of financial position reflects the assets, equity and liabilities of a business at *a specified point in time*. It has been compared to a photograph. A photograph 'freezes' a particular moment in time and will represent the situation only at that moment. Hence, events may be quite different immediately before and immediately after the photograph was taken. When examining a statement of financial position, therefore, it is important to establish the date for which it has been drawn up. This information should be prominently displayed in the heading to the statement, as shown above in Example 2.4. When we are trying to assess current financial position, the more recent the statement of financial position date, the more helpful it is likely to be.

A business will normally prepare a statement of financial position as at the close of business on the last day of its reporting period. In the UK, businesses are free to choose the date of the end of their reporting period and, once chosen, it will only normally change under exceptional circumstances. When making a decision on which year-end date to choose, commercial convenience can often be a deciding factor. For example, a business operating in the retail trade may choose to have a year-end date early in the calendar year (for example, 31 January) because trade tends to be slack during that period and more staff time is available to help with the tasks involved in the preparation of the annual financial statements (such as checking the amount of inventories held ('stocktaking')). Since trade is slack, it is also a time when the amount of inventories held by the retail business is likely to be unusually low as compared with other times of the year.

Activity (2.12)

Does this pose a problem for external users seeking to assess the business's financial health?

While the statement of financial position may provide a fair view of the inventories held at the time it was drawn up, it will not be typical of the position over the rest of the year.

The role of accounting conventions

Accounting has a number of conventions, or rules, that have evolved over time. They have evolved to deal with practical problems experienced by preparers and users of financial statements, rather than to reflect some theoretical ideal. In preparing the statements of financial position earlier in this chapter, we have followed various **accounting conventions**, although they have not been explicitly mentioned. We shall now identify and discuss the main conventions that we have applied.

Business entity convention

For accounting purposes, the business and its owner(s) are treated as being quite separate and distinct. This is why owners are treated as being claimants against their own business in respect of their investment. The **business entity convention** must be distinguished from the legal position that may exist between businesses and their owners. For sole proprietorships and partnerships, the law does not make any distinction between the business and its owner(s). For limited companies, on the other hand, there is a clear legal distinction between the business and its owners. (As we shall see in Chapter 4, the limited company is regarded as having a separate legal existence.) For accounting purposes, these legal distinctions are irrelevant and the business entity convention applies to all businesses.

Historic cost convention

The **historic cost convention** holds that the value of assets shown on the statement of financial position should be based on their historic cost (that is, acquisition cost). The use of historic cost means that problems of measurement reliability are minimised, as the amount paid for a particular asset is often a matter of demonstrable fact. Reliance on opinion is avoided, or at least reduced, which should enhance the credibility of the information in the eyes of users. A key problem, however, is that the information provided may not be relevant to user needs. Even quite early in the life of some assets, historic costs may become outdated compared to current market values. This can be misleading when assessing current financial position.

Many argue that recording assets at their current value would provide a more realistic view of financial position and would be relevant for a wide range of decisions. A system of measurement based on current value does, however, bring its own problems. The term 'current value' can be defined in different ways. It can be defined broadly as either the current replacement cost or the current realisable value (selling price) of an asset. These two types of valuation may result in quite different figures being produced to represent the current value of an item. Furthermore, the broad terms 'replacement cost' and 'realisable value' can be defined in different ways. We must therefore be clear about what kind of current value accounting we wish to use.

Activity 2.13 illustrates some of the problems associated with current value accounting.

Activity 2.13

Plumber and Company has a fleet of motor vans that are used for making deliveries to customers. The owners want to show these vans on the statement of financial position at their current values rather than at their historic cost. They would like to use either current replacement cost (based on how much would have to be paid to buy vans of a similar type, age and condition) or current realisable value (based on how much a motor van dealer would pay for the vans, if the business sold them).

Why is the choice between the two current valuation methods important? Why would both current valuation methods present problems in establishing reliable values?

The choice between the two current valuation methods is important because the values derived under each method are likely to be quite different. Normally, replacement cost values for the motor vans will be higher than their current realisable values.

Establishing current values will usually rely on opinions, which may well vary from one dealer to another. Thus, instead of a single, unambiguous figure for, say, the current replacement cost for each van, a range of possible current replacement costs could be produced. The same problem will arise when trying to establish the current realisable value for each van.

We should bear in mind that the motor vans discussed in Activity 2.13 are less of a problem than are many other types of asset. There is a ready market for motor vans, which means that a value can be obtained by contacting a dealer. For a custom-built piece of equipment, however, identifying a replacement cost or, worse still, a selling price, could be very difficult.

Where the current values of assets are based on the opinion of managers of the business, there is a greater risk that they will lack credibility. Some form of independent valuation, or verification, may therefore be required to reassure users.

Despite the problems associated with current values, they are increasingly used when reporting assets in the statement of financial position. This has led to a steady erosion in the importance of the historic cost convention. Thus, many businesses now prepare financial statements on a modified historic cost basis. We shall consider the valuation of assets in more detail a little later in the chapter.

Prudence convention

In broad terms, the **prudence convention** holds that caution should be exercised when preparing financial statements. This may not seem to be a contentious issue: it would, after all, be difficult to argue that an incautious approach should be taken. Nevertheless, the prudence convention has excited much debate over the years. The root cause has been the way in which the convention is interpreted. Reporting 'good news' (such as profits or gains in asset values) is usually seen as demanding a higher standard of evidence than reporting 'bad news' (such as losses). Furthermore, any 'bad news' should be reported earlier rather than later. This interpretation evolved to counteract possible excessive optimism among managers. Its ultimate purpose is to avoid the risk that the financial strength of a business will be overstated, thereby resulting in poor user decisions.

Activity 2.14

What sort of poor decisions may be made as a result of overstating the financial strength of a business? Try to think of at least two.

Examples of poor decisions may include:

- excessive amounts being paid out of profit to the owners, thereby, depleting their equity and undermining the financial health of the business;
- excessive bonuses being paid to managers based on overstated profits;
- new owners paying more to acquire a part, or the whole, of a business than is justified; and
- lenders providing funds to a business based on a rosier picture of financial strength than is warranted by the facts.

You may have thought of others.

By interpreting prudence in the way described, however, there is a risk that a business's financial strength will be understated. In other words, assets and profits will be understated and/or liabilities will be overstated. Just as overstatement may lead to poor user decisions, understatement may do the same. An unduly pessimistic portrayal of financial strength may result in existing owners selling their business too cheaply, lenders refusing a loan application and so on.

Any bias towards understatement of financial strength also clashes with the need for *neutrality* in preparing financial statements.

Activity 2.15

In Chapter 1 we discussed neutrality as a desirable element of one of the major qualitative characteristics of financial information. Can you remember which one?

Neutrality is one of three elements needed to ensure faithful representation. (The other two elements are completeness and freedom from error.)

Neutrality, by definition, requires that financial statements are not slanted or weighted so as to present either a favourable or unfavourable picture to users. To accommodate the requirement for neutrality, therefore, prudence must be interpreted differently than mentioned above. Adopting a cautious approach to preparing financial statements should not lead to the understatement of financial strength.

Going concern convention

According to the **going concern convention**, the financial statements should be prepared on the assumption that a business will continue operations for the foreseeable future, unless there is evidence to the contrary. In other words, it is assumed that there is no intention, or need, to sell off the non-current assets of the business.

Where a business is in financial difficulties, however, non-current assets may have to be sold to repay those with claims against the business. The realisable (sale) value of many non-current assets is often much lower than the values reported in the statement of financial position. In the event of a forced sale of assets, therefore, significant losses might arise. These losses must be anticipated and fully reported when, but only when, a business's going concern status is called into question.

Dual aspect convention

The **dual aspect convention** asserts that each transaction has two aspects, both of which will affect the statement of financial position. This means that, for example, the purchase of a computer for cash results in an increase in one asset (computer) and a decrease in another (cash). Similarly, the repayment of borrowings results in the decrease in a liability (borrowings) and the decrease in an asset (cash).

Activity 2.16

What are the two aspects of each of the following transactions?

1 Purchasing £1,000 of inventories on credit.
2 Owner withdrawing £2,000 in cash.
3 Paying a supplier £1,000 for inventories bought on credit a few weeks earlier.

Your answer should be as follows:

1 Inventories increase by £1,000, trade payables increase by £1,000.
2 Equity reduces by £2,000, cash reduces by £2,000.
3 Trade payables reduce by £1,000, cash reduces by £1,000.

Recording the dual aspect of each transaction ensures that the statement of financial position will continue to balance, that is the accounting equation will still hold.

Figure 2.5 summarises the main accounting conventions that exert an influence on what appears on the statement of financial position.

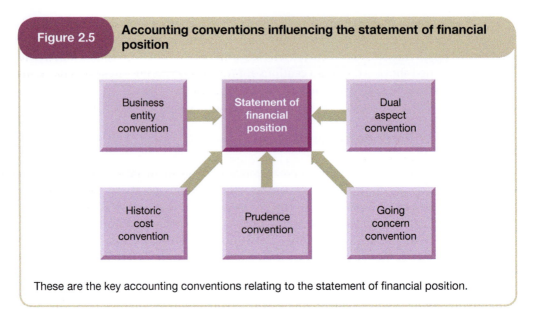

Figure 2.5 — Accounting conventions influencing the statement of financial position

These are the key accounting conventions relating to the statement of financial position.

Money measurement

We saw earlier that an economic resource will only normally be regarded as an asset, for inclusion in the statement of financial position, where it can be measured with a reasonable degree of certainty. Unless a monetary measure can faithfully portray a resource, it is unlikely to be useful.

Various resources of a business fail to meet this money measurement criterion and so are excluded from the statement of financial position.

Activity 2.17

Can you identify any of these resources? Try to think of at least two.

They may include:

- human resources;
- business reputation;
- business location; and/or
- customer and supplier relationships.

From time to time, attempts are made to try to measure and report these resources so as to provide a more complete picture of financial position. However, they usually garner little support from the users of financial statements. Monetary measures with a high degree of uncertainty produce inconsistency in reporting and create doubts in the minds of users. This, in turn, can undermine the integrity and credibility of financial statements.

Let us now move on to discuss some key economic resources that normally pose measurement problems.

Goodwill and brands

Some intangible non-current assets are similar to tangible non-current assets: they have a clear and separate identity and the cost of acquiring the asset can be measured with a reasonable degree of certainty. Examples normally include patents, trademarks, copyrights and licences. Other intangible non-current assets, however, are quite different. They lack a clear and separate identity and reflect a hotchpotch of attributes, which are part of the essence of the business. Goodwill and product brands are often examples of assets that lack a clear and separate identity.

The term '**goodwill**' is often used to cover various attributes such as the quality of the products, the skill of employees and the relationship with customers. The term 'product brands' is also used to cover various attributes, such as the brand image, the quality of the product, the trademark and so on. Where goodwill and product brands have been generated internally by the business, it is often difficult to determine their cost or to measure their current market value or even to be clear that they really exist. They are, therefore, excluded from the statement of financial position.

When such assets are acquired through an 'arm's-length transaction', however, the problems of uncertainty about their existence and measurement are resolved. (An arm's-length transaction is one that is undertaken between two unconnected parties.) If goodwill is acquired, when taking over another business, or if a business acquires a particular product brand, from another business, these items will be separately identified and a price agreed for them. Under these circumstances, they can be regarded as assets (for accounting purposes) by the business that acquired them and included in the statement of financial position.

To agree a price for acquiring goodwill or product brands means that some form of valuation must take place and this raises the question as to how it is done. Usually, the valuation will be based on estimates of future earnings from holding the asset – a process that is fraught with difficulties. Nevertheless, a number of specialist businesses now exist that are prepared to take on this challenge. **Real World 2.1** shows how one specialist business ranked and valued the top ten brands in the world for 2018.

Real World 2.1

Brand leaders

Brand Finance produces an annual ranking and valuation of the world's top 500 brands. For 2018, the top ten brands are as follows:

Rank		Brand	Value (US$)	
2018	2017		2018	2017
1	3	Amazon	150,811	106,396
2	2	Apple	146,311	107,141
3	1	Google	120,911	109,470
4	6	Samsung Group	92,289	66,218
5	9	Facebook	89,684	61,998
6	4	AT and T	82,422	87,016
7	5	Microsoft	81,163	76,265
8	7	Verizon	62,826	65,875
9	8	Walmart	61,480	62,211
10	10	ICBC	59,189	47,832

Source: Brand Finance Directory (2018) *Global 500*, www.brandirectory.com, accessed 5 November 2018.

We can see that US technology businesses dominate the rankings. We can also see that the valuations placed on the brands owned are quite staggering. These valuations, however, should be viewed with some degree of scepticism. There are significant variations in both the rankings and values assigned to brands between the various brand valuers.

Human resources

Attempts have been made to place a monetary measurement on the human resources of a business, but without any real success. There are, however, certain limited circumstances in which human resources are measured and reported in the statement of financial position. Professional football clubs provide an example of where these circumstances normally arise. While football clubs cannot own players, they can own the rights to the players' services. Where these rights are acquired by compensating other clubs for releasing the players from their contracts with those other clubs, an arm's-length transaction arises and the amounts paid provide a reliable basis for measurement. This means that the rights to services can be regarded as an asset of the club for accounting purposes (assuming, of course, the player will bring benefits to the club).

Real World 2.2 describes how one leading club reports its investment in players on the statement of financial position.

Real World 2.2

United players appear on the team sheet and on the statement of financial position

Manchester United Football Club has acquired several key players as a result of paying transfer fees to other clubs. In common with most UK football clubs. The club reports the investment in acquiring the rights to the players' services on its statement of financial position. The club's statement as at 30 June 2018 shows the total value of registering its squad of players at more than £785 million. The average annual net investment in player registrations over the five-year period to 30 June 2018 was more than £104 million. A total of 70 players were under contract at the year end, which included reserve team and youth team players. The club treats a proportion of each player's transfer fee as an expense each year. The exact proportion depends on the length of the particular player's contract.

The £785 million does not include 'home-grown' players such as Jesse Lingard, because United did not pay a transfer fee for them and no reasonably certain value can be placed on their services. During the year to 30 June 2018, the club was active in the transfer market and invested more than £243 million on acquiring new players, including Victor Lindelof, Nemanja Matic and Romelu Lukaku. Some players also left the club during the year, including Adnan Januzaj. The item of players' registrations is shown as an intangible asset in the statement of financial position as it is the rights to services, not the players, that are the assets. It is shown net of depreciation (or *amortisation* as it is usually termed for intangible non-current assets). The net amount at 30 June 2018 was more than £369 million and represented almost 24 per cent of Manchester United's total assets, as shown in the statement of financial position.

Sources: Manchester United plc, Annual Report 2018; and www.transfermarket.com.

Monetary stability

When using money as the unit of measurement, we normally fail to recognise the fact that it will change in value over time, despite the fact that in the UK, and throughout much of the world, inflation has been a persistent problem. This has meant that the value of money has declined in relation to other assets. In past years, high rates of inflation have resulted in statements of financial position, which were prepared on a historic cost basis, reflecting figures for assets that were much lower than if current values were employed. Rates of inflation have been relatively low in recent years and so the disparity between historic cost values and current values has been less pronounced. Nevertheless, it can still be significant. The problem of inflation has added fuel to the more general debate concerning how to measure asset values in the statement of financial position. It is to the issue of valuing assets that we now turn.

Valuing assets

We saw earlier that, when preparing the statement of financial position, the historic cost convention is normally applied for the reporting of assets. This point requires further explanation as, in practice, things are a little more complex than this. Large businesses throughout much of the world adhere to asset valuation rules set out in International Financial Reporting Standards. We shall now consider the key valuation rules.

Non-current assets

Non-current assets have useful lives that are either *finite* or *indefinite*. Those with a finite life provide benefits to a business for a limited period of time, whereas those with an indefinite life provide benefits without a foreseeable time limit. This distinction between the two types of non-current assets applies to both tangible and intangible assets.

Initially, non-current assets are recorded at their historic cost, which will include any amounts spent on getting them ready for use.

Non-current assets with finite lives

Benefits from assets with finite useful lives will be used up over time as a result of market changes, wear and tear and so on. The amount used up, which is referred to as *depreciation* (or *amortisation,* in the case of intangible non-current assets), must be measured for each reporting period for which the assets are held. Although we shall leave a detailed examination of depreciation until Chapter 3, we need to know that when an asset has been depreciated, this must be reflected in the statement of financial position.

The total depreciation that has accumulated over the period since the asset was acquired must be deducted from its cost. This net figure (that is, the cost of the asset less the total depreciation to date) is referred to as the **carrying amount**. It is sometimes also known as *net book value* or *written-down value.* The procedure just described is not really a contravention of the historic cost convention. It is simply recognition of the fact that a proportion of the historic cost of the non-current asset has been consumed in the process of generating, or attempting to generate, benefits for the business.

Activity 2.18

Try to identify two non-current assets with a finite useful life that can be classified as:

1 tangible and
2 intangible?

Tangible assets normally considered to have a finite life include:

● machinery and equipment;
● motor vehicles; and
● computers.

Intangible assets normally considered to have a finite life include:

● patents (many patents are granted for a period of 20 years);
● leases taken out on assets (such as a property); and
● licences (such as a taxi licence).

Non-current assets with indefinite useful lives

Benefits from assets with indefinite lives may, or may not, be used up over time. Property, in the form of land, is usually an example of a tangible non-current asset with an indefinite life. Purchased goodwill could be an example of an intangible one, though this is not always the case. These assets are not subject to routine depreciation each reporting period.

Fair values

Initially, non-current assets of all types (tangible and intangible) are recorded at cost. Subsequently, however, an alternative form of measurement may be allowed. Non-current assets may be recorded using **fair values** provided that these values can be measured with a fair degree of certainty. Fair values are market based. They represent the selling price that can be obtained in an orderly transaction under current market conditions. The use of fair values, rather than cost, provides users with more up-to-date information, which may be more relevant to their needs. It may also place the business in a better light, as assets such as property may have increased significantly in value over time. Increasing the statement of financial position value of an asset does not, of course, make that asset more valuable. Perceptions of the business may, however, be altered by such a move.

One consequence of upwardly revaluing non-current assets with finite lives is that the depreciation charge will be increased. This is because the depreciation charge is based on the new (increased) value of the asset.

Real World 2.3 shows the effect of the revaluation of non-current assets on the financial position of one large business.

Real World 2.3

Rising asset levels

During the year to 31 March 2010, Veolia Water UK plc, which owns Thames Water, changed its policy on the valuation of certain types of non-current assets. These assets included land and buildings, infrastructure assets and vehicles, plant and machinery. The business switched from the use of historic cost to the use of fair values and independent qualified valuers carried out a revaluation exercise.

The effect of this policy change was to report a revaluation gain of more than £436 million during the year. There was a 40 per cent increase in owners' (shareholders') equity, which was largely due to this gain.

Source: Veolia Water UK plc, Annual Report 2009/10.

Activity 2.19

Refer to the statement of financial position of Brie Manufacturing shown earlier in Example 2.4 (page 60). What would be the effect of revaluing the property to a figure of £110,000 in the statement of financial position? Show the revised statement.

The effect on the statement of financial position would be to increase the figure for property to £110,000 and the gain on revaluation (that is, £110,000 − £45,000 = £65,000) would be added to equity, as it is the owner(s) who will have benefited from the gain. The revised statement of financial position would therefore be as follows:

Brie Manufacturing
Statement of financial position as at 31 December 2018

	£000
ASSETS	
Non-current assets	
Property	110
Plant and equipment	30
Motor vans	19
	159
Current assets	
Inventories	23
Trade receivables	18
Cash at bank	12
	53
Total assets	212
EQUITY AND LIABILITIES	
Equity (60 + 65)	125
Non-current liabilities	
Long-term borrowings	50
Current liabilities	
Trade payables	37
Total equity and liabilities	212

Once non-current assets are revalued, the frequency of revaluation becomes an important issue. Reporting assets on the statement of financial position at out-of-date revaluations is the worst of both worlds. It lacks the objectivity and verifiability of historic cost; it also lacks the realism of current values. Thus, where fair values are used, revaluations should be frequent enough to ensure that the carrying amount of the revalued asset does not differ materially from its true fair value at the statement of financial position date.

When an item of property, plant or equipment (a tangible asset) is revalued on the basis of fair values, all assets within that particular group must be revalued. It is not, therefore, acceptable to revalue some items of property but not others. Although this rule provides some degree of consistency within a particular group of assets, it does not prevent the statement of financial position from containing a mixture of valuations.

Intangible assets are not usually revalued to fair values. This is because an active market is required to determine fair values. For most intangible assets, an active market does not exist. A few intangible assets, however, such as transferable taxi licences, fishing licences and production quotas, provide the exception.

It has been argued that recent emphasis on the use of fair values in accounting has resulted in the exercise of prudence becoming less important. **Real World 2.4** comprises extracts from an article by John Kay which explains why this change has taken place. The article, which is well worth reading in full, is highly critical of the change.

> ### Real World 2.4
>
> # It's really not fair
>
> Once upon a time, values were based on cost, unless assets were no longer worth their cost, in which case they had to be written down.
>
> A bird in the hand was worth more than any number in the bush: only when the bird emerged from the bush were you permitted to count it at all.
>
> Like finance, however, accounting became cleverer, and worse. By the 1980s accounting had become the principal means by which UK graduates prepared for business. Many of these trainees found jobs in the finance sector; others took jobs in non-financial business – and, since they were smart, many rose to senior positions. Young accountants were smarter, greedier, less schooled in prudence and better schooled in economics. 'Fair value' increasingly replaced conservatism (prudence) as a guiding principle. But this route to the 'true and fair view' – the traditional holy grail of the accountant – often led to an outcome that was just the opposite of fair.

    Source: Extracts from Kay, J. (2015) Playing dice with your money, ft.com, 4 September.
© The Financial Times Limited 2015. All Rights Reserved.

The impairment of non-current assets

All types of non-current asset are at risk of suffering a significant fall in value. This may be caused by changes in market conditions, technological obsolescence and so on. In some cases, this results in the carrying amount of the asset being higher than the amount that could be recovered from the asset; either through its continued use or through its sale. When this occurs, the asset value is said to be impaired and the general rule is to reduce the carrying amount on the statement of financial position to the recoverable amount. Unless this is done, the asset value will be overstated. The amount by which the asset value is reduced is known as an **impairment loss**.

This type of impairment in value should not be confused with routine depreciation of assets with finite lives. Routine depreciation arises from 'wear and tear' of the asset and/ or the passage of time. Impairment results from a fundamental shift in market conditions or technological obsolescence.

Activity 2.20

With which of the ideas discussed earlier in the chapter is this accounting treatment of impaired assets consistent?

The answer is *prudence,* which requires that we should adopt a cautious approach when preparing financial statements. The value of assets should not be overstated in the statement of financial position.

Real World 2.5 provides an example of where one large business incurred large impairment losses on the value of its assets.

Real World 2.5

All going impaired shape

The publisher of the Mirror and Express newspapers slumped to a first half loss of more than £100 million after slashing the value of regional titles, which include the Manchester Evening News, Birmingham Mail and Liverpool Echo.

Reach, the new name for the publisher Trinity Mirror, wrote down the value of its 160 local papers and websites by £150 million, reflecting the tough outlook for local newspapers in the digital age.

The impairment charge drove Reach to a pretax loss of £114.3 million in the first six months of the year, compared with a £38 million profit in the same period last year. The UK's largest publisher of local newspapers said it had cut the value of its portfolio by almost half – from £347 million to £197 million – to 'reflect a more challenging outlook for our regional businesses'. Simon Fox, chief executive of Reach, said the write-down reflected the poor long-term outlook for print sales and readership, not digital opportunity for local titles.

Source: Extract from Sweeney, M. (2018) Mirror parent slashes value of local newspapers by £150m, www.theguardian.com, 30 July.

Intangible non-current assets with indefinite useful lives must be tested for impairment as at the end of each reporting period. Other non-current assets, however, must also be tested where events suggest that impairment has taken place.

Activity 2.21

Why might it be a good idea to have impairment tests carried out by independent experts?

Impairment tests involve making judgements about the appropriate value to place on assets. Employing independent valuers to make these judgements will normally give users greater confidence in the information reported. There is always a risk that managers will manipulate impairment values to portray a picture that they would like users to see.

When a non-current asset with a finite useful life has its value impaired, the future, periodic, depreciation expense for that asset will be based on the new (lower) impaired value.

Inventories

It is not only non-current assets that run the risk of a significant fall in value. The inventories of a business could also suffer this fate as a result of changes in market taste, obsolescence, deterioration, damage and so on. Where a fall in value means that the amount likely to be recovered from the sale of the inventories will be lower than their cost, this loss must be reflected in the statement of financial position. Thus, if the net realisable value (that is, selling price less any selling costs) falls below the historic cost of inventories held, the former should be used as the basis of valuation. This reflects, once again, the influence of prudence in preparing the statement of financial position.

Real World 2.6 reveals how one well-known business wrote down some of its inventories.

Real World 2.6

Next to nothing

The fashion and home furnishing retailer Next plc saw some of its inventories fall in value during the year ended 27 January 2018. This led to a reported loss of £116.1 million, which represented the difference between their cost and net realisable value. (However, the operating profit for the year was £759.9 million overall.) To see this in context, the value of inventories held at the year-end was £490.1 million and the cost of inventories treated as an expense during the year was £1,433.9 million. In the previous year, there was a reported loss of £109.9 million for the same reason. Inventories held at the end of January 2017 were valued at £451.1 million and inventories treated as an expense during that year was £1,441.0 million.

The fashion business, particularly women's fashion, is very fast moving and so losses from holding such inventories are not altogether surprising.

Source: Information taken from Next plc, Annual Report and Accounts for the year ended 27 January 2018, pages 102, 104 and 116.

The published financial statements of large businesses will normally show the basis on which inventories are valued. **Real World 2.7** shows how one business reports this information.

Real World 2.7

Reporting inventories

The 2017/18 annual report of Ted Baker plc, a leading designer clothes brand, includes the following explanation concerning inventories:

> Inventories and work in progress are stated at the lower of cost and net realisable value. Cost includes materials, direct labour and inward transportation costs. Net realisable value is based on estimated selling price, less further costs expected to be incurred to completion and disposal.

Source: Ted Baker plc, Annual Report and Accounts 2017/18, page 93.

Meeting user needs

The statement of financial position is the oldest of the three main financial statements and may help users in the following ways:

- *It provides insights about how the business is financed and how its funds are deployed.* The statement of financial position shows how much finance the owners contribute and how much is contributed by outside lenders. It also shows the different kinds of assets acquired and how much is invested in each kind.
- *It can provide a basis for assessing the value of the business.* Since the statement of financial position lists, and places a value on, the various assets and claims, it can provide a starting point for assessing the value of the business. We have seen earlier, however, that account- ing rules may result in assets being shown at their historic cost, which may vary quite considerably from the current valuation, and that the restrictive definition of assets may completely exclude certain business resources from the statement of financial position.
- *Relationships between assets and claims can be assessed.* It can be useful to look at relation- ships between various statement of financial position items, for example the relation- ship between how much wealth is tied up in current assets and how much is owed in the short term (current liabilities). From this relationship, we can see whether the busi- ness has sufficient short-term assets to cover its maturing obligations. We shall look at this and other relationships between statement of financial position items in some detail in Chapter 7.
- *Performance can be assessed.* The effectiveness of a business in generating wealth can usefully be assessed against the amount of investment that was involved. Thus, the relationship between profit earned during a period and the value of the net assets invested can be helpful to many users, particularly owners and managers. This and similar relationships will also be explored in detail in Chapter 7.

Once armed with the insights that a statement of financial position can provide, users are better placed to make investment and other decisions. **Real World 2.8** shows how a small business was able to obtain a loan because its bank was impressed by its strong statement of financial position.

Real World 2.8

A sound education

Sandeep Sud is a qualified solicitor who also runs a school uniform business based in Hounslow, in partnership with his parents. The business, which has four full-time employ- ees, uses its statement of financial position to gauge how it is progressing. The statement has also been a key factor in securing a bank loan for the improvement and expansion of the business premises.

According to Sandeep,

Having a strong statement of financial position helped when it came to borrowing. When we first applied for a refurbishment loan we couldn't provide up-to-date accounts to the bank manager. This could have been a problem, but we quickly got our accounts in order and the loan was approved straight away. Because our statement of financial position was strong, the bank thought we were a good risk. Although we decided not to draw down on the loan – because we used cashflow instead – it did open our eyes to the importance of a strong statement of financial position.

Source: Adapted from: Balance sheets: the basics, www.businesslink.gov.uk, accessed 14 April 2010.

Self-assessment question 2.1

The following information relates to Simonson Engineering as at 30 September 2019:

	£
Plant and equipment	25,000
Trade payables	18,000
Short-term borrowings	26,000
Inventories	45,000
Property	72,000
Long-term borrowings	51,000
Trade receivables	48,000
Equity at 1 October 2017	117,500
Cash in hand	1,500
Motor vehicles	15,000
Fixtures and fittings	9,000
Profit for the year to 30 September 2018	18,000
Drawings for the year to 30 September 2018	15,000

Required:

(a) Prepare a statement of financial position for the business as at 30 September 2019 using the standard layout illustrated in Example 2.3.

(b) Comment on the financial position of the business based on the statement prepared in (a).

(c) Show the effect on the statement of financial position shown in (a) of a decision to revalue the property to £115,000 and to recognise that the net realisable value of inventories at the year end is £38,000.

The solution to this question can be found in at the back of the book on pages 749–750.

Summary

The main points of this chapter may be summarised as follows:

The major financial statements

● There are three major financial statements: the statement of cash flows, the income statement and the statement of financial position.

● The statement of cash flows shows the cash movements over a particular period.

● The income statement shows the wealth (profit) generated over a particular period.

● The statement of financial position shows the accumulated wealth at a particular point in time.

The statement of financial position

● The statement of financial position sets out the assets of the business, on the one hand, and the claims against those assets, on the other.

● Assets are resources of the business that have certain characteristics, such as the right to potential economic benefits.

- Claims are obligations on the part of the business to provide cash, or some other benefit, to outside parties.
- Claims are of two types: equity and liabilities.
- Equity represents the claim(s) of the owner(s) and liabilities represent the claims of others.
- The statement of financial position reflects the accounting equation:

$$\text{Assets} = \text{Equity} + \text{Liabilities}$$

Classification of assets and liabilities

- Assets are normally categorised as being current or non-current.
- Current assets are cash or near cash or are held for sale or consumption in the normal course of business, or for trading, or for the short term.
- Non-current assets are assets that are not current assets. They are normally held for the long-term operations of the business.
- Liabilities are normally categorised as being current or non-current liabilities.
- Current liabilities represent amounts due in the normal course of the business's operating cycle, or are held for trading, or are to be settled within a year of, or cannot be deferred for at least a year after, the end of the reporting period.
- Non-current liabilities represent amounts due that are not current liabilities.

Statement of financial position layouts

- The standard layout begins with assets at the top of the statement of financial position and places equity and liabilities underneath.
- A variation of the standard layout also begins with the assets at the top of the statement of financial position, but then the non-current and current liabilities are deducted from the total assets figure to arrive at a net assets figure. Equity is placed underneath.

Accounting conventions

- Accounting conventions are the rules of accounting that have evolved to deal with practical problems experienced by those preparing financial statements.
- The main conventions relating to the statement of financial position include the business entity, historic cost, prudence, going concern and dual aspect conventions.

Money measurement

- Using money as the unit of measurement limits the scope of the statement of financial position.
- Certain resources such as goodwill, product brands and human resources are difficult to measure. An 'arm's-length transaction' is normally required before such assets can be measured with reasonable certainty and reported on the statement of financial position.
- Money is not a stable unit of measurement – it changes in value over time.

Asset valuation

- The initial treatment is to show non-current assets at historic cost.

- Fair values may be used rather than historic cost, provided that they can be reliably obtained. This is rarely possible, however, for intangible non-current assets.
- Non-current assets with finite useful lives should be shown at cost (or fair value) less any accumulated depreciation (amortisation).
- Where the value of a non-current asset is impaired, it should be written down to its recoverable amount.
- Inventories are shown at the lower of cost or net realisable value.

The usefulness of the statement of financial position

- The statement of financial position shows how finance has been raised and how it has been deployed.
- It provides a basis for valuing the business, though it can only be a starting point.
- Relationships between various statement of financial position items can usefully be explored.
- Relationships between wealth generated and wealth invested can be a helpful indicator of business effectiveness.

Key terms

For definitions of these terms, see Appendix B.

statement of cash flows *p. 42*	non-current (fixed) asset *p. 56*
income statement *p. 42*	property, plant and equipment *p. 56*
statement of financial position *p. 42*	current liability *p. 58*
final accounts *p. 45*	non-current liability *p. 58*
assets *p. 46*	accounting convention *p. 62*
claims *p. 46*	business entity convention *p. 62*
trade receivable *p. 49*	historic cost convention *p. 62*
tangible asset *p. 50*	prudence convention *p. 64*
intangible asset *p. 50*	going concern convention *p. 65*
equity *p. 50*	dual aspect convention *p. 65*
liability *p. 50*	goodwill *p. 67*
trade payable *p. 52*	carrying amount *p. 69*
reporting period *p. 53*	fair value *p. 70*
current asset *p. 56*	impairment loss *p. 72*

Reference

1 International Accounting Standards Board (2018) *Conceptual Framework for Financial Reporting*, pages 28 to 31.

Further reading

If you would like to explore the topics covered in this chapter in more depth, we recommend the following:

Elliott, B. and Elliott, J. (2017) *Financial Accounting and Reporting,* 18th edn, Pearson, Chapters 17, 19 and 20.

International Accounting Standards Board, *IFRS Standards – Required 1 January 2018 (Blue Book) Part A,* IAS 16 *Property, Plant and Equipment* and IAS 38 *Intangible Assets.*

KPMG Audit Committee Institute, *Insights into IFRS: An Overview,* September 2018, Sections 3.2, 3.3, 3.8 and 3.10. (This publication is available free at www.kpmg.com.)

Melville, A. (2017) *International Financial Reporting: A Practical Guide,* 6th edn, Pearson, Chapters 5, 6 and 7.

Critical review questions

Solutions to these questions can be found at the back of the book on pages 771–772.

2.1 An accountant prepared a statement of financial position for a business. In this statement, the equity of the owner was shown next to the liabilities. This confused the owner, who argued, 'My equity is my major asset and so should be shown as an asset on the statement of financial position.' How would you explain this misunderstanding to the owner?

2.2 'The statement of financial position shows how much a business is worth.' Do you agree with this statement? Explain the reasons for your response.

2.3 The statement of financial position is sometimes seen as the least important of the three major financial statements discussed in this chapter. Can you see why this might be the case?

2.4 From time to time, there have been attempts to place a value on the 'human assets' of a business in order to derive a figure that can be included on the statement of financial position. Do you think humans should be treated as assets? Would 'human assets' meet the conventional definition of an asset for inclusion on the statement of financial position?

Exercises

Solutions to exercises with coloured numbers can be found at the back of the book on pages 785–787.

Basic-level exercises

2.1 On Thursday, the fourth day of his business venture, Paul, the street trader in wrapping paper (see earlier in the chapter, pages 42–45), bought more inventories for £53 cash. During the day he sold inventories that had cost £33 for a total of £47.

Required:
Draw up the three financial statements for Paul's business venture for Thursday.

2.2   The equity of Paul's business belongs to him because he is the sole owner of the business. Can you explain how the figure for equity by Thursday evening has arisen? You will need to look back at the events of Monday, Tuesday and Wednesday (pages 42–45) to do this.

Intermediate-level exercises

2.3   While on holiday, Helen had her credit cards and purse stolen from the beach while she was swimming. She was left with only £40, which she had kept in her hotel room, but she had three days of her holiday remaining. She was determined to continue her holiday and decided to make some money to enable her to do so. She decided to sell orange juice to holidaymakers using the local beach. On the first day, she bought 80 cartons of orange juice at £0.50 each for cash and sold 70 of these at £0.80 each. On the following day, she bought 60 cartons at £0.50 each for cash and sold 65 at £0.80 each. On the third and final day, she bought another 60 cartons at £0.50 each for cash. However, it rained and, as a result, business was poor. She managed to sell 20 at £0.80 each but sold off the rest of her inventories at £0.40 each.

Required:
Prepare an income statement and statement of cash flows for each day's trading and prepare a statement of financial position at the end of each day's trading.

2.4   On 1 March, Joe Conday started a new business. During his first week, he carried out the following transactions:

1 March	Deposited £20,000 in a newly opened business bank account.
2 March	Bought fixtures and fittings for £6,000 cash and inventories £8,000 on credit.
3 March	Borrowed £5,000 from a relative and deposited it in the bank.
4 March	Bought a motor car for £7,000 cash and withdrew £200 in cash for his own use.
5 March	Bought a further motor car costing £9,000. The motor car bought on 4 March was given in part exchange at a value of £6,500. The balance of the purchase price for the new car was paid in cash.
6 March	Conday won £2,000 in a lottery and paid the amount into the business bank account. He also repaid £1,000 of the borrowings.

Required:
Draw up a statement of financial position for the business at the end of each day.

2.5   The following is a list of assets and claims of a manufacturing business at a particular point in time:

	£
Short-term borrowings	22,000
Property	245,000
Inventories of raw materials	18,000
Trade payables	23,000
Plant and equipment	127,000
Loan from Manufacturing Finance Co. (long-term borrowing)	100,000
Inventories of finished goods	28,000
Delivery vans	54,000
Trade receivables	34,000

Required:
Write out a statement of financial position in the standard format incorporating these figures. (*Hint*: There is a missing item that needs to be deduced and inserted.)

Advanced-level exercises

2.6 The following is a list of the assets and claims of Crafty Engineering as at 30 June last year:

	£000
Trade payables	86
Motor vehicles	38
Long-term borrowing (loan from Industrial Finance Company)	260
Equipment and tools	207
Short-term borrowings	116
Inventories	153
Property	320
Trade receivables	185

Required:

(a) Prepare the statement of financial position of the business as at 30 June last year from the information provided, using the standard layout. (*Hint*: There is a missing item that needs to be deduced and inserted.)

(b) Discuss the significant features revealed by this financial statement.

2.7 The statement of financial position of a business at the start of the week is as follows:

	£
ASSETS	
Property	145,000
Furniture and fittings	63,000
Inventories	28,000
Trade receivables	33,000
Total assets	269,000
EQUITY AND LIABILITIES	
Equity	203,000
Short-term borrowing (bank overdraft)	43,000
Trade payables	23,000
Total equity and liabilities	269,000

During the week, the following transactions take place:

(a) Sold inventories for £11,000 cash; these inventories had cost £8,000.
(b) Sold inventories for £23,000 on credit; these inventories had cost £17,000.
(c) Received cash from trade receivables totalling £18,000.
(d) The owners of the business introduced £100,000 of their own money, which was placed in the business bank account.
(e) The owners brought a motor van, valued at £10,000, into the business.
(f) Bought inventories on credit for £14,000.
(g) Paid trade payables £13,000.

Required:

Show the statement of financial position after all of these transactions have been reflected.

CHAPTER 3

Measuring and reporting financial performance

Introduction

In this chapter, we continue our examination of the major financial statements by looking at the income statement. This statement was briefly considered in Chapter 2, but we shall now look at it in some detail. We shall see how it is prepared and how it links with the statement of financial position. We shall also consider some of the key measurement problems that have to be faced when preparing the income statement.

Learning outcomes

When you have completed this chapter, you should be able to:

● discuss the nature and purpose of the income statement;

● prepare an income statement from relevant financial information and interpret the information that it contains;

● discuss the main recognition and measurement issues that must be considered when preparing the income statement; and

● explain the main accounting conventions underpinning the income statement.

The income statement

Businesses exist for the primary purpose of generating wealth, or **profit**. The income statement – or *profit and loss account,* as it is sometimes called – measures and reports how much profit a business has generated over a period. It is, therefore, an immensely important financial statement for many users.

To measure profit for a particular period, the total **revenue** generated during that period must be identified. Revenue is simply a measure of the inflow of economic benefits arising from the ordinary operations of a business. These benefits result in either an increase in assets (such as cash or amounts owed to the business by its customers) or a decrease in liabilities. Different forms of business activities generate different forms of revenue. Some examples of the different forms that revenue can take are as follows:

- sales of goods (for example, by a manufacturer);
- fees for services (for example, of a solicitor);
- subscriptions (for example, of a club); and
- interest received (for example, on an investment fund).

Real World 3.1 shows the various forms of revenue generated by a leading football club.

Real World 3.1

Gunning for revenue

Arsenal Football Club generated total revenue of £424 million for the year ended 31 May 2017. Like other leading clubs, it relies on various forms of revenue to sustain its success. Figure 3.1 shows the contribution of each form of revenue for the year.

| Figure 3.1 | Arsenal's revenue for the year ended 31 May 2017 |

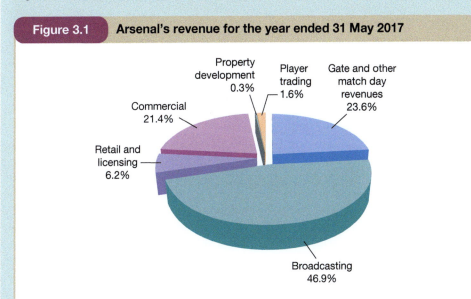

Gate receipts and broadcasting are Arsenal's main forms of revenue for 2017. Together, these account for around 70 per cent of the total revenue generated. Revenue during the year from player trading was insignificant by comparison.

Source: Based on information in Arsenal Holdings plc, Statement of Accounts and Annual Report 2016/2017, page 47.

The total **expenses** relating to each period must also be identified. Expense is really the opposite of revenue. It represents the outflow of economic benefits arising from the ordinary operations of a business. This outflow results in either a decrease in assets (such as cash) or an increase in liabilities (such as amounts owed to suppliers). Expenses are incurred in the process of generating revenue or, at least, in attempting to generate it. The nature of the business will again determine the type of expenses that will be incurred. Examples of some of the more common types of expense are:

- the cost of buying or making the goods that are sold during the period concerned – known as **cost of sales** or *cost of goods sold*;
- salaries and wages;
- rent;
- motor vehicle running expenses;
- insurance;
- printing and stationery;
- heat and light; and
- telephone and postage.

The income statement simply shows the total revenue generated during a particular reporting period and deducts from this the total expenses incurred in generating that revenue. The difference between the total revenue and total expenses will represent either profit (if revenue exceeds expenses) or loss (if expenses exceed revenue). Therefore:

> **Profit (or loss) for the period = Total revenue for the period − Total expenses incurred in generating that revenue**

Different roles

The income statement and the statement of financial position are not substitutes for one another. Rather, they perform different roles. The statement of financial position sets out the wealth held by the business at a single moment in time, whereas the income statement is concerned with the *flow* of wealth (profit) over a period of time. The two statements are, however, closely related.

The income statement links the statements of financial position at the beginning and the end of a reporting period. At the start of a new reporting period, the statement of financial position shows the opening wealth position of the business. At the end of that reporting period, an income statement is prepared to show the wealth generated during that period. A statement of financial position is then prepared to reveal the new wealth position at the end of the period. It will reflect changes in wealth that have occurred since the previous statement of financial position was drawn up.

We saw in Chapter 2 (pages 51–53) that the effect on the statement of financial position of making a profit (or loss) means that the accounting equation can be extended as follows:

> **Assets (at the end of the period) = Equity (amount at the start of the period)**
> **+ Profit (or − Loss) for the period**
> **+ Liabilities (at the end of the period)**

Activity 3.1

Can you recall from Chapter 2 how a profit, or loss, for a period is shown in the statement of financial position?

It is shown as an adjustment to owners' equity. Profit is added and a loss is subtracted.

The accounting equation can be further extended to:

Assets (at the end of the period) = Equity (amount at the start of the period)
+ (Sales revenue − Expenses)(for the period)
+ Liabilities (at the end of the period)

In theory, it is possible to calculate the profit (or loss) for the period by making all adjustments for revenue and expenses through the equity section of the statement of financial position. However, this would be rather cumbersome. A better solution is to have an 'appendix' to the equity section, in the form of an income statement. By deducting expenses from revenue for the period, the income statement derives the profit (or loss) by which the equity figure in the statement of financial position needs to be adjusted. Through this 'appendix', users are presented with a detailed and more informative view of performance.

Income statement layout

The layout of the income statement will vary according to the type of business to which it relates. To illustrate an income statement, let us consider the case of a retail business (that is, a business that buys goods in their completed state and resells them).

Example 3.1 sets out a typical layout for the income statement of a retail business.

Example 3.1

Better-Price Stores
Income statement for the year ended 30 June 2019

	£
Sales revenue	232,000
Cost of sales	(154,000)
Gross profit	78,000
Salaries and wages	(24,500)
Rent	(14,200)
Heat and light	(7,500)
Telephone and postage	(1,200)
Insurance	(1,000)
Motor vehicle running expenses	(3,400)
Depreciation – fixtures and fittings	(1,000)
– motor van	(600)
Operating profit	24,600
Interest received from investments	2,000
Interest on borrowings	(1,100)
Profit for the period	25,500

We saw in Chapter 2 that brackets are used to denote when an item is to be deducted. This convention is used by accountants in preference to + or − signs and will be used throughout the text.

We can see from Example 3.1 that three measures of profit have been calculated. Let us now consider each of these in turn.

Gross profit

The first part of the income statement is concerned with calculating the **gross profit** for the period. We can see that revenue, which arises from selling the goods, is the first item to appear. Deducted from this item is the cost of sales figure (also called cost of goods sold) during the period. This gives the gross profit, which represents the profit from buying and selling goods, without taking into account any other revenues or expenses associated with the business.

Operating profit

Operating expenses (overheads) incurred in running the business (salaries and wages, rent, insurance and so on) are deducted from the gross profit. The resulting figure is known as the **operating profit**. This represents the wealth generated during the period from the normal activities of the business. It does not take account of income from other activities. Better-Price Stores in Example 3.1 is a retailer, so interest received on some spare cash that the business has invested is not part of its operating profit. Costs of financing the business are also ignored in the calculation of the operating profit.

Profit for the period

Having established the operating profit, we add any non-operating income (such as interest receivable) and deduct any interest payable on borrowings to arrive at the **profit for the period** (or net profit). This final measure of wealth generated represents the amount attributable to the owner(s) and will be added to the equity figure in the statement of financial position. It is a residual: that is, the amount remaining after deducting all expenses incurred in generating the sales revenue and taking account of non-operating income and expenses.

Activity 3.2

Look back to Example 3.1 and assume that a trainee accountant had prepared the income statement. Subsequent checking by the chief financial officer revealed the following errors:

1 Sales performance bonuses payable to staff amounting to £12,500 had been charged to cost of sales.
2 The depreciation charge for fixtures and fittings should be £10,000, not £1,000.
3 Stationery costing £500 had been treated as interest on borrowings.

What will be the gross profit, operating profit and profit for the period after these errors have been corrected?

Staff bonuses should be treated as part of the salaries and wages expense of the business. This means that cost of sales will decrease by £12,500 and gross profit will increase by a corresponding amount. The corrected gross profit is therefore £90,500 (that is, £78,000 + £12,500).

The operating profit and profit for the period, however, will not be affected by this correction. Although the operating expense salaries and wages will increase, this is offset by a compensating increase in gross profit.

The increase in the depreciation charge from £1,000 to £10,000 will decrease operating profit by £9,000. Furthermore, by treating stationery correctly, operating expenses will increase by £500, thereby decreasing operating profit by a corresponding amount. The corrected operating profit figure is, therefore, £15,100 (that is, £24,600 − £9,500).

Finally, the corrected profit for the period is calculated by taking the corrected operating profit £15,100, adding the interest received from investments, £2,000, and deducting the correct amount of interest on borrowing £600 (that is, £1,100 − £500) = £16,500.

Further issues

Having set out the main principles involved in preparing an income statement, we need to consider some further points.

Cost of sales

The cost of sales (or cost of goods sold) for a period can be identified in different ways. In some businesses, the cost of sales for each individual item at the time of sale. By so doing, each item sold is matched with the relevant cost of that sale. Many large retailers (for example, supermarkets) have point-of-sale (checkout) devices that not only record each sale but also simultaneously pick up the cost of the goods that are the subject of the particular sale. Businesses that sell a relatively small number of high-value items (for example, an engineering business that produces custom-made equipment) also tend to match sales revenue for each item with the cost of the goods sold, at the time of sale. However, many businesses (for example, small retailers) may not find it practical to do this. Instead, they identify the cost of sales after the end of the reporting period.

To understand how this is done, we must remember that the cost of sales represents the cost of goods that were *sold* during the period rather than the cost of goods that were *bought* during the period. Part of the goods bought during the period may remain, as inventories, at the end of the period. These will normally be sold in the next period. To derive the cost of sales, we need to know the amount of opening and closing inventories for the period and the cost of goods bought during the period. Example 3.2 illustrates how the cost of sales is derived.

Example 3.2

Better-Price Stores, which we considered in Example 3.1, began the year with unsold inventories of £40,000 and during that year bought inventories at a cost of £189,000. At the end of the year, unsold inventories of £75,000 were still held by the business.

Example 3.2 *continued*

The opening (beginning of the year) inventories *plus* the goods bought during the year represent the total goods available for resale, as follows:

	£
Opening inventories	40,000
Purchases (goods bought)	189,000
Goods available for resale	229,000

The closing inventories represent that portion of the total goods available for resale that remains unsold at the end of the year. This means that the cost of goods actually sold during the year must be the total goods available for resale *less* the inventories remaining at the end of the year. That is:

	£
Goods available for resale	229,000
Closing inventories	(75,000)
Cost of sales (or cost of goods sold)	154,000

These calculations are sometimes shown on the face of the income statement as in Example 3.3.

Example 3.3

	£	£
Sales revenue		232,000
Cost of sales:		
Opening inventories	40,000	
Purchases (goods bought)	189,000	
Closing inventories	(75,000)	(154,000)
Gross profit		78,000

This is just an expanded version of the first section of the income statement for Better-Price Stores, as set out in Example 3.1. We have simply included the additional information concerning inventories balances and purchases for the year, provided in Example 3.2.

Classifying expenses

The classification of expense items is often a matter of judgement. For example, the income statement set out in Example 3.1 could have included the insurance expense with the telephone and postage expense under a single heading – say, 'general expenses'. Such decisions are normally based on how useful a particular classification will be to users. This will usually mean that expense items of material size will be shown separately. For businesses that trade as limited companies, however, rules dictate the classification of expense items for external reporting purposes. These rules will be discussed in Chapter 5.

Activity 3.3

The following information relates to the activities of H & S Retailers for the year ended 30 April 2019:

	£
Motor vehicle running expenses	1,200
Closing inventories	3,000
Rent payable	5,000
Motor vans – cost less depreciation	6,300
Annual depreciation – motor vans	1,500
Heat and light	900
Telephone and postage	450
Sales revenue	97,400
Goods purchased	68,350
Insurance	750
Loan interest payable	620
Balance at bank	4,780
Salaries and wages	10,400
Opening inventories	4,000

Prepare an income statement for the year ended 30 April 2019. (*Hint*: Not all items listed should appear on this statement.)

Your answer should be as follows:

H & S Retailers Income Statement for the year ended 30 April 2019

	£	£
Sales revenue		97,400
Cost of sales:		
Opening inventories	4,000	
Purchases	68,350	
Closing inventories	(3,000)	(69,350)
Gross profit		28,050
Salaries and wages		(10,400)
Rent payable		(5,000)
Heat and light		(900)
Telephone and postage		(450)
Insurance		(750)
Motor vehicle running expenses		(1,200)
Depreciation – motor vans		(1,500)
Operating profit		7,850
Loan interest		(620)
Profit for the period		7,230

Note that neither the motor vans nor the bank balance are included in this statement. This is because they are both assets and so are neither revenues nor expenses.

Figure 3.2 shows the layout of the income statement.

Figure 3.2   **The layout of the income statement**

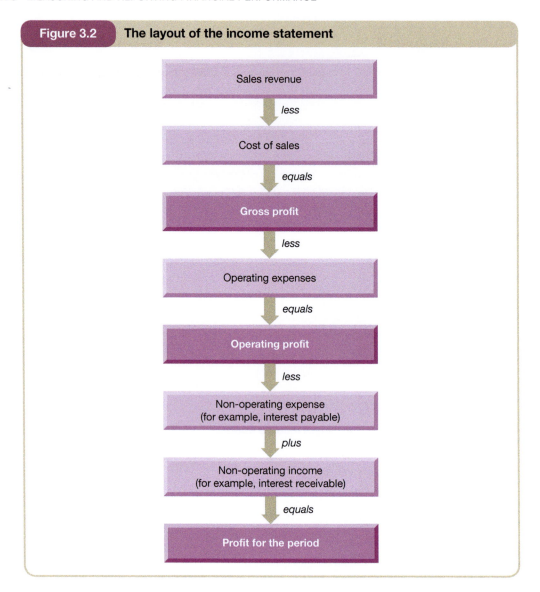

Recognising revenue

The amount to which a business is entitled for providing goods or services to a customer should be recognised as revenue. It should be recognised as soon as control of the goods or services is transferred to the customer. At this point, the business has satisfied its obligations towards the customer. To determine when control has passed, there are important indicators, such as when:

- physical possession passes to the customer;
- the business has the right to demand payment for the goods or services;
- the customer has accepted the goods or services;
- legal title passes to the customer; and
- significant risks and rewards of ownership passes to the customer.

If we take the example of a self-service store, where sales are for cash, the above indicators suggest that revenue can normally be recognised when the customer checks out. However, revenue recognition is not always so straightforward. Activity 3.4 provides the opportunity to apply the indicators to a slightly trickier situation.

Activity 3.4

A manufacturer produces and sells a standard product on credit, which is transported to customers using the manufacturer's delivery vans. Managers believe there are four different points in the production/selling cycle at which revenue *might* be recognised. These are:

1 when the goods are produced;
2 when an order is received from a customer;
3 when the goods are delivered to, and accepted by, the customer; or
4 when the cash is received from the customer.

At which of these points do you think the manufacturer should recognise revenue?

The indicators listed above point towards to point 3, that is when the goods are passed to, and accepted by, the customer. At this point, the customer acquires legal title, takes possession of the goods and so on.

The point at which revenue is recognised is not simply an academic issue. It can have a significant impact on reported revenues and, therefore, profit, for a period. Where a credit sale transaction straddles the end of a reporting period, the point chosen for recognising revenue can determine whether it is included in an earlier reporting period or a later one.

Revenue recognition and cash receipts

We can see from Activity 3.4 above that a sale on credit is usually recognised *before* the cash is received. This means that the total sales revenue shown in the income statement may include sales transactions for which the cash has yet to be received. The total sales revenue will, therefore, usually be different from the total cash received from sales during the period. For cash sales (that is, sales where cash is paid at the same time as the goods are transferred), there will be no difference in timing between reporting sales revenue and cash received.

Activity 3.5

Although revenue for providing services is often recognised before the cash is received, there are occasions when it is the other way around: a business will require payment before providing the service.
Can you think of two examples? (*Hint*: Try to think of services that you may use.)

Examples of cash being received in advance of the service being provided may include:

● rent received from letting premises;
● telephone line rental charges;
● TV licence (BBC) or subscription fees (for example, Sky); and
● subscriptions received by health clubs or golf clubs.

You may have thought of others.

Recognising revenue over time

Control of goods or services may be transferred to a customer over time rather than as a single 'one-off' event. When this occurs, the total revenue must be recognised over time. This situation may arise where:

- *the customer enjoys the benefits as the business carries out its obligations*. This can occur with service contracts, such as where an accounting firm undertakes employee payroll services for a large business or when an internet service is being provided.
- *the business creates, or improves, an asset held by the customer*. This can occur with building contracts, such as where a builder undertakes the refurbishment of a shop owned by a retailer or when a shipbuilder carries out extensive repairs to a large ship.
- *the business creates an asset with no alternative use and the customer has agreed to pay for work carried out*. This can apply to special orders, such as where an engineering business produces specially-designed equipment for a manufacturer or where a furniture manufacturer makes customised furniture for a hotel chain.

Where control is transferred over time, the total revenue will be spread across the reporting periods covered by the contract. In other words, part of the total contract price will be treated as revenue in each reporting period. To do this, however, it must be possible to measure progress towards complete fulfilment of the business's obligations towards the customer. Otherwise, the amount of progress made during a particular period cannot really be determined.

To determine the appropriate revenue for each period, some method of measuring progress towards transferring the goods or services is needed. Various methods are available. Some are based on outputs, or achievements, such as particular 'milestones' reached in completing the contract, the number of units delivered, the number of services provided. Others are based on inputs, or effort expended, such as costs incurred, materials consumed, or hours worked. There is no single correct method: it depends on the particular circumstances. Nevertheless, methods based on output usually provide a more direct measure of the value of goods or services transferred to customers than those based on inputs. Hence, output-based measures are often preferred.

Activity 3.6

Why might a business choose input-based methods to measure progress if they are generally considered to be inferior?

Where methods based on output are unreliable, or unavailable, methods based on input may be the only real choice.

To illustrate one approach to recognising revenue over time, let us take the example of a builder entering into a contract with a manufacturer to build a factory. The work will be carried out on land owned by the manufacturer and will take three years to complete. The contract recognises that building the factory can be broken down into the following stages:

- Stage 1 – clearing and levelling the land and putting in the foundations.
- Stage 2 – building the walls.
- Stage 3 – putting on the roof.
- Stage 4 – putting in the windows and completing all the interior work.

It is expected that Stage 1 of the contract will be completed by the end of Year 1, Stages 2 and 3 will be completed by the end of Year 2 and Stage 4 by the end of Year 3.

Once the performance obligations for a particular stage are satisfied, the builder can recognise the agreed proportion of the total contract price for that stage as revenue. Thus, the agreed proportion for completing Stage 1 will be reported as revenue in the income statement for Year 1 and so on. Normally, the contract would specify that the client would be required to pay the builder the appropriate proportion of the total contract price following successful completion of each stage.

Recognising expenses

Having considered the recognition of revenue, let us now turn to the recognition of expenses. The **matching convention** provides guidance on this. This convention states that expenses should be matched to the revenue that they helped to generate. In other words, the expenses associated with a particular item of revenue must be taken into account in the same reporting period as that in which the item of revenue is included. We saw how this convention is applied with the costs of sales for Better-Price Stores in Example 3.2. The appropriate expense was just the cost of inventories that were sold and not the whole cost of inventories that were available for sale, during the period.

Applying this convention often means that an expense reported in the income statement for a period may not be the same as the cash paid for that item during the period. The expense reported might be either more or less than the cash paid during the period. Examples 3.4 and 3.5 illustrate this point.

When the expense for the period is more than the cash paid during the period

Example 3.4

Domestic Ltd, a retailer, sells household electrical appliances. It pays its sales staff a commission of 2 per cent of sales revenue generated. Total sales revenue for last year amounted to £300,000. This means that the commission to be paid on sales for the year will be £6,000. However, by the end of the year, the amount of sales commission actually paid was only £5,000. If the business reported this amount as the sales commission expense, it would mean that the income statement would not reflect the full expense for the year. This would contravene the matching convention because not all of the expenses associated with the revenue of the year would have been matched with it in the income statement. This will be remedied as follows:

- Sales commission expense in the income statement will include the amount paid plus the amount outstanding (that is £6,000 = 5,000 + 1,000).
- The amount outstanding (£1,000) represents an outstanding liability at the end of the year and will be included under the heading **accrued expenses**, or 'accruals', in the statement of financial position. As this item will have to be paid within 12 months of the year-end, it will be treated as a current liability.
- The cash will already have been reduced to reflect the commission paid (£5,000) during the period.

Example 3.4 *continued*

These points are illustrated in Figure 3.3.

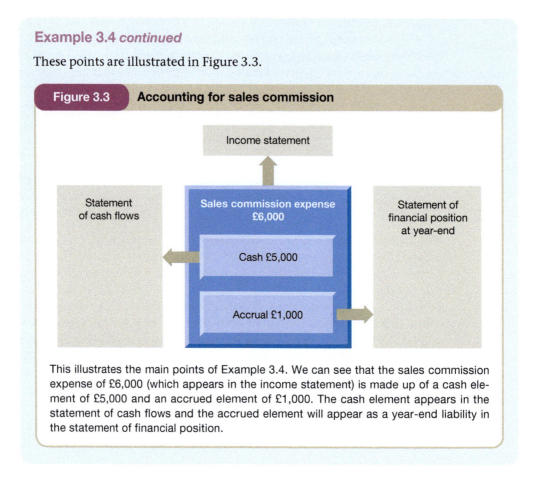

| Figure 3.3 | **Accounting for sales commission** |

This illustrates the main points of Example 3.4. We can see that the sales commission expense of £6,000 (which appears in the income statement) is made up of a cash element of £5,000 and an accrued element of £1,000. The cash element appears in the statement of cash flows and the accrued element will appear as a year-end liability in the statement of financial position.

In principle, all expenses should be matched to the period in which the sales revenue to which they relate is reported. It is sometimes difficult, however, to match certain expenses to sales revenue in the same precise way that we have matched sales commission to sales revenue. For example, electricity charges incurred often cannot be linked directly to particular sales in this way. As a result, the electricity charges incurred by, say, a retailer would be matched to the *period* to which they relate. Example 3.5 illustrates this.

Example 3.5

Domestic Ltd, a retailer, has reached the end of its reporting period and has only paid for electricity for the first three quarters of the year (amounting to £1,900). This is simply because the electricity company has yet to send out bills for the quarter that ends on the same date as Domestic Ltd's year-end. The amount of Domestic Ltd's bill for the last quarter of the year is £500. In this situation, the amount of the electricity expense outstanding is dealt with as follows:

- Electricity expense in the income statement will include the amount paid, plus the amount of the bill for the last quarter of the year (that is, £1,900 + 500 = £2,400) in order to cover the whole year.
- The amount of the outstanding bill (£500) represents a liability at the end of the year and will be included under the heading 'accrued expenses' in the statement

of financial position. This item would normally have to be paid within 12 months of the year-end and will, therefore, be treated as a current liability.

- The cash will already have been reduced to reflect the amount (£1,900) paid for electricity during the period.

This treatment will mean that the correct figure for the electricity expense for the year will be included in the income statement. It will also have the effect of showing that, at the end of the reporting period, Domestic Ltd owed the amount of the last quarter's electricity bill. Dealing with the outstanding amount in this way reflects the dual aspect of the item and will ensure that the accounting equation is maintained.

Domestic Ltd may wish to draw up its income statement before it is able to discover how much it owes for the last quarter's electricity. In this case, it is quite normal to make an estimate of the amount of the bill and to use this amount as described above.

Activity 3.7

How will the eventual payment of the outstanding sales commission (Example 3.4) and the electricity bill for the last quarter (Example 3.5) be dealt with in the accounting records of Domestic Ltd?

When these amounts are eventually paid, they will be dealt with as follows:

- reduce cash by the amounts paid; and
- reduce the amount of the accrued expense as shown on the statement of financial position by the same amounts.

Other expenses, apart from electricity charges, may also be matched to the period to which they relate.

Activity 3.8

Can you think of other expenses for a retailer that cannot be linked directly to sales revenue and for which matching will therefore be done on a time basis? Try to think of at least two examples.

You may have thought of the following:

- rent payable;
- insurance;
- interest payable; and
- licence fees payable.

This is not an exhaustive list. You may have thought of others.

When the amount paid during the period is more than the full expense for the period

It is not unusual for a business to be in a situation where it has paid more during the year than the full expense for that year. Example 3.6 illustrates how we deal with this.

Example 3.6

Images Ltd, an advertising agency, normally pays rent for its premises quarterly in advance (on 1 January, 1 April, 1 July and 1 October). On the last day of the last reporting period (31 December), it paid the next quarter's rent (£4,000) to the following 31 March, which was a day earlier than required. This would mean that a total of five quarters' rent was paid during the year. If Images Ltd reports all of the cash paid as an expense in the income statement, this would be more than the full expense for the year. This would contravene the matching convention because a higher figure than the expenses associated with the revenue of the year would appear in the income statement.

The problem is overcome by dealing with the rental payment as follows:

- Show the rent for four quarters as the appropriate expense in the income statement (that is, 4 × £4,000 = £16,000).
- The cash (that is, 5 × £4,000 = £20,000) would already have been paid during the year.
- Show the quarter's rent paid in advance (£4,000) as a prepaid expense under assets in the statement of financial position. (The rent paid in advance will appear as a current asset in the statement of financial position, under the heading **prepaid expenses** or 'prepayments'.)

In the next reporting period, this prepayment will cease to be an asset and will become an expense in the income statement of that period. This is because the rent prepaid relates to the next period during which it will be 'used up'.

These points are illustrated in Figure 3.4.

Figure 3.4   Accounting for rent payable

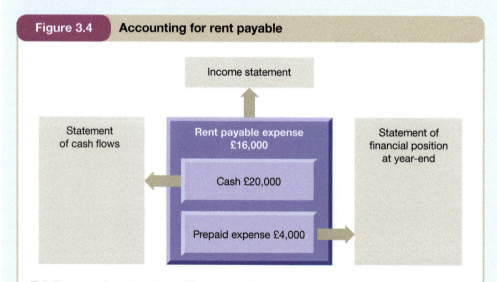

This illustrates the main points of Example 3.6. We can see that the rent expense of £16,000 (which appears in the income statement) is made up of four quarters' rent at £4,000 per quarter. This is the amount that relates to the period and is 'used up' during the period. The cash paid, £20,000 (which appears in the statement of cash flows), is made up of the cash paid during the period, which is five quarters at £4,000 per quarter. Finally, the prepayment of £4,000 (which appears on the statement of financial position) represents the payment made on 31st December and relates to the next reporting period.

In practice, the treatment of accruals and prepayments will be subject to the **materiality convention**. This convention states that, where the amounts involved are trivial, we should consider only what is expedient. This will usually mean treating an item as an expense in the period in which it is first recorded, rather than strictly matching it to the revenue to which it relates. For example, a large business may find that, at the end of a reporting period, it holds £20 worth of unused stationery. The time and effort taken to record this as a prepayment would outweigh the negligible effect on the measurement of profit or financial position. As a result, it would be treated as an expense of the current period and ignored in the following period.

Profit, cash and accruals accounting

We have seen that, normally, for a particular reporting period, total revenue is not the same as total cash received and total expenses are not the same as total cash paid. As a result, the profit for the period (that is, total revenue minus total expenses) will not normally represent the net cash generated during that period. This reflects the difference between profit and liquidity. Profit is a measure of achievement, or productive effort, rather than a measure of cash generated. Although making a profit increases wealth, cash is only one possible form in which that wealth may be held.

These points are reflected in the **accruals convention**, which asserts that profit is the excess of revenue over expenses for a period, not the excess of cash receipts over cash payments. Leading on from this, the approach to accounting that is based on the accruals convention is frequently referred to as **accruals accounting**. The statement of financial position and the income statement are both prepared on the basis of accruals accounting.

Activity 3.9

What about the statement of cash flows that we came across in Chapter 1? Is it prepared on an accruals accounting basis?

No. The statement of cash flows simply deals with cash receipts and payments.

One major organisation, the UK government, has only recently adopted accruals accounting, despite the fact that this approach has been standard practice in all private-sector organisations, and many public-sector ones, for very many years. **Real World 3.2** is based on a *Financial Times* article that discusses the change of approach.

Real World 3.2

Casting light on the UK economy

Only fairly recently (2014) has the UK government started using accruals accounting principles in its assessment of national output, for example, as measured by gross domestic product (GDP). Until then, it based its assessments of national economic output on a cash receipts and payments basis.

The main effect of the new accruals approach is that certain 'investments' will be recognised as such and will not simply be treated as 'expenses' in the year incurred, as they tend to be with a cash-based approach. Areas most affected by the switch to accruals accounting are:

- research and development, that is the acquisition of economically valuable knowledge;
- expenditure on weapons systems; and
- cash invested in pension schemes.

It is estimated that the effect of introducing accruals accounting will raise GDP by between 3.5 per cent and 5 per cent. Similar changes in the accounting approach taken in the United States added 3.5 per cent to its GDP.

Depreciation

The expense of **depreciation**, which we have already come across, requires further examination. Most non-current assets do not have a perpetual existence, but have finite, or limited, lives. They are eventually 'used up' in the process of generating revenue for the business. This 'using up' may relate to physical deterioration (as with a motor vehicle). It may, however, be linked to obsolescence (as with some IT software that is no longer useful) or the mere passage of time (as with a purchased patent, which has a limited period of validity).

In essence, depreciation is an attempt to measure that portion of the cost (or fair value) of a non-current asset that has been depleted in generating the revenue recognised during a particular period. In the case of intangibles, the expense is usually referred to as **amortisation** rather than *depreciation*.

Calculating the depreciation expense

To calculate a depreciation expense for a period, four factors have to be considered:

- the cost (or fair value) of the asset;
- the useful life of the asset;
- the residual value of the asset; and
- the depreciation method.

The cost (or fair value) of the asset

The cost of an asset will include all costs incurred by the business to bring the asset to its required location and to make it ready for use. This means that, in addition to the cost of acquiring the asset, any delivery costs, installation costs (for example, setting up a new machine) and legal costs incurred in the transfer of legal title (for example, in purchasing a lease on property) will be included as part of the total cost of the asset. Similarly, any costs incurred in improving or altering an asset to make it suitable for use will also be included as part of the total cost.

Activity 3.10

Andrew Wu (Engineering) Ltd bought a new motor car for its marketing director. The invoice received from the motor car supplier showed the following:

	£
New BMW 325i	28,350
Delivery charge	280
Alloy wheels	860
Sun roof	600
Petrol	80
Number plates	130
Road fund licence	150
	30,450
Part exchange – Reliant Robin	(1,000)
Amount outstanding	29,450

What is the total cost of the new car to be treated as part of the business's property, plant and equipment?

The cost of the new car will be as follows:

	£
New BMW 325i	28,350
Delivery charge	280
Alloy wheels	860
Sun roof	600
Number plates	130
Total cost	30,220

This cost includes delivery charges, which are necessary to bring the asset into use, and it includes number plates, as they are a necessary and integral part of the asset. Improvements (alloy wheels and sun roof) are also regarded as part of the total cost of the car. The petrol and road fund licence, however, are costs of operating the asset. These amounts will, therefore, be treated as expenses.

The part-exchange figure shown is part payment of the total amount outstanding and so is not relevant to a consideration of the total cost.

The fair value of an asset was defined in Chapter 2 as the selling price that could be obtained in an orderly transaction under market conditions. As we saw, assets may be revalued to fair value only if this can be measured reliably. Where fair values have been applied, the depreciation expense should be based on those fair values, rather than on the historic costs.

The useful life of the asset

A non-current asset has both a *physical life* and an *economic life*. The physical life will be exhausted through the effects of wear and tear and/or the passage of time. The economic life is decided by the effects of technological progress, by changes in demand or by changes in the way that the business operates. The benefits provided by the asset are eventually outweighed by the costs as it becomes unable to compete with newer assets, or becomes irrelevant to the needs of the business. The economic life of an asset may be much shorter than its physical life. For example, a computer may have a physical life of eight years and an economic life of three years.

The economic life determines the expected *useful life* of an asset for depreciation purposes. It is often difficult to estimate, however, as technological progress and shifts in consumer tastes can be swift and unpredictable.

Residual value (disposal value)

When a business disposes of a non-current asset that may still be of value to others, some payment may be received. This payment will represent the **residual value**, or *disposal value,* of the asset. To calculate the total amount to be depreciated, the residual value must be deducted from the cost (or fair value) of the asset. The likely amount to be received on disposal can, once again, be difficult to predict. The best guide is often past experience of similar assets sold.

Depreciation method

Once the amount to be depreciated (that is, the cost, or fair value, of the asset less any residual value) has been estimated, the business must select a method of allocating this depreciable amount between the reporting periods covering the asset's useful life. Although there are various ways in which this may be done, there are only two methods that are commonly used in practice.

The first of these is known as the **straight-line method**. This method simply allocates the amount to be depreciated evenly over the useful life of the asset. In other words, there is an equal depreciation expense for each year that the asset is held. Example 3.7 illustrates this.

Example 3.7

Consider the following information:

Cost of machine	£78,124
Estimated residual value at the end of its useful life	£2,000
Estimated useful life	4 years

To arrive at the depreciation expense for each year, the total amount to be depreciated must be calculated. This will be the total cost less the estimated residual value: that is, £78,124 − £2,000 = £76,124. The annual depreciation expense can then be derived by dividing the amount to be depreciated by the estimated useful life of the asset of four years. The calculation is therefore:

$$\frac{£76,124}{4} = £19,031$$

This means that the annual depreciation expense that appears in the income statement in relation to this asset will be £19,031 for each of the four years of the asset's life.

The amount of depreciation relating to the asset will be accumulated for as long as the asset continues to be owned by the business or until the accumulated depreciation amounts to the cost less residual value. This accumulated depreciation figure will increase each year as a result of the annual depreciation expense in the income statement. This accumulated amount will be deducted from the cost of the asset in the statement of financial position. At the end of the second year, for example, the accumulated depreciation will be £19,031 × 2 = £38,062. The asset details will appear on the statement of financial position as follows:

	£
Machine at cost	78,124
Accumulated depreciation	(38,062)
	40,062

As we saw in Chapter 2, this balance of £40,062 is referred to as the **carrying amount** (sometimes also known as the **written-down value** or **net book value**) of the asset. It represents that portion of the cost (or fair value) of the asset that has still to be treated as an expense (written off) in future years plus the residual value. This carrying-amount figure does not, except by coincidence, represent the current market value, which may be quite different. The only point at which the carrying amount is intended to represent the market value of the asset is at the time of its disposal. In Example 3.7, at the end of the four-year life of the machine, the carrying amount would be £2,000; its estimated disposal value.

The straight-line method derives its name from the fact that the carrying amount of the asset at the end of each year, when plotted against time, will result in a straight line, as shown in Figure 3.5.

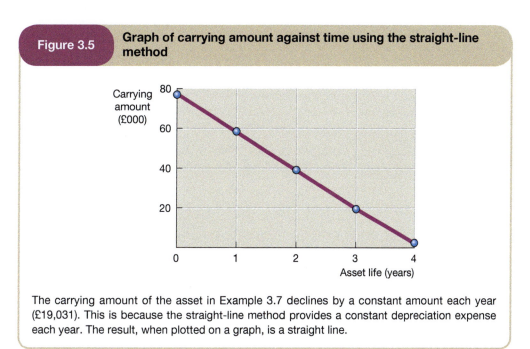

Figure 3.5 **Graph of carrying amount against time using the straight-line method**

The carrying amount of the asset in Example 3.7 declines by a constant amount each year (£19,031). This is because the straight-line method provides a constant depreciation expense each year. The result, when plotted on a graph, is a straight line.

The second approach to calculating the depreciation expense for a period is referred to as the **reducing-balance method**. This method applies a fixed percentage rate of depreciation to the carrying amount of the asset each year. The effect of this will be high annual depreciation expenses in the early years and lower expenses in the later years. To illustrate this method, let us take the same information that was used in Example 3.7. By using a fixed percentage of 60 per cent of the carrying amount to determine the annual depreciation expense, the effect will be to reduce the carrying amount to £2,000 after four years. The calculations will be as follows:

	£
Cost of machine	78,124
Year 1 depreciation expense (60%* of cost)	(46,874)
Carrying amount	31,250
Year 2 depreciation expense (60% of carrying amount)	(18,750)
Carrying amount	12,500
Year 3 depreciation expense (60% of carrying amount)	(7,500)
Carrying amount	5,000
Year 4 depreciation expense (60% of carrying amount)	(3,000)
Residual value	2,000

*See the box below for an explanation of how to derive the fixed percentage.

Deriving the fixed percentage

Deriving the fixed percentage to be applied requires the use of the following formula:

$$P = (1 - \sqrt[n]{R/C} \times 100\%)$$

where

P = the depreciation percentage
n = the useful life of the asset (in years)
C = the residual value of the asset
R = the cost, or fair value, of the asset.

The fixed percentage rate will, however, be given in all examples used in this book.

We can see that the pattern of depreciation is quite different between the two methods. If we plot against time the carrying amount of the asset that has been derived using the reducing-balance method, the result will be as shown in Figure 3.6.

Figure 3.6 **Graph of carrying amount against time using the reducing-balance method**

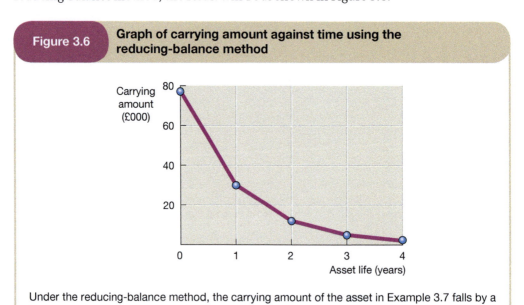

Under the reducing-balance method, the carrying amount of the asset in Example 3.7 falls by a larger amount in the earlier years than in the later years. This is because the depreciation expense is based on a fixed percentage of the carrying amount.

Activity 3.11

Assume that the machine in Example 3.7 was owned by a business that made a profit before depreciation of £40,000 for each of the four years in which the asset was held.

Calculate the profit for the business for each year under each depreciation method, and comment on your findings.

Your answer should be as follows:

Straight-line method

	(a) Profit before depreciation £	(b) Depreciation £	(a − b) Profit £
Year 1	40,000	19,031	20,969
Year 2	40,000	19,031	20,969
Year 3	40,000	19,031	20,969
Year 4	40,000	19,031	20,969

Reducing-balance method

	(a) Profit before depreciation £	(b) Depreciation £	(a − b) Profit £
Year 1	40,000	46,874	(6,874)
Year 2	40,000	18,750	21,250
Year 3	40,000	7,500	32,500
Year 4	40,000	3,000	37,000

The straight-line method of depreciation results in the same profit figure for each year of the four-year period. This is because both the profit before depreciation and the depreciation expense are constant over the period. The reducing-balance method, however, results in very different profit figures for the four years, despite the fact that in this example the pre-depreciation profit is the same each year. In the first year, a loss is reported and, thereafter, a rising profit.

Although the *pattern* of profit over the four-year period will be quite different, depending on the depreciation method used, the *total* profit for the period (£83,876) will remain the same. This is because both methods of depreciating will allocate the same amount of total depreciation (£76,124) over the four-year period. It is only the amount allocated *between years* that will differ.

In practice, the use of different depreciation methods may not have such a dramatic effect on profits as suggested in Activity 3.11. This is because businesses typically have more than one depreciating non-current asset. Where a business replaces some of its assets each year, the total depreciation expense calculated under the reducing-balance method will reflect a range of expenses (from high through to low), as assets will be at different points in their economic lives. This could mean that each year's total depreciation expense may not be significantly different from that which would have been derived under the straight-line method.

Selecting a depreciation method

The appropriate depreciation method to choose is the one that reflects the consumption of economic benefits provided by the asset. Where the economic benefits are consumed evenly over time (for example, with buildings) the straight-line method is usually appropriate. Where the economic benefits consumed decline over time (for example, with certain types of machinery that lose their efficiency) the reducing-balance method may be more appropriate. Where the pattern of economic benefits consumed is uncertain, the straight-line method is normally chosen.

There is an International Financial Reporting Standard (or International Accounting Standard) to deal with the depreciation of property, plant and equipment. As we shall see in Chapter 5, the purpose of accounting standards is to narrow areas of accounting difference and to ensure that information provided to users is transparent and comparable. The relevant standard endorses the view that the depreciation method chosen should reflect the pattern of consumption of economic benefits but does not specify particular methods to be used. It states that the useful life, depreciation method and residual values for property, plant and equipment should be reviewed at least annually and adjustments made where appropriate. For intangible non-current assets with finite lives, there is a separate standard containing broadly similar rules. It does state, however, that the straight-line method must be chosen where the pattern of consumption of economic benefits is not clear.

Real World 3.3 sets out the depreciation policies of one large business.

Real World 3.3

Depreciating assets

Mothercare plc is a leading retailer that is focused on the needs of parents and young children. The annual reports of the business for the 52 weeks ended 24 March 2018 set out the following depreciation policies.

Property, plant and equipment

Property, plant and equipment is carried at cost less accumulated depreciation and any recognised impairment losses. Depreciation is charged so as to write off the cost or valuation of assets, other than land and assets in the course of construction, over their estimated useful lives, using the straight-line method, on the following bases:

> Freehold buildings – 50 years
> Fixed equipment in freehold buildings – 20 years
> Leasehold improvements – the lease term
> Fixtures, fittings and equipment – 3 to 20 years

Intangible assets – software

Where computer software is not an integral part of a related item of computer hardware, the software is classified as an intangible asset. The capitalised costs of software for internal use include external direct costs of materials and services consumed in developing or obtaining the software and payroll and payroll-related costs for employees who are directly associated with and who devote substantial time to the project.

These costs are amortised on a straight-line basis over their expected useful lives, which is normally five years.

Source: Extracts from Mothercare plc, Annual Report and Accounts 2018, p. 99, www.mothercare.com.

Mothercare plc is typical of most UK businesses in that it uses the straight-line method of depreciation. The reducing-balance method is very much less popular.

The approach taken to calculating depreciation is summarised in Figure 3.7.

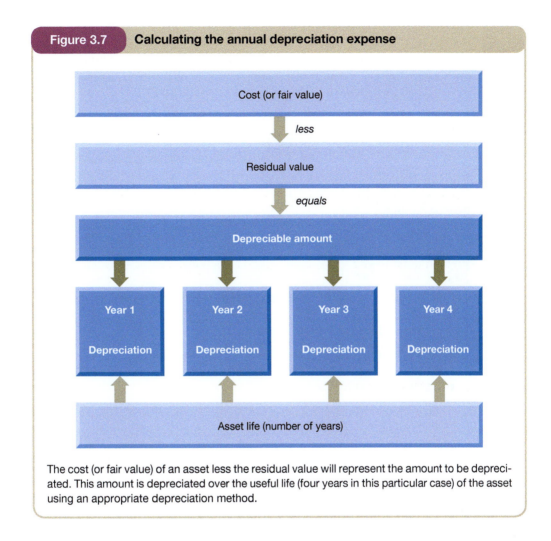

Figure 3.7 **Calculating the annual depreciation expense**

The cost (or fair value) of an asset less the residual value will represent the amount to be depreciated. This amount is depreciated over the useful life (four years in this particular case) of the asset using an appropriate depreciation method.

Impairment and depreciation

We saw in Chapter 2 that all non-current assets could be subjected to an impairment test. Where a non-current asset with a finite life has its carrying amount reduced following an impairment test, depreciation expenses for future reporting periods should be based on the impaired value.

Depreciation and asset replacement

Some appear to believe that the purpose of depreciation is to provide the funds for the replacement of a non-current asset when it reaches the end of its useful life. However, this is not the case. It was mentioned earlier that depreciation represents an attempt to allocate the cost or fair value (less any residual value) of a non-current asset over its expected useful life. The depreciation expense for a particular reporting period is used in calculating profit for that period. If a depreciation charge is excluded from the income statement, we shall not have a fair measure of financial performance. Whether or not the business intends to replace the asset in the future is irrelevant.

Where an asset is to be replaced, the depreciation expense in the income statement will not ensure that liquid funds are set aside specifically for this purpose. Although the depreciation expense will reduce profit and, therefore, reduce the amount that the owners may decide to withdraw, the amounts retained within the business as a result may be invested in ways that are unrelated to the replacement of the asset.

Depreciation and judgement

From our discussions about depreciation, it is clear that accounting is not as precise and objective as it is sometimes portrayed as being. There are areas where subjective judgement is required.

Activity 3.12

What judgements must be made to calculate a depreciation expense for a period?

You may have thought of the following:

- the expected residual or disposal value of the asset;
- the expected useful life of the asset; and
- the choice of depreciation method.

Making different judgements on these matters would result in a different pattern of depreciation expenses over the life of the asset and, therefore, in a different pattern of reported profits. However, any underestimations or overestimations that are made will be adjusted for in the final year of an asset's life. As a result, the total depreciation expense (and total profit) over the asset's life will not be affected by estimation errors.

Real World 3.4 describes the effect on annual performance of extending the useful life of a non-current asset held by a well-known business.

Real World 3.4

Engineering an improvement?

BA reported a loss of £358 million for the 2008/09 reporting period. This loss, however, would have been significantly higher had the business not changed its depreciation policies. The 2008/09 annual report of the business states:

> During the prior year, the Group changed the depreciation period for the RB211 engine, used on Boeing 747 and 767 fleets, from 54 months to 78 months. The change resulted in a £33 million decrease in the annual depreciation charge for this engine type.

Source: British Airways, Annual Report and Accounts 2008/09, Note 15, www.britishairways.com.

Activity (3.13)

Sally Dalton (Packaging) Ltd purchased a machine for £40,000. At the end of its useful life of four years, the amount received on sale was £4,000. When the asset was purchased, the business received two estimates of the likely residual value of the asset. These were: (a) £8,000 and (b) zero.

Show the annual depreciation expenses over the four years and the total depreciation expenses for the asset under each of the two estimates. The straight-line method should be used to calculate the annual depreciation expenses.

The depreciation expense, assuming estimate (a), will be £8,000 a year (that is, (£40,000 – £8,000)/4). The depreciation expense, assuming estimate (b), will be £10,000 a year (that is, £40,000/4). As the actual residual value is £4,000, estimate (a) will lead to under-depreciation of £4,000 (that is, £8,000 – £4,000) over the life of the asset and estimate (b) will lead to over-depreciation of £4,000 (that is, £0 – £4,000). These under- and overestimations will be dealt with in Year 4.

The pattern of depreciation and total depreciation expenses will therefore be:

		Estimate	
		(a)	(b)
Year		£	£
1	Annual depreciation	8,000	10,000
2	Annual depreciation	8,000	10,000
3	Annual depreciation	8,000	10,000
4	Annual depreciation	8,000	10,000
		32,000	40,000
4	Under/(over)-depreciation	4,000	(4,000)
	Total depreciation	36,000	36,000

The final adjustment for under-depreciation of an asset is often referred to as 'loss (or deficit) on disposal of a non-current asset', as the amount actually received is less than the residual value. Similarly, the adjustment for over-depreciation is often referred to as 'profit (or surplus) on disposal of a non-current asset'. These final adjustments are normally made as an addition to the expense (or a reduction in the expense) for depreciation in the reporting period during which the asset is disposed of.

Activity (3.14)

In practice, would you expect it to be more likely that the amount of depreciation would be overestimated or underestimated? Why?

We might expect there to be systematic overestimations of the annual depreciation expense. The prudence convention tends to encourage a cautious approach to estimating the lives and residual values of assets. Where this occurs, the result will be an overestimate for the annual depreciation charge.

Costing inventories

The cost of inventories is important in determining financial performance and position. The cost of inventories sold during a reporting period will affect the calculation of profit and the cost of inventories held at the end of the reporting period will affect the portrayal of assets held.

To calculate the cost of inventories, an assumption must be made about the physical flow of inventories through the business. This assumption need not have anything to do with how inventories *actually* flow through the business. It is concerned only with providing useful measures of performance and position.

Three common assumptions used are:

- **first in, first out (FIFO)**, in which inventories are costed *as if* the earliest acquired inventories held are the first to be used;
- **last in, first out (LIFO)**, in which inventories are costed *as if* the latest acquired inventories held are the first to be used; and
- **weighted average cost (AVCO)**, in which inventories are costed *as if* inventories acquired lose their separate identity and go into a 'pool'. Any issues of inventories from this pool will reflect the weighted average cost of inventories held.

During a period of changing prices, the choice of assumption used in costing inventories can be important. Example 3.8 provides an illustration of how each assumption is applied and the effect of each on financial performance and position.

Example 3.8

A business that supplies grass seed to farmers and horticulturalists has the following transactions during a period:

		Tonnes	Cost/tonne £
1 May	Opening inventories	100	100
2 May	Bought	500	110
3 May	Bought	800	120
		1,400	
6 May	Sold	(900)	
	Closing inventories	500	

First in, first out (FIFO)

Using the FIFO approach, the first 900 tonnes of seed bought are treated as if these are the ones that are sold. This will consist of the opening inventories (100 tonnes), the purchases made on 2 May (500 tonnes) and some of the purchases made on 3 May (300 tonnes). The remainder of the 3 May purchases (500 tonnes) will comprise the closing inventories. This means that we have:

	Cost of sales			Closing inventories		
	Tonnes	Cost/tonne £	Total £000	Tonnes	Cost/tonne £	Total £000
1 May	100	100	10.0			
2 May	500	110	55.0			
3 May	300	120	36.0	500	120	60.0
Cost of sales			101.0	**Closing inventories**		60.0

Last in, first out (LIFO)

Using the LIFO assumption, the later purchases will be treated as if these were the first to be sold. This is the 3 May purchases (800 tonnes) and some of the 2 May purchases (100 tonnes). The earlier purchases (the rest of the 2 May purchase and the opening inventories) will comprise the closing inventories. This can be set out as follows:

	Cost of sales			Closing inventories		
	Tonnes	Cost/tonne £	Total £000	Tonnes	Cost/tonne £	Total £000
3 May	800	120	96.0			
2 May	100	110	11.0	400	110	44.0
1 May				100	100	10.0
Cost of sales			107.0	**Closing inventories**		54.0

Figure 3.8 contrasts LIFO and FIFO.

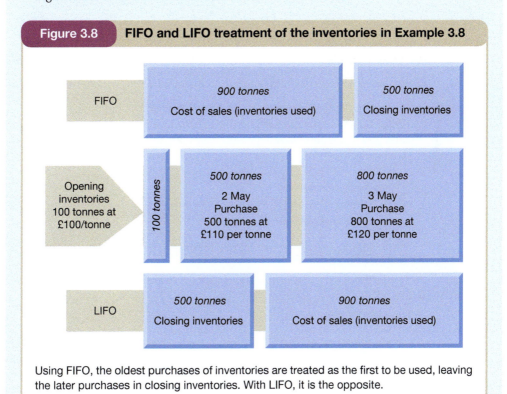

Figure 3.8   FIFO and LIFO treatment of the inventories in Example 3.8

Using FIFO, the oldest purchases of inventories are treated as the first to be used, leaving the later purchases in closing inventories. With LIFO, it is the opposite.

Example 3.8 *continued*

Weighted average cost (AVCO)

Using the AVCO assumption, a weighted average cost will be determined that will be used to derive both the cost of goods sold and the cost of the remaining inventories held. This simply means that the total cost of the opening inventories and of the 2 May and 3 May purchases are added together and divided by the total number of tonnes to obtain the weighted average cost per tonne. Both the cost of sales and closing inventories values are based on that average cost per tonne. This means that we have:

	Tonnes	Cost/tonne £	Total £000
1 May	100	100	10.0
2 May	500	110	55.0
3 May	800	120	96.0
	1,400		161.0

The average cost is £161,000/1,400 = £115 per tonne.

Cost of sales			Closing inventories		
Tonnes	Cost/tonne £	Total £000	Tonnes	Cost/tonne £	Total £000
900	115	103.5	500	115	57.5

Activity 3.15

Suppose the 900 tonnes of inventories in Example 3.8 were sold for £150 per tonne.

(a) Calculate the gross profit for this sale under each of the three methods.
(b) What observations concerning the portrayal of financial position and performance can you make about each method when prices are rising?

Your answer should be along the following lines:
(a) Gross profit calculation:

	FIFO £000	LIFO £000	AVCO £000
Sales revenue (900 @ £150)	135.0	135.0	135.0
Cost of sales	(101.0)	(107.0)	(103.5)
Gross profit	34.0	28.0	31.5
Closing inventories	60.0	54.0	57.5

(b) These figures reveal that FIFO will give the highest gross profit during a period of rising prices. This is because sales revenue is matched with the earlier (and cheaper) purchases. LIFO will give the lowest gross profit because sales revenue is matched against the more recent (and dearer) purchases. The AVCO method will normally give a figure that is between these two extremes.

The closing inventories figure in the statement of financial position will be highest with the FIFO method. This is because the cost of goods still held will be based on the more recent (and dearer) purchases. LIFO will give the lowest closing inventories figure, as the goods held will be based on the earlier (and cheaper) purchases. Once again, the AVCO method will normally give a figure that is between these two extremes.

Activity 3.16

Assume that prices are falling rather than rising. How would your observations concerning the portrayal of financial performance and position be different for the various costing methods?

When prices are falling, the positions of FIFO and LIFO are reversed. FIFO will give the lowest gross profit as sales revenue is matched against the earlier (and dearer) goods bought. LIFO will give the highest gross profit as sales revenue is matched against the more recent (and cheaper) goods bought. AVCO will give a cost of sales figure between these two extremes. The closing inventories figure in the statement of financial position will be lowest under FIFO, as the cost of inventories will be based on the more recent (and cheaper) purchases. LIFO will provide the highest closing inventories figure and AVCO will provide a figure between the two extremes.

The different costing assumptions only have an effect on reported profit from one reporting period to the next. The figure derived for closing inventories will be carried forward and matched with sales revenue in a later period. If the cheaper purchases of inventories are matched to sales revenue in the current period, it will mean that the dearer purchases will be matched to sales revenue in a later period. Over the life of the business, therefore, total profit will be the same either way.

Inventories – some further issues

We saw in Chapter 2 that the convention of prudence requires that inventories be valued at the lower of cost and net realisable value. (The net realisable value of inventories is the estimated selling price less any further costs necessary to complete the goods and any costs involved in selling and distributing them.) In theory, this means that the valuation method applied to inventories could switch each year, depending on which of cost and net realisable value is the lower. In practice, however, the cost of the inventories held is usually below the current net realisable value – particularly during a period of rising prices. It is, therefore, the cost figure that will normally appear in the statement of financial position.

Activity 3.17

Can you think of any circumstances where the net realisable value will be lower than the cost of inventories held, even during a period of generally rising prices? Try to think of at least two.

The net realisable value may be lower where:

- goods have deteriorated or become obsolete;
- there has been a fall in the market price of the goods;
- the goods are being used as a 'loss leader', that is, they are deliberately going to be sold at a price lower than their cost; and/or
- bad buying decisions have been made.

There is also an International Financial Reporting Standard that deals with inventories. It states that, when preparing financial statements for external reporting, the cost of inventories should normally be determined using either FIFO or AVCO. The LIFO assumption is not acceptable for external reporting. (There is no reason, however, that a business should not apply LIFO when preparing financial statements for use by its own managers.) The standard also requires the 'lower of cost and net realisable value' rule to be used, thereby supporting the application of prudence.

Activity 3.18

Where inventories are written down (reduced) to their net realisable value, how do you think this should be treated in the financial statements?

The amount written down should be treated as an expense in the income statement of the period in which the write down occurs. The value of inventories shown in the statement of financial position should then report the inventories at their net realisable value rather than their cost.

Real World 3.5 sets out the inventories' costing methods used by some of the UK's leading businesses.

Real World 3.5

Counting the cost

Inventories costing methods used by some large UK businesses are as follows:

Name	Type of business	Costing method used
J Sainsbury plc	Supermarket	AVCO
Babcock International plc	Engineering support services	FIFO
British American Tobacco plc	Tobacco manufacturer	AVCO
Premier Foods plc	Food manufacturer	FIFO
Marks and Spencer plc	Food and clothing retailer	AVCO
Diageo plc	Alcoholic beverages	AVCO
Tate and Lyle plc	Food ingredients	FIFO or AVCO
AstraZeneca plc	Pharmaceuticals	FIFO or AVCO
Mothercare plc	Retailer	AVCO

Source: Annual reports of the relevant businesses for 2017 or 2018.

Note that Tate and Lyle plc and AstraZeneca plc employ more than one inventories' costing method. Tate and Lyle plc state that the choice of costing method will depend on the materials and production processes used. AstraZeneca plc does not state what determines the choice of costing method. However, it will probably vary according to location, production processes or some other key factor.

The table simply sets out a small, non-random sample of well-known businesses and so we cannot assess the relative popularity of the three methods in practice on the basis of this.

Costing inventories and depreciation provide two examples where the **consistency convention** should be applied. This convention holds that once a particular method of accounting is selected, it should be applied consistently over time. It would not be acceptable to switch from, say, FIFO to AVCO between periods (unless exceptional circumstances make it appropriate). The purpose of this convention is to help users make valid comparisons of performance and position from one period to the next.

Activity 3.19

Reporting inventories in the financial statements provides a further example of the need to apply subjective judgement. For the inventories of a retail business, what are the main judgements that are required?

The main judgements are:

● the choice of costing method (FIFO, LIFO, AVCO); and
● deducing the net realisable value figure for inventories held.

One final point before leaving this topic. Costing inventories using FIFO, LIFO and AVCO applies to items that are interchangeable. Where they are not, as would be the case with custom-made items, the specific cost of the individual items must be used.

Trade receivables problems

We have seen that, when businesses sell goods or services on credit, revenue will usually be recognised before the customer pays the amounts owing. Recording the dual aspect of a credit sale will involve increasing sales revenue and increasing trade receivables by the amount of the revenue from the credit sale.

With this type of sale, there is always the risk that the customer will not pay the amount due. Where it becomes reasonably certain that the customer will not pay, the amount owed is considered to be a **bad debt**, which must be taken into account when preparing the financial statements.

Activity 3.20

What would be the effect on the income statement, and on the statement of financial position, of not taking into account the fact that a debt is bad?

The effect would be to overstate the assets (trade receivables) on the statement of financial position and to overstate profit in the income statement, as the revenue that has been recognised will not result in any future benefit.

To provide a more realistic picture of financial performance and position, the bad debt must be 'written off'. This will involve reducing the trade receivables and increasing expenses (by creating an expense known as 'bad debts written off') by the amount of the bad debt. The matching convention requires that the bad debt is written off in the same period as the sale that gave rise to the debt is recognised.

Note that, when a debt is bad, the accounting response is not simply to cancel the original sale. If this were done, the income statement would not be so informative. Reporting the bad debts as an expense can be extremely useful in assessing management performance.

Real World 3.6 indicates the level of bad debts incurred among small and medium size businesses European businesses.

Real World 3.6

Bad news

A survey of small and medium size businesses across 29 European countries, and generating a total of 9,607 responses, revealed the following level of bad debts within various industry sectors:

Proportion of yearly revenues written off 2017

	Percentage
Agriculture, forestry and fishing	1.68
Mining and quarrying	3.67
Electricity, gas, steam, water and air conditioning supply	1.89
Manufacturing	1.70
Construction	2.03
Wholesale and retail trade	1.57
Transport and storage	1.88
Accommodation and food service activities	1.28
Information and communication	1.84
Financial and insurance activities	2.45
Real estate activities	1.26
Professional, scientific, technical, administration and support service activities	1.69
Public administration, defence, education, human health and social work activities	1.46
European average	1.69

We can see that mining and quarrying suffers the most from bad debts with real estate activities suffering the least.

Source: European Payment Industry White Paper 2018, page 12, www.intrum.com.

Doubtful debts

At the end of a reporting period, it may not be possible to identify, with certainty, all bad debts arising from credit sales made. Doubts may surround certain trade receivables, but it may only be at a later date that the true position will become clear. Nevertheless, the possibility that some trade receivables will not be paid should not be ignored. It would not be prudent, nor would it comply with the need to match expenses to the period in which the associated revenue is recognised.

The business must try to determine the amount of trade receivables that, at the end of the period, are doubtful (that is, there is a possibility that they may eventually prove to be bad). This amount may be derived by examining individual trade receivables accounts or by taking a proportion (the exact proportion being based on past experience) of the total trade receivables outstanding.

Once a figure has been derived, an expense known as an **allowance for trade receivables** should be recognised. This will be shown as an expense in the income statement and deducted from the total trade receivables figure in the statement of financial position. In this way, full account is taken, in the appropriate reporting period, of those trade receivables where there is a risk of non-payment. This accounting treatment of these 'doubtful' trade receivables will be in addition to the treatment of the more definite bad debts described above.

Example 3.9 illustrates the reporting of bad debts and allowances for trade receivables.

Example 3.9

Desai Enterprises had trade receivables of £350,000 outstanding at the end of the reporting period to 30 June 2019. Investigation of these trade receivables revealed that £10,000 would probably be irrecoverable and that there was doubt concerning the recoverability of a further £30,000.

Relevant extracts from the income statement for that year would be as follows:

Income statement (extracts) for the year ended 30 June 2019

	£
Bad debts written off	10,000
Allowances for trade receivables	30,000

Statement of financial position (extracts) as at 30 June 2019

	£
Trade receivables	340,000*
Allowances for trade receivables	(30,000)
	310,000

*That is, £350,000 less £10,000 irrecoverable trade receivables.

The allowances for trade receivables figure is, of course, an estimate; it is quite likely that the actual amount of trade receivables that prove to be bad will be different from the estimate. Let us say that, during the next reporting period, it was discovered that, in fact, £26,000 of the trade receivables considered doubtful proved to be irrecoverable. These trade receivables must now be written off as follows:

- reduce trade receivables by £26,000; and
- reduce allowances for trade receivables by £26,000.

However, allowances for trade receivables of £4,000 will remain. This amount represents an overestimate made when creating the allowance as at 30 June 2019. As the allowance is no longer needed, it should be eliminated. Remember that the allowance was made by creating an expense in the income statement for the year to 30 June 2019. As the expense was too high, the amount of the overestimate should be 'written back' in the next reporting period. In other words, it will be treated as revenue for the year to 30 June 2020. This will mean:

- reducing the allowances for trade receivables by £4,000; and
- increasing revenue by £4,000.

Ideally, of course, the amount should be written back to the 2019 income statement; however, it is too late to do this. At the end of the year to 30 June 2020, not only will 2019's overestimate be written back, but a new allowance should be created to take account of the trade receivables arising from 2020's credit sales that are considered doubtful.

Activity 3.21

Clayton Conglomerates had trade receivables of £870,000 outstanding at the end of the reporting period to 31 March 2018. The chief accountant believed £40,000 of those trade receivables to be irrecoverable and a further £60,000 to be doubtful. In the subsequent year, it was found that an over-pessimistic estimate of those trade receivables considered doubtful had been made and that only a further £45,000 of trade receivables had actually proved to be bad.

Show the relevant income statement extracts for both 2018 and 2019 to report the bad debts written off and the allowances for trade receivables. Also show the relevant statement of financial position extract as at 31 March 2018.

Your answer should be as follows:

Income statement (extract) for the year ended 31 March 2018

	£
Bad debts written off	40,000
Allowances for trade receivables	60,000

Income statement (extract) for the year ended 31 March 2019

	£
Allowances for trade receivables written back (revenue)	15,000

(*Note*: This figure will usually be netted off against any allowances for trade receivables created in respect of 2019.)

Statement of financial position (extract) as at 31 March 2018

	£
Trade receivables	830,000
Allowances for trade receivables	(60,000)
	770,000

Activity 3.22

The accounting treatment of bad debts and allowances for trade receivables are two further examples where judgement is needed to derive an appropriate expense figure.

What will be the effect of different judgements concerning the appropriate amount of bad debts expense and allowances for trade receivables expense on the profit for a particular period and on the total profit reported over the life of the business?

The judgement concerning whether to write off a debt as bad will affect the expenses for the period and, therefore, the reported profit. Over the life of the business, however, total reported profit would not be affected, as incorrect judgements made in one period will be adjusted for in a later period.

Suppose that a debt of £100 was written off in a period and that, in a later period, the amount owing was actually received. The increase in expenses of £100 in the period in which the bad debt was written off would be compensated for by an increase in revenue of £100 when the amount outstanding was finally received (bad debt recovered). If, on the other hand, the amount owing of £100 was never written off in the first place, the profit for the two periods would not be affected by the bad debt adjustment and would, therefore, be different – but the total profit for the two periods would be the same.

A similar situation would apply where there are differences in judgements concerning allowances for trade receivables.

Uses and usefulness of the income statement

The income statement may help in providing information on:

- *How effective the business has been in generating wealth.* Since wealth generation is the primary reason for most businesses to exist, assessing how much wealth has been created is an important issue. The income statement reveals the profit for the period, or *bottom line* as it is sometimes called. This provides a measure of the wealth created for the owners. Gross profit and operating profit are also useful measures of wealth creation.
- *How profit was derived.* In addition to providing various measures of profit, the income statement provides other information needed for a proper understanding of business performance. It reveals the level of sales revenue and the nature and amount of expenses incurred, which can help in understanding how profit was derived. The analysis of financial performance will be considered in detail in Chapter 7.

Self-assessment question 3.1

TT and Co. is a new business that started trading on 1 January 2018. The following is a summary of transactions that occurred during the first year of trading:

1. The owners introduced £50,000 of equity, which was paid into a bank account opened in the name of the business.
2. Premises were rented from 1 January 2018 at an annual rental of £20,000. During the year, rent of £25,000 was paid to the owner of the premises.
3. Rates (a tax on business premises) were paid during the year as follows:

For the period 1 January 2018 to 31 March 2018	£500
For the period 1 April 2018 to 31 March 2019	£1,200

4. A delivery van was bought on 1 January 2018 for £12,000. This is expected to be used in the business for four years and then to be sold for £2,000.
5. Wages totalling £33,500 were paid during the year. At the end of the year, the business owed £630 of wages for the last week of the year.
6. Electricity bills for the first three quarters of the year were paid totalling £1,650. After 31 December 2018, but before the financial statements had been finalised for the year, the bill for the last quarter arrived showing a charge of £620.
7. Inventories totalling £143,000 were bought on credit.
8. Inventories totalling £12,000 were bought for cash.
9. Sales revenue on credit totalled £152,000 (cost of sales £74,000).
10. Cash sales revenue totalled £35,000 (cost of sales £16,000).
11. Receipts from trade receivables totalled £132,000.
12. Payments of trade payables totalled £121,000.
13. Van running expenses paid totalled £9,400.

Self-assessment question 3.1 *continued*

At the end of the year it was clear that a credit customer who owed £400 would not be able to pay any part of the debt. All of the other trade receivables were expected to be settled in full.

The business uses the straight-line method for depreciating non-current assets.

Required:
Prepare a statement of financial position as at 31 December 2018 and an income statement for the year to that date.

The solution to this question can be found at the back of the book on pages 751–752.

Summary

The main points of this chapter may be summarised as follows:

The income statement (profit and loss account)

- Reveals how much profit (or loss) has been generated over a period and links the statements of financial position at the beginning and end of a reporting period.
- Profit (or loss) is the difference between total revenue and total expenses for a period.
- Three main measures of profit are shown:
  - gross profit – which is calculated by deducting the cost of sales from the sales revenue;
  - operating profit – which is calculated by deducting overheads from the gross profit;
  - profit for the period – which is calculated by adding non-operating income and deducting non-operating (for example, finance) costs from the operating profit.

Expenses and revenue

- Cost of sales can be identified by matching the cost of each sale to the particular sale or by adjusting the goods bought during a period by the opening and closing inventories.
- Classifying expenses is often a matter of judgement, although there are rules for businesses that trade as limited companies.
- Revenue is recognised when a business has performed its obligations: that is, when control of the goods or services is passed to the customer.
- Revenue can be recognised over a period of time or at a particular point in time.
- The matching convention states that expenses should be matched to the revenue that they help generate.
- An expense reported in the income statement may not be the same as the cash paid. This can result in accruals or prepayments appearing in the statement of financial position.

- The materiality convention states that where the amounts are immaterial, we should consider only what is expedient.
- The accruals convention states that profit = revenue − expenses (not cash receipts – cash payments).

Depreciation of non-current assets

- Depreciation requires a consideration of the cost (or fair value), useful life and residual value of an asset. It also requires a consideration of the method of depreciation.
- The straight-line method of depreciation allocates the amount to be depreciated evenly over the useful life of the asset.
- The reducing-balance method applies a fixed percentage rate of depreciation to the carrying amount of an asset each year.
- The depreciation method chosen should reflect the pattern of consumption of economic benefits of an asset.
- Depreciation allocates the cost (or fair value), less the residual value, of an asset over its useful life. It does not provide funds for replacement of the asset.

Costing inventories

- The way in which we derive the cost of inventories is important in the calculation of profit and the presentation of financial position.
- The first in, first out (FIFO) assumption is that the earliest inventories held are the first to be used.
- The last in, first out (LIFO) assumption is that the latest inventories are the first to be used.
- The weighted average cost (AVCO) assumption applies an average cost to all inventories used.
- When prices are rising, FIFO gives the lowest cost of sales figure and highest closing inventories figure and for LIFO it is the other way around. AVCO gives figures for cost of sales and closing inventories that lie between FIFO and LIFO.
- When prices are falling, the positions of FIFO and LIFO are reversed.
- Inventories are shown at the lower of cost and net realisable value.
- When a particular method of accounting, such as a depreciation method, is selected, it should be applied consistently over time.

Bad debts

- Where it is reasonably certain that a credit customer will not pay, the debt is regarded as 'bad' and written off.
- Where it is doubtful that a credit customer will pay, an allowance for trade receivables expense should be created.

Uses of the income statement

- It provides measures of profit generated during a period.
- It provides information on how the profit was derived.

Key terms

For definitions of these terms, see Appendix B.

profit *p. 83*	**amortisation** *p. 98*
revenue *p. 83*	**residual value** *p. 100*
expense *p. 84*	**straight-line method** *p. 100*
cost of sales *p. 84*	**carrying amount** *p. 101*
gross profit *p. 86*	**written-down value** *p. 101*
operating profit *p. 86*	**net book value** *p. 101*
profit for the period *p. 86*	**reducing-balance method** *p. 101*
matching convention *p. 93*	**first in, first out (FIFO)** *p. 108*
accrued expense *p. 93*	**last in, first out (LIFO)** *p. 108*
prepaid expense *p. 96*	**weighted average cost (AVCO)** *p. 108*
materiality convention *p. 97*	**consistency convention** *p. 113*
accruals convention *p. 97*	**bad debt** *p. 113*
accruals accounting *p. 97*	**allowance for trade receivables**
depreciation *p. 98*	*p. 114*

Further reading

If you would like to explore the topics covered in this chapter in more depth, we recommend the following:

Alexander, D. and Nobes, C. (2016) *Financial Accounting: An International Introduction,* 6th edn, Pearson, Chapters 2, 3, 9 and 10.

Elliott, B. and Elliott, J. (2016) *Financial Accounting and Reporting,* 18th edn, Pearson, Chapters 2, 11, 20 and 21.

International Accounting Standards Board, *IFRS Standards – Required 1 January 2018 (Blue Book) Part A* IAS 2 *Inventories* and IFRS 15 *Revenue from Contracts with Customers.*

KPMG Audit Committee Institute, *Insights into IFRS: An Overview,* September 2018, Sections 3.2, 3.3, 3.8, 3.10 and 4.2. (This publication is available free at www.kpmg.com.)

Critical review questions

Solutions to these questions can be found at the back of the book on pages 772–773.

3.1   'Although the income statement is a record of past achievement, the calculations required for certain expenses involve estimates of the future.' What does this statement mean? Can you think of examples where estimates of the future are used?

3.2   'Depreciation is a process of allocation and not valuation.' What do you think is meant by this statement?

3.3   What is the convention of consistency? Does this convention help users in making a more valid comparison between businesses?

3.4   'An asset is similar to an expense.' In what ways in this true or untrue?

Exercises

Solutions to exercises with coloured numbers can be found at the back of the book on pages 788–789.

Basic-level exercises

3.1 You have heard the following statements made. Comment critically on them.

(a) 'Equity only increases or decreases as a result of the owners putting more cash into the business or taking some out.'
(b) 'An accrued expense is one that relates to next year.'
(c) 'Unless we depreciate this asset we shall be unable to provide for its replacement.'
(d) 'There is no point in depreciating the factory building. It is appreciating in value each year.'

3.2 Singh Enterprises, which started business on 1 January 2016, has a reporting period to 31 December and uses the straight-line method of depreciation. On 1 January 2016, the business bought a machine for £10,000. The machine had an expected useful life of four years and an estimated residual value of £2,000. On 1 January 2017, the business bought another machine for £15,000. This machine had an expected useful life of five years and an estimated residual value of £2,500. On 31 December 2018, the business sold the first machine bought for £3,000.

Required:
Show the relevant income statement extracts and statement of financial position extracts for the years 2016, 2017 and 2018.

3.3 The owner of a business is confused and comes to you for help. The financial statements for the business, prepared by an accountant, for the last reporting period revealed a profit of £50,000. However, during the reporting period the bank balance declined by £30,000. What reasons might explain this apparent discrepancy?

Intermediate-level exercises

3.4 Fill in the values (a) to (f) in the following table on the assumption that there were no opening balances involved.

	Relating to period		At end of period	
	Paid/received	Expense/revenue for period	Prepaid	Accruals/deferred revenues
	£	£	£	£
Rent payable	10,000	**(a)**	1,000	
Rates and insurance	5,000	**(b)**		1,000
General expenses	**(c)**	6,000	1,000	
Interest payable on borrowings	3,000	2,500	**(d)**	
Salaries	**(e)**	9,000		3,000
Rent receivable	**(f)**	1,500		1,500

3.5 Spratley Ltd is a builders' merchant. On 1 September the business had, as part of its inventories, 20 tonnes of sand at a cost of £18 per tonne and, therefore, at a total cost of £360. During the first week in September, the business bought the following amounts of sand:

	Tonnes	Cost per tonne £
2 September	48	20
4 September	15	24
6 September	10	25

On 7 September, the business sold 60 tonnes of sand to a local builder.

Required:
Calculate the cost of goods sold and of the remaining inventories using the following costing methods:
(a) first in, first out;
(b) last in, first out;
(c) weighted average cost.

Advanced-level exercises

3.6 The following is the statement of financial position of TT and Co. (see Self-Assessment Question 3.1 on page 117) at the end of its first year of trading:

Statement of financial position as at 31 December 2018

ASSETS	£
Non-current assets	
Property, plant and equipment:	
Delivery van at cost	12,000
Depreciation	(2,500)
	9,500
Current assets	
Inventories	65,000
Trade receivables	19,600
Prepaid expenses*	5,300
Cash	750
	90,650
Total assets	100,150
EQUITY AND LIABILITIES	
Equity	
Original	50,000
Retained earnings	26,900
	76,900
Current liabilities	
Trade payables	22,000
Accrued expenses†	1,250
	23,250
Total equity and liabilities	100,150

*The prepaid expenses consisted of rates (£300) and rent (£5,000).
†The accrued expenses consisted of wages (£630) and electricity (£620).

During 2019, the following transactions took place:

1 The owners withdrew £20,000 of equity as cash.
2 Premises continued to be rented at an annual rental of £20,000. During the year, rent of £15,000 was paid to the owner of the premises.
3 Rates on the premises £1,300 were paid for the period 1 April 2019 to 31 March 2020.
4 A second delivery van was bought on 1 January 2019 for £13,000. This is expected to be used in the business for four years and then to be sold for £3,000.
5 Wages totalling £36,700 were paid during the year. At the end of the year, the business owed £860 of wages for the last week of the year.
6 Electricity bills for the first three quarters of the year and £620 for the last quarter of the previous year were paid totalling £1,820. After 31 December 2019, but before the financial statements had been finalised for the year, the bill for the last quarter arrived showing a charge of £690.
7 Inventories totalling £67,000 were bought on credit.
8 Inventories totalling £8,000 were bought for cash.
9 Sales revenue on credit totalled £179,000 (cost £89,000).
10 Cash sales revenue totalled £54,000 (cost £25,000).
11 Receipts from trade receivables totalled £178,000.
12 Payments to trade payables totalled £71,000.
13 Van running expenses paid totalled £16,200.

The business uses the straight-line method for depreciating non-current assets.

Required:
Prepare a statement of financial position as at 31 December 2019 and an income statement for the year to that date.

3.7 The following is the income statement for Nikov and Co. for the year ended 31 December 2018, along with information relating to the preceding year.

Income statement for the year ended 31 December

	2018 £000	2017 £000
Sales revenue	420.2	382.5
Cost of sales	(126.1)	(114.8)
Gross profit	294.1	267.7
Salaries and wages	(92.6)	(86.4)
Selling and distribution costs	(98.9)	(75.4)
Rent and rates	(22.0)	(22.0)
Bad debts written off	(19.7)	(4.0)
Telephone and postage	(4.8)	(4.4)
Insurance	(2.9)	(2.8)
Motor vehicle expenses	(10.3)	(8.6)
Depreciation – delivery van	(3.1)	(3.3)
– fixtures and fittings	(4.3)	(4.5)
Operating profit	35.5	56.3
Loan interest	(4.6)	(5.4)
Profit for the year	30.9	50.9

Required:
Analyse the performance of the business for the year to 31 December 2018 insofar as the information allows.

Accounting for limited companies (1)

Introduction

Most businesses in the UK, from the very largest to some of the very smallest, operate in the form of limited companies. Around four million limited companies now exist, accounting for the majority of business activity and employment. The economic significance of this type of business is not confined to the UK; it can be seen in virtually all of the world's developed countries.

In this chapter, we shall consider the nature of limited companies and how they differ from sole-proprietorship businesses and partnerships. This expands on the discussion of various business forms that we met in Chapter 1. The nature of limited companies leads to a need to distinguish between various elements of equity finance, according to how that aspect arose. We shall examine these various elements along with the restrictions that owners face when seeking to withdraw part of their equity.

The financial statements prepared for a limited company reflect certain key features of this type of business. We shall consider how the financial statements dealt with in the previous two chapters are adapted to accommodate these. As we shall see, these adaptations relate to matters of detail rather than of underlying principle.

Many large businesses operate as a group of companies rather than as a single company. We end this chapter by discussing the reasons for this and by describing the main features of financial statements prepared for groups of companies.

Learning outcomes

When you have completed this chapter, you should be able to:

● discuss the nature and financing of a limited company;

● describe the main features of the equity in a limited company and the restrictions placed on owners seeking to withdraw part of their equity;

● explain how the income statement and statement of financial position of a limited company differ in detail from those of sole proprietorships and partnerships; and

● discuss the reasons for the formation of groups of companies and the main features of financial statements prepared for groups of companies.

The main features of limited companies

Legal nature

Let us begin our examination of limited companies by discussing their legal nature. A *limited company* has been described as an artificial person that has been created by law. This means that a company has many of the rights and obligations that 'real' people have. It can, for example, enter into contracts in its own name. It can also sue other people (real or corporate) and they can sue it. This contrasts sharply with unincorporated businesses, such as sole proprietorships and partnerships, where it is the owner(s) rather than the business that must enter into contracts, sue and so on. This is because those businesses have no separate legal identity.

With the rare exceptions of those that are created by Act of Parliament, or by Royal Charter, all UK companies are created (or *incorporated*) by registration. To create a company the person or persons wishing to create it (usually known as *promoters*) fill in a few simple forms and pay a modest registration fee. After having ensured that the necessary formalities have been met, the Registrar of Companies, a UK government official, enters the name of the new company on the Registry of Companies. Thus, in the UK, companies can be formed very easily and cheaply (for about £100).

A limited company may be owned by just one person, but most have more than one owner and some have many owners. The owners are usually known as *members* or *shareholders*. The ownership of a company is normally divided into a number of shares, each of equal size. Each owner, or shareholder, owns one or more shares in the company. Large companies typically have a very large number of shareholders. For example, at 31 March 2018, BT Group plc, the telecommunications business, had more than 763,000 different shareholders. These shareholders held nearly 10 billion shares between them.

Since a limited company has its own legal identity, it is regarded as being quite separate from those that own and manage it. It is worth emphasising that this legal separateness of owners and the company has no connection with the business entity convention discussed in Chapter 2. This accounting convention applies equally to all business types, including sole proprietorships and partnerships where there is no legal distinction between the owner(s) and the business.

The legal separateness of the limited company and its shareholders leads to two important features of the limited company: perpetual life and limited liability. These are now explained.

Perpetual life

A company is normally granted a perpetual existence and so will continue even where an owner of some, or even all, of the shares in the company dies. The shares of the deceased person will simply pass to the beneficiary of his or her estate. The granting of perpetual existence means that the life of a company is quite separate from the lives of those individuals who own or manage it. It is not, therefore, affected by changes in ownership that arise when individuals buy and sell shares in the company.

Although a company may be granted a perpetual existence when it is first formed, it is possible for either the shareholders or the courts to bring this existence to an end. When this is done, the assets of the company are usually sold to generate cash to meet the outstanding liabilities. Any amounts remaining after all liabilities have been met will then be distributed between the shareholders. Shareholders may agree to end the life of a company where it has achieved the purpose for which it was formed or where they feel that the company has no real future. The courts may bring the life of a company to an end where creditors (those owed money by the company) have applied to the courts for this to be done because they have not been paid.

Where shareholders agree to end the life of a company, it is referred to as a 'voluntary liquidation'. **Real World 4.1** describes the demise of one company by this method.

Real World 4.1

Monotub Industries in a spin as founder gets Titan for £1

Monotub Industries, maker of the Titan washing machine, yesterday passed into corporate history with very little ceremony and with only a whimper of protest from minority shareholders.

At an extraordinary meeting held in a basement room of the group's West End headquarters, shareholders voted to put the company into voluntary liquidation and sell its assets and intellectual property to founder Martin Myerscough for £1. [The shares in the company were at one time worth 650p each.]

The only significant opposition came from Giuliano Gnagnatti who, along with other shareholders, has seen his investment shrink faster than a wool twin-set on a boil wash.

The not-so-proud owner of 100,000 Monotub shares, Mr Gnagnatti, the managing director of an online retailer, described the sale of Monotub as a 'free gift' to Mr Myerscough. This assessment was denied by Ian Green, the chairman of Monotub, who said the closest the beleaguered company had come to a sale was an offer for £60,000 that gave no guarantees against liabilities, which are thought to amount to £750,000.

The quiet passing of the washing machine, eventually dubbed the Titanic, was in strong contrast to its performance in many kitchens.

Originally touted as the 'great white goods hope' of the washing machine industry with its larger capacity and removable drum, the Titan ran into problems when it kept stopping during the spin cycle, causing it to emit a loud bang and leap into the air.

Summing up the demise of the Titan, Mr Green said: 'Clearly the machine had some revolutionary aspects, but you can't get away from the fact that the machine was faulty and should not have been launched with those defects.'

The usually-vocal Mr Myerscough, who has promised to pump £250,000 into the company and give Monotub shareholders £4 for every machine sold, refused to comment on his plans for the Titan or reveal who his backers were. But . . . he did say that he intended to 'take the Titan forward'.

 Source: Urquhart, L. (2003) Monotub Industries in a spin as founder gets Titan for £1, *Financial Times*, 23 January.
© The Financial Times Limited 2012. All Rights Reserved.

Limited liability

Since the company is a legal person in its own right, it must take responsibility for its own debts and losses. This means that, once the shareholders have paid what they have agreed to pay for the shares, their obligation to the company, and to the company's creditors, is satisfied. Thus, shareholders can limit their losses to the amount that they have paid, or agreed to pay, for their shares. This is of great practical importance to potential shareholders since they know that what they can lose, as part owners of the business, is limited.

Contrast this with the position of sole proprietors or partners. They cannot 'ring-fence' assets that they do not want to put into the business. If a sole-proprietorship or partnership business finds itself in a position where liabilities exceed the business assets, the law gives unsatisfied creditors the right to demand payment out of what the sole proprietor or partner may have regarded as 'non-business' assets. Thus, the sole proprietor or partner could lose everything – house, car, the lot. This is because the law sees Jill, the sole proprietor, as being the same as Jill the private individual.

Real World 4.2 gives an example of a well-known case where the shareholders of a particular company were able to avoid any liability to those that had lost money as a result of dealing with the company.

Real World 4.2

Carlton and Granada 1 – Nationwide Football League 0

Two television broadcasting companies, Carlton and Granada, each owned 50 per cent of a separate company, ITV Digital (formerly ON Digital). ITV Digital signed a contract to pay the Nationwide Football League (in effect the three divisions of English football below the Premiership) more than £89 million on both 1 August 2002 and 1 August 2003 for the rights to broadcast football matches over three seasons. ITV Digital was unable to sell enough subscriptions for the broadcasts and so collapsed because it was unable to meet its liabilities. The Nationwide Football League tried to force Carlton and Granada (ITV Digital's only two shareholders) to meet ITV Digital's contractual obligations. It was unable to do so because the shareholders could not be held legally liable for the amounts owing.

Carlton and Granada subsequently merged into one business, but at the time of ITV Digital were two independent companies.

Activity 4.1

The fact that shareholders can limit their losses to that which they have paid, or have agreed to pay, for their shares is of great practical importance to potential shareholders.

Can you think of any practical benefit to a private-sector economy, in general, of this ability of shareholders to limit losses?

Business is a risky venture – in some cases very risky. People will usually be happier to invest money when they know the limit of their liability. If investors are given limited liability, new businesses are more likely to be formed and existing ones are likely to find it easier to raise more finance. This is good for the private-sector economy and may ultimately lead to the generation of greater wealth for society as a whole.

Although **limited liability** has this advantage to the providers of equity finance (the shareholders), it is not necessarily to the advantage of all of the others who have a stake in the business, as we saw in the case of the Nationwide Football League clubs in Real World 4.2. Limited liability is attractive to shareholders because they can, in effect, walk away from the unpaid debts of the company if their committed contribution is not enough to cover those debts. As a consequence, individuals, or businesses, may be wary of entering into a contract with a limited company. This can be a real problem for smaller, less established companies. Suppliers may insist on cash payment before delivery of goods or the rendering of a service. Alternatively, they may require a personal guarantee from a major shareholder, or some other individual, that the debt will be paid before allowing trade credit. In this way, the supplier circumvents the company's limited liability status by demanding the personal liability of an individual. Larger, more established companies, on the other hand, once having gained the confidence of suppliers, tend to be able to retain it.

Legal safeguards

Various safeguards exist to protect individuals and businesses contemplating dealing with a limited company. They include the requirement to indicate limited liability status in the name of the company. This should alert prospective suppliers and lenders to the potential risks involved.

A further safeguard is the restrictions placed on the ability of shareholders to withdraw their equity from the company.

Activity 4.2

Can you think why these restrictions on the withdrawal of equity are imposed?

They are designed to prevent shareholders from protecting their own investment and, as a result, leaving lenders and suppliers in an exposed position.

We shall consider this point in more detail later in the chapter.

Finally, limited companies are required to produce annual financial statements (income statements, statements of financial position and statements of cash flows) and make these publicly available. This means that anyone interested can gain an impression of the financial performance and position of the company. The form and content of the first two of these statements are considered in some detail later in this chapter and in Chapter 5. The statement of cash flows is considered in Chapter 6.

Public and private companies

When a company is registered with the Registrar of Companies, it must be registered either as a public or as a private company. The main practical difference between these is that a **public limited company** can offer its shares for sale to the general public, but a **private limited company** cannot. A public limited company must signal its status to all interested parties by having the words 'public limited company', or its abbreviation 'plc', in its name. For a private limited company, the word 'limited', or 'Ltd', must appear as part of its name.

Private limited companies tend to be smaller businesses where the ownership is divided among relatively few shareholders who are usually fairly close to one another – for example, a family company. There are vastly more private limited companies in the UK than public limited companies. Of almost 4 million UK private and public limited companies in existence at the end of March 2018, only 5,902 (representing 0.2 per cent of the total) were public limited companies. Figure 4.1 shows the trend in the numbers of public and private limited companies in recent years.

Figure 4.1 Numbers of public and private limited companies in the UK, 2012/13 to 2017/18

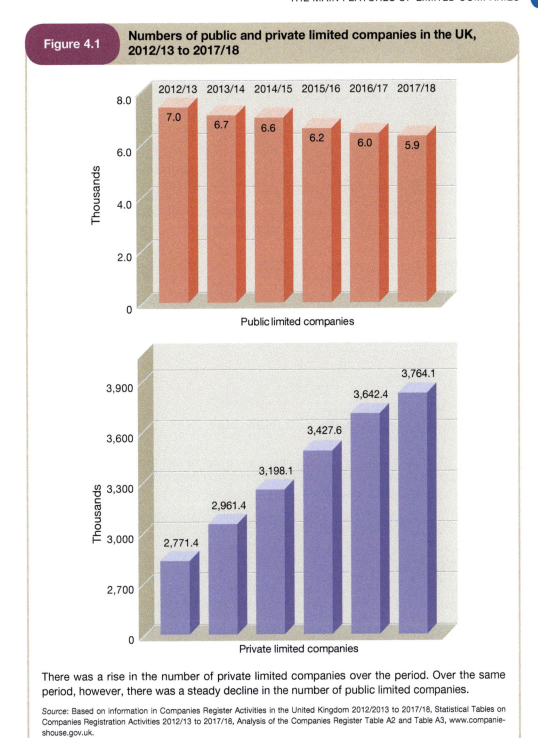

There was a rise in the number of private limited companies over the period. Over the same period, however, there was a steady decline in the number of public limited companies.

Source: Based on information in Companies Register Activities in the United Kingdom 2012/2013 to 2017/18, Statistical Tables on Companies Registration Activities 2012/13 to 2017/18, Analysis of the Companies Register Table A2 and Table A3, www.companie-shouse.gov.uk.

Since individual public companies tend to be larger, they are often economically more important. In some industry sectors, such as banking, insurance, oil refining and grocery retailing, they are completely dominant. Although some private limited companies are large, many are little more than the vehicle through which one-person businesses operate.

Real World 4.3 shows the extent of the market dominance of public limited companies in one particular business sector.

Real World 4.3

A big slice of the market

The grocery sector is dominated by four large players: Tesco, Sainsbury, Morrison and Asda. The first three are public limited companies and the fourth, Asda, is owned by a large US public company, Wal-Mart Inc. However, in April 2018, Sainsbury agreed to buy a majority stake in Asda. At the time of writing, the proposed merger of Sainsbury and Asda had not been finalised. Figure 4.2 shows the share of the grocery market of each during the 12-week period to 7 October 2018.

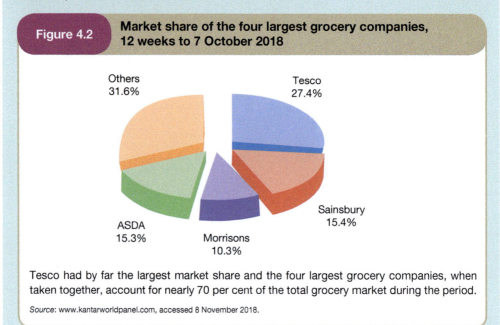

Figure 4.2	Market share of the four largest grocery companies, 12 weeks to 7 October 2018

Tesco had by far the largest market share and the four largest grocery companies, when taken together, account for nearly 70 per cent of the total grocery market during the period.

Source: www.kantarworldpanel.com, accessed 8 November 2018.

Taxation

Another consequence of the legal separation of the limited company from its owners is that companies must be accountable to the tax authorities for tax on their profits and gains. This leads to the reporting of tax in the financial statements of limited companies. The charge for tax is shown in the income statement. The tax charge for a particular year is based on that year's profit. For many companies, only 50 per cent of the tax liability is due for payment during the year concerned, so the other 50 per cent will appear on the end-of-year statement of financial position as a current liability. This will be illustrated a little later in the chapter.

Companies are charged **corporation tax** on their profits and gains. It is levied on the company's taxable profit, which may differ from the profit shown on the income statement. This is because tax law does not follow normal accounting rules in every respect. Generally, however, taxable profit and accounting profit are pretty close to one another. The percentage rate of corporation tax tends to vary over time. For the corporation tax year commencing 1 April 2019, the rate is set at 19 per cent. For the tax year commencing 1 April 2020, the rate will be reduced to 18 per cent.

The tax position of companies contrasts with that of sole proprietorships and partnerships, where tax is levied not on the business but on the owner(s). This means that tax will not be reported in the financial statements of unincorporated businesses, as it is a matter between the owner(s) and the tax authorities. There can be tax advantages to trading as a limited company, rather than as a sole proprietor or partner, though these advantages have been somewhat diminished by recent legislation. This may partly explain the rise in popularity of private limited companies over recent years. It will be interesting to see whether this increase in popularity continues in the light of legislative changes.

The role of the Stock Exchange

A **Stock Exchange** typically acts as both an important *primary* and *secondary* capital market for companies. As a primary market, its function is to enable companies to raise new finance. As a secondary market, its function is to enable investors to sell their securities (including shares and loan notes) with ease. We have already seen that shares in a company may be transferred from one owner to another. The wish of some investors to sell their shares, coupled with the wish of others to buy those shares, has led to the creation of a formal market in which shares are bought and sold.

As with most stock exchanges, only the shares of certain companies (*listed* companies) may be traded on the **London Stock Exchange**. As at 31 October 2018, 943 UK companies were listed. This represents only about one in 4,000 of all UK companies (public and private) and roughly one in six public limited companies. However, many of these listed companies are massive. Nearly all of the UK businesses that are 'household names' (for example, Tesco, Next, BT, Vodafone, BP and so on) are listed companies.

Activity **4.3**

As mentioned earlier, the change in ownership of shares does not directly affect a particular company. Why, in that case, do many public companies seek to have their shares traded in a recognised Stock Exchange?

Investors are generally reluctant to pledge their money unless they can see some way of turning their investment back into cash. The shares of a particular company may be valuable because it has bright prospects. Unless this value can be turned into cash, however, the benefit to investors is dubious. After all, we cannot spend shares; we normally need cash. Thus, investors are more likely to buy new shares from a company where they can liquidate their investment (turn it into cash) as and when they wish. Stock Exchanges provide shareholders with this 'exit route' and, by so doing, make it easier for a company to raise new share capital.

We shall consider the role of the Stock Exchange in rather more detail in Chapter 15.

Managing a company

A limited company may have a legal personality, but it is not a human being capable of making decisions and plans about the business and exercising control over it. People must undertake these management tasks. The most senior level of management of a company is the board of directors.

Directors are elected by shareholders to manage the company on a day-to-day basis on their behalf. By law there must be at least one director for a private limited company and two for a public limited company. In a small company, the board may be the only level of management and consist of all of the shareholders. In larger companies, the board may consist of 10 or so directors out of many thousands of shareholders. (The directors are normally shareholders although they do not have to be.) Below the board of directors of the typical large company could be several layers of management comprising many thousands of people.

Financing limited companies

Equity (the owners' claim)

The equity of a sole proprietorship is normally encompassed in one figure on the statement of financial position. In the case of companies, things are a little more complicated, although the same broad principles apply. With companies, equity is divided between shares (for example, the original investment), on the one hand, and **reserves** (that is, profits and gains subsequently made), on the other. There is also the possibility that there will be more than one type of shares and of reserves. Thus, within the basic divisions of share capital and reserves, there will usually be further subdivisions. This might seem quite complicated, but we shall shortly consider the reasons for these subdivisions and all should become clearer.

The basic division

When a company is first formed, those who take steps to form it (the promoters) will decide how much needs to be raised from potential shareholders to set the company up with the necessary assets to operate. Example 4.1 illustrates this.

Example 4.1

Some friends decide to form a company to operate an office cleaning business. They estimate that the company will need £50,000 to obtain the necessary assets. Between them, they raise the cash, which they use to buy shares in the company, on 31 March 2018, with a **nominal value** (or **par value**) of £1 each.

At this point the statement of financial position of the company would be:

Statement of financial position as at 31 March 2018

	£
Net assets (all in cash)	50,000
Equity	
Share capital:	
50,000 shares of £1 each	50,000

The company now buys the necessary non-current assets (vacuum cleaners and so on) and inventories (cleaning materials) and starts to trade. During the first year, the company makes a profit of £10,000. This, by definition, means that the equity expands by £10,000. During the year, the shareholders (owners) make no drawings of their equity, so at the end of the year the summarised statement of financial position looks like this:

Statement of financial position as at 31 March 2019

	£
Net assets (various assets less liabilities*)	60,000
Equity	
Share capital:	
50,000 shares of £1 each	50,000
Reserves (revenue reserve)	10,000
Total equity	60,000

* We saw in Chapter 2 that Assets = Equity + Liabilities. We also saw that this can be rearranged so that Assets − Liabilities = Equity.

The profit is shown as a reserve, known as a **revenue reserve**, because it arises from generating revenue (making sales). Note that we do not simply merge the profit with the share capital: we must keep the two amounts separate in order to satisfy company law. There is a legal restriction on the maximum drawings of their equity (for example, as a **dividend**) that the shareholders can make. This maximum is defined by the amount of revenue reserves and so it is helpful to show these separately. We shall look at why there is this restriction, and how it works, a little later in the chapter.

Share capital

Ordinary shares

Ordinary shares represent the basic units of ownership of a business. They are issued by all companies and are often known as *equities*. Ordinary shareholders are the primary risk takers as they share in the profits of the company only after other claims have been satisfied. There are no upper limits, however, on the amount by which they may benefit. The potential rewards available to ordinary shareholders reflect the risks that they are prepared to take. Since ordinary shareholders take most of the risks, power normally rests in their hands. Usually, only the ordinary shareholders are able to vote on issues that affect the company, such as the appointment of directors.

The nominal value of such shares is at the discretion of the people who start up the company. For example, if the initial share capital is to be £50,000 this could be two shares of £25,000 each, 5 million shares of one penny each or any other combination that gives a total of £50,000. All shares must have equal value.

Activity 4.4

The initial financial requirement for a new company is £50,000. There are to be two equal shareholders. Would you advise them to issue two shares of £25,000 each? Why?

Such large-denomination shares tend to be unwieldy and difficult to sell. If one of the shareholders wished to liquidate her shareholding, she would have to find a single buyer. Where, however, the shareholding consisted of shares of smaller denomination, the price per share would be lower and the whole shareholding could probably be sold more easily to various potential buyers. It would also be possible for the original shareholder to sell just part of the shareholding and retain a part.

In practice, £1 is the normal maximum nominal value for shares. Shares of 25 pence each and 50 pence each are probably the most common. BT plc, the telecommunications business, has ordinary shares with a nominal value of 5 pence each (although their market value at 7 November 2018 was 249.25p per share).

Preference shares

In addition to ordinary shares, some companies issue **preference shares**. These shares guarantee that *if a dividend is paid,* the preference shareholders will be entitled to the first part of it up to a maximum value. This maximum is normally defined as a fixed percentage of the nominal value of the preference shares. If, for example, a company issues one million preference shares of £1 each with a dividend rate of 6 per cent, this means that the preference shareholders are entitled to receive the first £60,000 (that is, 6 per cent of £1 million) of any dividend that is paid by the company for a particular year. Any dividend payment in excess of £60,000 goes to the ordinary shareholders.

Real World 4.4 describes the types of preference shares issued by one large company.

Real World 4.4

Having a preference

BP plc, the energy company, has two types of £1 preference share in issue, one with a dividend rate of 8 per cent and another with a dividend rate of 9 per cent. Both types of preference share are cumulative, which means that any unpaid dividends are carried forward for payment when a dividend is next declared. The unpaid dividends will be paid before ordinary shareholders receive a dividend. Although BP's preference shares are cumulative, those issued by other companies may not be. Where non-cumulative preference shares are issued, any dividends not paid for a particular period are foregone.

Source: BP plc, Share information, www.bp.com, accessed 8 November 2018.

It is open to the company to issue shares of various classes – perhaps with some having unusual conditions – but in practice it is rare to find other than straightforward ordinary and preference shares. Even preference shares are not very common. Although a company may have different classes of shares with each class giving holders different rights, within each class all shares must have equal rights. The rights of the various classes of shareholders, as well as other matters relating to a particular company, are contained in that company's set of rules, known as the *memorandum and articles of association*. A copy of these rules must be lodged with the Registrar of Companies, who makes it available for inspection by the general public.

Altering the nominal value of shares

As we have already seen, the promoters of a new company may make their own choice of the nominal (par) value of the shares. This value need not be permanent. At a later date, the shareholders can decide to change it.

Suppose that a company has one million ordinary shares of £1 each and a decision is made to change the nominal value of the shares from £1 to £0.50 – in other words to halve the value. To maintain the total nominal value of the share capital intact, the company would then issue each shareholder exactly twice as many shares, each with half the original nominal value. Thus, each shareholder would retain a holding of the same total nominal value as before. This process is known, not surprisingly, as **splitting** the shares. The opposite, reducing the number of shares and increasing their nominal value per share to compensate, is known as **consolidating**. Since each shareholder would be left, after a split or consolidation, with exactly the same proportion of ownership of the company's assets as before, the process should have no effect on the total value of the shares held.

Both splitting and consolidating may be used to help make the shares more marketable. Splitting may help avoid share prices becoming too high and consolidating may help avoid share prices becoming too low. It seems that investors do not like either extreme. In addition, some Stock Exchanges do not allow shares to be traded at too low a price.

Real World 4.5 provides an example of a share consolidation by one business.

Real World 4.5

Doing the splits

Air Partner plc, the UK based international private charter flight provider, announced a share split where in place of each five pence share, shareholders will receive five one penny shares. The business explained the reason for this as follows:

> The Board of directors believes that the Company's share price has risen to a point where it is appropriate to recommend that each existing ordinary share of five pence be split into five new ordinary shares of one penny each. The Board believes that this split will improve the liquidity of the market in the Company's shares, reduce the percentage spread between the bid and offer prices and increase the attractiveness of the Company's shares to potential investors. A long-term aim of the Board is to attract and retain a diverse shareholder base with an appropriate balance between retail and institutional investors for a public company listed on the premium segment of the London Stock Exchange.

Source: Air Partner plc (2017) Statement from the business, 6 January.

Reserves

The shareholders' equity consists of share capital and reserves. As mentioned earlier, reserves are profits and gains that a company has made and which still form part of the shareholders' equity. One reason that past profits and gains may no longer continue to be part of equity is that they have been paid out to shareholders (as dividends and so on). Another reason is that reserves will be reduced by the amount of any losses that the company might suffer. In the same way that profits increase equity, losses reduce it.

Activity 4.5

Are reserves amounts of cash? Can you think of a reason why this is an odd question?

To deal with the second point first, it is an odd question because reserves are a claim, or part of one, on the assets of the company, whereas cash is an asset. So, reserves cannot be cash.

Reserves are classified as either revenue reserves or **capital reserves**. In Example 4.1 we came across a revenue reserve. This reserve represents the company's retained trading profits as well as gains on the disposal of non-current assets. *Retained earnings,* as they are most often called, represent overwhelmingly the largest source of new finance for UK companies. Capital reserves arise for two main reasons:

● issuing shares at above their nominal value (for example, issuing £1 shares at £1.50); and
● revaluing (upwards) non-current assets.

Where a company issues shares at above their nominal value, UK law requires that the excess of the issue price over the nominal value be shown separately.

Activity 4.6

Can you think why shares might be issued at above their nominal value? (*Hint*: This would not usually happen when a company is first formed and the initial shares are being issued.)

Once a company has traded and has been successful, the shares would normally be worth more than the nominal value at which they were issued. If additional shares are to be issued to new shareholders to raise finance for further expansion, unless they are issued at a value higher than the nominal value, the new shareholders will be gaining at the expense of the original ones.

Example 4.2 shows how this works.

Example 4.2

Based on future prospects, the net assets of a company are worth £1.5 million. There are currently one million ordinary shares in the company, each with a nominal value of £1. The company wishes to raise an additional £0.6 million of cash for expansion and has decided to raise it by issuing new shares. If the shares are issued for £1 each (that is 600,000 shares), the total number of shares will be:

$$1.0\,m + 0.6\,m = 1.6\,m$$

and their total value will be the value of the existing net assets plus the new injection of cash:

$$£1.5\,m + £0.6\,m = £2.1\,m$$

This means that the value of each share after the new issue will be:

$$£2.1\,m/1.6\,m = £1.3125$$

The current value of each share is:

$$£1.5\,m/1.0\,m = £1.50$$

so the original shareholders will lose:

$$£1.50 - £1.3125 = £0.1875 \text{ a share}$$

and the new shareholders will gain:

$$£1.3125 - £1.0 = £0.3125 \text{ a share.}$$

The new shareholders will, no doubt, be delighted with this outcome; the original ones will not.

Things could be made fair between the two sets of shareholders described in Example 4.2 by issuing the new shares at £1.50 each. In this case, it would be necessary to issue 400,000 shares to raise the necessary £0.6 million. £1 a share of the £1.50 is the nominal value and will be included with share capital in the statement of financial position (£400,000 in total). The remaining £0.50 is a share premium, which will be shown as a capital reserve known as the **share premium account** (£200,000 in total).

It is not clear why UK company law insists on the distinction between nominal share values and the premium. In some other countries (for example, the United States) with similar laws governing the corporate sector, there is not this distinction. Instead, the total value at which shares are issued is shown as one comprehensive figure on the company's statement of financial position.

Real World 4.6 shows the equity of one very well-known business.

Real World 4.6

Flying funds

Ryanair Holdings plc, the budget airline, had the following share capital and reserves as at 31 March 2018:

	€ million
Share capital (10p ordinary shares)	7.0
Share premium	719.4
Other capital	3.0
Retained earnings	4,077.9
Other reserves	(338.4)
Total equity	4,468.9

Note how the nominal share capital figure is only a small fraction of the share premium account figure. This implies that Ryanair has issued shares at much higher prices than the

Real World 4.6 *continued*

10p a share nominal value. This reflects its trading success over time. Although other reserves held by the business are negative overall, the retained earnings are huge and account for 91 per cent of the total shareholder equity.

Source: Ryanair Holdings plc, Annual Report 2018, p. 147.

Bonus shares

It is always open to a company to take reserves of any kind (irrespective of whether they are capital or revenue) and turn them into share capital. This will involve transferring the desired amount from the reserve concerned to share capital and then distributing the appropriate number of new shares to the existing shareholders. New shares arising from such a conversion are known as **bonus shares**. Example 4.3 illustrates how bonus issues work.

Example 4.3

The summary statement of financial position of a company at a particular point in time is as follows:

Statement of financial position

	£
Net assets (various assets less liabilities)	128,000
Equity	
Share capital:	
50,000 shares of £1 each	50,000
Reserves	78,000
Total equity	128,000

The directors decide that the company will issue existing shareholders with one new share for every share currently owned by each shareholder. The statement of financial position immediately following this will appear as follows:

Statement of financial position

	£
Net assets (various assets less liabilities)	128,000
Equity	
Share capital:	
100,000 shares of £1 each	100,000
Reserves	28,000
Total equity	128,000

We can see that the reserves have decreased by £50,000 and share capital has increased by the same amount. To complete the transaction, 50,000 new ordinary shares of £1 each, which have been created from reserves, will be issued to the existing shareholders.

Activity (4.7)

A shareholder of the company in Example 4.3 owned 100 shares before the bonus issue. How will things change for this shareholder as regards the number of shares owned and the value of the shareholding?

The answer should be that the number of shares would double, from 100 to 200. Now the shareholder owns one five-hundredth of the company (that is, 200/100,000). Before the bonus issue, the shareholder also owned one five-hundredth of the company (that is, 100/50,000). The company's assets and liabilities have not changed as a result of the bonus issue and so, logically, one five-hundredth of the value of the company should be identical to what it was before. Thus, each share is worth half as much as it used to be.

A bonus issue simply takes one part of the equity (a reserve) and puts it into another part (share capital). The transaction has no effect on the company's assets or liabilities, so there is no effect on shareholders' wealth. Issues of bonus shares have become less common in recent years, perhaps because of the lack of business profitability during the current economic climate.

Note that a bonus issue is not the same as a share split. A split does not affect the reserves.

Activity (4.8)

Can you think of any reasons why a company might want to make a bonus issue if it has no economic consequence? Try to think of at least one reason.

We think that there are three possible reasons:

- *Share price.* To lower the value of each share in order to make the shares more marketable. This has a similar effect to share splitting.
- *Shareholder confidence.* To provide the shareholders with a 'feel-good factor'. It is believed that shareholders like bonus issues because they seem to make them better off, although in practice they should not affect their wealth.
- *Lender confidence.* Where reserves arising from operating profits and/or realised gains on the sale of non-current assets (revenue reserves) are used to make the bonus issue, it has the effect of taking part of that portion of the shareholders' equity that could be withdrawn by the shareholders, and locking it up. The amount transferred becomes part of the permanent equity base of the company. (We shall see a little later in this chapter that there are severe restrictions on the extent to which shareholders may make drawings from their equity.) An individual or business contemplating lending money, or advancing credit, to the company may insist that the extent that shareholders can withdraw their funds is restricted as a condition of making the loan or giving credit.

The last point in the answer to Activity 4.8 will be examined in more detail shortly.

Real World 4.7 provides an example of a bonus share issue, where it seemed that the main motive was to make the share price more manageable. The 'feel-good' factor, however, also seems to be playing a part.

> ### Real World 4.7
>
> ### Is it really a bonus?
>
> Medusa Mining is a gold producer that is listed on various international stock markets. In 2010, it announced a one-for-ten bonus issue of shares to all shareholders of the company.
>
> In a statement, the company said that it had achieved several significant milestones in the last calendar year and that the bonus issue was in recognition of the invaluable support the company had received from its shareholders. The bonus issue was also designed to encourage greater liquidity in Medusa shares.
>
> Geoff Davis, managing director of Medusa, said: 'The board is extremely pleased to be in a position to reward shareholders as a result of the company having rapidly expanded its production over the last 12 months and having met all targets on time.'
>
> *Source*: Adapted from Medusa Mining, www.proactiveinvestors.co.uk, 8 March 2010.

It seems that bonus issues have become relatively rare events in recent times.

Share capital jargon

Before leaving our detailed discussion of share capital, it might be helpful to clarify some of the jargon relating to shares that is used in company financial statements.

Share capital that has been issued to shareholders is known as the **issued share capital** (or **allotted share capital**). Sometimes, but not very often, a company may not require shareholders to pay the whole amount that is due to be paid for the shares at the time of issue. This may happen where the company does not need the money all at once. Some money would normally be paid at the time of issue and the company would 'call' for further instalments until the shares were **fully paid shares**. That part of the total issue price that has been called is known as the **called-up share capital**. That part that has been called and paid is known as the **paid-up share capital**.

Borrowings

Most larger companies borrow money to supplement funds raised from share issues and ploughed-back profits. Company borrowing is often on a long-term basis, perhaps on a 10-year contract. The contract, which is legally binding, will specify the rate of interest, the interest payments date and the repayment date for the amount borrowed. Lenders may be banks and other professional providers of loan finance, such as pension funds and insurance companies.

Many companies borrow in such a way that individual investors are able to lend only part of the total amount required. This is particularly the case with the larger, Stock Exchange listed, companies and involves them making an issue of **loan notes**. Although such an issue may be large, private individuals and investing institutions can take it up in small slices. In some cases, these slices of loans can be bought and sold through the Stock Exchange. This means that investors do not have to wait the full term of their loan to obtain repayment. They can sell their slice of the loan to another would-be lender at intermediate points during the loan term. This flexibility can make loan notes an attractive investment to certain investors. Loan notes are often known as **loan stock**, **bonds** or **debentures**.

Some of the features of financing by loan notes, particularly the possibility that the loan notes may be traded on the Stock Exchange, can lead to confusing loan notes with shares. We should be clear, however, that shares and loan notes are not the same thing.

Activity (4.9)

What is the essential difference in status within a company between ordinary shareholders and a loan notes holders?

Ordinary shareholders are the owners of the company who share in the profits and losses of the company. We saw earlier that they are the main risk takers and are given voting rights. Holders of loan notes are simply lenders that receive interest on their investment. They have no ownership stake in the company.

Long-term loans are usually secured on assets of the company. This would give the lender the right, if the company fails to make the contractual payments, to seize the assets concerned, sell them and use the cash to rectify this failure. A mortgage granted to a private individual buying a house or an apartment is a very common example of a secured loan.

Long-term financing of companies can be depicted as in Figure 4.3.

Figure 4.3	**Sources of long-term finance for a typical limited company**

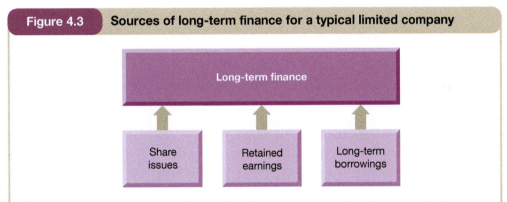

Companies derive their long-term finance from three sources: new share issues, retained earnings and long-term borrowings. For a typical company, the sum of the first two (jointly known as 'equity finance') exceeds the third. Retained earnings usually exceed either of the other two in terms of the amount of finance raised in most years.

It is important to the prosperity and stability of a company that it strikes a suitable balance between finance provided by the shareholders (equity) and from borrowing. This topic will be explored in Chapter 7.

Real World 4.8 shows the long-term borrowings of Rolls-Royce Holdings plc, the engine-building business, at 31 December 2017.

Real World 4.8

Borrowing at Rolls-Royce

The following extract from the annual financial statements of Rolls-Royce plc sets out the sources of the company's long-term borrowings (non-current liabilities) as at 31 December 2017.

Real World 4.8 continued

	£m
Unsecured	
Bank loans	572
6.75% notes 2019	519
2.375% notes 2020	362
2.125% notes 2021	701
3.625% notes 2025	726
3.375% notes 2026	412
Secured	
Obligations under finance leases	114
	3,406

Source: Rolls-Royce Holdings plc, Annual Report and Accounts 2017, p.148, note 15.

Note the large number of sources of the company borrowings. This is typical of most large companies and probably reflects a desire to exploit all available means of raising finance, each of which may have advantages and disadvantages. Normally, a lender would accept a lower rate of interest where the loan is secured, as there is less risk involved. It should be said that whether a loan to a company like Rolls-Royce is secured or unsecured is usually pretty academic. It is unlikely that such a large and profitable company would fail to meet its obligations.

Raising share capital

After an initial share issue a company may decide to make further issues of new shares in order to finance its operations. These new share issues may be carried out in various ways. They may involve direct appeals to investors or may employ the services of financial intermediaries. The most common methods of share issue are:

- *rights issues* – issues made to existing shareholders, in proportion to their existing shareholding;
- *public issues* – issues made to the general investing public; or
- *private placings* – issues made to selected individuals who are usually approached and asked if they would be interested in taking up new shares.

During its lifetime, a company may use all three of these approaches to raising funds through issuing new shares (although only public companies can make appeals to the general public).

These approaches will be discussed in detail in Chapter 15.

Withdrawing equity

As we have seen, companies are legally obliged to distinguish, in the statement of financial position, between that part of the shareholders' equity that may be withdrawn and that part which may not. The withdrawable part consists of profits arising from trading and from the disposal of non-current assets. It is represented in the statement of financial position by *revenue reserves*.

Paying dividends is the most usual way of enabling shareholders to withdraw part of their equity. An alternative is for the company to buy its own shares from those shareholders wishing to sell them. This is usually known as a *share repurchase*. The company would then normally cancel the shares concerned. Share repurchases usually involve only a small proportion of the shareholders, unlike a dividend which involves them all.

The total of revenue reserves appearing in the statement of financial position is rarely the total of all trading profits and profits on disposals of non-current assets generated by the company since it was first formed. This total will normally have been reduced by at least one of the following:

- corporation tax paid on those profits;
- any dividends paid or amounts paid to purchase the company's own shares; and
- any losses from trading and the disposal of non-current assets.

The non-withdrawable part consists of share capital plus profits arising from shareholders buying shares in the company and from upward revaluations of assets still held. It is represented in the statement of financial position by *share capital* and *capital reserves*.

Figure 4.4 shows the important division between the part of the shareholders' equity that can be withdrawn and the part that cannot.

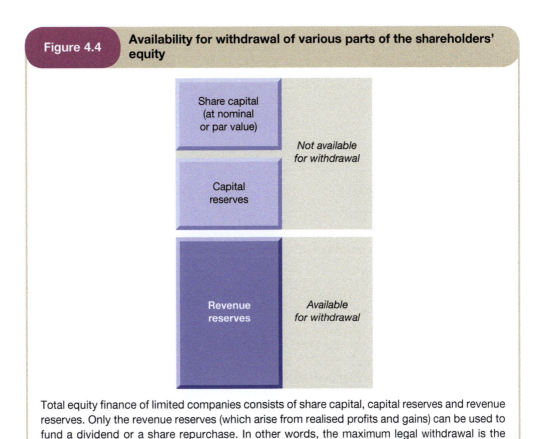

Figure 4.4   **Availability for withdrawal of various parts of the shareholders' equity**

Total equity finance of limited companies consists of share capital, capital reserves and revenue reserves. Only the revenue reserves (which arise from realised profits and gains) can be used to fund a dividend or a share repurchase. In other words, the maximum legal withdrawal is the amount of the revenue reserves.

The law does not specify the size of the non-withdrawable part of shareholders' equity. However, for a company to gain the confidence of prospective lenders and suppliers, the bigger the non-withdrawable part, the better.

Real World 4.9 describes how one company contravened the rules concerning the withdrawal of equity.

Activity 4.10

Why are limited companies required to distinguish different parts of their shareholders' equity, whereas sole-proprietorship and partnership businesses are not?

The reason stems from the limited liability that company shareholders enjoy but which owners of unincorporated businesses do not. If a sole proprietor or partner withdraws all of the equity, the position of the lenders and credit suppliers of the business is not weakened since they can legally enforce their claims against the sole proprietor or partner as an individual. With a limited company, however, the right to enforce claims against individual owners does not exist. To protect the company's lenders and credit suppliers, therefore, the law insists that the non-withdrawable part of shareholders' equity is clearly distinguished.

Let us now look at Example 4.4, which illustrates how this protection of lenders and suppliers works.

Example 4.4

The summary statement of financial position of a company at a particular date is as follows:

Statement of financial position

	£
Total assets	43,000
Equity	
Share capital:	£
20,000 shares of £1 each	20,000
Reserves (revenue)	23,000
Total equity	43,000

A bank has been asked to make a £25,000 long-term loan to the company. If the loan is granted, the statement of financial position immediately following would appear as follows:

Statement of financial position (after the loan)

	£
Total assets	68,000
Equity	
Share capital:	£
20,000 shares of £1 each	20,000
Reserves (revenue)	23,000
	43,000
Non-current liability	
Borrowings – loan	25,000
Total equity and liabilities	68,000

As things stand, there are assets with a total carrying amount of £68,000 to meet the bank's claim of £25,000. It would be possible and perfectly legal, however, for the company to withdraw part of the shareholders' equity (through a dividend or share repurchase) equal to the total revenue reserves (£23,000). The statement of financial position would then appear as follows:

Statement of financial position (after withdrawal)

	£
Total assets (£68,000 − £23,000)	45,000
Equity	
Share capital:	£
20,000 shares of £1 each	20,000
Reserves [revenue (£23,000 − £23,000)]	–
	20,000
Non-current liabilities	
Borrowings – bank loan	25,000
Total equity and liabilities	45,000

Example 4.4 *continued*

This leaves the bank in a very much weaker position, in that there are now total assets with a carrying amount of £45,000 to meet a claim of £25,000. Note that the difference between the amount of the borrowings (bank loan) and the total assets equals the equity (share capital and reserves) total. Thus, the equity represents a margin of safety for lenders and suppliers. The larger the amount of the equity withdrawable by the shareholders, the smaller is the potential margin of safety for lenders and suppliers.

Activity 4.11

Can you recall the circumstances in which the non-withdrawable part of a company's capital could be reduced, without contravening the law? This was mentioned earlier in the chapter.

It can be reduced as a result of the company sustaining trading losses, or losses on disposal of non-current assets, which exceed the withdrawable amount of shareholders' equity.

The main financial statements

The financial statements of a limited company are, in essence, the same as those of a sole proprietor or partnership. There are, however, some differences of detail. We shall now consider these. Example 4.5 sets out the income statement and statement of financial position of a limited company.

Example 4.5

Da Silva plc

Income statement for the year ended 31 December 2018

	£m
Revenue	840
Cost of sales	(520)
Gross profit	320
Wages and salaries	(98)
Heat and light	(18)
Rent and rates	(24)
Motor vehicle expenses	(20)
Insurance	(4)
Printing and stationery	(12)
Depreciation	(45)
Audit fee	(4)
Operating profit	95
Interest payable	(10)
Profit before taxation	85
Taxation	(24)
Profit for the year	61

Statement of financial position as at 31 December 2018

	£m
ASSETS	
Non-current assets	
Property, plant and equipment	203
Intangible assets	100
	303
Current assets	
Inventories	65
Trade receivables	112
Cash	36
	213
Total assets	516
EQUITY AND LIABILITIES	£
Equity	
Ordinary shares of £0.50 each	200
Share premium account	30
Other reserves	50
Retained earnings	25
	305
Non-current liabilities	
Borrowings	100
Current liabilities	
Trade payables	99
Taxation	12
	111
Total equity and liabilities	516

Let us now go through these statements and pick out those aspects that are unique to limited companies.

The income statement

The main points for consideration in the income statement are as follows:

Profit

We can see that, following the calculation of operating profit, two further measures of profit are shown.

- The first of these is the **profit before taxation**. Interest charges are deducted from the operating profit to derive this figure. In the case of a sole proprietor or partnership business, the income statement would end here.

● The second measure of profit is the profit for the reporting period (usually a year). As the company is a separate legal entity, it is liable to pay tax (known as corporation tax) on the profits generated. This measure of profit represents the amount that is available for the shareholders.

Audit fee

Companies beyond a certain size are required to have their financial statements audited by an independent firm of accountants, for which a fee is charged. As we shall see in Chapter 5, the purpose of the audit is to lend credibility to the financial statements. Although it is also open to sole proprietorships and partnerships to have their financial statements audited, relatively few do so. Audit fee is, therefore, an expense that is most often seen in the income statement of a company.

Figure 4.5 shows an outline of the income statement for a limited company.

| Figure 4.5 | The layout of the income statement for a limited company |

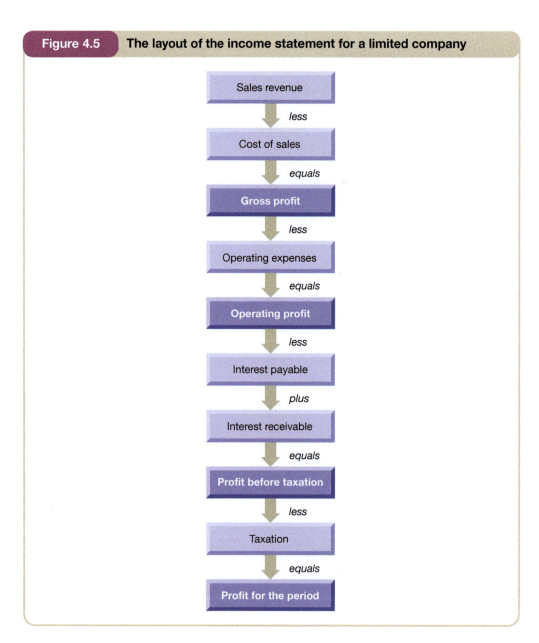

The statement of financial position

The main points for consideration in the statement of financial position are as follows:

Taxation

For many companies, the amount that appears as part of the current liabilities represents 50 per cent of the tax on the profit for the year 2018. It is, therefore, 50 per cent (£12 million) of the charge that appears in the income statement (£24 million); the other 50 per cent will already have been paid. The unpaid 50 per cent will be paid shortly after the statement of financial position date. These payment dates are set down by law.

Other reserves

This will include any reserves that are not separately identified on the face of the statement of financial position. It may include a *general reserve,* which normally consists of trading profits that have been transferred to this separate reserve for reinvestment ('ploughing back') into the operations of the company. It is not necessary to set up a separate reserve for this purpose. The trading profits could remain unallocated and still swell the retained earnings of the company. It is not entirely clear why directors decide to make transfers to general reserves, since the profits concerned remain part of the revenue reserves and, as such, they still remain available for dividend.

Activity 4.12

Can you think of a reason why the directors may wish to make a transfer to general reserves from retained earnings?

The most plausible explanation seems to be that directors feel that placing profits in a separate reserve indicates an intention to invest the funds, represented by the reserve, permanently in the company and, therefore, not to use them to pay a dividend or to fund a share repurchase.

Retained earnings appearing on the statement of financial position are, of course, also a reserve, but that fact is not indicated in its title.

Dividends

Although most companies pay dividends to shareholders, they are under no legal obligation to do so. The decision whether to pay dividends will be influenced by commercial factors such as the financial resources of the company, future commitments and shareholder expectations. It must also take account of the legal restraints on the withdrawal of equity, as discussed earlier.

Dividends are paid out of the revenue reserves and should be deducted from these reserves (usually retained earnings) when preparing the statement of financial position. Shareholders are often paid an annual dividend, perhaps in two parts. An 'interim' dividend may be paid part way through the year and a 'final' dividend shortly after the year end.

Dividends declared by the directors during the year but still unpaid at the year end *may* appear as a liability in the statement of financial position. To be recognised as a liability, however, they must be properly authorised before the year-end date. This normally means that the shareholders must approve the dividend by that date.

Large companies tend to have their own clear and consistent policy towards the payment of dividends. Any change in the policy provokes considerable interest and is usually interpreted by shareholders as a signal of the directors' views concerning the future. For example, an increase in dividends may be taken as a signal from the directors that future prospects are bright: a higher dividend is seen as tangible evidence of their confidence.

Real World 4.10 provides an example of one well-known business that restored its dividend after a difficult period.

Real World 4.10

Sending a signal

Tesco chief Dave Lewis will this week attempt to confirm the supermarket giant's comeback by restoring its dividend, even as the alleged 'colossal fraud' that blew a hole in its finances is laid bare in court.

Mr Lewis, who was drafted in to lead a salvage operation at Tesco three years ago after investigators uncovered hundreds of millions of pounds of missing profits, scrapped the dividend months into his reign to help repair the balance sheet.

Its expected return as part of Tesco's half-year results on Wednesday comes as investor nerves are tested by the three former senior executives accused of masterminding a scheme to 'cook the books'. The trial of Christopher Bush, Tesco UK's former managing director, Carl Rogberg, the company's former UK finance director, and John Scouler, former food commercial director, began on Friday.

Bruno Monteyne, an analyst at Bernstein, has said that, while the size of any dividend may be small, it will be 'important symbolically, signalling the next stage of the Tesco recovery to the market'.

Source: Extract from Armstrong, A. (2017) Tesco to signal comeback with return to dividend, *Daily Telegraph,* 30 September.

Accounting for groups of companies

Most large businesses, including nearly all of the well-known ones, operate not as a single company but as a group of companies. In these circumstances, one company (the **parent company** (or 'parent') or **holding company**) is able to control various subsidiary companies, normally as a result of owning more than 50 per cent of their shares. Many larger businesses have numerous subsidiary companies, with each subsidiary operating some aspect of the group's activities. The reasons why many businesses operate in the form of groups include:

- a desire for each part of the business to have its own limited liability, so that financial problems in one part of a business cannot have an adverse effect on other parts; and
- an attempt to make each part of the business have some sense of independence and autonomy and, perhaps, to create or perpetuate a market image of a smaller independent business.

Each company within a group will prepare its own individual annual financial statements. The law also requires, however, that the parent company prepares **group financial statements**, also known as **consolidated financial statements**. These group financial statements amalgamate the financial statements of all of the group members. Thus, the group income statement includes the total revenue figure for all group companies to customers who are not members of the same group, the statement of financial position includes the property, plant and equipment for all group companies and so on. This means that the group financial statements will look like the financial statements of the parent company, had it owned and operated all of the assets of the business directly, instead of through subsidiary companies.

In view of what we have just seen, it may not be possible to detect whether the business operates through a single company or through a large number of subsidiaries, simply by looking at a set of group financial statements. Only by referring to the heading at the top of each statement, which should mention the word 'consolidated' or 'group', might we find this out. In many cases, however, one or two items will be reported that are peculiar to group financial statements. These items are:

- *Goodwill arising on consolidation.* This occurs when a parent acquires a subsidiary from previous owners and pays more for the subsidiary than the subsidiary's individual assets (net of liabilities) appear to be worth. This excess may represent such things as the value of a good reputation that the new subsidiary already has in the market, or the value of its having a loyal and skilled workforce. Goodwill arising on consolidation will appear as an intangible non-current asset on the group statement of financial position.
- *Non-controlling interests (NCI).* One of the principles followed when preparing group financial statements is that *all* of the revenue, expenses, assets, liabilities and cash flows of each subsidiary are reflected *to their full extent* in the group financial statements. This is true whether or not the parent owns all of the shares in each subsidiary, provided that the parent has control. (Control normally means owning more than 50 per cent of the subsidiary's ordinary shares.) Where not all of the shares are owned by the parent, the investment of those shareholders in the subsidiary, other than the parent company, appears as part of the shareholders' equity in the group statement of financial position. This shows that, although the net assets of the group are being financed mainly by the parent company's shareholders, 'outside' shareholders also finance a part. Similarly, the group income statement reflects the fact that not all of the profit of the group is attributable to the shareholders of the parent company; a part of it is attributable to the 'outside' shareholders. The interests, or claims, of outside shareholders are known as **non-controlling interests**.

Example 4.6 shows how the statement of financial position of Major plc and its subsidiary is drawn up. Note that the group statement of financial position closely resembles that of an individual company.

Example 4.6

Major plc has just bought, from the previous shareholders, 45 million (out of 60 million) ordinary shares in Minor plc, paying £75 million for them. The remaining 15 million Minor plc shares are owned by other shareholders. These shareholders are now referred to by Major plc as the non-controlling interests. Minor plc is now a subsidiary of Major plc and, as is clear from Major plc's statement of financial position, its only subsidiary company.

Example 4.6 *continued*

The statements of financial position of the two companies immediately following the **takeover** (that is, the acquisition of control) of Minor plc by Major plc were as follows:

Statements of financial position

	Major plc £m	Minor plc £m
ASSETS		
Non-current assets		
Property, plant and equipment	63	67
Intangible – 45 million shares in Minor plc	75	–
	138	67
Current assets		
Inventories	37	21
Trade receivables	22	12
Cash	16	2
	75	35
Total assets	213	102
EQUITY AND LIABILITIES		
Equity		
Ordinary shares of £1 each	100	60
Reserves	60	20
	160	80
Non-current liabilities		
Borrowings – loan notes	35	13
Current liabilities		
Trade payables	18	9
Total equity and liabilities	213	102

As would be normal practice, the statement of financial position of the subsidiary (Minor plc) has been revised so that the values of the individual assets are based on *fair values,* rather than what Minor plc originally paid for them. Fair values are those that would be agreed as the selling price between a buyer and a seller, both of whom are knowledgeable and willing. In this context, they probably equate to the values that Major plc would have placed on the individual tangible assets when assessing Minor plc's value.

If a statement of financial position for the group were to be drawn up immediately following the takeover, it would be as follows:

Statements of financial position of Major plc and its subsidiary

	£m
ASSETS	
Non-current assets	
Property, plant and equipment (63 + 67)	130
Intangible – goodwill (75 − ($^{45}/_{60}$ × 80))	15
	145
Current assets	
Inventories (37 + 21)	58
Trade receivables (22 + 12)	34

	£m
Cash (16 + 2)	18
	110
Total assets	255
EQUITY AND LIABILITIES	
Equity	
Ordinary shares of £1 each	100
Reserves	60
Equity attributable to equity holders of the parent	160
Non-controlling interests ($^{15}/_{60} \times 80$)	20
Total equity	180
Non-current liabilities	
Borrowings – loan notes (35 + 13)	48
Current liabilities	
Trade payables (18 + 9)	27
Total equity and liabilities	255

Note that all of the items, except two, in the group statement of financial position are simply the figures for the item concerned, in each of the two statements, added together. This is despite the fact that Major plc owns only three-quarters of the shares of Minor plc. The logic of group financial statements is that if the parent owns enough shares to control its subsidiary, all of the subsidiary's assets and claims should be reflected on the group statement of financial position.

As we have seen, there are two exceptions to this approach: goodwill and non-controlling interests. Goodwill is simply the excess of what Major paid for the shares over their fair value. Major plc bought 45 million of 60 million shares, paying £75 million. According to Minor plc's statement of financial position, there were net assets (non-current and current assets, less current and non-current liabilities) of £80 million.

Activity 4.13

Can you figure out how much Major plc paid for goodwill?

Major plc paid £75 million for £60 million (that is, $^{45}/_{60} \times$ £80 million) of net assets – an excess of £15 million. This is the goodwill amount.

The excess represents the goodwill element and is usually referred to as 'goodwill arising on consolidation'. This asset is seen as being the value of a loyal workforce, a regular and profitable customer base and so on, that a new business setting up would not have. The relevant International Financial Reporting Standard (IFRS 3) demands that goodwill be reviewed at least annually: if its value has been impaired, it must be written down to the lower value.

The NCI take account of the fact that, although Major plc may control all of the assets and liabilities of Minor plc, it only provides the equity finance for three-quarters of them. The other quarter, £20 million (that is, $^{15}/_{60} \times$ £80 million), is still provided by shareholders in Minor plc, other than Major plc. (Note that IFRS 3 allows an alternative method of calculating goodwill on consolidation and NCI for reporting purposes, but this is beyond the scope of this chapter.)

Example 4.7 shows the income statement of Major plc and its subsidiary (Minor plc) for the first year following the takeover. As with the statement of financial position, the various revenue and expense figures are simply the individual figures for each company added together. The non-controlling interests figure (£2 million) represents $^{15}/_{60}$ of the after-tax profit of Minor plc, which is assumed to be £8 million. The parent's equity holders share of the profit for the year consists of 75 per cent of Minor plc's profit (£6 million), plus all of Major plc's profit (assumed to be £10 million).

Example 4.7

Income statement for the first year

	£m
Revenue	123
Cost of sales	(56)
Gross profit	67
Administration expenses	(28)
Distribution expenses	(9)
Profit before tax	30
Taxation	(12)
Profit for the year	18
Attributable to:	
Equity holders of the parent	16
Non-controlling interests	2
	18

Self-assessment question 4.1

The summarised statement of financial position of Dev Ltd at a particular point in time is as follows:

Statement of financial position

	£
Net assets (various assets less liabilities)	235,000
Equity	
Share capital: 100,000 shares of £1 each	100,000
Share premium account	30,000
Revaluation reserve	37,000
Retained earnings	68,000
Total equity	235,000

Required:

(a) Without any other transactions occurring at the same time, the company made a one-for-five rights share issue at £2 per share payable in cash. This means that each shareholder was offered one share for every five already held. All shareholders took up their rights. Immediately afterwards, the company made a one-for-two bonus issue. Show the statement of financial position immediately following the bonus issue, assuming that the directors wanted to retain the maximum dividend payment potential for the future.

(b) Explain what external influence might cause the directors to choose not to retain the maximum dividend payment possibilities.

(c) Show the statement of financial position immediately following the bonus issue, assuming that the directors wanted to retain the *minimum* dividend payment potential for the future.

(d) What is the maximum dividend that could be paid before and after the events described in (a) if the minimum dividend payment potential is achieved?

(e) Lee owns 100 shares in Dev Ltd before the events described in (a). Assuming that the net assets of the company have a value equal to their carrying amount on the statement of financial position, show how these events will affect Lee's wealth.

(f) Looking at the original statement of financial position of Dev Ltd, shown above, what four things do we know about the company's status and history that are not specifically stated on the statement of financial position?

The solution to this question can be found at the back of the book on pages 752–753.

Summary

The main points of this chapter may be summarised as follows:

Main features of a limited company

- It is an artificial person created by law.
- It has a separate life to its owners and is granted a perpetual existence.
- It must take responsibility for its own debts and losses, but its owners are granted limited liability.
- To safeguard those dealing with a limited company, limited liability status is included as part of the business name, restrictions are placed on the ability of owners to withdraw equity and annual financial statements are made publicly available.
- A public company can offer its shares for sale to the public; a private company cannot.
- A limited company is governed by a board of directors elected by the shareholders.

Financing the limited company

- The share capital of a company can be of two main types: ordinary shares and preference shares.
- Holders of ordinary shares (equities) are the main risk takers and are given voting rights; they form the backbone of the company.
- Holders of preference shares are given a right to a fixed dividend before ordinary shareholders receive a dividend.

- Reserves are profits and gains made by the company and form part of the ordinary shareholders' claim.
- Borrowings provide another major source of finance.

Share issues

- Bonus shares are issued to existing shareholders when part of the reserves of the company is converted into share capital. No funds are raised.
- Shares may be issued for cash through a rights issue, a public issue or a public placing.
- The shares of a public company may be traded on the London Stock Exchange.

Withdrawing equity

- Reserves are of two types: revenue reserves and capital reserves.
- Revenue reserves arise from trading profits and from realised profits on the sale of non-current assets.
- Capital reserves arise from the issue of shares above their nominal value or from the upward revaluation of non-current assets.
- Revenue reserves can be withdrawn as dividends by the shareholders whereas capital reserves normally cannot.

Financial statements of limited companies

- The financial statements of limited companies are based on the same principles as those of sole-proprietorship and partnership businesses. However, there are some differences in detail.
- The income statement has two measures of profit displayed after the operating profit figure: profit before taxation and profit for the year.
- The income statement also shows audit fees and tax on profits for the year.
- The statement of financial position will show any unpaid tax and any unpaid, but authorised, dividends as current liabilities.
- The share capital plus the reserves make up 'equity'.

Groups of companies

- Parent companies are required to produce group financial statements incorporating the results of all companies controlled by the parent.
- A group statement of financial position is prepared by adding like items of assets and liabilities based on 'fair values' together, as if all of the trading is undertaken through the parent company.
- A 'goodwill arising on consolidation' figure often emerges in the group statement of financial position.
- Where the parent does not own all of the shares of each subsidiary, a non-controlling interests (NCI) figure will appear in the statement of financial position, representing the outside shareholders' investment.
- A group income statement is drawn up following similar logic to that applied to the group statement of financial position.

Key terms

For definitions of these terms, see Appendix B.

limited liability *p. 127*	**bonus share** *p. 138*
public limited company *p. 128*	**issued share capital** *p. 140*
private limited company *p. 128*	**allotted share capital** *p. 140*
corporation tax *p. 130*	**fully paid share** *p. 140*
Stock Exchange *p. 131*	**called-up share capital** *p. 140*
London Stock Exchange *p. 131*	**paid-up share capital** *p. 140*
director *p. 132*	**loan note** *p. 140*
reserve *p. 132*	**loan stock** *p. 140*
nominal value *p. 132*	**bond** *p. 140*
par value *p. 132*	**debenture** *p. 140*
revenue reserve *p. 133*	**profit before taxation** *p. 147*
dividend *p. 133*	**parent company** *p. 150*
ordinary share *p. 133*	**holding company** *p. 150*
preference share *p. 134*	**group financial statement** *p. 151*
splitting *p. 135*	**consolidated financial**
consolidating *p. 135*	**statement** *p. 151*
capital reserve *p. 136*	**non-controlling interest** *p. 151*
share premium account *p. 137*	**takeover** *p. 152*

Further reading

If you would like to explore the topics covered in this chapter in more depth, we recommend the following:

Alexander, D., Britton, A., Jorissen, A., Hoogendorn, M. and Van Mourik, C. (2017) *International Financial Reporting and Analysis,* 7th edn, Cengage Learning EMEA, Chapter 10.

Elliott, B. and Elliott, J. (2017) *Financial Accounting and Reporting,* 18th edn, Pearson, Chapters 3, 12 and 22.

Maynard, J. (2017) *Financial Accounting, Reporting and Analysis,* 2nd edn, Oxford University Press, Chapter 17.

Melville, A. (2017) *International Financial Reporting: A Practical Guide,* 6th edn, Pearson, Chapter 1.

Critical review questions

Solutions to these questions can be found at the back of the book on page 773.

4.1 You and a friend have decided to set up in business offering a bicycle delivery service in your local area. You feel that you can raise enough funds from your own resources to get the business going. You have calculated that you can finance your planned future expansion from profits. You intend to create a limited company to own the business. Would a public limited company or a private one be more appropriate? Explain your reasons.

4.2 The London Stock Exchange has the power to suspend dealing in shares of businesses that have failed to comply with particular regulations. Why is this seen as a sanction for the business concerned?

4.3 Is limited liability a wholly good idea? Can you think of any arguments against it?

4.4   An established company listed on the London Stock Exchange has decided to raise further funds through an issue of shares. The board of directors has decided to issue preference shares rather than ordinary shares in order to raise the funds required. What factors may have lead them to make such a decision?

Exercises

Solutions to exercises with **coloured numbers** can be found at the back of the book on pages **789–791**.

Basic-level exercises

4.1   Comment on the following quote:
'Limited companies can set a limit on the amount of debts that they will meet. They tend to have reserves of cash as well as share capital, and they can use these reserves to pay dividends to the shareholders. Many companies have preference shares as well as ordinary shares. The preference shares give a guaranteed dividend. The shares of many companies can be bought and sold on the Stock Exchange. Shareholders selling their shares can represent a useful source of new finance to the company.'

4.2   Comment on the following quotes:
(a) 'Bonus shares increase the shareholders' wealth because, after the issue, they have more shares, but each one of the same nominal value as they had before.'
(b) 'By law, once shares have been issued at a particular nominal value, they must always be issued at that value in any future share issues.'
(c) 'By law, companies can pay as much as they like by way of dividends on their shares, provided that they have sufficient cash to do so.'
(d) 'Companies do not have to pay tax on their profits because the shareholders have to pay tax on their dividends.'

4.3   Briefly explain each of the following expressions that you have seen in the financial statements of a limited company:
(a) dividend;
(b) audit fee;
(c) share premium account.

Intermediate-level exercises

4.4   Iqbal Ltd started trading on 1 July 2014. During the first five years of trading, the following occurred:

Year ended 30 June	Trading profit/ (loss)	Profit/(loss) on sale of non-current assets	Upward revaluation of non-current assets
	£	£	£
2015	(15,000)	–	–
2016	8,000	–	10,000
2017	15,000	5,000	–
2018	20,000	(6,000)	–
2019	22,000	–	–

Required:

Assume that the company paid the maximum legal dividend each year. Under normal circumstances, how much would each year's dividend be?

4.5 Hudson plc's outline statement of financial position as at a particular date was as follows:

	£m
Net assets (assets less liabilities)	72
Equity	
Ordinary shares	40
General reserve	32
Total equity	72

The directors made a one-for-four bonus issue, immediately followed by a one-for-four rights issue at a price of £1.80 per share.

Required:

Show the statement of financial position of Hudson plc immediately following the two share issues.

Advanced-level exercises

4.6 The following is a draft set of simplified financial statements for Pear Limited for the year ended 30 September 2019.

Income statement for the year ended 30 September 2019

	£000
Revenue	1,456
Cost of sales	(768)
Gross profit	688
Salaries	(220)
Depreciation	(249)
Other operating costs	(131)
Operating profit	88
Interest payable	(15)
Profit before taxation	73
Taxation at 30%	(22)
Profit for the year	51

Statement of financial position as at 30 September 2019

	£000
ASSETS	
Non-current assets	
Property, plant and equipment:	
Cost	1,570
Depreciation	(690)
	880
Current assets	
Inventories	207
Trade receivables	182
Cash at bank	21
	410
Total assets	1,290

	£000
EQUITY AND LIABILITIES	
Equity	
Share capital	300
Share premium account	300
Retained earnings at beginning of year	104
Profit for year	51
	755
Non-current liabilities	
Borrowings (10% loan notes repayable 2025)	300
Current liabilities	
Trade payables	88
Other payables	20
Taxation	22
Borrowings (bank overdraft)	105
	235
Total equity and liabilities	1,290

The following information is available:

1. Depreciation has not been charged on office equipment with a carrying amount of £100,000 This class of assets is depreciated at 12 per cent a year using the reducing-balance method.
2. A new machine was purchased, on credit, for £30,000 and delivered on 29 September 2019 but has not been included in the financial statements. (Ignore depreciation.)
3. A sales invoice to the value of £18,000 for September 2019 has been omitted from the financial statements. (The cost of sales figure is stated correctly.)
4. A dividend of £25,000 had been approved by the shareholders before 30 September 2019, but was unpaid at that date. This is not reflected in the financial statements.
5. The interest payable on the loan notes for the second half-year was not paid until 1 October 2019 and has not been included in the financial statements.
6. An allowance for trade receivables is to be made at the level of 2 per cent of trade receivables.
7. An invoice for electricity to the value of £2,000 for the quarter ended 30 September 2019 arrived on 4 October 2019 and has not been included in the financial statements.
8. The charge for taxation will have to be revised to take account of any amendments to the taxable profit arising from items 1 to 7. Make the simplifying assumption that tax is payable shortly after the end of the year, at the rate of 30 per cent of the profit before tax.

Required:

Prepare a revised set of financial statements for the year ended 30 September 2019 incorporating the additional information in 1 to 8 above. (Work to the nearest £1,000.)

4.7 Rose Limited is a wholesaler and retailer of high-quality teas and coffees. Approximately half of sales are on credit. Abbreviated and unaudited financial statements are as follows:

Rose Limited
Income statement for the year ended 31 March 2019

	£000
Revenue	12,080
Cost of sales	(6,282)
Gross profit	5,798
Labour costs	(2,658)
Depreciation	(625)
Other operating costs	(1,003)
Operating profit	1,512

	£000
Interest payable	(66)
Profit before taxation	1,446
Taxation	(434)
Profit for the year	1,012

Statement of financial position as at 31 March 2019

	£000
ASSETS	
Non-current assets	2,728
Current assets	
Inventories	1,583
Trade receivables	996
Cash	26
	2,605
Total assets	5,333
EQUITY AND LIABILITIES	
Equity	
Share capital (50p shares, fully paid)	750
Share premium	250
Retained earnings	1,468
	2,468
Non-current liabilities	
Borrowings – secured loan notes (2025)	300
Current liabilities	
Trade payables	1,118
Other payables	417
Tax	434
Borrowings – overdraft	596
	2,565
Total equity and liabilities	5,333

Since the unaudited financial statements for Rose Limited were prepared, the following information has become available:

1 An additional £74,000 of depreciation should have been charged on fixtures and fittings.
2 Invoices for credit sales on 31 March 2019 amounting to £34,000 have not been included; cost of sales is not affected.
3 Trade receivables totalling £21,000 are recognised as having gone bad, but they have not yet been written off.
4 Inventories which had been purchased for £2,000 have been damaged and are unsaleable. This is not reflected in the financial statements.
5 Fixtures and fittings to the value of £16,000 were delivered just before 31 March 2019, but these assets were not included in the financial statements and the purchase invoice had not been processed.
6 Wages for Saturday-only staff, amounting to £1,000, have not been paid for the final Saturday of the year. This is not reflected in the financial statements.
7 Tax is payable at 30 per cent of profit before taxation. Assume that it is payable shortly after the year-end.

Required:
Prepare revised financial statements for Rose Limited for the year ended 31 March 2019, incorporating the information in 1 to 7 above. (Work to the nearest £1,000.)

CHAPTER 5

Accounting for limited companies (2)

Introduction

This chapter continues our examination of the financial statements of limited companies. We begin by considering the importance of accounting rules in preparing financial statements and the main sources of these rules. We then go on to discuss the conceptual framework that underpins these rules.

Over the years, the published annual financial reports of larger companies have greatly increased in scope. They now include a comprehensive set of financial statements for users. A detailed consideration of the various rules relating to these statements is beyond the scope of this book; however, we shall take a look at the key rules that shape their form and content. To accompany the financial statements, the directors must provide comments, and supplementary information, concerning the performance and position of the company. In this chapter, we outline the key topics that the directors must address.

Corporate governance, which concerns the way in which companies are directed and controlled, has become an important issue. In recent years, strenuous efforts have been made to improve standards of corporate governance, particularly for large listed companies. In this chapter, we consider the framework of rules that has been created to try to protect the interests of shareholders.

Despite the proliferation of accounting rules and the increasing supply of financial information to users, concerns have been expressed over the quality of some published financial reports. We end the chapter by looking at some well-publicised accounting scandals and the problem of creative accounting.

Learning outcomes

When you have completed this chapter, you should be able to:

- discuss the framework of accounting rules and the conceptual framework that help to shape the form and content of annual financial statements;

- prepare a statement of financial position, statement of comprehensive income and statement of changes in equity in accordance with International Financial Reporting Standards;

- describe the role and content of the directors' report and the strategic report;

- explain the principles upon which corporate governance rules are based and describe the framework of rules created to protect the interests of shareholders; and

- discuss the threat posed by creative accounting and outline the main methods employed to distort the fair presentation of position and performance.

The directors' duty to account

For most large companies, it is not possible for all shareholders to be involved in the management of the company. Instead, they appoint directors to act on their behalf. This separation of ownership from day-to-day control creates a need for directors to be accountable for their stewardship (management) of the company's assets. To fulfil this need, the directors must prepare financial statements that provide a fair representation of the financial position and performance of the business. This means that they must select appropriate accounting policies, make reasonable accounting estimates and adhere to all relevant accounting rules when preparing the statements. To avoid any misleading information in the financial statements, whether from fraud or error, they must also maintain appropriate internal control systems.

Activity 5.1

Do you think that, in practice, the directors will undertake the task of preparing the financial statements themselves?

Probably not – they will normally delegate this task to the accounting staff. Nevertheless, they will retain responsibility for the financial statements and must monitor the work done.

Each of the company's shareholders has the right to be sent a copy of the financial statements produced by the directors. These statements must also be made available to the general public. A copy must also be sent to the Registrar of Companies, which is then made available for public inspection. A Stock Exchange listed company has the additional obligation to publish its financial statements on its website.

Activity 5.2

It can be argued that the publication of financial statements is vital to a well-functioning private sector. Why might this be the case? Try to think of at least one reason.

There are at least two reasons:

- Unless shareholders receive regular information about the performance and position of a business, they will have problems in appraising their investment. As a result, they would probably be reluctant to invest.

Activity 5.2 *continued*

- Unless suppliers of labour, goods, services and finance, particularly those supplying credit (loans) or goods and services on credit, receive information about a company's financial health they may be reluctant to engage in commercial relationships. The fact that a company has limited liability increases the risks involved in dealing with it.

In both cases, the functioning of the private sector of the economy will be adversely affected by the absence of financial statements.

The need for accounting rules

The obligation on directors to prepare and publish financial statements has led to the creation of a framework of rules concerning their form and content. Without rules, there is a much greater risk that unscrupulous directors will adopt accounting policies and practices that portray an unrealistic view of financial health. There is also a much greater risk that the financial statements will not be comparable over time, or with those of other businesses. Accounting rules can narrow areas of differences and reduce the variety of accounting methods. This should help ensure that all businesses treat similar transactions in a similar way.

Example 5.1 illustrates the problems that can arise where businesses are allowed to exercise choice over their accounting policies.

Example 5.1

Rila plc and Pirin plc are both wholesalers of electrical goods. Both commenced trading on 1 March 2018 with an identical share capital. Both acquired identical property, plant and equipment on 1 March and both achieved identical trading results during the first year of trading. The following financial information relating to both businesses is available:

	£m
Ordinary £1 shares fully paid on 1 March 2018	60
Non-current assets (at cost) acquired on 1 March 2018	40
Revenue for the year to 28 February 2019	100
Purchases of inventories during the year to 28 February 2019	70
Expenses for the year to 28 February 2019 (excluding depreciation)	20
Trade receivables as at 28 February 2019	37
Trade payables as at 28 February 2019	12
Cash as at 28 February 2019	5

The non-current assets held by both businesses are leasehold buildings that have five years left to run on the lease. Inventories for both businesses have been valued at the year-end at £16 million on a FIFO basis and £12 million on a LIFO basis.

When preparing their financial statements for the first year of trading,

- Rila plc decided to write off the cost of the leasehold premises at the end of the lease period. Pirin plc adopted the straight-line basis of depreciation for the leasehold buildings.
- Rila plc adopted the FIFO method of inventories valuation and Pirin plc adopted the LIFO method.

The income statements and the statements of financial position for the two businesses, ignoring taxation, will be as follows:

Income statements for the year to 28 February 2019

	Rila plc £m	Pirin plc £m
Revenue	100	100
Cost of sales:		
Rila plc (£70m − £16m)	(54)	
Pirin plc (£70m − £12m)	—	(58)
Gross profit	46	42
Expenses (excluding depreciation)	(20)	(20)
Depreciation:		
Rila plc	(−)	
Pirin plc (£40m/5)	—	(8)
Profit for the year	26	14

Statements of financial position as at 28 February 2019

	Rila plc £m	Pirin plc £m
ASSETS		
Non-current assets		
Property, plant and equipment at cost	40	40
Accumulated depreciation	(−)	(8)
	40	32
Current assets		
Inventories	16	12
Trade receivables	37	37
Cash	5	5
	58	54
Total assets	98	86
EQUITY AND LIABILITIES		
Equity		
Share capital	60	60
Retained earnings	26	14
	86	74
Current liabilities		
Trade payables	12	12
Total equity and liabilities	98	86

Although the two businesses are identical in terms of funding and underlying trading performance, the financial statements create an impression that the financial health of each business is quite different. The accounting policies selected by Rila plc help to portray a much rosier picture. We can see that Rila plc reports a significantly higher profit for the year and higher assets at the year-end.

Depreciation and inventories valuation are not the only areas where choices might be exercised. Nevertheless, they illustrate the potential impact of different accounting choices over the short term.

Accounting rules should help to create greater confidence in the integrity of financial statements. This should make it easier to raise funds from investors and to build stronger relationships with customers and suppliers. We must be realistic, however, about what can be achieved through regulation. Problems of manipulation and of concealment can still occur even within a highly-regulated environment (and examples of both will be considered later in the chapter). Nevertheless, the scale of these problems should be reduced where accounting rules are in place.

Problems of comparability between businesses can also still occur. Accounting is not a precise science. Even within a regulated environment, estimates and judgements must be made and these may vary according to who makes them. Furthermore, no two businesses are identical (unlike the companies in Example 5.1). Different accounting policies may therefore be applied to fit different circumstances.

Sources of accounting rules

In recent years, there has been an increasing trend towards both the internationalisation of business and the integration of financial markets. This has helped to strengthen the case for the international harmonisation of accounting rules. By adopting a common set of rules, users of financial statements are better placed to compare the financial health of companies based in different countries. It can also relieve international companies of some of the burden of preparing financial statements. Different financial statements are no longer needed to comply with the rules of the particular countries in which these companies operate.

The International Accounting Standards Board (IASB) is an independent body that is at the forefront of the move towards harmonisation. The Board, which is based in the UK, is dedicated to developing a single set of high-quality, global accounting rules. These rules aim to provide transparent and comparable information in financial statements. They are known as **International Financial Reporting Standards** (IFRSs) (or **International Accounting Standards** (IASs)) and deal with key issues such as:

- what information should be disclosed;
- how information should be presented;
- how assets and liabilities should be valued; and
- how profit should be measured.

Activity 5.3

We have already come across some IASs and IFRSs in earlier chapters. Try to recall at least two topics where financial reporting standards were mentioned.

We came across financial reporting standards when considering:

- the valuation and impairment of assets (Chapter 2);
- depreciation and impairment of non-current assets (Chapter 3); and
- the valuation of inventories (Chapter 3).

The growing authority of the IASB

Over recent years the authority of the IASB has gone from strength to strength. The first major boost came when the European Commission required nearly all companies listed on the stock exchanges of European Union member states to adopt IFRSs for reporting periods commencing on or after 1 January 2005. As a result, nearly 7,000 companies in 25 different countries switched to IFRSs. Since this landmark development, the authority of the IASB has continued to grow. Of the 166 countries that the IASB profiles, 144 (87 per cent) require the use of IFRS Standards for all, or most, public companies and financial institutions in their capital markets (such as stock exchanges). (See Reference 1 at the end of the chapter.) Non-listed UK companies are not required to adopt IFRSs but have the option to do so.

Adopting IFRSs

Figure 5.1 sets out the main sources of accounting rules for Stock Exchange listed companies.

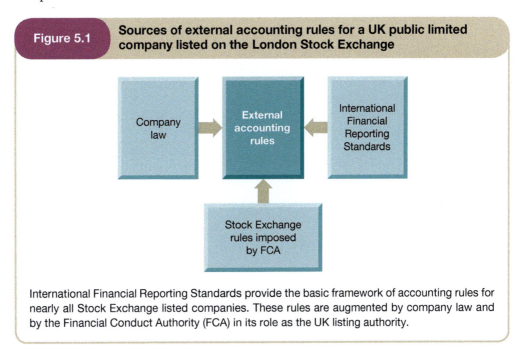

Figure 5.1 Sources of external accounting rules for a UK public limited company listed on the London Stock Exchange

International Financial Reporting Standards provide the basic framework of accounting rules for nearly all Stock Exchange listed companies. These rules are augmented by company law and by the Financial Conduct Authority (FCA) in its role as the UK listing authority.

Real World 5.1 provides a list of IASB standards that were in force as at 10 November 2018. It gives some idea of the range of topics that are covered. The IASB continues its work and so changes to this list will occur over time.

Real World 5.1

International standards

The following is a list of the International Accounting Standards (IASs) and International Financial Reporting Standards (IFRSs) in force as at 10 November 2018. (The latter term is used for standards issued from 2003 onwards.) Several standards have been issued and subsequently withdrawn, which explains the gaps in the numerical sequence. In addition, several have been revised and reissued.

IAS 1	*Presentation of Financial Statements*
IAS 2	*Inventories*
IAS 7	*Statement of Cash Flows*
IAS 8	*Accounting Policies, Changes in Accounting Estimates and Errors*

Real World 5.1 *continued*

IAS 10	*Events after the Reporting Period*
IAS 11	*Construction Contracts**
IAS 12	*Income Taxes*
IAS 16	*Property, Plant and Equipment*
IAS 17	*Leases***
IAS 18	*Revenue****
IAS 19	*Employee Benefits*
IAS 20	*Accounting for Government Grants and Disclosure of Government Assistance*
IAS 21	*The Effects of Changes in Foreign Exchange Rates*
IAS 23	*Borrowing Costs*
IAS 24	*Related Party Disclosures*
IAS 26	*Accounting and Reporting by Retirement Benefit Plans*
IAS 27	*Separate Financial Statements*
IAS 28	*Investments in Associates*
IAS 29	*Financial Reporting in Hyperinflationary Economies*
IAS 32	*Financial Instruments: Presentation*
IAS 33	*Earnings per Share*
IAS 34	*Interim Financial Reporting*
IAS 36	*Impairment of Assets*
IAS 37	*Provisions, Contingent Liabilities and Contingent Assets*
IAS 38	*Intangible Assets*
IAS 39	*Financial Instruments: Recognition and Measurement*****
IAS 40	*Investment Property*
IAS 41	*Agriculture*
IFRS 1	*First-time Adoption of International Financial Reporting Standards*
IFRS 2	*Share-based Payment*
IFRS 3	*Business Combinations*
IFRS 4	*Insurance Contracts*
IFRS 5	*Non-current Assets Held for Sale and Discontinued Operations*
IFRS 6	*Exploration for and Evaluation of Mineral Resources*
IFRS 7	*Financial Instruments: Disclosures*
IFRS 8	*Operating Segments*
IFRS 9	*Financial Instruments*
IFRS 10	*Consolidated Financial Statements*
IFRS 11	*Joint Arrangements*
IFRS 12	*Disclosure of Interests in Other Entities*
IFRS 13	*Fair Value Measurement*
IFRS 14	*Regulatory Deferral Accounts*
IFRS 15	*Revenue from Contracts with Customers*
IFRS 16	*Leases*
IFRS 17	*Insurance Contracts*

* Will be superseded by IFRS 15
** Will be superseded by IFRS 16
*** Will be superseded by IFRS 15
**** Will be superseded by IFRS 9

Source: Adapted from list on International Accounting Standards Board website, www.ifrs.org, accessed 10 November 2018.

The need for a conceptual framework

In Chapters 2 and 3 we came across various accounting conventions such as the prudence, historic cost and going concern conventions. These were developed as a practical response to particular problems that were confronted when preparing financial statements. They have stood the test of time and are still of value to preparers today. However, they do not provide, and were never designed to provide, a **conceptual framework**, or framework of principles, to guide the development of financial statements. As we grapple with increasingly complex financial reporting problems, the need to have a better understanding of *why* we account for things in a particular way becomes more pressing. Knowing *why* we account, rather than simply *how* we account, is vital if we are to improve the quality of financial statements.

In recent years, much effort has been expended in various countries, including the UK, to develop a clear conceptual framework that will guide us in the development of accounting. This framework should provide clear answers to such fundamental questions as:

- Who are the main users of financial statements?
- What is the purpose of financial statements?
- What qualities should financial information possess?
- What are the main elements of financial statements?
- How should these elements be defined, recognised and measured?

If these questions can be answered, accounting rule makers, such as the IASB, will be in a stronger position to identify best practice and to develop more coherent rules. This should, in turn, increase the credibility of financial reports in the eyes of users. It may even help reduce the possible number of rules.

Activity 5.4

Can you think how it may help reduce the number of rules required?

Some issues may be resolved by reference to the application of general principles rather than by the generation of further rules.

The IASB framework

The quest for a conceptual framework began in earnest in the 1970s when the Financial Accounting Standards Board (FASB) in the USA devoted a large amount of time and resources to this task. This resulted in a broad framework, which other rule-making bodies, including the IASB, then drew upon to develop their own frameworks. The main aim of the IASB conceptual framework is to provide a firm foundation for the development of International Financial Reporting Standards (IFRSs). This can be achieved if they are underpinned by a clear set of principles.

History shows that the IASB conceptual framework is not set in stone. It is revised over time to take account of developments in accounting and the changing business environment. In 2018, the IASB produced its latest version of the *Conceptual Framework for*

Financial Reporting. This states that the objective of general purpose financial reporting is 'to provide financial information about the reporting entity that is useful to existing and potential investors, lenders and other creditors in making decisions relating to providing resources to the entity'. Note that it is the providers of finance that are seen as the primary users of general-purpose financial reports. This is because investors, lenders and other creditors largely rely on these reports to make their investment decisions. Although other users may find general-purpose financial reports useful, the reports are not particularly aimed at them.

The IASB framework sets out the qualitative characteristics that make financial statements useful. These are the same as those discussed in Chapter 1.

Activity 5.5

Can you recall what they are?

The fundamental characteristics identified are relevance and faithful representation: it is these characteristics that make information useful. Characteristics that enhance the quality of financial reports are comparability, timeliness, verifiability and understandability. These enhancing characteristics are of secondary importance. In absence of relevance and faithful representation, they cannot make information useful.

The IASB conceptual framework also recognises that producing financial information incurs costs, which should be justified by the benefits provided.

The framework discusses three important accounting conventions that were covered in earlier chapters: going concern, prudence and accruals. It states that financial statements should normally be prepared on the assumption that a business is a going concern. Where, however, this assumption cannot be applied, a different basis for preparation must be used. This basis must then be described in the financial statements.

The IASB framework defines prudence as the exercise of caution when making judgements under conditions of uncertainty. More controversially, prudence is seen as supporting the concept of *neutrality,* a component of faithful representation. This is a point to which we shall return later. The framework regards the accruals convention as a better way of assessing past and future performance than using cash inflows and outflows. Nevertheless, information concerning cash flows is still seen as helpful when assessing certain aspects of financial health such as financing and investing activities and liquidity.

The IASB framework goes on to identify and define the main elements of financial statements. Those relating to the measurement of financial position are assets, liabilities and equity. Those relating to the measurement of performance are income and expense. The definition for each of these elements has been used to form the basis of our discussions in Chapters 2 and 3. Procedures for recognising each element, as well as how each should be presented and disclosed in the financial statements, are also described in the framework.

Finally, the IASB conceptual framework discusses different measurement bases for assets and liabilities. These include historic cost and current value measures, such as current cost and fair value, which we have already come across. No attempt is made to support a particular measurement basis. It is merely stated that, when selecting a particular measurement basis, the nature of the information produced must be considered. This information must be useful to users, which means that it must be possess the qualitative characteristics of relevance, faithful representation and so on. However, cost should be taken into account when selecting an appropriate measurement basis. (See Reference 2 at the end of the chapter.)

Activity 5.6

Which do you think is likely to be the less costly measurement basis to employ: one based on historic cost or one based on current values?

One based on historic cost will normally be far less costly. Establishing the cost of acquisition is usually fairly straightforward, assuming proper records are kept. Establishing current values, on the other hand, can be time consuming and can involve out-of-pocket search costs. (Similar costs, however, can be incurred under historic cost when calculating impairment and depreciation charges.)

Criticisms of the framework

The general approach to developing a conceptual framework has attracted some criticism. It has been argued, for example, that the IASB framework is too broad in nature to provide useful guidance for the development of financial reporting standards, or to deal with emerging accounting issues. It has also been argued that the framework is merely descriptive and fails to provide a solid theoretical underpinning to the financial statements.

There has also been criticism of specific issues covered. The idea that prudence supports the concept of neutrality, for example, has created some debate. It runs counter to traditional thinking, where prudence and neutrality are not regarded as comfortable bedfellows. Prudence is normally taken to mean that more convincing evidence is required for recognising assets and income than for recognising liabilities and expenses. Despite such criticism, however, the IASB's efforts in trying to develop a principles-led approach to standard setting are generally supported.

The auditors' role

Shareholders are required to elect a qualified and independent person or, more usually, a firm to act as **auditors**. The auditors' main duty is to report whether, in their opinion, the financial statements do what they are supposed to do, namely to show a true and fair view of the financial performance, position and cash flows of the company. To form an opinion, auditors must carefully scrutinise the financial statements and the underlying evidence upon which those statements are based. This will involve an examination of the accounting principles followed, the accounting estimates made and the robustness of the company's internal control systems. Following this examination, the auditors should be able to assess the risks of misstatements arising from either fraud or error. Their opinion must accompany the financial statements provided for shareholders and the Registrar of Companies.

The relationship between the shareholders, the directors and the auditors is illustrated in Figure 5.2. This shows that the shareholders elect the directors to act on their behalf, in the day-to-day running of the company. The directors are then required to 'account' to the shareholders on the performance, position and cash flows of the company, on an annual basis. The shareholders also elect the auditors, who then report back to the shareholders.

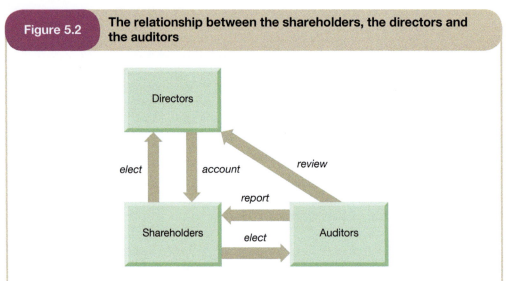

| Figure 5.2 | The relationship between the shareholders, the directors and the auditors |

The directors are appointed by the shareholders to manage the company on the shareholders' behalf. The directors are required to report each year to the shareholders, principally by means of financial statements, on the company's performance, position and cash flows. To give greater confidence in the statements, the shareholders also appoint auditors to investigate the reports and to express an opinion on their reliability.

The framework of annual financial reports

Over the years, there has been a trend towards higher and higher levels of disclosure within annual financial reports. Various reasons have been suggested for this trend. They include the increasing complexity of business, the increasing sophistication of users and an increasing recognition that other groups, and not just shareholders, have a stake in the success of a business.

The content of annual financial reports of companies now goes way beyond the main financial statements. A wide range of information is provided and the reporting boundaries are ill defined. As well as financial information, annual reports often contain information concerning social matters (such as community involvement) and environmental matters (such as carbon emissions). This has led to a growing debate as to whether such information should be included. Questions raised include: 'Does this information really fit with the objectives of financial reporting? Should more appropriate forms of reporting be devised to convey this information?'

Whatever the outcome of this debate, its very existence has highlighted the need for a more coherent reporting framework. A useful starting point in the search for such a framework is to try to identify the core components of financial reports. It has been suggested that three core components have evolved in practice. (See Reference 3 at the end of the chapter.) These are set out in Figure 5.3.

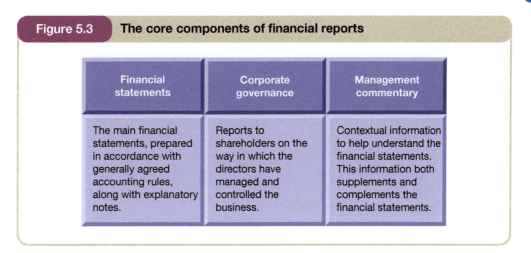

Figure 5.3   The core components of financial reports

Financial statements	Corporate governance	Management commentary
The main financial statements, prepared in accordance with generally agreed accounting rules, along with explanatory notes.	Reports to shareholders on the way in which the directors have managed and controlled the business.	Contextual information to help understand the financial statements. This information both supplements and complements the financial statements.

In the sections that follow, we shall consider each of these three components in turn. We should bear in mind, however, that these are not clearly distinguished in the financial reports. In practice, the information is often poorly organised and overlaps occur.

Presenting the financial statements

Let us now turn our attention to the main rules to be followed in the presentation of financial statements. We shall focus on the IASB rules and, in particular, those contained in IAS 1 *Presentation of Financial Statements*. This standard is very important as it sets out the structure and content of financial statements and the principles to be followed in preparing these statements.

It might be helpful to have a set of the most recent financial statements of a Stock Exchange listed company available as you work through this section. They should all be available on the internet. Select a listed company that interests you and go to its website.

The financial statements identified in IAS 1 are as set out in Figure 5.4.

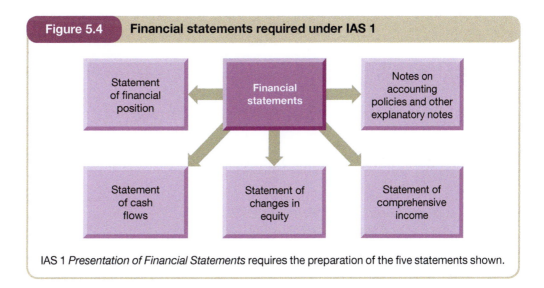

Figure 5.4   Financial statements required under IAS 1

IAS 1 *Presentation of Financial Statements* requires the preparation of the five statements shown.

Each of the financial statements identified should be presented with equal prominence.

According to the standard, these financial statements should normally cover a one-year period and should be accompanied by comparative information for the previous year. Thus, at the end of each reporting period companies should normally produce two of each of the statements, plus the related notes. In practice, virtually all companies satisfy this requirement by showing the equivalent figures for the previous year in a separate column in the current year's statements.

Comparative narrative information should also be provided if needed for a better grasp of current period results – for example, as background to an ongoing legal dispute.

Fair representation

Before we consider the financial statements in detail, it is important to note that IAS 1 contains an overriding requirement that these statements provide a *fair representation* of a company's financial position, financial performance and cash flows. There is a presumption that this will occur as long as they are drawn up in accordance with current IASB standards. Only in very rare circumstances, would this not be the case. Where the financial statements have applied all relevant IASB standards, this should be stated in the notes.

Activity 5.7

IAS 1 says that the financial statements are required to show a 'fair representation' of financial health. It does not say that the statements should show a 'correct' or an 'accurate' representation of financial health. Why, in your opinion, does it not use those words? (*Hint*: Think of depreciation of non-current assets.)

Accounting can never really be said to be 'correct' or 'accurate' as these words imply that there is a precise value that an asset, claim, revenue or expense could have. This is simply not true in many, if not most, cases.

Depreciation provides a good example of where 'correct' or 'accurate' would not be appropriate. The annual depreciation expense is based on judgements about the future concerning the expected useful life and residual value of an asset. If all relevant factors are taken into account and reasonable judgements are applied, it may be possible to achieve a fair representation of the amount of the cost or fair value of the asset that is consumed for a particular reporting period. However, a uniquely correct figure for depreciation for a period cannot be achieved.

Let us now consider each of the financial statements in turn.

Statement of financial position

IAS 1 does not prescribe the layout for this financial statement but does set out the *minimum* information that should be presented on the face of the statement of financial position. This includes the following:

● property, plant and equipment;
● investment property;
● intangible assets;

- financial assets (such as shares and loan notes of other companies held as assets);
- inventories;
- trade and other receivables;
- cash and cash equivalents;
- trade and other payables;
- provisions (a provision is a liability that is of uncertain timing or amount – such as a possible obligation arising from a legal case against the company that has yet to be determined);
- financial liabilities (other than payables and provisions shown above);
- tax liabilities; and
- issued share capital and reserves (equity).

Additional information should be also shown where relevant to an understanding of the financial position of the business.

The standard requires that, on the statement of financial position, a distinction is normally made between current assets and non-current assets and between current liabilities and non-current liabilities. However, for certain types of business, such as financial institutions (for example, a bank), the standard accepts that it may be more appropriate to order items according to their liquidity (that is, their nearness to cash).

Some of the assets and claims listed above may have to be sub-classified to comply with particular standards or because of their size or nature. Thus, sub-classifications are required for assets such as property, plant and equipment, trade receivables and inventories as well as for claims such as provisions and reserves. Certain details relating to share capital, such as the number of issued shares and their nominal value, must also be shown. To avoid cluttering up the statement of financial position, however, this additional information can be shown in the notes. In practice, most companies use notes for this purpose.

Statement of comprehensive income

This statement extends the conventional income statement to include certain other gains and losses that affect shareholders' equity. It may be presented either in the form of a single statement or as two separate statements, comprising an income statement (such as we have considered so far) and a **statement of comprehensive income**.

Again, the format of the statement of comprehensive income is not prescribed, but IAS 1 sets out the *minimum* information to be presented on the face of the statement. This includes:

- revenue;
- finance costs;
- impairment losses;
- profits or losses arising from discontinued operations;
- tax expense;
- profit or loss;
- total other comprehensive income (as well as certain line items such as the share of other comprehensive income from associate and joint ventures); and
- total comprehensive income (profit or loss plus other comprehensive income).

As a further aid to understanding, all material expenses should be separately disclosed. However, they need not be shown on the face of the income statement: they can appear in the notes to the financial statements. The kind of material items that may require separate disclosure include:

- write-down of inventories to net realisable value;
- write-down of property, plant and equipment;

- disposals of investments;
- restructuring costs;
- discontinued operations; and
- litigation settlements.

This is not an exhaustive list and, in practice, other material expenses may require separate disclosure.

The standard suggests two possible ways in which expenses can be presented on the face of the income statement. Expenses can be presented either:

- according to their nature, for example as depreciation, employee expenses and so on; or
- according to business functions, such as administrative activities and distribution (where, for example, depreciation of delivery lorries will be included in distribution expenses).

The choice between the two possible ways of presenting expenses will depend on which one the directors believe will provide the more relevant and reliable information.

To understand what other information must be presented in this statement, apart from that already contained in a conventional income statement, we should remember that, broadly, the conventional income statement shows all *realised* gains and losses for the period. It also includes some unrealised losses (that is, losses relating to assets still held).

Activity 5.8

Identify two types of unrealised loss that may appear in the conventional income statement. (*Hint*: Think back to Chapter 3.)

Unrealised losses may include:

- impairment losses following the revaluation of non-current assets; and
- inventories written down to net realisable value.

Unrealised gains and some unrealised losses, however, do not pass through the conventional income statement, but, instead, go directly to equity. In the case of limited companies, a separate revaluation reserve (forming part of total equity) is created for each type of revaluation. In an earlier chapter, we came across an example of an unrealised gain from an asset that did not pass through the conventional income statement.

Activity 5.9

Can you remember what this example was?

The example is where a business revalues its property. The gain arising is not shown in the conventional income statement, but is transferred to a revaluation reserve, which forms part of the equity. (We met this example in Activity 2.19 on p. 71.)

Property is not the only asset to which this rule relates, but this type of asset, in practice, provides the most common example of unrealised gains.

An example of unrealised gains, or losses, that has not been mentioned so far, arises from those arising from holding marketable equity shares. Any such gains, or losses, will bypass the income statement and be taken directly to a reserve.

A weakness of conventional accounting is that there is no robust principle that can be applied to determine precisely what should, and what should not, be included in the income statement. Losses arising from the impairment of non-current assets, as we have seen, appear in the income statement. However, losses arising from holding marketable equity shares that are available for sale do not. In principle, there is no significant difference between these two types of loss, but the difference in treatment is ingrained in conventional accounting practice.

The statement of comprehensive income attempts to overcome the deficiencies mentioned by taking into account unrealised gains as well as any unrealised losses not reported in the conventional income statement. It extends the conventional income statement by including these items immediately beneath the *profit for the year* figure. An illustration of this statement is shown in Example 5.2. Here, expenses are presented according to business function and comparative figures for the previous year are shown alongside the figures for the current year.

Example 5.2

Malik plc

Statement of comprehensive income for the year ended 30 June 2019

	2019	2018
	£m	£m
Revenue	100.6	97.2
Cost of sales	(60.4)	(59.1)
Gross profit	40.2	38.1
Other income	4.0	3.5
Distribution expenses	(18.2)	(16.5)
Administration expenses	(10.3)	(11.2)
Other expenses	(2.1)	(2.4)
Operating profit	13.6	11.5
Finance charges	(2.0)	(1.8)
Profit before tax	11.6	9.7
Tax	(2.9)	(2.4)
Profit for the year	8.7	7.3
Other comprehensive income		
Revaluation of property, plant and equipment	20.3	6.6
Foreign currency translation differences for foreign operations	12.5	4.0
Tax on other comprehensive income	(6.0)	(2.6)
Other comprehensive income for the year, net of tax	26.8	8.0
Total comprehensive income for the year	35.5	15.3

This example adopts a single-statement approach to presenting comprehensive income. The alternative two-statement approach simply divides the information shown into two separate parts. The income statement, which is the first statement, begins with the revenue and ends with the profit for the year. The statement of comprehensive income, which is the second statement, begins with the profit for the year and ends with the total comprehensive income.

Statement of changes in equity

The **statement of changes in equity** reveals the changes in share capital and reserves that took place during the reporting period. It reconciles the figures for these items at the beginning of the period with those at the end. This is achieved by showing the effect of the total comprehensive income for the reporting period on the share capital and reserves as well as share issues and redemptions during the period. The effect of dividends during the period may also be shown in this statement, although dividends can be shown in the notes instead.

To see how a statement of changes in equity may be prepared, let us consider Example 5.3.

Example 5.3

At 1 January 2018 Miro plc had the following equity:

Miro plc

	£m
Share capital (£1 ordinary shares)	100
Revaluation reserve	20
Translation reserve	40
Retained earnings	150
Total equity	310

During 2018, the company made a profit for the year from normal business operations of £42 million and reported an upward revaluation of property, plant and equipment of £120 million (net of any tax payable if the unrealised gains were realised). A loss on exchange differences on translating the results of foreign operations of £10 million was also reported. To strengthen its financial position, the company issued 50 million ordinary shares during the year at a premium of £0.40. Dividends for the year were £27 million.

This information for 2018 can be set out in a statement of changes in equity as follows:

Statement of changes in equity for the year ended 31 December 2018

	Share capital £m	Share premium £m	Revaluation reserve £m	Translation reserve £m	Retained earnings £m	Total £m
Balance as at 1 January 2018	100	–	20	40	150	310
Changes in equity for 2018						
Issue of ordinary shares[1]	50	20	–	–	–	70
Dividends[2]	–	–	–	–	(27)	(27)
Total comprehensive income for the year[3]	–	–	120	(10)	42	152
Balance at 31 December 2018	150	20	140	30	165	505

[1] The premium on the share price is transferred to a specific reserve.

[2] We have chosen to show dividends in the statement of changes in equity rather than in the notes. They represent an appropriation of equity and are deducted from retained earnings.

[3] The effect of each component of comprehensive income on the various elements of shareholders' equity must be separately disclosed. The revaluation gain and the loss on translating foreign operations are each allocated to a specific reserve. The profit for the year is added to retained earnings.

Statement of cash flows

The statement of cash flows should help users to assess the ability of a company to generate cash and to assess the company's need for cash. The presentation requirements for this statement are set out in IAS 7 *Statement of Cash Flows,* which we shall consider in some detail in the next chapter.

Notes

The notes play an important role in helping users to understand the financial statements. They will normally contain the following:

- a declaration that the financial statements comply with relevant accounting standards;
- a summary of the measurement bases used and other significant accounting policies applied (for example, the basis of inventories valuation);
- any dividends proposed;
- information concerning the objectives and policies for managing capital;
- information relevant to an understanding of the financial statements but not presented elsewhere;
- information required by accounting standards but not presented elsewhere; and
- key assumptions made concerning the future and major sources of estimation uncertainty.

These notes to accompany the financial statements should be presented in an orderly manner.

General points

The standard provides support for three key accounting conventions when preparing the financial statements. These are:

- the going concern convention;
- the accruals convention (except for the statement of cash flows); and
- the consistency convention.

These conventions were discussed in Chapters 2 and 3.
Finally, to improve the transparency of financial statements, the standard states that:

- offsetting liabilities against assets, or expenses against income, is not allowed unless specifically permitted by a particular accounting standard. It is not acceptable, for example, to offset a bank overdraft against a positive bank balance (where a company has both); and
- material items must be shown separately.

Segmental financial reports

Most large businesses are engaged in a number of different operations, with each having its own levels of risk, growth and profitability. Information relating to each type of business operation, however, is normally aggregated (added together) in the financial statements so as to provide a picture of financial health for the business as a whole. For example, the revenue figure at the top of the income statement represents the business's revenues from all its different operations. Although aggregating may provide a useful overall picture, comparisons over time or between businesses can become difficult. For a sound understanding of financial health, we need some idea of the range and scale of each of the main business operations. As a result, it is often necessary to disaggregate the information contained within the financial statements. This disaggregated information is disclosed in **segmental financial reports**.

By breaking down the financial information according to each type of business operation, or operating segment, we can evaluate the relative risks and profitability of each segment. Better comparisons with other businesses, or other business operating segments can be made. We can also monitor trends for each operating segment over time and so identify more accurately the growth prospects for the business as a whole. We should also be able to assess more easily how changes in market conditions relating to particular operating segments will affect the business as a whole.

It can also be argued that disclosure of information relating to the performance of each operating segment may also help to improve the efficiency of the business.

Activity 5.10

Can you think why this may be the case?

Operating segments that are performing poorly will be revealed, which should put pressure on managers to take corrective action.

Segmental reporting rules

The IASB standard (IFRS 8 *Operating Segments*) requires listed companies to disclose information about their various operating segments. Defining an operating segment, however, can lead to much head scratching. The IASB has opted for definition based on a 'management approach'. This means that an operating segment is defined according to how managers have segmented their particular business for internal reporting purposes. An operating segment is, therefore, defined as a part of the business that:

- generates revenues and expenses;
- has its own separate financial statements; and
- has its results regularly reviewed for resource-allocation and assessment purposes.

Not all parts of the business will meet the criteria identified. The headquarters of the business ('head office'), for example, is unlikely to do so.

Activity 5.11

What do you think are the main advantages of adopting the management approach? Try to think of at least one.

Three advantages spring to mind:

1 Shareholders will receive similar reports to the internal reports produced for managers, which means that they can assess business performance from the same viewpoint.
2 There will fewer delays in reporting the information to shareholders as the information has already been produced.
3 Additional, perhaps significant, reporting costs will be avoided for the same reason as mentioned in 2 above.

There are, of course, other ways of identifying an operating segment. One approach would be to define a segment according to the industry to which it relates. This, however, may lead to endless definition and classification problems.

To be reported separately, an operating segment must be of significant size. This normally means that it must account for 10 per cent or more of the combined revenue, profits or assets of all operating segments. A segment that does not meet this size threshold may be combined with other similar segments to produce a reportable segment, or separately reported despite its size, at the directors' discretion. If neither of these options is chosen, it should be reported with other segments under a separate category of 'all other segments'.

Segmental disclosure

Financial information to be disclosed includes some profit (/loss) measure (for example, operating profit) for each segment, along with the following income statement items, provided that they are regularly reported to management:

- revenue, distinguishing between revenue from external customers and revenue from other segments of the business;
- interest revenue and interest expense;
- depreciation and other material non-cash items;
- material items of income and expense;
- any profit (loss) from associate companies or joint ventures; and
- corporation tax (where it is separately reported for a segment).

The business must also disclose the total assets for each segment and, if they are reported to management, the total liabilities. Any additions to non-current assets during the period must also be reported. Where these items are not regularly reported to management, they need not be included in the published segmental report.

Example 5.4 provides an illustrative segmental financial report for a business.

Example 5.4

Goya Plc

Segmental report for the year ended 31 May 2019

	Publishing £m	Film-making £m	All other £m	Totals £m
Revenue from external customers	150	200	25	375
Inter-segment revenue	20	10	–	30
Interest revenue	10	–	–	10
Interest expense	–	15	–	15
Depreciation	40	20	5	65
Reportable segment profit	15	19	4	38
Other material non-cash items:				
Impairment of assets	–	10	–	10
Reportable segment assets	60	80	12	152
Expenditures for reportable				
segment non-current assets	12	18	2	32
Reportable segment liabilities	25	32	4	61

We can see that information relating to each segment as well as a combined total for all operating segments is shown.

Key items, which include revenues, profits, assets and liabilities, must be reconciled with the corresponding amounts for the business as a whole. For example, Goya plc's income statement should show revenue of £375 million for the business as a whole. When carrying out a reconciliation, we should bear in mind that:

- inter-segment revenues should be eliminated as no transaction with external parties occurs – only sales to customers outside the business are deemed to be sales of the business as a whole;
- any profit arising from inter-segment transfers should also be eliminated; and
- assets and liabilities that have not been allocated to a particular segment should be taken into account.

The last item normally refers to assets and liabilities relating to business-wide activities. Thus, head office buildings may provide an example of unallocated assets, and staff pension liabilities may provide an example of unallocated liabilities.

IFRS 8 also requires certain non-financial information concerning segments to be disclosed, including the basis for identifying operating segments and the types of products and services that each segment provides. It also requires disclosure of business-wide information such as geographical areas of operations and reliance on major customers.

Segmental reporting problems

When preparing segmental reports, various problems can arise, not least of which is how a segment is defined. We saw earlier that the IASB opts for a definition based on the internal reporting procedures of the business.

Activity 5.12

Can you think how defining a segment in this way could create problems for external users, such as investors?

While this may be the most practical course of action, comparisons between segments in other businesses may be impossible because of the different ways in which they are defined.

Problems may also arise where trading occurs between operating segments within the same business. A **transfer price** for each of the various items of goods, or services, being traded must be set. These transfer prices can have a considerable impact on reported profits for each segment. They can also be used to manipulate revenues and profits for different operating segments.

Activity 5.13

Why might a business wish to do this?

There are probably three main reasons:

1 Where a business operates in different countries, it may try to report high profits in a country that has low tax rates and to report low profits (or even losses) in a country with high tax rates.
2 To give an impression that a particular segment is more, or less, profitable than it really is. Managers may, for example, wish to close an operating segment and transfer pricing can be used to provide a (false) impression of the segment's performance. (Low transfer prices will, of course, also appear to make other segments more profitable.)
3 To mislead competitors as to the profitability of a business operation.

Real World 5.2 indicates the extent of the use of transfer pricing by multinational businesses to avoid UK tax.

Real World 5.2

A taxing issue

Multinationals avoided paying as much as £5.8 billion in UK corporate taxes last year by booking profits in overseas entities, a 50 per cent increase over previous government forecasts, according to newly published estimates from British tax authorities.

'The standards of what is acceptable in transfer pricing have changed,' said Sanjay Mehta, a partner at law firm Katten Muchin Rosenman. 'HMRC has invested heavily in the area of transfer pricing as this is an area of growing complexity and there is a recognition of historic underpayment of tax by some large corporates.' Transfer pricing now represents almost a quarter of the total £25 billion tax potentially underpaid by large businesses last year – up from 17 per cent the previous year, according to Pinsent Masons, the law firm.

FT *Source*: Extracts from: Marriage, M. (2017) Multinationals avoid up to £5.8bn in UK tax, HMRC finds, ft.com, 24 October.
© The Financial Times Limited 2017. All Rights Reserved.

IFRS 8 recognises the impact of transfer pricing policies on segmental revenues and profit by stating that the basis for accounting for transactions between segments must be disclosed.

A final problem is that some expenses and assets may relate to more than one operating segment and their allocation between segments may vary between businesses. Again, this may hinder comparisons of segmental profits and profitability between businesses.

Management commentary

Many businesses have complex organisational structures, operating systems and financing methods. These features must be taken into account if the financial statements are to faithfully portray financial position and performance. This can, however, lead to financial statements that are lengthy, detailed and difficult to understand. To provide a clearer picture, a management commentary may prove helpful to users. It can review the results and provide further information relating to an understanding of financial health.

Activity 5.14

What do you think are the main qualitative characteristics that information contained in a management commentary should possess? (*Hint*: Think back to Chapter 1.)

To be useful, the information should exhibit the characteristics for accounting information in general, which we identified in Chapter 1. Thus, the information should be relevant, faithfully represented, comparable, verifiable, timely and understandable. The fact that we are often dealing with narrative information does not alter the need for these characteristics to be present.

In the UK, a management commentary has become an established part of the financial reporting landscape. Two narrative reports will now be considered, the directors' report and the strategic report. These form an important part of a management commentary designed to supplement and complement the main financial statements.

Directors' report

For many years, the directors have been required to prepare a report to shareholders relating to each financial period. The content of the **directors' report** is prescribed by law and includes assorted topics such as current year's performance and position, future prospects of the business and social aspects. For larger companies, the report must cover, amongst other things, the following matters:

- the names of those who were directors during the reporting period;
- any recommended dividend;
- the acquisition by a public listed company of its own shares;
- the involvement of employees in the affairs of the company;
- the employment and training of disabled persons;
- important events affecting the company since the year end;
- financial risk management objectives and policies;
- greenhouse gas emissions by a public listed company;
- likely future developments in the business; and
- research and development activities.

In addition to disclosing the information mentioned above, the directors' report must contain a declaration that the directors are not aware of any other information that the auditors might need in preparing their audit report. There must also be a declaration that the directors have taken steps to ensure that the auditors are aware of all relevant information. The auditors do not carry out an audit of the directors' report. However, they do check to see that the information in the report is consistent with that contained in the audited financial statements.

Criticisms of the directors' report

While the directors' report provides useful information, there is a strong case for revising its role, form and content. It contains a disjointed collection of items that lacks an underlying theme. It appears little more than a repository for miscellaneous items. The structure and presentation of the report is not tightly prescribed and so, in practice, comparisons between companies can be difficult. Furthermore, its relationship with the strategic report, which also provides additional narrative information about the business, and which we shall now discuss, is not clear.

Strategic report

The overall aim of the **strategic report** is to provide context for the financial statements and so help shareholders assess how well the directors have performed in promoting the success of the company. The content of the report has five main themes, which are summarised in Figure 5.5.

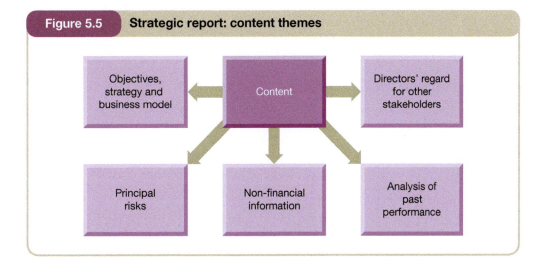

Figure 5.5   Strategic report: content themes

Directors of all but the smallest companies are legally obliged to produce a strategic report. The report produced should be fair, balanced and understandable. This means that both the good and the bad aspects of performance, position and future prospects must be covered. The report should be unbiased and there should be no omissions of important information. It should also convey all information relevant to an understanding of business performance and position in as concise a way as possible.

The strategic reports prepared by Stock Exchange listed companies must disclose more than those of other companies, including disclosures concerning its strategy and business model. Figure 5.6 summarises their main features.

Figure 5.6 The main features of the strategic report

Strategic management	Business environment	Business performance
How the entity intends to generate and preserve value	*The internal and external environment in which the entity operates*	*How the entity has developed and performed and its position at the year-end*
Strategy	Principal risks and uncertainties	Analysis of performance and position
Business model	Environmental, employee, social, community, human rights, anti-corruption and anti-bribery matters	Key performance indicators (KPIs)
		Employee gender diversity

We can see that the strategic report covers three broad areas. These are interrelated and should not be treated in isolation.

Source: Guidance on the Strategic Report, Financial Reporting Council, July 2018, p.40.

Activity 5.15

Stock Exchange listed companies are required to disclose more information about their business than other companies? Try to think of at least one reason for this requirement.

Various arguments can be made in favour of greater accountability from such companies. They include:

- Greater transparency concerning the companies' business operations should help investors make more informed decisions. This is particularly important with Stock Exchange listed companies since their shares are frequently traded.
- Stock Exchange listed companies tend to be larger, have more economic power and have more stakeholders than other companies. Their impact on the economy and society as a whole, therefore, tends to be greater. This, in turn, creates an obligation for them to account more fully for their operations and actions.

The auditors have the same duty towards the strategic report as that of the directors' report. They must give an opinion as to whether the information it contains is consistent with the financial statements and complies with legal requirements. Where there are any material misstatements they must be disclosed. Both narrative reports are, therefore, subject to independent scrutiny.

We saw earlier that Stock Exchange listed companies must, along with other matters, report on their strategy and business model. **Real World 5.3** illustrates how one listed company reports these elements.

Real World 5.3

Equipped for the future

VP plc is a specialist equipment rental group operating in the UK, Ireland and mainland Europe. It offers products and services to a diverse range of markets including rail, transmission, water, civil engineering, construction, house building, oil and gas. The business has summed up its strategy and business model as follows (see Figure 5.7):

> Our aim is to generate sustainable value creation for shareholders and other stakeholders through our expertise in asset management, by exceeding customer expectations, maintaining and utilising our financial strength and retaining and attracting the best people.

Figure 5.7	VP plc business model

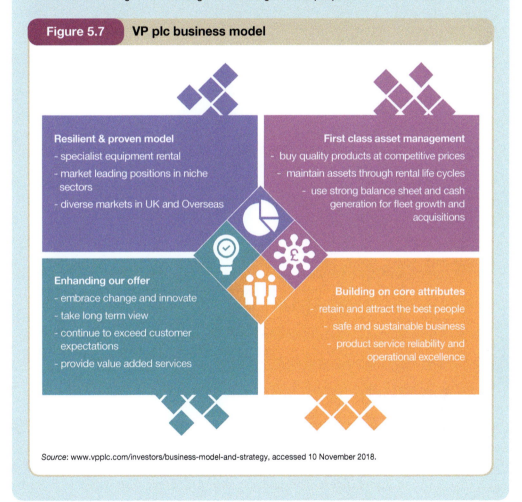

Resilient & proven model
- specialist equipment rental
- market leading positions in niche sectors
- diverse markets in UK and Overseas

First class asset management
- buy quality products at competitive prices
- maintain assets through rental life cycles
- use strong balance sheet and cash generation for fleet growth and acquisitions

Enhanding our offer
- embrace change and innovate
- take long term view
- continue to exceed customer expectations
- provide value added services

Building on core attributes
- retain and attract the best people
- safe and sustainable business
- product service reliability and operational excellence

Source: www.vpplc.com/investors/business-model-and-strategy, accessed 10 November 2018.

Corporate governance

In recent years, the issue of **corporate governance** has generated much debate. The term is used to describe the ways in which companies are directed and controlled. The issue of corporate governance is important because, with larger companies, those who own the company (that is, the shareholders) are usually divorced from the day-to-day control of the business. The shareholders employ directors to manage the company for them. Given this position, it may seem reasonable to assume that the best interests of shareholders will guide the directors' decisions. In practice, however, this is not always the case. The directors may be more concerned with pursuing their own interests, such as increasing their pay and 'perks' (such as expensive motor cars, overseas visits and so on) and improving their job security and status. As a result, a conflict can occur between the interests of shareholders and the interests of directors.

Where directors pursue their own interests at the expense of the shareholders, there is clearly a problem for the shareholders. It may also be a problem, however, for society as a whole.

Activity 5.16

Can you think of a reason why directors pursuing their own interests may be a problem for society as a whole?

If shareholders feel that their funds are likely to be mismanaged, they will be reluctant to invest. A shortage of funds will lead to companies making fewer investments. Furthermore, the costs of finance will increase as companies compete for what limited funds are available. A lack of concern for shareholders can therefore have a profound effect on the performance of individual companies and, with this, the health of the economy.

To avoid these problems, most competitive market economies have a framework of rules to help monitor and control the behaviour of directors. These rules are usually based around three guiding principles:

- *Disclosure.* This lies at the heart of good corporate governance. Adequate and timely disclosure can help shareholders to judge the performance of the directors. Where performance is considered unsatisfactory, this will be reflected in the price of shares. Changes should then be made to ensure the directors regain the confidence of shareholders.
- *Accountability.* This involves setting out the duties of the directors and establishing an adequate monitoring process. In the UK, company law requires that the directors act in the best interests of the shareholders. This means, among other things, that they must not try to use their position and knowledge to make gains at the expense of the shareholders. The law also requires larger companies to have their annual financial statements independently audited. As we saw earlier, the purpose of an independent audit is to lend credibility to the financial statements prepared by the directors.
- *Fairness.* Directors should not be able to benefit from access to 'inside' information that is not available to shareholders. As a result, both the law and the Stock Exchange place restrictions on the ability of directors to buy and sell the shares of the company. This means, for example, that the directors cannot buy or sell shares immediately before the announcement of the annual profits or before the announcement of a significant event such as a planned merger.

These principles are set out in Figure 5.8.

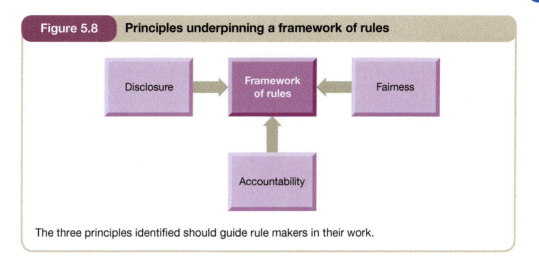

Figure 5.8   Principles underpinning a framework of rules

The three principles identified should guide rule makers in their work.

Strengthening the framework of rules

The number of rules designed to safeguard shareholders has increased considerably over the years. This has been in response to weaknesses in corporate governance procedures, which have been exposed through well-publicised business failures and frauds, excessive pay increases to directors and evidence that some financial reports were being 'massaged' so as to mislead shareholders.

Many believe, however, that the shareholders must shoulder some of the blame for any weaknesses. Ownership, by market value, of the shares listed on the London Stock Exchange is dominated by investing institutions such as insurance businesses, banks and pension funds, as we shall see in Chapter 15. These are often massive operations, owning large quantities of the shares of the companies in which they invest. These institutional investors employ specialist staff to manage their share portfolios. Yet, despite their size and relative expertise, they have not always been active in corporate governance matters. As a consequence, directors' behaviour has not been closely monitored. More recently, however, there has been a sea change. Institutional investors are now engaging much more with the companies in which they invest.

A real effort has been made by regulatory authorities to address the problems of poor corporate governance. This has led to the creation of a code of best practice, known as the **UK Corporate Governance Code**. The UK Code is produced by the Financial Reporting Council, an independent regulator seeking to promote high quality corporate governance and accountability. The first version of the UK Code was published in 1992 and revised versions have been published every few years since then. The 2018 version is divided into five sections and sets out a number of key principles. **Real World 5.4** below describes these principles.

Real World 5.4

The UK Corporate Governance Code

The UK Code is based on the following key principles:

Board leadership and company purpose

- A successful company is led by an effective and entrepreneurial board, whose role is to promote the long-term sustainable success of the company, generating value for shareholders and contributing to wider society.

Real World 5.4 *continued*

- The board should establish the company's purpose, values and strategy, and satisfy itself that these and its culture are aligned. All directors must act with integrity, lead by example and promote the desired culture.
- The board should ensure that the necessary resources are in place for the company to meet its objectives and measure performance against them. The board should also establish a framework of prudent and effective controls, which enable risk to be assessed and managed.
- In order for the company to meet its responsibilities to shareholders and stakeholders, the board should ensure effective engagement with, and encourage participation from, these parties.
- The board should ensure that workforce policies and practices are consistent with the company's values and support its long-term sustainable success. The workforce should be able to raise any matters of concern.

Division of responsibilities

- The chair leads the board and is responsible for its overall effectiveness in directing the company. They should demonstrate objective judgement throughout their tenure and promote a culture of openness and debate. In addition, the chair facilitates constructive board relations and the effective contribution of all non-executive directors, and ensures that directors receive accurate, timely and clear information.
- The board should include an appropriate combination of executive and non-executive (and, in particular, independent non-executive) directors, such that no one individual or small group of individuals dominates the board's decision-making. There should be a clear division of responsibilities between the leadership of the board and the executive leadership of the company's business.
- Non-executive directors should have sufficient time to meet their board responsibilities. They should provide constructive challenge, strategic guidance, offer specialist advice and hold management to account.
- The board, supported by the company secretary, should ensure that it has the policies, processes, information, time and resources it needs in order to function effectively and efficiently.

Company success and evaluation

- Appointments to the board should be subject to a formal, rigorous and transparent procedure, and an effective succession plan should be maintained for board and senior management. Both appointments and succession plans should be based on merit and objective criteria and, within this context, should promote diversity of gender, social and ethnic backgrounds, cognitive and personal strengths.
- The board and its committees should have a combination of skills, experience and knowledge. Consideration should be given to the length of service of the board as a whole and membership regularly refreshed.
- Annual evaluation of the board should consider its composition, diversity and how effectively members work together to achieve objectives. Individual evaluation should demonstrate whether each director continues to contribute effectively.

Audit, risk and internal control

- The board should establish formal and transparent policies and procedures to ensure the independence and effectiveness of internal and external audit functions and satisfy itself on the integrity of financial and narrative statements.
- The board should present a fair, balanced and understandable assessment of the company's position and prospects.
- The board should establish procedures to manage risk, oversee the internal control framework, and determine the nature and extent of the principal risks the company is willing to take in order to achieve its long-term strategic objectives.

Remuneration

- Remuneration policies and practices should be designed to support strategy and promote long-term sustainable success. Executive remuneration should be aligned to company purpose and values, and be clearly linked to the successful delivery of the company's long-term strategy.
- A formal and transparent procedure for developing policy on executive remuneration and determining director and senior management remuneration should be established. Individual directors should not be involved in deciding their own remuneration outcome.
- Directors should exercise independent judgement and discretion when authorising remuneration outcomes, taking account of company and individual performance, and wider circumstances.

Source: Extracts from *The UK Corporate Governance Code*, July 2018, pages 4 to 13, Financial Reporting Council, www.frc.org.uk.

The 2018 UK Code places great emphasis on how the principles described above are applied in practice. Listed companies are required to provide a statement to shareholders on the approach taken. Because of its importance, companies are discouraged from adopting a formulaic approach. The UK Code makes it clear that a 'tick box' approach, which has been a growing trend in corporate governance reporting, is unacceptable.

The Code has the backing of the London Stock Exchange. This means that companies listed on the London Stock Exchange are expected to comply with the requirements of the Code or must give their shareholders good reason why they do not (that is, comply or explain). Failure to do one or other of these can lead to the company's shares being suspended from listing.

Activity 5.17

Why might suspension from listing be an important sanction against a non-compliant company?

A major advantage of a Stock Exchange listing is that it enables investors to sell their shares whenever they wish. A company that is suspended from listing would find it hard and, therefore, expensive to raise funds from investors because there would be no ready market for the shares.

It is widely accepted that the existence of the Code has improved the quality of information available to shareholders. It has also resulted in better checks on the powers of directors, and provided greater transparency in corporate affairs. However, rules can only be a partial answer. Ultimately, good corporate governance behaviour depends on a healthy **corporate culture**. This term refers to the values, attitudes and behaviour displayed towards the company's various stakeholders and to the wider community. To be effective, therefore, governance rules rely on corporate decision making that reflect high standards of integrity, openness and accountability.

Rulemaking is a tricky business. Where corporate governance rules are too tightly drawn, entrepreneurial spirit may be stifled and risk taking may be discouraged. However, problems can also arise where rules are too loosely drawn.

Activity 5.18

Can you think of a possible problem with corporate governance rules that are too loosely drawn?

In this case, it would be easier for unscrupulous directors to find ways around them.

Thus, when creating corporate governance rules, a balance must somehow be struck between the need to protect shareholders (and other stakeholders) and the need to encourage an entrepreneurial behaviour.

Creative accounting

Despite the proliferation of rules and the independent checks that are imposed, concerns over the quality of published financial statements surface from time to time. There are occasions when directors apply particular accounting policies, or structure particular transactions, in such a way as to portray a picture of financial health that is in line with what they want users to see, rather than what is a true and fair view of financial position and performance. Misrepresenting the performance and position of a business in this way is often called **creative accounting** and it poses a major problem for accounting rule makers and for society generally.

Activity 5.19

Why might the directors of a company engage in creative accounting? Try to think of at least two reasons.

There are many reasons, including:

- to get around restrictions (for example, to report sufficient profit to pay a dividend);
- to avoid government action (for example, the taxation of profits);
- to hide poor management decisions;
- to achieve sales revenue or profit targets, thereby ensuring that performance bonuses are paid to the directors;
- to attract new share capital or long-term borrowing by showing an apparently healthy financial position; and
- to satisfy the demands of major investors concerning levels of return.

Creative accounting methods

There are many ways in which unscrupulous directors can manipulate the financial statements. They usually involve adopting novel or unorthodox practices for reporting key elements of the financial statements, such as revenue, expenses, assets and liabilities. They may also involve the use of complicated or obscure transactions in an attempt to hide the underlying economic reality. The manipulation carried out may be designed either to bend the rules or to break them.

We shall now consider some of the more important ways in which rules may be bent or broken.

Misstating revenue

Some creative accounting methods are designed to overstate the revenue for a period. These methods often involve the early recognition of sales revenue or the reporting of sales transactions that have no real substance. **Real World 5.5** provides examples of both types of revenue manipulation.

Real World 5.5

Overstating revenue

Types of revenue manipulation include:

- *Early recognition of revenue.* A business may report the sale of goods as soon as an order has been placed, rather than when the goods are delivered to, and accepted by, the customer. This will boost current revenues and profits and is known as 'pre-dispatching'.
- *Passing goods to distributors.* A business may force its distributors to accept more goods that they can sell. This will again boost current revenues and profits and is known as 'channel stuffing' or 'trade loading'.
- *Artificial trading.* This involves businesses in the same industry selling the same items between themselves to boost sales revenue. One example is where telecoms businesses sell unused fibre optic capacity to each other. This is known as 'hollow swaps'. Another example is where energy businesses sell energy between themselves for the same price and at the same time. This is known as 'round tripping' or 'in and out trading'.

Note that artificial trading between similar businesses will inflate the sales revenue for a period but will not inflate reported profits. Nevertheless, this may still benefit the business. Sales revenue growth has become an important yardstick of performance for some investors and can affect the value they place on the business.

Source: Based on information in *The Times* (2002) Dirty laundry: how companies fudge the numbers, *The Times, Business Section*, 22 September.

The manipulation of revenue has been at the heart of many of the accounting scandals recently exposed. Given its critical role in the measurement of performance, this is, perhaps, not surprising. **Real World 5.6** discusses how the reported revenues of one UK software business have been hotly disputed. It was acquired by a US computer giant, which concluded that, as a result of this and other alleged irregularities, the price paid was far too much. It, therefore, reported a huge impairment charge soon after the acquisition.

Real World 5.6

Recomputing the numbers

Autonomy, the UK software company at the centre of massive fraud allegations, booked revenues from uncompleted transactions at the end of a number of quarters to meet sales targets, according to claims levelled in a document from the US Air Force.

The accusations, made against Autonomy founder Mike Lynch and five other former executives, contain the first details of the alleged accounting irregularities that US computer group Hewlett-Packard has said forced it to take an $8.8 billion write-off in 2012, a year after buying the UK company. Also named in the letter are two US government contractors, MicroTech and Capax Global, that acted as resellers of Autonomy's software and played a role in the disputed transactions. A representative for Mr Lynch responded that Autonomy's accounting had been in compliance with international accounting standards.

The allegations, which were first reported by the Washington Post, detail three transactions that had not been completed when Autonomy recorded revenues on them. One of the deals later fell through, while another was completed for less than the amount Autonomy recorded.

→

Real World 5.6 *continued*

Under one of the contracts, Autonomy was said to have booked $11 million in revenue at the end of March 2010 on a transaction involving MicroTech and an unnamed end customer. The final sale failed to materialise, with Autonomy only receiving $500,000 on the contract. After an auditor queried the large uncollected debt from MicroTech at the end of the year, according to the claims, Autonomy made a payment of $9.6 million to the contractor under the heading 'Advanced technology innovation centre' and Micro-Tech wired back the same amount to cover some of the money it owed Autonomy.

Autonomy booked a further $15.7 million of revenue in two instalments on the final days of March and June the following year on a separate deal involving Capax, even though the ultimate sales transactions had not been completed, according to the Air Force document. The deal was later completed for $14.1 million. In the third case, a $1.95 million sale was booked in December 2010, six months before it was finalised.

 Source: Extracts from Waters, R. (2014) Autonomy beset by revenues allegation, ft.com, 5 January.
© The Financial Times Ltd 2014. All Rights Reserved.

Massaging expenses

Some creative accounting methods focus on the manipulation of expenses. Those expenses that rely on directors' estimates of the future or their choice of accounting policy are particularly vulnerable to manipulation.

Activity 5.20

Can you identify the kind of expenses where the directors make estimates or choices in the ways described? Think back to Chapter 3 and try to identify at least two.

These include certain expenses that we discussed in Chapter 3, such as:

- depreciation of property, plant and equipment;
- amortisation of intangible assets, such as goodwill;
- inventories (cost of sales); and
- allowances for trade receivables.

By changing estimates about the future (for example, the useful life or residual value of an asset), or by changing accounting policies (for example, switching from FIFO to AVCO), it may be possible to derive an expense figure and, consequently, a profit figure that suits the directors.

In may also be possible for a business to redefine what constitutes an expense. **Real World 5.7** provides an example of one business that paid some of its staff salaries in the form of shares in the business, rather than in cash, and then failed to treat this as an expense.

Real World 5.7

Taking stock

Examples of businesses using financial engineering to boost their statements of financial position are all too easy to find. A recent one features Microsoft's takeover of LinkedIn.

A possible reason that LinkedIn wanting to be taken over may have been that it had been applying rather dubious approach to accounting. Employees were being remunerated by being given the business's shares rather the normal cash payments. This was being accounted for a simple share issue, rather than treating it as an expense. This led to the business's profit figure being artificially inflated to a significant extent.

This type of dubious practice is by no means restricted to LinkedIn. Seemingly most larger US stock market listed businesses do it. Recently, however, Facebook has shown shares, issued to employees as part of their remuneration, as an expense and the mood now seems to be to pressure businesses to do the same so that the reported profit figure is a fairer reflection of reality. Whether employees are paid in shares or in cash, it's still an expense and should be accounted for as such.

Source: Information taken from Faroohar, R. (2016) Why the creative accounting in the Microsoft–LinkedIn deal is so disturbing, *Time Magazine*, 15 June.

Finally, the incorrect 'capitalisation' of expenses may be used as a means of manipulation. This involves treating expenditure as though it was incurred to acquire or develop non-current assets, even though the benefits were consumed during the current year. Expenses will, therefore, be understated. Businesses that build their own assets are often best placed to undertake this form of malpractice.

Activity 5.21

What would be the effect on the profits and total assets of a business that incorrectly capitalises expenses?

Both would be artificially inflated. Reported profits would increase because expenses would be reduced. Total assets would be increased because the expenses would be incorrectly treated as non-current assets.

Concealing 'bad news'

Some creative accounting methods focus on the concealment of losses or liabilities. The financial statements can look much healthier if these can somehow be eliminated. One way of doing this is to create a 'separate' entity that will take over the losses or liabilities.

Real World 5.8 describes the, now, almost legendary, case of one large business concealing losses and liabilities.

Real World 5.8

For a very special purpose

Perhaps the most well-known case of concealment of losses and liabilities concerned the Enron Corporation. This was a large US energy business that used 'special purpose entities' (SPEs) as a means of concealment. SPEs were used by Enron to rid itself of problem assets

Real World 5.8 *continued*

that were falling in value, such as its broadband operations. In addition, liabilities were transferred to these entities to help Enron's statement of financial position look healthier. The company had to keep its gearing ratios (the relationship between borrowing and equity) within particular limits to satisfy credit-rating agencies and SPEs were used to achieve this. The SPEs used for concealment purposes were not independent of the company and should have been consolidated in the statement of financial position of Enron, along with their losses and liabilities.

When these, and other accounting irregularities, were discovered in 2001, there was a restatement of Enron's financial performance and position to reflect the consolidation of the SPEs, which had previously been omitted. As a result of this restatement, the company recognised $591 million in losses over the preceding four years and an additional $628 million worth of liabilities at the end of 2000.

The company collapsed at the end of 2001.

Source: William Thomas, C. (2002) The rise and fall of Enron, *Journal of Accountancy*, vol. 194, no. 3. This article represents the opinions of the author, which are not necessarily those of the Texas Society of Certified Public Accountants.

Misstating assets

There are various ways in which assets may be misstated. These include:

- using asset values that are higher than the assets' fair market values;
- capitalising costs that should have been written off as expenses, as described earlier; and
- recording assets that are not owned, or which simply do not exist.

Real World 5.9 describes how one large business is alleged to have overstated some of its assets.

Real World 5.9

It's worth ... less

Anglo-Australian mining giant Rio Tinto has been charged with fraud in the US and fined £27.4 million in the UK after being accused of overstating the value of African coal assets. The FTSE 100 company and two of its top former executives were charged in the US of hiding losses by inflating the value of assets in Mozambique, which Rio bought in 2011 for $3.7 billion and sold a few years later for $50 million.

America's financial regulator, the Securities and Exchange Commission, filed a complaint in federal court in Manhattan. It alleges that Rio Tinto, its former chief executive, Tom Albanese, and its former chief financial officer, Guy Elliott, failed to follow accounting standards and company policies to accurately value and record its assets.

As the project began to suffer setbacks, resulting in the rapid decline of the value of the coal assets, Albanese and Elliott sought to hide or delay disclosure of the nature and extent of the adverse developments from Rio Tinto's board of directors, auditors, and investors, the SEC alleges.

'Rio Tinto and its top executives allegedly failed to come clean about an unsuccessful deal that was made under their watch. They tried to save their own careers at the expense of investors by hiding the truth.' said Steven Peikin, co-director of the SEC's enforcement division.

The miner said it intends to 'vigorously defend itself' against the allegations.

Source: Extract from Rio Tinto charged with fraud in US and fined £27.4m in UK, www.theguardian.com, 18 October 2017.

Inadequate disclosure

Directors may misrepresent or try to conceal certain information. This may relate to commitments made, key changes in accounting policies or estimates, significant events and so on. **Real World 5.10** reveals how one large bank allegedly tried to conceal its actions in order to avoid the legal consequences.

Real World 5.10

Standard practice?

New York State's financial watchdog has accused Standard Chartered of hiding $250 billion of transactions with the Iranian government, leaving 'the US financial system vulnerable to terrorists, weapons dealers, drug kingpins and corrupt regimes'. The UK-based bank's shares fell more than 6 per cent after the New York state Department of Financial Services (DFS) issued an order just before the London market closed on Monday, which included a threat to revoke the bank's licence to operate in the state, and called it a 'rogue institution'.

The order said that between 2001 and 2010 Standard Chartered concealed from US authorities roughly 60,000 transactions for Iranian clients, amounting to about $250 billion and generating 'hundreds of millions of dollars' in fees for the bank. Among the Iranian clients were the Central Bank of Iran and two state-owned institutions, Bank Saderat and Bank Melli. The US has had economic sanctions in place against Iran since 1979. They were toughened in 1995 to place strict limits on dealing with Iranian customers by US banks, including foreign banks with operations in the US. The New York regulator, led by Benjamin Lawsky, superintendent of financial services, alleged that StanChart had falsified records and evaded US sanctions.

FT   *Source*: Braithewaite, T. and Goff, S. (2012) StanChart accused of hiding Iran dealings, ft.com, 7 August.
© The Financial Times Limited 2012. All Rights Reserved.

Figure 5.9 summarises the main methods of creative accounting.

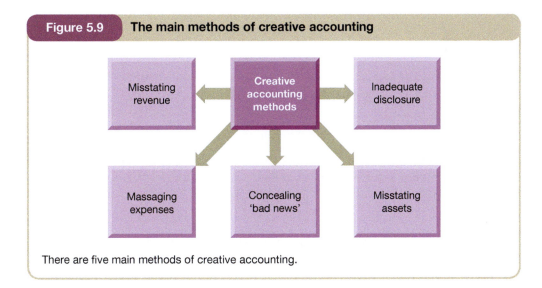

Figure 5.9   The main methods of creative accounting

There are five main methods of creative accounting.

Checking for creative accounting

When the financial statements of a business are being examined, a number of checks may be carried out to help gain a feel for their reliability. These can include checks to see whether:

- the reported profits are significantly higher than the operating cash flows for the period (as shown in the business's statement of cash flows), which may suggest that profits have been overstated;
- the tax charge is low in relation to reported profits, which may suggest, again, that profits are overstated, although there may be other, more innocent, explanations;
- the valuation methods used for assets held are based on historic cost or fair values and, if the latter approach has been used, why and how the fair values were determined;
- there have been changes in accounting policies over the period, particularly in key areas such as revenue recognition, inventories valuation and depreciation;
- the accounting policies adopted are in line with those adopted by the rest of the industry;
- the auditors' report gives a 'clean bill of health' to the financial statements; and
- the 'small print' (that is the notes to the financial statements) is being used to hide significant events or changes.

Real World 5.11 describes the emphasis that one analyst places on this last check.

Real World 5.11

Taking note

Alistair Hodgson, investment manager at private client stockbroker Pilling and Co, says 'I almost look at the notes more than I look at the main figures at first. The notes tend to hold the key to anything that looks strange. I look to pick out things that the auditor has told the company to declare – the kind of thing they might not want to declare, but they have got to do so in order to make the accounts honest.'

FT *Source*: Extract from Smith, S. (2005) Read between the lines, *Financial Times*, 16 September.
© The Financial Times Limited 2012. All Rights Reserved.

Checks may also be carried out to provide confirmation of positive financial health. These may include checks to see whether:

- the business is paying increased dividends; and/or
- the directors are buying shares in the business.

Although the various checks described are useful, they cannot be used to guarantee the reliability of the financial statements. Some creative accounting practices may be very deeply seated and may go undetected for years.

Creative accounting and economic growth

Some years ago, there was a wave of creative accounting scandals, particularly in the USA but also in Europe. It seems, however, that this wave has now subsided. As a result of the actions taken by various regulatory bodies, and by accounting rule makers, creative accounting has become a more risky and difficult process for those who attempt it. It will never disappear completely, however, and a further wave of creative accounting scandals may occur in the future.

The wave of creative accounting scandals coincided with a period of strong economic growth. During good economic times, investors and auditors become less vigilant, making it easier to manipulate the figures. We must not, therefore, become too complacent. Things may change again when we next experience a period of strong growth.

Real World 5.12 concludes this chapter by identifying some key features of businesses that engage in creative accounting.

Real World 5.12

Spotting a wrong 'un

We all know why companies manipulate their earnings. They do it because they can. Accounting principles necessarily allow some discretion beyond the direct moves that show up in cash terms each quarter. And there are rewards for manipulation – stronger earnings will be greeted by higher share prices. That means cheaper equity finance for the company, and more pay for any executives whose remuneration is linked to share performance. The tricky part is to work out who is manipulating. That requires a good grasp of forensic accounting. And the really useful knowledge for investors would be to spot companies before they start cooking their books. New research from a group of academics at the University of Southern California, the University of Houston, the University of Hong Kong and Cambridge University's Judge Business School appears to do just that. After studying all the companies that fell foul of US regulators for manipulation between 1985 and 2010, they boiled down the search for future manipulators into internal and external factors.

Internally the key driver, and this should surprise nobody, is the power of the chief executive officer. CEOs with power concentrated in themselves – measured by standard corporate governance measures such as whether they also have the role of chairman, and how many independent directors sit on the board – tend to get their own way. Manipulation is much more likely.

Externally, the key factor is earnings expectations themselves. Once companies see that brokers' analysts have higher forecasts for them, they feel pressure from the market to try harder (through manipulation) to beat those forecasts. Also, as big institutions raise their stakes, they feel greater pressure to meet expectations.

Perhaps the most surprising finding is that legitimately consistent and rising earnings are a first warning flag. There is what Jennifer Chu of the Judge Business School describes as a 'slippery slope'. Companies with a regular record of growth and of outperforming expectations become accustomed to the rich equity valuation that comes with it. They do not want to suffer the sharp sell-off that would accompany an admission of reality.

FT *Source:* Extract from Authers, J. (2017) How to spot companies at risk of earnings manipulation: Academic research underlines the dangers of chief executives with too much power, ft.com, 7 September.

Self-assessment question **5.1**

(a) You have overheard the following statements:
1 'Dividends paid during a reporting period must be shown on the face of the Statement of changes in equity for that period.'
2 'IAS 1 provides support for three key accounting conventions – accruals, historic cost and consistency.'
3 'IAS 1 permits bank overdrafts to be offset against positive bank balances when preparing the statement of financial position.'

Self-assessment question 5.1 *continued*

Critically comment on each of the statements.

(b) Segmental information relating to Dali plc for the year to 31 May 2019 is:

	Car parts £m	Aircraft parts £m	Boat parts £m	Total £m
Revenues from external customers	360	210	85	655
Inter-segment revenues	95	40	–	135
Interest revenue	34	–	–	34
Interest expense	–	28	8	36
Depreciation	80	55	15	150
Reportable segment profit	20	24	18	62
Other material non-cash items				
Impairment of assets	–	39	–	39
Reportable segment assets	170	125	44	339
Expenditures for reportable segment non-current assets	28	23	26	77
Reportable segment liabilities	85	67	22	174

Required:

Analyse the performance of each of the three main business segments of Dali plc for the year and comment on your results.

The solution to this question can be found at the end of the book on pages 753–754.

Summary

The main points of this chapter may be summarised as follows:

Directors' duty

- Separation of ownership from day-to-day control creates a need for directors to be accountable.
- To fulfil this need, the directors have a duty to prepare and publish financial statements.
- These financial statements must provide a fair representation of the financial health of the business.

The need for accounting rules

- Accounting rules are needed to avoid unacceptable accounting practices and to improve the comparability of financial statements.
- This should give greater confidence in the integrity of financial statements.

Sources of accounting rules

- The International Accounting Standards Board (IASB) has become an important source of rules.

- Company law and the London Stock Exchange are also sources of rules for UK companies.
- Accounting conventions and principles followed in preparing the statements also contribute towards the framework of rules.

Conceptual framework

- This helps to underpin financial reporting standards.
- The IASB framework sets out the objective of general purpose financial reports, the primary user groups, the qualitative characteristics, the elements of financial statements and the different measurement bases that may be used.

The auditors' role

- Auditors are required to report to shareholders whether, in their opinion, the financial statements provide a true and fair view of the financial health of a business.
- They are elected by the shareholders and are accountable to them.

Financial reporting framework

- Company annual reports have three core components: the main financial statements, corporate governance and management commentary.

Presenting financial statements

- IAS 1 sets out the structure and content of financial statements.
- It requires preparation of a statement of financial position, a statement of comprehensive income, a statement of changes in equity and a statement of cash flows. In addition, explanatory notes are required.
- The financial statements must provide a fair representation of the financial health of a company and this will only normally be achieved by adherence to relevant IASB standards.
- IAS 1 sets out information to be shown in the various financial statements and some of the accounting conventions and principles to be followed in preparing the statements.

Segmental reports

- Segmental reports disaggregate information on the financial statements to help users to achieve a better understanding of financial health.
- An operating segment is defined by the IASB using the 'management approach'.
- IFRS 8 requires certain information relating to each segment to be shown.

Management commentary

- A management commentary reviews the financial results. It aims to complement and supplement the financial statements.
- The directors' report contains information of a financial and non-financial nature. It includes such diverse matters as any recommended dividend, the involvement of employees in company affairs and important events since the year-end. It is rather disjointed and lacks an underlying theme.
- The strategic report aims to provide context for the financial statements and so help shareholders assess how well the directors have performed in promoting the success of the company. It should be fair, balanced and understandable.
- The strategic report of Stock Exchange listed companies must provide additional information, including the strategy and business model adopted.

Corporate governance

- Corporate governance issues arise because of the separation of ownership from control of the company.

- Corporate governance rules are based around the principles of disclosure, accountability and fairness.

- The UK Corporate Governance Code, which applies to UK Stock Exchange listed companies, adopts a 'comply-or-explain' approach. It contains principles and guidance on corporate governance matters as well as annual reporting requirements.

Creative accounting

- This involves using accounting practices to show what the directors would like users to see rather than what is a fair representation of reality.

- The main forms of creative accounting involve misstating revenues, massaging expenses, concealing bad news, misstating assets and inadequate disclosure.

Key terms

For definitions of these terms, see Appendix B.

International Financial Reporting
   Standards   *p. 166*
International Accounting
   Standards   *p. 166*
conceptual framework   *p. 169*
auditors   *p. 171*
statement of comprehensive
   income   *p. 175*
statement of changes in equity   *p. 178*

segmental financial report   *p. 180*
transfer price   *p. 182*
directors' report   *p.184*
strategic report   *p. 185*
corporate governance   *p. 187*
UK Corporate Governance
   Code   *p. 189*
corporate culture   *p. 191*
creative accounting   *p. 192*

References

1 IFRS Foundation, *Use of IFRS Standards Around the World 2018,* www.ifrs.org.

2 International Accounting Standards Board (2018) *Conceptual Framework for Financial Reporting,* pages 28 to 31.

3 Financial Reporting Council (2012) *Thinking about disclosures in a broader context: a roadmap for a disclosure framework,* Discussion paper, October, www.frc.org.uk, accessed 3 August 2015.

Further reading

If you would like to explore the topics covered in this chapter in more depth, we recommend the following:

Alexander, D., Britton, A., Jorissen, A., Hoogendoorn, M. and Van Mourik, C. (2017) *International Financial Reporting and Analysis,* 7th edn, Cengage Learning EMEA, Chapters 2, 3 and 8.

Elliott, B. and Elliott, J. (2017) *Financial Accounting and Reporting,* 18th edn, Pearson, Chapters 3, 6 and 7.

International Accounting Standards Board (2018) *The Conceptual Framework for Financial Reporting,* 2018.

Melville, A. (2017) *International Financial Reporting: A Practical Guide,* 6th edn, Pearson, Chapter 3.

Critical review questions

Solutions to these questions can be found at the back of the book on pages 773–774.

5.1 'Searching for an agreed conceptual framework for accounting rules is likely to be a journey without an ending.' Discuss.

5.2 There is a risk that managers will be inhibited from providing meaningful management commentaries. Instead, commentaries may be uninformative and written in a bland form. Can you think why managers may feel inhibited? What might be done to overcome any concerns they may have?

5.3 Why are accounting rules needed when preparing financial statements? Can you see any difficulties arising from harmonising accounting rules between different countries?

5.4 What are the main methods of creative accounting? How might the problem of creative accounting in developing countries be mitigated by harmonising accounting rules across national boundaries?

Solutions to exercises with coloured numbers can be found at the back of the book on pages 791–793.

Basic-level exercises

5.1 The size of annual financial reports published by limited companies has increased steadily over the years. Can you think of any reasons, apart from the increasing volume of accounting regulation, why this has occurred?

5.2 It has been suggested that too much information may be as bad as too little information for users of annual reports. Explain.

Intermediate-level exercises

5.3 The following information was extracted from the financial statements of I. Ching (Booksellers) plc for the year to 31 May 2019:

	£000
Finance charges	40
Cost of sales	460
Distribution expenses	110
Revenue	943
Administrative expenses	212
Other expenses	25
Gain on revaluation of property, plant and equipment	20
Loss on foreign currency translations on foreign operations	15
Tax on profit for the year	24
Tax on other components of comprehensive income	1

Required:

Prepare a statement of comprehensive income for the year ended 31 May 2019 that is set out in accordance with the requirements of IAS 1 *Presentation of Financial Statements*.

5.4   Manet plc had the following share capital and reserves as at 1 June 2018:

	£m
Share capital (£0.25 ordinary shares)	250
Share premium account	50
Revaluation reserve	120
Currency translation reserve	15
Retained earnings	380
Total equity	**815**

During the year to 31 May 2019, the company revalued property, plant and equipment upwards by £30 million and made a loss on foreign exchange translation of foreign operations of £5 million. The company made a profit for the year from normal operations of £160 million during the year and the dividend was £80 million.

Required:

Prepare a statement of changes in equity for the year ended 31 May 2019 in accordance with the requirements of IAS 1 *Presentation of Financial Statements.*

Advanced-level exercises

5.5   (a)   'The UK system of corporate governance for Stock Exchange listed companies adopts a "comply or explain" approach.' What does this mean? Set out one advantage and one disadvantage of this approach.

(b)   'The strategic report should be prepared by the company's accountants and not the directors.' Do you agree? Discuss.

5.6   You have overheard the following statements:

(a)   'The role of independent auditors is to prepare the financial statements of the company.'

(b)   'International Accounting Standards (IASs) apply to all UK companies, but London Stock Exchange listed companies must also adhere to International Financial Reporting Standards (IFRSs).'

(c)   'All listed companies in the European Union states must follow IASs and IFRSs.'

(d)   'According to IAS 1, companies' financial statements must show an "accurate representation" of what they purport to show.'

(e)   'IAS 1 leaves it to individual companies to decide the format that they use in the statement of financial position.'

(f)   'The statement of changes in equity deals with unrealised profits and gains, for example an upward revaluation of a non-current asset.'

(g)   'If a majority of the shareholders of a listed company agree, the company need not produce a full set of financial statements, but can just produce summary financial statements.'

Critically comment on each of these statements.

5.7   Segmental information relating to Turner plc for the year to 30 April 2019 is:

	Software £m	Electronics £m	Engineering £m	Total £m
Revenues from external customers	250	230	52	532
Inter-segment revenues	45	25	–	70
Interest revenue	18	–	–	18
Interest expense	–	25	–	25
Depreciation	60	35	10	105
Reportable segment profit	10	34	12	56
Other material non-cash items:				
Impairment of assets	–	5	–	5
Reportable segment assets	140	90	34	264
Expenditures for reportable segment non-current assets	22	12	10	44
Reportable segment liabilities	55	38	4	97

Required:

Analyse the performance of each of the three main business segments for the year and comment on your results.

CHAPTER 6

Measuring and reporting cash flows

Introduction

This chapter is devoted to the first major financial statement identified in Chapter 2: the statement of cash flows. This statement reports the movements of cash during a period and the effect of these movements on the cash position of the business. It is an important financial statement because cash is vital to the survival of a business. Without cash, a business cannot operate.

In this chapter, we shall see how the statement of cash flows is prepared and how the information that it contains may be interpreted. We shall also see why the inability of the income statement to identify and explain cash flows makes a separate statement necessary.

The statement of cash flows is being considered after the chapters on limited companies because the format of the statement on which we focus requires an understanding of this type of business.

Learning outcomes

When you have completed this chapter, you should be able to:

- discuss the crucial importance of cash to a business;

- explain the nature of the statement of cash flows and discuss how it can be helpful in identifying cash flow problems;

- prepare a statement of cash flows; and

- interpret a statement of cash flows.

Why is cash so important?

It is worth asking why cash is so important that it justifies having a major financial statement devoted to it. In one sense, it is just another asset that the business needs to enable it to function. Hence, it is no different from inventories or non-current assets.

The importance of cash lies in the fact that people will only normally accept cash in settlement of their claims. If a business wants to employ people, it must pay them in cash. If it wants to buy a new non-current asset, it must normally pay the seller in cash (perhaps after a short period of credit). When businesses fail, it is the lack of cash to pay amounts owed that really pushes them under. Cash generation is vital for businesses to survive and to be able to take advantage of commercial opportunities. This is what makes make cash the pre-eminent business asset. During an economic downturn, the ability to generate cash takes on even greater importance. Banks become more cautious in their lending and businesses with weak cash flows often find it difficult to obtain finance.

Real World 6.1 is taken from an article by Luke Johnson who is a 'serial entrepreneur'. Among other things, he was closely involved with taking Pizza Express from a business that owned just 12 restaurants to over 250 and, at the same time, increasing its share price from 40 pence to over £9. In the article, he highlights the importance of cash flow in managing a business.

Real World 6.1

Cash flow is king

Wise entrepreneurs learn that profits are not necessarily cash. But many founders never understand this essential accounting truth. A cash flow projection is a much more important document than a profit and loss (income) statement. A lack of liquidity can kill you, whereas a company can make paper losses for years and still survive if it has sufficient cash. It is amazing how financial journalists, fund managers, analysts, bankers and company directors can still focus on the wrong numbers in the accounts – despite so many high-profile disasters over the years.

FT *Source:* Extract from Johnson, L. (2013) The most dangerous unforced errors, ft.com, 9 July.
© The Financial Times Ltd 2013. All Rights Reserved.

Real World 6.2 is taken from a column written by John Timpson, which appeared in the *Daily Telegraph.* Timpson was the chief executive of the successful, high street shoe repairing and key cutting business that bears his name. In the column, he highlights the importance of cash reporting in managing the business.

Real World 6.2

Cash is key

Every day the figure I look for is our bank balance. By concentrating on the cash, I can stay in control of the business.

Keeping a close eye on the cash not only gives peace of mind, it also provides the best measure of your company's performance. The aim of the game is to make money – in other words, to create cash. The trick is to compare your bank balance with exactly the same date last year and be able to explain the difference.

My daily cash flow email compares the bank balance with the figure we forecast yesterday. I don't like surprises, but if things go awry, I want the surprise spotted straight away.

Source: Extracts from Timpson, J. (2016) Ask John, *The Daily Telegraph Business,* 29 August.

Real World 6.3 reveals that cash flow problems are quite common among smaller UK businesses and discusses why this may be the case.

Real World 6.3

Big problems for small businesses

There is a saying in business that sales revenue is vanity, profit is sanity but cash is reality. To this we might add that cash flow problems are a particularly harsh form of reality. Nevertheless, many smaller businesses experience such problems. One survey of 500 UK small and medium-size businesses revealed that nearly four-in-ten (38 per cent) experienced cashflow problems in recent years. The survey also found that nearly three quarters (71 per cent) of smaller business owners cited the risk of cash shortages as being their greatest headache. According to the survey, the main difficulties confronted by a lack of cash were an inability: to pay suppliers (41 per cent), to fulfil debt obligations (30 per cent), to buy inventories (29 per cent) and to pay employees (24 per cent).

According to Joanne Cains of accounting firm Bishop Fleming, the underlying causes of cash flow problems among smaller businesses can vary. They include insufficient sales revenue, poor pricing policies, inadequate credit control, poor management of inventories, growing the business too quickly and seasonal fluctuations. Some of these reasons may be attributed to a lack of financial expertise among the smaller business owners. However, not everything is within their control. Economic downturns and a weak bargaining position in relation to large business customers can badly affect the ability of smaller businesses to collect cash that is due.

Sources: Based on information in Williams, M. (2016) Cash flow is king: how to look after the money, www.guardian.co.uk, 9 June; and Amicus plc (2016) Cashflow problems undermine four in ten small firms, https://amicusplc.co.uk, 7 December.

Having established that cash is of the utmost importance to businesses of all sizes, let us now go on to examine the financial statement that deals with movements in this asset.

The statement of cash flows and its relation to the other major financial statements

The statement of cash flows is, along with the income statement and the statement of financial position, a major financial statement. The statement of cash flows is a fairly late addition to the annual published financial statements. At one time, companies were only required to publish an income statement and a statement of financial position. It seems the prevailing view was that all the financial information needed by users would be contained within these two statements. This view may have been based partly on the assumption that, if a business were profitable, it would also have plenty of cash. While in the long run this is likely to be true, it is not necessarily true in the short-to-medium term.

We saw in Chapter 3 that the income statement sets out the revenue and expenses, for the period, rather than the cash inflows and outflows. This means that the profit (or loss), which represents the difference between the revenue and expenses for the period, may have little or no relation to the cash generated during the period.

To illustrate this point, let us take the example of a business making a sale (generating revenue). This may well lead to an increase in wealth that will be reflected in the income statement. However, if the sale is made on credit, no cash changes hands – at least not at the time of the sale. Instead, the increase in wealth is reflected in another asset: trade receivables. Furthermore, if an item of inventories is the subject of the sale, wealth is lost to the business through the reduction in inventories. This means that an expense is incurred in making the sale, which will also be shown in the income statement. Once again, however, no cash changes hands at the time of sale. For such reasons, the profit and the cash generated during a period rarely go hand in hand.

Activity 6.1 helps to underline how particular transactions and events can affect profit and cash for a period differently.

Activity 6.1

The following is a list of business/accounting events. In each case, state the immediate effect (increase, decrease or none) on both profit and cash:

	Effect	
	on profit	*on cash*
1 Repayment of borrowings	____	____
2 Making a profitable sale on credit	____	____
3 Buying a non-current asset on credit	____	____
4 Receiving cash from a credit customer (trade receivable)	____	____
5 Depreciating a non-current asset	____	____
6 Buying some inventories for cash	____	____
7 Making a share issue for cash	____	____

You should have come up with the following:

	Effect	
	on profit	*on cash*
1 Repayment of borrowings	none	decrease
2 Making a profitable sale on credit	increase	none
3 Buying a non-current asset on credit	none	none
4 Receiving cash from a credit customer (trade receivable)	none	increase
5 Depreciating a non-current asset	decrease	none
6 Buying some inventories for cash	none	decrease
7 Making a share issue for cash	none	increase

The reasons for these answers are as follows:

1 Repaying borrowings requires that cash be paid to the lender. This means that two figures in the statement of financial position will be affected, but none in the income statement.
2 Making a profitable sale on credit will increase the sales revenue and profit figures. No cash will change hands at this point, however.
3 Buying a non-current asset on credit affects neither the cash balance nor the profit figure.
4 Receiving cash from a credit customer increases the cash balance and reduces the credit customer's balance. Both of these figures are on the statement of financial position. The income statement is unaffected.
5 Depreciating a non-current asset means that an expense is recognised. This causes a decrease in profit. No cash is paid or received.
6 Buying some inventories for cash means that the value of the inventories will increase and the cash balance will decrease by a similar amount. Profit is not affected.
7 Making a share issue for cash increases the shareholders' equity and increases the cash balance. Profit is not affected.

From what we have seen so far, it is clear that the income statement is not the place to look if we are to gain insights about cash movements over time. We need a separate financial statement.

The relationship between the three statements is shown in Figure 6.1. The statement of financial position shows the various assets (including cash) and claims (including the shareholders' equity) of the business *at a particular point in time.* The statement of cash flows and the income statement explain the *changes over a period* to two of the items in the statement of financial position. The statement of cash flows explains the changes to cash. The income statement explains changes to equity, arising from trading operations.

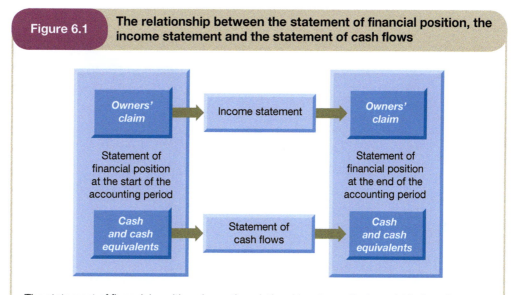

| Figure 6.1 | The relationship between the statement of financial position, the income statement and the statement of cash flows |

The statement of financial position shows the relationship, at a particular point in time, between the business's assets and claims. The income statement explains how, over a period between two statements of financial position, the equity figure in the first statement of financial position has altered as a result of trading operations. The statement of cash flows also looks at changes over the reporting period, but this statement explains the alteration in the cash (and cash equivalent) balances from the first to the second of the two consecutive statements of financial position.

The main features of the statement of cash flows

The statement of cash flows summarises the inflows and outflows of cash (and cash equivalents) for a business over a period. To aid user understanding, these cash flows are divided into categories (for example, those relating to investments in non-current assets). Cash inflows and outflows falling within each category are added together and the totals for each category are reported on the statement of cash flows. By adding the totals for each category together, an overall total is achieved that reveals the net increase or decrease in cash (and cash equivalents) over the period.

When describing in detail how this statement is prepared and presented, we shall follow the requirements of International Accounting Standard (IAS) 7 *Statement of Cash Flows.* This standard applies to Stock Exchange listed companies.

A definition of cash and cash equivalents

IAS 7 defines cash as notes and coins in hand and deposits in banks and similar institutions that are accessible to the business on demand. Cash equivalents are short-term, highly liquid investments that can be readily convertible to known amounts of cash. They are also subject to an insignificant risk of changes of value. Figure 6.2 sets out this definition of cash equivalents in the form of a decision chart.

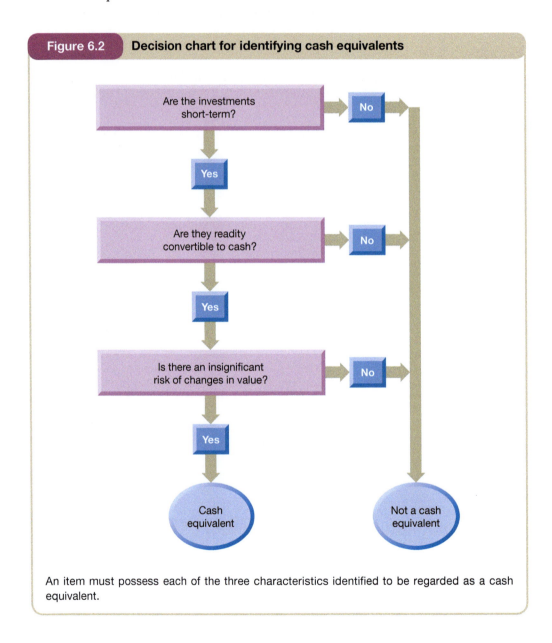

Figure 6.2   **Decision chart for identifying cash equivalents**

An item must possess each of the three characteristics identified to be regarded as a cash equivalent.

Activity 6.2 should clarify the types of items that fall within the definition of 'cash equivalents'.

Activity 6.2

At the end of its reporting period, Zeneb plc's statement of financial position included the following items:

1 A bank deposit account where one month's notice of withdrawal is required.
2 Ordinary shares in Jones plc (a Stock Exchange listed business).
3 A high-interest bank deposit account that requires six months' notice of withdrawal.
4 An overdraft on the business's bank current account.

Which (if any) of these four items would be included in the figure for cash and cash equivalents?

Your response should have been as follows:

1 A cash equivalent. It is readily withdrawable and there is no risk of a change of value.
2 Not a cash equivalent. It can be converted into cash because it is Stock Exchange listed. There is, however, a significant risk that the amount expected (hoped for!) when the shares are sold may not actually be forthcoming.
3 Not a cash equivalent because it is not readily convertible into liquid cash.
4 This is cash itself, though a negative amount of it. The only exception to this classification would be where the business is financed in the longer term by an overdraft, when it would be part of the financing of the business, rather than negative cash.

The layout of the statement of cash flows

As mentioned earlier, the cash flows of a business are divided into categories. The various categories and the way in which they are presented in the statement of cash flows are shown in Figure 6.3.

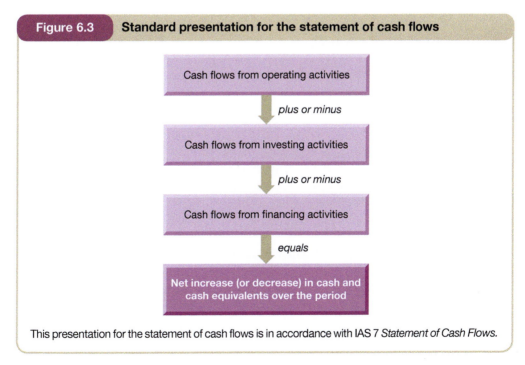

Figure 6.3   Standard presentation for the statement of cash flows

Cash flows from operating activities

plus or minus

Cash flows from investing activities

plus or minus

Cash flows from financing activities

equals

Net increase (or decrease) in cash and cash equivalents over the period

This presentation for the statement of cash flows is in accordance with IAS 7 *Statement of Cash Flows*.

Let us now consider each of the categories that have been identified.

Cash flows from operating activities

These represent the cash inflows and outflows arising from normal day-to-day trading, after taking account of the tax paid and financing costs (equity and borrowings) relating to it. The cash inflows for the period are the amounts received from trade receivables (credit customers settling their accounts) and from cash sales for the period. The cash outflows for the period are the amounts paid for inventories, operating expenses (such as rent and wages) corporation tax, interest and dividends.

Note that it is the cash inflows and outflows during a period that appear in the statement of cash flows, not revenue and expenses for that period. Similarly, tax and dividends that appear in the statement of cash flows are those actually paid during the period. Many companies pay tax on their annual profits in four equal instalments. Two of these are paid during the year concerned and the other two are paid during the following year. Thus, by the end of each year, half of the tax will have been paid and the remaining half will still be outstanding, to be paid during the following year. This means that the tax payment during a year is normally equal to half of the previous year's tax charge and half of that of the current year and it is this total that should appear in the current year's statement of cash flows.

Cash flows from investing activities

These include cash outflows to acquire non-current assets and cash inflows from their disposal. In addition to items, such as property, plant and equipment, non-current assets might include financial investments made in loans or shares in another business.

This section of the statement of cash flows also includes cash inflows *arising from* financial investments (loans and shares).

> ### Activity 6.3
>
> **What might be included as cash inflows from financial investments?**
>
> This can include interest received from loans that have been made and dividends received from shares in other companies.

Under IAS 7, interest received and dividends received could be classified under *Cash flows from operating activities*. This alternative treatment is available as these items appear in the calculation of profit. For the purpose of this chapter, however, we shall include them in *Cash flows from investing activities*.

Cash flows from financing activities

These represent cash inflows and outflows relating to the long-term financing of the business.

Activity 6.4

What might be included as cash inflows from financing activities?

This would include cash movements relating to the raising and redemption of both long-term borrowings and shares.

Under IAS 7, interest and dividends paid by the business could, if the directors chose, appear under this heading as outflows. This alternative to including them in *Cash flows from operating activities* is available as they represent a cost of raising finance. For the purpose of this chapter, however, we shall not use this alternative treatment.

Whichever treatment for interest and dividends (both paid and received) is chosen, it should be applied consistently.

Net increase or decrease in cash and cash equivalents

The final total shown on the statement will be the net increase or decrease in cash and cash equivalents over the period. It will be deduced from the totals from each of the three categories mentioned above.

Real World 6.4 shows a summarised statement of cash flows of Tesco plc, the UK-based supermarket company.

Real World 6.4

Cashing in

A summary of the statement of cash flows for the business for the year ended 24 February 2018 shows the cash flows of the business under each of the headings described above.

Summary group statement of cash flows Year ended 24 February 2018

	£m
Cash generated from operations	3,309
Interest paid	(351)
Corporation tax paid	(176)
Net cash generated from operating activities	2,782
Net cash generated from investing activities	666
Net cash used in financing activities	(3,236)
Net increase in cash and cash equivalents	212

Source: Adapted from Tesco plc, Annual Report and Financial Statements 2018, p. 78 www.tescoplc.com.

As we shall see shortly, more detailed information under each of the main categories is provided in the statement of cash flows presented to shareholders and other users.

The normal direction of cash flows

The effect on a business's cash and cash equivalents of activities relating to each category is shown in Figure 6.4. The arrows show the *normal* direction of cash flow for the typical, profitable, business in a typical reporting period.

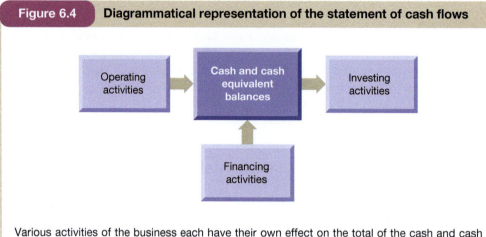

Figure 6.4	Diagrammatical representation of the statement of cash flows

Various activities of the business each have their own effect on the total of the cash and cash equivalents, either positive (increasing the total) or negative (reducing it). The net increase or decrease in the cash and cash equivalents over a period will be the sum of these individual effects, taking account of the direction (cash in or cash out) of each activity.

Note that the direction of the arrow shows the *normal* direction of the cash flow in respect of each activity. In certain circumstances, each of these arrows could be reversed in direction.

Normally, *operating activities* provide positive cash flows and, therefore, increase the business's cash resources. For most UK businesses, cash generated from day-to-day trading, even after deducting tax, interest and dividends, is by far the most important source of new finance.

Activity 6.5

Last year's statement of cash flows for Angus plc showed a negative cash flow from operating activities. What could be the reason for this and should the business's management be alarmed by it? (*Hint*: We think that there are two broad possible reasons for a negative cash flow.)

The two reasons are:

1 The business is unprofitable. This leads to more cash being paid out to employees, to suppliers of goods and services, for interest and so on than is received from trade receivables. This should be of concern as a major expense for most businesses is depreciation. Since depreciation does not lead to a cash flow, it is not considered in *Net cash inflows from operating activities*. A negative operating cash flow might well indicate, therefore, a much larger trading loss – in other words, a significant loss of the business's wealth. This is likely to be a source of concern for management.

2 The business is expanding its activities (level of sales revenue). Although the business may be profitable, it may be spending more cash than is being generated from sales. Cash will be spent on acquiring more assets, non-current and current, to accommodate increased demand. For example, a business may need to have inventories in place before additional sales can be made. Similarly, staff will have to be employed and paid. Even when additional sales are made, they would normally be made on credit, with the cash inflow lagging behind the sales. This means that there would be no immediate cash benefit.

Expansion often causes cash flow strains for new businesses, which will be expanding inventories and other assets from zero. They would also need to employ and pay staff. To add to this problem, increased profitability may encourage a feeling of optimism, leading to a lack of attention being paid to the cash flows. Although the cause of the cash flow problem is less disturbing than a lack of profitability, the effect could be a severe strain on cash resource and the consequent dangers of this.

Investing activities typically cause net negative cash flows. This is because many non-current assets either wear out or become obsolete and need to be replaced. Businesses may also expand their asset base. Non-current assets may, of course, be sold, which would give rise to positive cash flows. In net terms, however, the cash flows are normally negative, with cash spent on new assets far outweighing that received from the sale of old ones.

Financing activities can go in either direction, depending on the financing strategy at the time. Since businesses seek to expand, however, there is a tendency for these activities to result in cash inflows rather than cash outflows.

Before leaving this section let us consider **Real World 6.5.** It explains how, in recent years, many US businesses have experienced cash outflows that exceed their cash flows from operating activities. This has resulted in a need for greater borrowing. It also points out that the cash outflows were often not incurred for re-investment purposes.

Real World 6.5

Spend, spend, spend!

Corporate America is swimming in cash. There is no great news about this, and no great mystery about where it came from. Seven years of historically low interest rates will prompt companies to borrow. A new development, however, is that investors are starting to ask in more detail what companies are doing with their cash. And they are starting to revolt against signs of over-borrowing. That over-borrowing has grown most blatant in the last year, as earnings growth has petered out and, in many cases, turned negative. This has made the sharp increases in corporate debt look far harder to sustain.

Perhaps the most alarming illustration of the problem compares annual changes in net debt with the annual change in earnings before interest, tax, depreciation and amortization (EBITDA), which is a decent approximation for the operating cash flow (cash flow from operating activities) from which they can expect to repay that debt. As the chart [see Figure 6.5] shows, debt has grown at almost 30 per cent over the past year; the cash flow to pay it has fallen slightly.

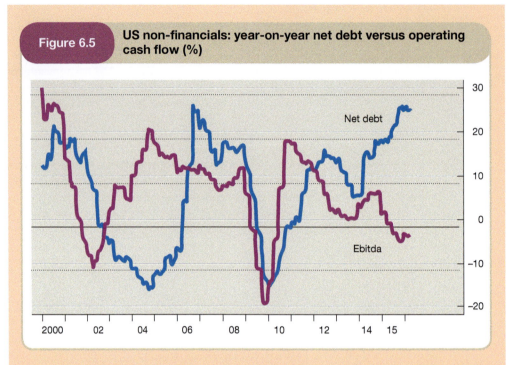

Figure 6.5   **US non-financials: year-on-year net debt versus operating cash flow (%)**

According to Andrew Lapthorne of Société Générale, the reality is that 'US corporates appear to be spending way too much (over 35 per cent more than their gross operating cash flow, the biggest deficit in over 20 years of data) and are using debt issuance to make up the difference'. The decline in earnings and cash flows in the past year has accentuated the problem, and brought it to the top of investors' consciousness.

A further issue is the uses to which the debt has been put. As pointed out many times in the post-crisis years, it has generally not gone into capital expenditures (property, plant and equipment), which might arguably be expected to boost the economy. It has instead been deployed to pay dividends, or to buy back shares – or to buy other companies.

Preparing the statement of cash flows

Deducing net cash flows from operating activities

As we have seen, the first category within the statement of cash flows is the *Cash flows from operating activities*. There are two approaches that can be taken to deriving this figure: the **direct method** and the **indirect method**.

The direct method

The direct method involves an analysis of the cash records of the business for the period, identifying all payments and receipts relating to operating activities. These receipts and payments are then summarised to provide the total figures for inclusion in the statement of cash flows. Since accounting records are normally computerised, this is a fairly simple matter. Nevertheless, very few businesses adopt the direct method.

The indirect method

The indirect method is a much more popular approach. It relies on the fact that, sooner or later, sales revenue gives rise to cash inflows and expenses give rise to outflows. This means that the figure for profit for the year will be linked to the net cash flows from operating activities. Since businesses have to produce an income statement, the information that it contains can be used as a starting point to deduce the cash flows from operating activities.

With credit sales, the cash receipt arises at some point after the sale is made. Thus, sales made towards the end of the current reporting period may result in the cash being received after the end of the period. The income statement for the current period will include all sales revenue generated during that period. Where cash relating to those sales is received after the end of the period, it will be included in the statement of cash flows for the following period. While profit for the period will not normally equal the net cash inflows from operating activities, there is a clear link between them. This means that we can, for example, deduce the cash inflows from sales if we have the relevant income statement and statements of financial position, as we shall see in Activity 6.6.

Activity 6.6

What information contained within the income statement and statement of financial position for a business can help us deduce the cash inflows from sales?

The income statement tells us the sales revenue figure. The statement of financial position will tell us how much was owed in respect of credit sales at the beginning and end of the reporting period (trade receivables).

If we adjust the sales revenue figure by the increase or decrease in trade receivables over the period, we deduce the cash from sales for the period. Example 6.1 shows how this is done.

Example 6.1

The sales revenue figure for a business for the year was £34 million. The trade receivables totalled £4 million at the beginning of the year, but had increased to £5 million by the end of the year.

Basically, the trade receivables figure is dictated by sales revenue and cash receipts. It is increased when a sale is made and decreased when cash is received from a credit customer. If, over the year, the sales revenue and the cash receipts had been equal, the beginning-of-year and end-of-year trade receivables figures would have been equal. Since the trade receivables figure increased, it must mean that less cash was received than sales revenues were made. In fact, the cash receipts from sales must have been £33 million (that is, 34 − (5 − 4)).

Put slightly differently, we can say that as a result of sales, assets of £34 million flowed into the business. If £1 million of this went to increasing the asset of trade receivables, this leaves only £33 million that went to increase cash.

The same general point is true in respect of nearly all of the other items that are taken into account in deducing the operating profit figure. The main exception is depreciation. This expense is not normally associated with any movement in cash during that same period.

All of this means that we can take the *profit before taxation* (that is, the profit after interest but before taxation) for the year, add back the depreciation and interest expense charged in arriving at that profit, and adjust this total by movements in inventories, trade (and other) receivables and payables. If we then go on to deduct payments made during the reporting period for taxation, interest on borrowings and dividends, we have the net cash from operating activities. Example 6.2 illustrates this process.

Example 6.2

The relevant information from the financial statements of Dido plc for last year is as follows:

	£m
Profit before taxation (after interest)	122
Depreciation charged in arriving at profit before taxation	34
Interest expense	6
At the beginning of the year:	
Inventories	15
Trade receivables	24
Trade payables	18
At the end of the year:	
Inventories	17
Trade receivables	21
Trade payables	19

The following further information is available about payments during last year:

	£m
Taxation paid	32
Interest paid	5
Dividends paid	9

The cash flow from operating activities is derived as follows:

	£m
Profit before taxation (after interest)	122
Depreciation	34
Interest expense	6
Increase in inventories (17 − 15)	(2)
Decrease in trade receivables (21 − 24)	3
Increase in trade payables (19 − 18)	1
Cash generated from operations	164
Interest paid	(5)
Taxation paid	(32)
Dividends paid	(9)
Net cash from operating activities	118

As we can see, the net increase in **working capital*** (that is, current assets less current liabilities) as a result of trading was £162 million (that is, 122 + 34 + 6). Of this, £2 million went into increased inventories. More cash was received from trade receivables than sales revenue was made. Similarly, less cash was paid to trade payables than purchases of goods and services on credit. Both of these had a favourable effect on cash. Over the year, therefore, cash increased by £164 million. When account was taken of the payments for interest, tax and dividends, the net cash from operating activities was £118 million (inflow).

Note that we needed to adjust the profit before taxation (after interest) by the depreciation and interest expenses to derive the profit before depreciation, interest and taxation.

* Working capital is a term widely used in accounting and finance, not just in the context of the statement of cash flows. We shall encounter it several times in later chapters.

Activity 6.7

In deriving the cash generated from operations, we add the depreciation expense for the period to the profit before taxation. Does this mean that depreciation is a source of cash?

No. Depreciation is a not source of cash. The periodic depreciation expense is irrelevant to cash flow. Since the profit before taxation is derived *after* deducting the depreciation expense for the period, we need to eliminate the impact of depreciation by adding it back to the profit figure. This will give us the profit before tax *and before* depreciation, which is what we need.

We should be clear why we add back an amount for interest at the start of the derivation of cash flow from operating activities only to deduct an amount for interest further down. The reason is that the first is the *interest expense* for the reporting period, whereas the second is the amount of *cash paid out for interest* during that period. These may well be different amounts, as was the case in Example 6.2.

The indirect method of deducing the net cash flow from operating activities is summarised in Figure 6.6.

Let us now turn our attention to how, in practice, *cash flows from operating activities* is used as a measure of performance. Before doing so, however, it is useful to emphasise an important point. The fact that we can work from the profit before taxation to derive the cash flows from operating activities should not lead us to conclude that these two figures are broadly in line. Typically, adjustments made to the profit figure to derive net cash flows from operating activities are significant in size.

Figure 6.6	**The indirect method of deducing the net cash flows from operating activities**

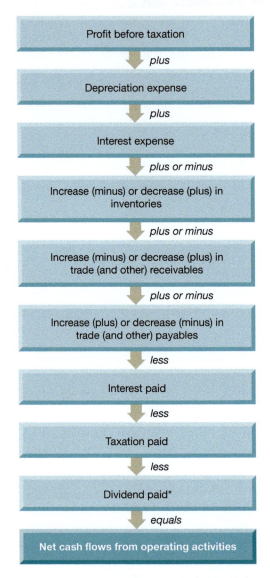

Determining the net cash from operating activities firstly involves adding back the depreciation and the interest expense to the profit before taxation. Next, adjustment is made for increases or decreases in inventories, receivables and payables. Lastly, cash paid for interest, taxation and dividends is deducted.

* Note that dividends could alternatively be included under the heading 'Cash flows from financing activities'.

Activity 6.8

The relevant information from the financial statements of Pluto plc for last year is as follows:

	£m
Profit before taxation (after interest)	165
Depreciation charged in arriving at operating profit	41
Interest expense	21
At the beginning of the year:	
Inventories	22
Trade receivables	18
Trade payables	15
At the end of the year:	
Inventories	23
Trade receivables	21
Trade payables	17

The following further information is available about payments during last year:

	£m
Taxation paid	49
Interest paid	25
Dividends paid	28

What figure should appear in the statement of cash flows for *Net cash from operating activities*?

Cash flow from operating activities:

	£m
Profit before taxation (after interest)	165
Depreciation	41
Interest expense	21
Increase in inventories (23 − 22)	(1)
Increase in trade receivables (21 − 18)	(3)
Increase in trade payables (17 − 15)	2
Cash generated from operations	225
Interest paid	(25)
Taxation paid	(49)
Dividends paid	(28)
Net cash from operating activities	123

Assessing performance using cash flows from operating activities

Cash flows from operating activities are regarded by many businesses as a key performance indicator. **Real World 6.6** explains why one well-known business regards this measure as being important as well as revealing its recent performance using this yardstick.

Real World 6.6

Turning energy into cash

Royal Dutch Shell plc, the energy business, employs cash flows from operating activities as one of its key indicators of financial performance. It points out that this measure indicates the ability of the business to pay its debts, undertake investments and make cash distributions to shareholders. The performance of the business over the four years ending 31 December 2017 is set out in Figure 6.7.

Figure 6.7 **Royal Dutch Shell plc: cash flows from operating activities 2014–2017**

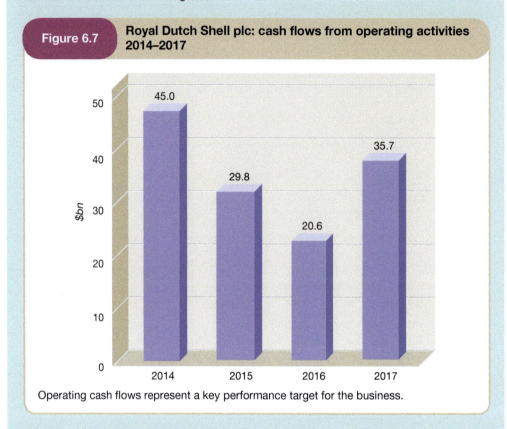

Operating cash flows represent a key performance target for the business.

In its 2017 annual report, the business explained the increase in this key performance indicator over time as follows:

> Cash flow from operating activities in 2017 was an inflow of $35.7 billion. The increase from $20.6 billion in 2016 was mainly due to higher earnings. The decrease in cash flow from operating activities in 2016 compared with $29.8 billion in 2015 mainly reflected unfavourable working capital impacts.

Shell bases part of the remuneration of senior staff on its various key performance indicators, including cash flow from operating activities.

Source: Graph produced from information in Shell, 2017 Annual Report, p. 22. Quote from p. 55 of the report.

The relationship between revenue generated during a period and cash flows from operating activities can help assess the outcome of productive effort. This relationship reveals how successful a business has been in converting the revenue generated into surplus cash. **Real World 6.7** outlines the findings of a recent survey, which indicate that large businesses are finding this conversion process increasingly difficult.

Real World 6.7

Cash conversion

PwC's annual global *Working Capital Study 2018/19* indicates that the world's largest listed businesses are finding it harder to convert revenue generated into operating cash flows (that is, cash flows from operating activities). The survey, using data from 14,694 businesses, reveals a decline of 6.5 per cent in operating cash flows relative to revenue when compared with the preceding year. It is not entirely clear why this decline has occurred, although it may well reflect a more challenging economic environment. Figure 6.8 shows the overall performance of large businesses in recent years according to this measure.

Figure 6.8	Trend in operating cash flows to revenue

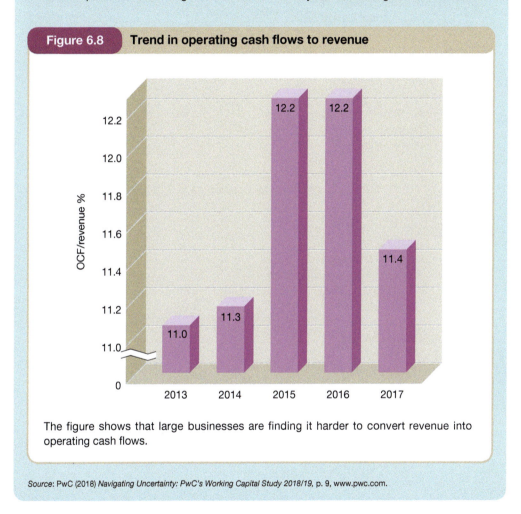

The figure shows that large businesses are finding it harder to convert revenue into operating cash flows.

Source: PwC (2018) *Navigating Uncertainty: PwC's Working Capital Study 2018/19*, p. 9, www.pwc.com.

Deducing the other areas of the statement of cash flows

Deriving the *cash flows from investing activities* and the *cash flows from financing activities* is much easier than deriving *cash flows from operating activities*. It largely involves a comparison of the opening and closing statements of financial position to detect movements in non-current assets, non-current liabilities and equity over the period. We show how this is done in Example 6.3, which prepares a complete statement of cash flows.

Example 6.3

Torbryan plc's income statement for the year ended 31 December 2018 and the statements of financial position as at 31 December 2017 and 2018 are as follows:

Income statement for the year ended 31 December 2018

	£m
Revenue	576
Cost of sales	(307)
Gross profit	269
Distribution expenses	(65)
Administrative expenses	(26)
	178
Other operating income	21
Operating profit	199
Interest receivable	17
Interest payable	(23)
Profit before taxation	193
Taxation	(46)
Profit for the year	147

Statements of financial position as at 31 December 2017 and 2018

	2017 £m	2018 £m
ASSETS		
Non-current assets		
Property, plant and equipment		
Land and buildings	241	241
Plant and machinery	309	325
	550	566
Current assets		
Inventories	44	41
Trade receivables	121	139
	165	180
Total assets	715	746
EQUITY AND LIABILITIES		
Equity		
Called-up ordinary share capital	150	200
Share premium account	–	40
Retained earnings	26	123
	176	363
Non-current liabilities		
Borrowings – loan notes	400	250
Current liabilities		
Borrowings (all bank overdraft)	68	56
Trade payables	55	54
Taxation	16	23
	139	133
Total equity and liabilities	715	746

During 2018, the business spent £95 million on additional plant and machinery. There were no other non-current-asset acquisitions or disposals. A dividend of £50 million was paid on ordinary shares during the year. The interest receivable revenue and the interest payable expense for the year were each equal to the cash inflow and outflow respectively. Loan notes of £150 million were redeemed at their nominal (par) value.

The statement of cash flows would be:

Statement of cash flows for the year ended 31 December 2018

	£m
Cash flows from operating activities	
Profit before taxation (after interest) (see Note 1 below)	193
Adjustments for:	
Depreciation (Note 2)	79
Interest receivable (Note 3)	(17)
Interest payable (Note 4)	23
Increase in trade receivables (139 − 121)	(18)
Decrease in trade payables (55 − 54)	(1)
Decrease in inventories (44 − 41)	3
Cash generated from operations	262
Interest paid	(23)
Taxation paid (Note 5)	(39)
Dividend paid	(50)
Net cash from operating activities	150
Cash flows from investing activities	
Payments to acquire tangible non-current assets	(95)
Interest received (Note 3)	17
Net cash used in investing activities	(78)
Cash flows from financing activities	
Repayments of loan notes	(150)
Issue of ordinary shares (Note 6)	90
Net cash used in financing activities	(60)
Net increase in cash and cash equivalents	12
Cash and cash equivalents at 1 January 2018 (Note 7)	(68)
Cash and cash equivalents at 31 December 2018	(56)

Notes:
1 This is simply taken from the income statement for the year.
2 Since there were no disposals, the depreciation charges must be the difference between the start and end of the year's plant and machinery (non-current assets) values, adjusted by the cost of any additions.

	£m
Carrying amount at 1 January 2018	309
Additions	95
	404
Depreciation (balancing figure)	(79)
Carrying amount at 31 December 2018	325

3 Interest receivable must be deducted to work towards what the profit would have been before it was added in the income statement, because it is not part of operations but of investing activities. The cash inflow from this source appears under the *Cash flows from investing activities* heading.

Example 6.3 *continued*

4 The interest payable expense must be taken out, by adding it back to the profit figure. We subsequently deduct the cash paid for interest payable during the year. In this case, the two figures are identical.

5 Taxation is paid by many companies in instalments: 50 per cent during their reporting year and 50 per cent in the following year. As a result, the 2018 payment would have been half the tax on the 2017 profit (that is, the figure that would have appeared in the current liabilities at the end of 2017), plus half of the 2018 taxation charge (that is, $16 + (\frac{1}{2} \times 46) = 39$). Probably the easiest way to deduce the amount paid during the year to 31 December 2018 is by following this approach:

	£m
Taxation owed at start of the year (from the statement of financial position as at 31 December 2017)	16
Taxation charge for the year (from the income statement)	46
	62
Taxation owed at the end of the year (from the statement of financial position as at 31 December 2018)	(23)
Taxation paid during the year	39

This follows the logic that if we start with what the business owed at the beginning of the year, add what was owed as a result of the current year's taxation charge and then deduct what was owed at the end, the resulting figure must be what was paid during the year.

6 The share issue raised £90 million, of which £50 million went into the share capital total on the statement of financial position and £40 million into share premium.

7 There were no 'cash equivalents', just cash (though negative).

Reconciliation of liabilities from financing activities

IAS 7 requires businesses to provide a reconciliation that shows the link between liabilities at the beginning and end of the reporting period that relate to *Cash flows from financing activities* in the statement of cash flows. This reconciliation sets out movements in liabilities, such as long-term borrowings and lease liabilities, over the reporting period. A separate reconciliation is required for each type of liability.

The reconciliation appears as a note to the statement of cash flows and is designed to help track any changes occurring in the liabilities of the business. Example 6.4 illustrates how this reconciliation may be presented.

Example 6.4

Based on the information set out in the financial statements of Torbryan plc for the financial years ended 31 December 2017 and 2018 (see Example 6.3), the following reconciliation of long-term liabilities for the year to 31 December 2018 can be carried out:

Reconciliation of liabilities from financing activities for the year to 31 December 2018

	£m
Loan notes outstanding at 1 January 2018	400
Cash paid to redeem loan notes	(150)
Loan notes outstanding at 31 December 2018	250

Activity 6.9

IAS 7 requires a statement reconciling movements in liabilities, for the reporting period, but does not require a reconciliation of movements of equity. Can you suggest why this is?

The reason is that such a statement (statement of changes in equity) is required under IAS 1 *Presentation of Financial Statements,* as we saw in Chapter 5.

What does the statement of cash flows tell us?

The statement of cash flows tells us how the business has generated cash during the period and how that cash was used. This is potentially very useful information. Tracking the sources and uses of cash over time may reveal trends that could help a user to assess likely future cash movements for the business.

Looking specifically at the statement of cash flows for Torbryan plc, in Example 6.3, we can see the following:

- Net cash flow from operations seems strong, much larger than the profit for the year, after taking account of the dividend paid. This might be expected as depreciation is deducted in arriving at profit.
- Working capital has absorbed some cash, which may indicate an expansion of activity (sales revenue) over the year. As we have only one year's income statement, however, we cannot tell whether this has occurred.
- There were net outflows of cash for investing activities, but this would not be unusual. Many types of non-current assets have limited lives and need to be replaced. Expenditure during the year was not out of line with the depreciation expense for the year, which is to be expected for a business with a regular replacement programme for its non-current assets.
- There was a major outflow of cash to redeem borrowings, which was partly offset by the proceeds of a share issue. This may well represent a change of financing strategy.

Activity 6.10

Why might this be the case? What has been the impact of these changes on the long-term financing of the business?

The financing changes, together with the retained earnings for the year, have led to a significant shift in the equity/borrowings balance.

Real World 6.8 identifies the important changes in the cash flows of Ryanair plc during the year ended 31 March 2018.

Real World 6.8

Flying high

Ryanair's summarised statement of cash flows for the year ended 31 March 2018:

	€m
Net cash provided by operating activities	2,233.2
Net cash from (used in) investing activities	(719.4)
Net cash from (used in) financing activities	(1,222.8)
Net decrease in cash and cash equivalents	291.0

We can see that there was a net increase in cash and cash equivalents of €291.0 million during the year. Cash and cash equivalents increased from €1,224.0 million at 31 March 2017 to €1,515.0 million at 31 March 2018. Both are very large balances and represent 10 per cent and 12 per cent, respectively, of total assets held.

The net cash inflow from operating activities during the year to 31 March 2018 was €2,233.2 million. This was higher than the previous year's figure of €1,927.2 million. The increase of €306 million over 2017 was largely due to an increase in profit after tax of €134.3 million along with higher depreciation charges and higher receipts from customers for future flights.

The net cash outflow from investing activities during the year totalled €719.4 million, which was down from the previous year's figure by €2,604.6 million. The 2018 figure included an outflow of €1,470.6 million for the purchase of property, plant and equipment. This represented an increase over recent years and was mostly due to the purchase of new aircraft. This large capital outlay was partly offset, however, by the sale of financial investments (with a maturity of more than three months) for €774.0 million.

The net cash outflow from financing activities was €1,222.8 million. This huge outflow largely reflected repayments of long-term borrowings of €458.9 million and returns to shareholders of €829.1 million.

Source: Information taken from Ryanair plc, Annual Report 2018, pages 105, 106 and 151.

Problems with IAS 7

IAS 7 *Statement of Cash Flows* does not enjoy universal acclaim. Its critics argue that the standard is too permissive in the description and classification of important items.

Some believe that the standard would give users greater confidence if it insisted that only the direct method be used to calculate cash flows from operating activities. Supporters of the direct method argue that, being cash-based, it provides greater clarity by setting out operating cash receipts and payments. No accrual-based adjustments are made, which means that it is less susceptible to manipulation than the indirect approach. This greater transparency 'would enable the market to distinguish between the weak and the strong – the better companies would be safe, and the worse would be more exposed'. (See Reference 1 at the end of the chapter.) In its defence, however, it should be said that the indirect approach might help to shed light on the quality of reported profits by reconciling profit with the net cash from operating activities for a period. A business must demonstrate an ability to convert profits into cash. Revealing the link between profits and cash is, therefore, very helpful.

Self-assessment question 6.1

Touchstone plc's income statements for the years ended 31 December 2017 and 2018 and statements of financial position as at 31 December 2017 and 2018 are as follows:

Income statements for the years ended 2017 and 2018

	2017 £m	2018 £m
Revenue	173	207
Cost of sales	(96)	(101)
Gross profit	77	106
Distribution expenses	(18)	(20)
Administrative expenses	(24)	(26)
Other operating income	3	4
Operating profit	38	64
Interest payable	(2)	(4)
Profit before taxation	36	60
Taxation	(8)	(16)
Profit for the year	28	44

Statements of financial position as at 31 December 2017 and 2018

	2017 £m	2018 £m
ASSETS		
Non-current assets		
Property, plant and equipment		
Land and buildings	94	110
Plant and machinery	53	62
	147	172
Current assets		
Inventories	25	24
Treasury bills (short-term investments)	–	15
Trade receivables	16	26
Cash at bank and in hand	4	4
	45	69
Total assets	192	241
EQUITY AND LIABILITIES		
Equity		
Called-up ordinary share capital	100	100
Retained earnings	30	56
	130	156
Non-current liabilities		
Borrowings – loan notes (10%)	20	40
Current liabilities		
Trade payables	38	37
Taxation	4	8
	42	45
Total equity and liabilities	192	241

Self-assessment question 6.1 *continued*

Notes:

1 Included in 'cost of sales', 'distribution expenses' and 'administrative expenses', depreciation was as follows:

	2017 £m	2018 £m
Land and buildings	5	6
Plant and machinery	6	10

2 The interest payable expense equalled the cash payment made during each of the years.
3 The business paid dividends on ordinary shares of £14 million during 2017 and £18 million during 2018.
4 The Treasury bills represent a short-term investment of funds that will be used shortly in operations. There is insignificant risk that this investment will lose value.
5 There were no non-current asset disposals in either year.

Required:

Prepare a statement of cash flows for the business for 2018.

The solution to this question can be found at the back of the book on page 755.

Summary

The main points of this chapter may be summarised as follows:

The need for a statement of cash flows

- Cash is important because no business can operate without it.
- The statement of cash flows is specifically designed to reveal movements in cash over a period.
- Cash movements cannot be readily detected from the income statement, which focuses on revenue and expenses rather than on cash inflows and outflows.
- Profit (or loss) and cash generated for the period are rarely equal.
- The statement of cash flows is a major financial statement, along with the income statement and the statement of financial position.

Preparing the statement of cash flows

- The statement of cash flows has three major categories of cash flows: cash flows from operating activities, cash flows from investing activities and cash flows from financing activities.
- The total of the cash movements under these three categories will provide the net increase or decrease in cash and cash equivalents for the period.
- A reconciliation can be undertaken to check that the opening balance of cash and cash equivalents plus the net increase (or decrease) for the period equals the closing balance.

Calculating the cash generated from operations

- The net cash flows from operating activities can be derived by either the direct method or the indirect method.

- The direct method is based on an analysis of the cash records for the period, whereas the indirect method uses information contained within the income statement and statements of financial position.

- The indirect method takes the operating profit for the period, adds back any depreciation charge and then adjusts for changes in inventories, receivables and payables during the period.

Interpreting the statement of cash flows

- The statement of cash flows shows the main sources and uses of cash.

- Tracking the cash movements over several periods may reveal financing and investing patterns and may help predict future management action.

Reconciliation of liabilities from financing activities

- IAS 7 requires businesses to provide a reconciliation that shows the link between liabilities at the beginning and end of the reporting period that relate to *Cash flows from financing activities* in the statement of cash flows.

- The reconciliation shows how borrowings and other non-equity finance have changed over the reporting period. Each type of non-equity finance needs to be separately reconciled.

Problems with IAS 7

- IAS 7 has been criticised for being too permissive over the description and classification of important items and for allowing businesses to adopt the indirect method for determining net cash from operating activities.

Key terms

For definitions of these terms, see Appendix B.

direct method *p. 216*   working capital *p. 219*
indirect method *p. 216*

Reference

1 Clacher, D. (2013) Why the numbers add up for direct cash flow statements, *Financial Director,* 17 December.

Further reading

If you would like to explore the topics covered in this chapter in more depth, we recommend the following:

Alexander, D. and Nobes, C. (2016) *Financial Accounting: An International Introduction,* 6th edn, Pearson, Chapter 13.

Elliott, B. and Elliott, J. (2017) *Financial Accounting and Reporting,* 18th edn, Pearson, Chapter 5.

IFRS Standards (2018) (Red Book) *IAS 7 Statement of Cash Flows,* January, IFRS Foundation.

Melville, A. (2017) *International Financial Reporting: A Practical Guide,* 6th edn, Pearson, Chapter 16.

Critical review questions

Solutions to these questions can be found at the back of the book on pages 774–775.

6.1 The typical business outside the service sector has about 50 per cent more of its resources tied up in inventories than in cash, yet there is no call for a 'statement of inventories flows' to be prepared. Why is cash regarded as more important than inventories?

6.2 What is the difference between the direct and indirect methods of deducing cash generated from operations? Can you see an advantage of using the indirect method rather than the direct method from the perspective of an external user of financial statements?

6.3 IAS 7 carefully defines cash (and cash equivalents). Can you explain why the authors of this standard were so careful and precise in their definition?

6.4 'Profit should more or less equal the net cash inflow for a period?' Do you agree? Explain your reasoning.

Exercises

Solutions to exercises with coloured numbers can be found at the back of the book on pages 793–796.

Basic-level exercises

6.1 How will each of the following events ultimately affect the amount of cash?
(a) An increase in the level of inventories
(b) A rights issue of ordinary shares
(c) A bonus issue of ordinary shares
(d) Writing off part of the value of some inventories
(e) The disposal of a large number of the business's shares by a major shareholder
(f) Depreciating a non-current asset.

6.2 The following information has been taken from the financial statements of Juno plc for last year and the year before last:

	Year before last £m	Last year £m
Operating profit	156	187
Depreciation charged in arriving at operating profit	47	55
Inventories held at end of year	27	31
Trade receivables at end of year	24	23
Trade payables at end of year	15	17

Required:
What is the figure for cash generated from the operations for Juno plc for last year?

Intermediate-level exercises

6.3 Torrent plc's income statement for the year ended 31 December 2018 and the statements of financial position as at 31 December 2017 and 2018 are as follows:

Income statement for the year ended 31 December 2018

	£m
Revenue	623
Cost of sales	(353)
Gross profit	270
Distribution expenses	(71)
Administrative expenses	(30)
Other operating income	27
Operating profit	196
Interest payable	(26)
Profit before taxation	170
Taxation	(36)
Profit for the year	134

Statements of financial position as at 31 December 2017 and 2018

	2017 £m	2018 £m
ASSETS		
Non-current assets		
Property, plant and equipment		
Land and buildings	310	310
Plant and machinery	325	314
	635	624
Current assets		
Inventories	41	35
Trade receivables	139	145
	180	180
Total assets	815	804
EQUITY AND LIABILITIES		
Equity		
Called-up ordinary share capital	200	300
Share premium account	40	–
Revaluation reserve	69	9
Retained earnings	123	197
	432	506

	2017 £m	2018 £m
Non-current liabilities		
Borrowings – loan notes	250	150
Current liabilities		
Borrowings (all bank overdraft)	56	89
Trade payables	54	41
Taxation	23	18
	133	148
Total equity and liabilities	815	804

During 2018, the business spent £67 million on additional plant and machinery. There were no other non-current asset acquisitions or disposals.

There was no share issue for cash during the year. The interest payable expense was equal in amount to the cash outflow. A dividend of £60 million was paid.

Required:

Prepare the statement of cash flows for Torrent plc for the year ended 31 December 2018.

6.4 Chen plc's income statements for the years ended 31 December 2017 and 2018 and the statements of financial position as at 31 December 2017 and 2018 are as follows:

Income statements for the years ended 31 December 2017 and 2018

	2017 £m	2018 £m
Revenue	207	153
Cost of sales	(101)	(76)
Gross profit	106	77
Distribution expenses	(22)	(20)
Administrative expenses	(20)	(28)
Operating profit	64	29
Interest payable	(4)	(4)
Profit before taxation	60	25
Taxation	(16)	(6)
Profit for the year	44	19

Statements of financial position as at 31 December 2017 and 2018

	2017 £m	2018 £m
ASSETS		
Non-current assets		
Property, plant and equipment		
Land and buildings	110	130
Plant and machinery	62	56
	172	186
Current assets		
Inventories	24	25
Trade receivables	26	25
Cash at bank and in hand	19	–
	69	50
Total assets	241	236

	2017 £m	2018 £m
EQUITY AND LIABILITIES		
Equity		
Called-up ordinary share capital	100	100
Retained earnings	56	57
	156	157
Non-current liabilities		
Borrowings – loan notes (10%)	40	40
Current liabilities		
Borrowings (all bank overdraft)	–	2
Trade payables	37	34
Taxation	8	3
	45	39
Total equity and liabilities	241	236

Included in 'cost of sales', 'distribution expenses' and 'administrative expenses', depreciation was as follows:

	2017 £m	2018 £m
Land and buildings	6	10
Plant and machinery	10	12

There were no non-current asset disposals in either year. The amount of cash paid for interest equalled the expense in each year. Dividends were paid totalling £18 million in each year.

Required:
Prepare a statement of cash flows for the business for 2018.

6.5 The following are the financial statements for Nailsea plc for the years ended 30 June 2018 and 2019:

Income statement for years ended 30 June

	2018 £m	2019 £m
Revenue	1,230	2,280
Operating expenses	(722)	(1,618)
Depreciation	(270)	(320)
Operating profit	238	342
Interest payable	–	(27)
Profit before taxation	238	315
Taxation	(110)	(140)
Profit for the year	128	175

Statements of financial position as at 30 June

	2018 £m	2019 £m
ASSETS		
Non-current assets		
Property, plant and equipment (at carrying amount)		
Land and buildings	1,500	1,900
Plant and machinery	810	740
	2,310	2,640

	2018 £m	2019 £m
Current assets		
Inventories	275	450
Trade receivables	100	250
Bank	–	118
	375	818
Total assets	2,685	3,458
EQUITY AND LIABILITIES		
Equity		
Share capital (fully paid £1 shares)	1,400	1,600
Share premium account	200	300
Retained earnings	828	958
	2,428	2,858
Non-current liabilities		
Borrowings – 9% loan notes (repayable 2025)	–	300
Current liabilities		
Borrowings (all bank overdraft)	32	–
Trade payables	170	230
Taxation	55	70
	257	300
Total equity and liabilities	2,685	3,458

There were no disposals of non-current assets in either year. Dividends were paid in 2018 and 2019 of £40 million and £45 million, respectively.

Required:
Prepare a statement of cash flows for Nailsea plc for the year ended 30 June 2019.

Advanced-level exercises

6.6   The following financial statements for Blackstone plc are a slightly simplified set of published accounts. Blackstone plc is an engineering business that developed a new range of products in 2015. These products now account for 60 per cent of its sales revenue.

Income statement for the years ended 31 March

	Note	2018 £m	2019 £m
Revenue		7,003	11,205
Cost of sales		(3,748)	(5,809)
Gross profit		3,255	5,396
Operating expenses		(2,205)	(3,087)
Operating profit		1,050	2,309
Interest payable	1	(216)	(456)
Profit before taxation		834	1,853
Taxation		(210)	(390)
Profit for the year		624	1,463

Statements of financial position as at 31 March

	Notes	2018 £m	2019 £m
ASSETS			
Non-current assets			
Property, plant and equipment	2	4,300	7,535
Intangible assets	3	–	700
		4,300	8,235
Current assets			
Inventories		1,209	2,410
Trade receivables		641	1,173
Cash at bank		123	–
		1,973	3,583
Total assets		6,273	11,818
EQUITY AND LIABILITIES			
Equity			
Share capital		1,800	1,800
Share premium		600	600
Capital reserves		352	352
Retained earnings		685	1,748
		3,437	4,500
Non-current liabilities			
Borrowings – bank loan (repayable 2024)		1,800	3,800
Current liabilities			
Trade payables		931	1,507
Taxation		105	195
Borrowings (all bank overdraft)		–	1,816
		1,036	3,518
Total equity and liabilities		6,273	11,818

Notes:

1 The expense and the cash outflow for interest payable are equal for each year.

2 The movements in property, plant and equipment during the year are:

	Land and buildings £m	Plant and machinery £m	Fixtures and fittings £m	Total £m
Cost				
At 1 April 2018	4,500	3,850	2,120	10,470
Additions	–	2,970	1,608	4,578
Disposals	–	(365)	(216)	(581)
At 31 March 2019	4,500	6,455	3,512	14,467
Depreciation				
At 1 April 2018	1,275	3,080	1,815	6,170
Charge for year	225	745	281	1,251
Disposals	–	(305)	(184)	(489)
At 31 March 2019	1,500	3,520	1,912	6,932
Carrying amount at 31 March 2019	3,000	2,935	1,600	7,535

3 Intangible assets represent the amounts paid for the goodwill of another engineering business acquired during the year.

4 Proceeds from the sale of non-current assets in the year ended 31 March 2019 amounted to £54 million.

5 £300 million was paid in dividends on ordinary shares in 2018, and £400 million in 2019.

Required:

Prepare a statement of cash flows for Blackstone plc for the year ended 31 March 2019. (*Hint:* A loss (deficit) on disposal of non-current assets is simply an additional amount of depreciation and should be dealt with as such in preparing the statement of cash flows.)

6.7 Simplified financial statements for York plc are:

Income statement for the year ended 30 September 2019

	£m
Revenue	290.0
Cost of sales	(215.0)
Gross profit	75.0
Operating expenses (Note 1)	(62.0)
Operating profit	13.0
Interest payable (Note 2)	(3.0)
Profit before taxation	10.0
Taxation	(2.6)
Profit for the year	7.4

Statement of financial position as at 30 September

	2018 £m	2019 £m
ASSETS		
Non-current assets (Note 4)	80.0	85.0
Current assets		
Inventories and trade receivables	119.8	122.1
Cash at bank	9.2	16.6
	129.0	138.7
Total assets	209.0	223.7
EQUITY AND LIABILITIES		
Equity		
Share capital	35.0	40.0
Share premium account	30.0	30.0
Reserves	31.0	34.9
	96.0	104.9
Non-current liabilities		
Borrowings	32.0	35.0
Current liabilities		
Trade payables	80.0	82.5
Taxation	1.0	1.3
	81.0	83.8
Total equity and liabilities	209.0	223.7

Notes:

1 Operating expenses include depreciation of £13 million and a surplus of £3.2 million on the sale of non-current assets.
2 The expense and the cash outflow for interest payable are equal.
3 A dividend of £3.5 million was paid during 2019.
4 Non-current asset costs and depreciation:

	Cost	Accumulated depreciation	Carrying amount
	£m	£m	£m
At 1 October 2018	120.0	40.0	80.0
Disposals	(10.0)	(8.0)	(2.0)
Additions	20.0	–	20.0
Depreciation	–	13.0	(13.0)
At 30 September 2019	130.0	45.0	85.0

Required:

Prepare a statement of cash flows for York plc for the year ended 30 September 2019.

CHAPTER 7

Analysing and interpreting financial statements

Introduction

In this chapter, we consider the analysis and interpretation of the financial statements discussed in Chapters 2, 3 and 6. We shall see how the use of financial (or accounting) ratios can help to assess the financial performance and position of a business. We shall also take a look at the problems encountered when applying financial ratios.

Financial ratios can be used to examine various aspects of financial health and are widely employed by external users, such as shareholders and lenders, and by managers. They can be very helpful to managers in a wide variety of decision areas, such as profit planning, pricing, working capital management and financial structure.

Learning outcomes

When you have completed this chapter, you should be able to:

- identify the major categories of ratios that can be used for analysing financial statements;

- calculate key ratios for assessing the financial performance and position of a business and explain their significance;

- discuss the use of ratios in helping to predict financial failure; and

- discuss the limitations of ratios as a tool of financial analysis.

Financial ratios

Financial ratios provide a quick and relatively easy means of assessing the financial health of a business. A ratio simply relates one figure appearing in the financial statements to another figure appearing there (for example operating profit in relation to sales revenue) or, perhaps, to some non-financial resource of the business (for example, operating profit per employee).

Ratios can be very helpful when comparing the financial health of different businesses. Differences may exist between businesses in the scale of operations. As a result, a direct comparison of, say, the operating profit generated by each business may be misleading. By expressing operating profit in relation to some other measure (for example, capital employed), the problem of scale is eliminated. This means that a business with an operating profit of £10,000 and capital employed of £100,000 can be compared with a much larger business with an operating profit of £80,000 and capital employed of £1,000,000 by the use of a simple ratio. The operating profit to capital employed ratio for the smaller business is 10 per cent (that is, (10,000/100,000) × 100%) and the same ratio for the larger business is 8 per cent (that is, (80,000/1,000,000) × 100%). These ratios can be directly compared, whereas a comparison of the absolute operating profit figures might be much less meaningful. The need to eliminate differences in scale through the use of ratios can also apply when comparing the performance of the same business from one time period to another.

By calculating a small number of ratios, it is often possible to build up a revealing picture of the position and performance of a business. It is not surprising, therefore, that ratios are widely used by those who have an interest in businesses and business performance. Ratios are not difficult to calculate but they can be difficult to interpret.

Ratios tend to identify which questions to ask, rather than provide the answers. They help to highlight the financial strengths and weaknesses of a business, but cannot explain why those strengths or weaknesses exist or why certain changes have occurred. They provide a starting point for further analysis. Only a detailed investigation will reveal the underlying reasons.

Ratios can be expressed in various forms, for example as a percentage or as a proportion. The way that a particular ratio is presented will depend on the needs of those who will use the information. Although it is possible to calculate a large number of ratios, only a few, based on key relationships, tend to be helpful to a particular user. Many ratios that could be calculated from the financial statements (for example, rent payable in relation to current assets) may not be considered because there is not usually any clear or meaningful relationship between the two items.

There is no generally accepted list of ratios that can be applied to the financial statements, nor is there a standard method of calculating many ratios. Variations in both the choice of ratios and their calculation will be found in practice. It is important, therefore, to be consistent in the way in which ratios are calculated for comparison purposes. The ratios that we shall discuss are very popular – presumably because they are seen as useful for decision-making purposes.

Financial ratio classifications

Ratios tend to be grouped into categories, with each category relating to a particular aspect of financial performance or position. The following broad categories are those that are usually found in practice. There are five of them:

- *Profitability*. Businesses generally exist with the primary purpose of creating wealth for their owners. Profitability ratios provide some indication of the degree of success in achieving this. These ratios express the profit made in relation to other key figures in the financial statements or to some business resource.
- *Efficiency*. Ratios may be used to measure the efficiency with which particular resources, such as inventories or employees, have been used within the business. These ratios are also referred to as *activity* ratios.
- *Liquidity*. It is vital to the survival of a business that there are sufficient liquid resources available to meet maturing obligations (that is, amounts owing that must be paid in the near future). Liquidity ratios examine the relationship between liquid resources, or cash generated, and amounts due for payment in the near future.
- *Financial gearing*. This is the relationship between the contribution to financing a business made by the owners and the contribution made by others, in the form of loans. This relationship is important because the level of gearing has an important effect on the level of risk associated with a business. Gearing ratios help to reveal the extent to which loan finance is employed and the consequent effect on the level of risk borne by a business.
- *Investment*. Certain ratios are concerned with assessing the returns and performance of shares in a particular business from the perspective of shareholders who are not involved with the management of the business.

These five key aspects of financial health that ratios seek to examine are summarised in Figure 7.1.

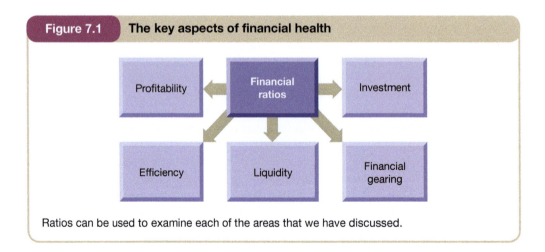

Figure 7.1	The key aspects of financial health

Ratios can be used to examine each of the areas that we have discussed.

The analyst must be clear *who* the target users are and *why* they need the information. Different users of financial information are likely to have different information needs. This will, in turn, determine the ratios that they find useful. Shareholders, for example, are likely to be interested in their returns in relation to the level of risk associated with their investment. Profitability, investment and gearing ratios should, therefore, be of particular interest. Long-term lenders are likely to be concerned with the long-term viability of the business and, to assess this, profitability and gearing ratios should be of interest. Short-term lenders, such as suppliers of goods and services on credit, are likely to be interested in the ability of the business to repay the amounts owing in the short term. Liquidity ratios should, therefore, be of particular interest.

The need for comparison

Merely calculating a ratio will not tell us very much about the position or performance of a business. For example, if a ratio revealed that a retail business was generating £100 in sales revenue per square metre of floor space, it would not be possible to deduce from this information alone whether this particular level of performance was good, bad or indifferent. It is only when we compare this ratio with some 'benchmark' that the information can be interpreted and evaluated.

Activity 7.1

Can you think of any bases that could be used to compare a ratio that you have calculated from the financial statements of your business for a particular period? (*Hint*: There are three main possibilities.)

You may have thought of the following bases:

- past periods for the same business;
- similar businesses for the same or past periods; and/or
- planned performance for the business.

Let us now take a closer look at each of these in turn.

Past periods

By comparing the ratio that we have calculated with the same ratio, but for a previous period, it is possible to detect whether there has been an improvement or deterioration in performance. Indeed, it is often useful to track particular ratios over time (say, five or 10 years) to see whether it is possible to detect trends. The comparison of ratios from different periods brings certain problems, however. In particular, there is always the possibility that trading conditions were quite different in the periods being compared. There is the further problem that, when comparing the performance of a single business over time, operating inefficiencies may not be clearly exposed. For example, the fact that sales revenue per employee has risen by 10 per cent over the previous period may at first sight appear to be satisfactory. This may not be the case, however, if similar businesses have shown an improvement of 50 per cent for the same period or had much better sales revenue per employee ratios to start with. Finally, there is the problem that inflation may have distorted the figures on which the ratios are based. Inflation can lead to an overstatement of profit and an understatement of asset values, as will be discussed later in the chapter.

Similar businesses

In a competitive environment, a business must consider its performance in relation to that of other businesses operating in the same industry. Survival may depend on its ability to achieve comparable levels of performance. A useful basis for comparing a particular ratio, therefore, is the ratio achieved by similar businesses during the same period. This basis is not, however, without its problems. Competitors may have different year-ends and so trading conditions may not be identical. They may also have different accounting policies, which can have a significant effect on reported profits and asset values (for example, different methods of calculating depreciation or valuing inventories). Finally, it may be difficult to obtain the financial statements of competitor businesses. Sole proprietorships and partnerships, for example, are not obliged to make their financial statements available to the public. In the case of limited companies, there is a legal obligation to do so. However, a diversified business may not provide a breakdown of activities that is sufficiently detailed to enable comparisons with other businesses. This is despite the requirement for diversified businesses to report certain information on their different segments, that we discussed in Chapter 5.

Planned performance

Planned performance often provides the most valuable benchmark against which managers may assess their own business. Ratios based on the actual results may be compared with targets that management developed before the start of the period under review. This comparison can be a useful way of assessing the level of achievement attained. However, planned performance must be based on realistic assumptions if it is to be worthwhile for comparison purposes.

Planned, or target, ratios may be prepared for each aspect of the business's activities. When developing these ratios, account will normally be taken of past performance and the performance of other businesses. This does not mean, however, that the business should seek to achieve either of these levels of performance. Neither may provide an appropriate target.

We should bear in mind that those outside the business do not normally have access to the business's plans. For such people, past performance and the performances of other, similar, businesses may provide the only practical benchmarks.

The three most used bases of comparison for financial ratios are shown in Figure 7.2.

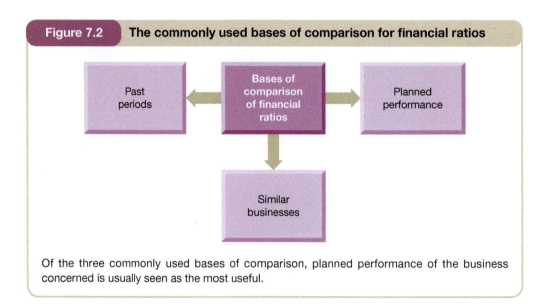

Figure 7.2 **The commonly used bases of comparison for financial ratios**

Of the three commonly used bases of comparison, planned performance of the business concerned is usually seen as the most useful.

Calculating the ratios

Probably the best way to explain financial ratios is through an example. Example 7.1 provides a set of financial statements from which we can calculate important ratios.

Example 7.1

The following financial statements relate to Alexis plc, which operates a wholesale carpet business:

Statements of financial position (balance sheets) as at 31 March

	2018 £m	2019 £m
ASSETS		
Non-current assets		
Property, plant and equipment (at cost less depreciation)		
Land and buildings	381	427
Fixtures and fittings	129	160
	510	587
Current assets		
Inventories	300	406
Trade receivables	240	273
Cash at bank	4	–
	544	679
Total assets	1,054	1,266
EQUITY AND LIABILITIES		
Equity		
£0.50 ordinary shares (Note 1)	300	300
Retained earnings	263	234
	563	534
Non-current liabilities		
Borrowings – 9% loan notes (secured)	200	300
Current liabilities		
Trade payables	261	354
Taxation	30	2
Short-term borrowings (all bank overdraft)	–	76
	291	432
Total equity and liabilities	1,054	1,266

Income statements for the year ended 31 March

	2018 £m	2019 £m
Revenue (Note 2)	2,240	2,681
Cost of sales (Note 3)	(1,745)	(2,272)
Gross profit	495	409
Operating expenses	(252)	(362)
Operating profit	243	47
Interest payable	(18)	(32)
Profit before taxation	225	15
Taxation	(60)	(4)
Profit for the year	165	11

→

Example 7.1 *continued*

Statement of cash flows for the year ended 31 March

	2018 £m	2019 £m
Cash flows from operating activities		
Profit, after interest, before taxation	225	15
Adjustments for:		
Depreciation	26	33
Interest expense	18	32
	269	80
Increase in inventories	(59)	(106)
Increase in trade receivables	(17)	(33)
Increase in trade payables	58	93
Cash generated from operations	251	34
Interest paid	(18)	(32)
Taxation paid	(63)	(32)
Dividend paid	(40)	(40)
Net cash from/(used in) operating activities	130	(70)
Cash flows from investing activities		
Payments to acquire property, plant and equipment	(77)	(110)
Net cash used in investing activities	(77)	(110)
Cash flows from financing activities		
Issue of loan notes	–	100
Net cash from financing activities	–	100
Net increase in cash and cash equivalents	53	(80)
Cash and cash equivalents at start of year		
Cash/(overdraft)	(49)	4
Cash and cash equivalents at end of year		
Cash/(overdraft)	4	(76)

Notes:
1. The market value of the shares of the business at the end of the reporting period was £2.50 for 2018 and £1.50 for 2019.
2. All sales and purchases are made on credit.
3. The cost of sales figure can be analysed as follows:

	2018 £m	2019 £m
Opening inventories	241	300
Purchases (Note 2)	1,804	2,378
	2,045	2,678
Closing inventories	(300)	(406)
Cost of sales	1,745	2,272

4. At 31 March 2017, the trade receivables stood at £223 million and the trade payables at £183 million.
5. A dividend of £40 million had been paid to the shareholders in respect of each of the years.
6. The business employed 13,995 staff at 31 March 2018 and 18,623 at 31 March 2019.
7. The business expanded its capacity during the year to 31 March 2019 by setting up a new warehouse and distribution centre.
8. At 1 April 2017, the total of equity stood at £438 million and the total of equity and non-current liabilities stood at £638 million.

A brief overview

Before we start our detailed look at the ratios for Alexis plc (see Example 7.1), it is helpful to take a quick look, without calculating any ratios, at what information is obvious from the financial statements. This will usually pick up some issues that ratios may not be able to identify. It may also highlight some points that could help us in our interpretation of the ratios. Starting at the top of the statement of financial position, the following points can be noted:

- *Expansion of non-current assets.* These have increased by about 15 per cent (from £510 million to £587 million). Note 7 mentions a new warehouse and distribution centre, which may account for much of the additional investment in non-current assets. We are not told when this new facility was established, but it is quite possible that it was well into the year. This could mean that not much benefit was reflected in terms of additional sales revenue or cost saving during 2019. Sales revenue, in fact, expanded by about 20 per cent (from £2,240 million to £2,681 million); this is greater than the expansion in non-current assets.
- *Major expansion in the elements of working capital.* Inventories increased by about 35 per cent, trade receivables by about 14 per cent and trade payables by about 36 per cent between 2018 and 2019. These are major increases, particularly in inventories and payables (which are linked because the inventories are all bought on credit – see Note 2).
- *Reduction in the cash balance.* The cash balance fell from £4 million (in funds) to a £76 million overdraft between 2018 and 2019. The bank may be putting the business under pressure to reverse this, which could create difficulties.
- *Apparent debt capacity.* Comparing the non-current assets with the long-term borrowings implies that the business may well be able to offer security on further borrowing. This is because potential lenders usually look at the value of assets that can be offered as security when assessing loan requests. Lenders seem particularly attracted to land and buildings as security. For example, at 31 March 2019, non-current assets had a carrying amount (the value at which they appeared in the statement of financial position) of £587 million, but long-term borrowing was only £300 million (though there was also an overdraft of £76 million). Carrying amounts are not normally, of course, market values. On the other hand, land and buildings tend to have a market value higher than their value as shown on the statement of financial position due to a general tendency to inflation in property values.
- *Lower operating profit.* Although sales revenue expanded by 20 per cent between 2018 and 2019, both cost of sales and operating expenses rose by a greater percentage, leaving both gross profit and, particularly, operating profit massively reduced. The level of staffing, which increased by about 33 per cent (from 13,995 to 18,623 employees – see Note 6), may have greatly affected the operating expenses. (Without knowing when the additional employees were recruited during 2019, we cannot be sure of the effect on operating expenses.) Increasing staffing by 33 per cent must put an enormous strain on management, at least in the short term. It is not surprising, therefore, that the year to 31 March 2019 was not successful for the business – not, at least, in profit terms.

Having had a quick look at what is fairly obvious, without calculating any financial ratios, we shall now go on to calculate and interpret those relating to profitability, efficiency, liquidity, gearing and investment.

Profitability

The following ratios may be used to evaluate the profitability of the business:

- return on ordinary shareholders' funds;
- return on capital employed;
- operating profit margin; and
- gross profit margin.

We shall now look at each of these in turn.

Return on ordinary shareholders' funds

The **return on ordinary shareholders' funds ratio (ROSF)** compares the amount of profit for the period available to owners with their average investment in the business during that same period. The ratio (which is normally expressed in percentage terms) is as follows:

$$\text{ROSF} = \frac{\text{Profit for the year (less any preference dividend)}}{\text{Ordinary share capital} + \text{Reserves}} \times 100$$

The profit for the year (less any preference dividend) is used in calculating the ratio, because this figure represents the amount of profit that is attributable to the owners.

In the case of Alexis plc, the ratio for the year ended 31 March 2018 is:

$$\text{ROSF} = \frac{165}{(438 + 563)/2} \times 100 = 33.0\%$$

Note that, when calculating the ROSF, the average of the figures for ordinary shareholders' funds as at the beginning and at the end of the year has been used. This is because an average figure is normally more representative. The amount of shareholders' funds was not constant throughout the year, yet we want to compare it with the profit earned during the whole period. We know, from Note 8, that the amount of shareholders' funds at 1 April 2017 was £438 million. By a year later, however, it had risen to £563 million, according to the statement of financial position as at 31 March 2018.

The easiest approach to calculating the average amount of shareholders' funds is to take a simple average based on the opening and closing figures for the year. This is often the only information available, as is the case with Example 7.1. Averaging is normally appropriate for all ratios that combine a figure for a period (such as profit for the year) with one taken at a point in time (such as shareholders' funds).

Where not even the beginning-of-year figure is available, it will be necessary to rely on just the year-end figure. This is not ideal but, when this approach is consistently applied, it can still produce useful ratios.

Activity 7.2

Calculate the ROSF for Alexis plc for the year ended 31 March 2019.

The ratio for 2019 is:

$$\text{ROSF} = \frac{11}{(563 + 534)/2} \times 100 = 2.0\%$$

Broadly, businesses seek to generate as high a value as possible for this ratio. This is provided that it is not achieved at the expense of jeopardising future returns by, for example, taking on more risky activities. In view of this, the 2019 ratio is very poor by any standards; a bank deposit account will normally yield a better return. We need to find out why things went so badly wrong in the year to 31 March 2019. As we look at other ratios, we should find some clues.

Return on capital employed

The **return on capital employed ratio (ROCE)** is a fundamental measure of business performance. This ratio expresses the relationship between the operating profit generated during a period and the average long-term capital invested in the business.

The ratio is expressed in percentage terms and is as follows:

$$ROCE = \frac{\text{Operating profit}}{\text{Share capital} + \text{Reserves} + \text{Non-current liabilities}} \times 100$$

Note, in this case, that the profit figure used is the operating profit (that is, the profit *before* interest and taxation), because the ratio attempts to measure the returns to all suppliers of long-term finance before any deductions for interest payable on borrowings, or payments of dividends to shareholders, are made.

For the year to 31 March 2018, the ratio for Alexis plc is:

$$ROCE = \frac{243}{(638 + 763)/2} \times 100 = 34.7\%$$

(The capital employed figure, which is the total equity plus non-current liabilities, at 1 April 2017 is given in Note 8.)

ROCE is considered by many to be a primary measure of profitability. It compares inputs (capital invested) with outputs (operating profit) so as to reveal the effectiveness with which funds have been deployed. Once again, an average figure for capital employed should be used where the information is available.

Activity 7.3

Calculate the ROCE for Alexis plc for the year ended 31 March 2019.

The ratio for 2019 is:

$$ROCE = \frac{47}{(763 + 834)/2} \times 100 = 5.9\%$$

This ratio tells much the same story as ROSF; namely a poor performance, with the return on the assets being less than the rate that the business pays for most of its borrowed funds (that is, 9 per cent for the loan notes).

Real World 7.1 shows how financial ratios are used by businesses as a basis for setting profitability targets.

Real World 7.1

Targeting profitability

The ROCE ratio is widely used by businesses when establishing targets for profitability. These targets are sometimes made public and here are some examples:

- Barratt Developments plc, the builder, has a target ROCE on all new land acquisitions of 25 per cent.
- Vattenfall, a Swedish power company, has a target ROCE of 8 per cent.
- UDG Healthcare plc, a healthcare services provider, has a target ROCE of 15 per cent.
- Bovis Homes plc, the housebuilder, has a medium-term ROCE of 25 per cent.
- Tyman plc, a supplier of building products, has a medium-term target ROCE of 15 per cent.

Real World 7.1 *continued*

- Ramirent plc, the rental equipment business, has a target ROCE of 16 per cent to be achieved by the end of 2020.
- Countryside Properties plc, the housebuilders, has a target ROCE of 28 per cent for 2018.
- Smurfit Kappa Group plc, the packaging manufacturer, has a target ROCE of 17 per cent.

Sources: Information taken from Barratt Developments plc, Key performance indicators, www.barrattdevelopments.com, accessed 16 November 2018; Company Announcements: Vattenfall, markets.ft.com, 20 November 2017; Company Announcements: UDG Healthcare plc, markets.ft.com, 3 July 2018; Vincent, M. (2018) Opening quote: Royal Mail – vote of little confidence, ft.com, 15 November; Tyman plc, Preliminary results for the year ended 31 December 2017, www.tymanplc.com; Ramirent pl,c Interim Report Q3 January–September 2018; Countryside Properties plc, Annual Report 2017, p.7, https://assets.ctfassets.net; and Smurfit Kappa plc, Half year report 2018, www.businesswire.com.

Real World 7.2 provides some indication of the levels of ROCE achieved by businesses in different European countries.

Real World 7.2

Comparing profitability

Average ROCE ratios for non-financial businesses in different European countries for the five-year period ending in 2017 are shown in Figure 7.3.

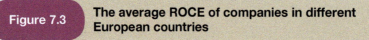

Figure 7.3 **The average ROCE of companies in different European countries**

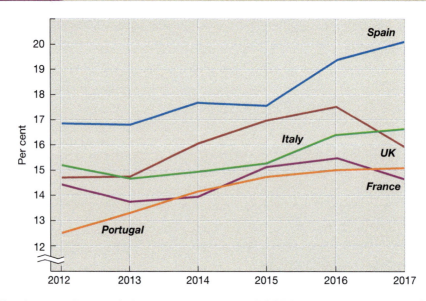

The chart reveals a steady improvement in average ROCE for businesses in three of the five different countries over the period. For Italy and France, there has also been an improvement but it has been less steady over time.

Source: Figure taken from Gross return on capital employed, before taxes, of non-financial corporations, Eurostat database, https://ec.europa.eu

Operating profit margin

The **operating profit margin ratio** relates the operating profit for the period to the sales revenue. The ratio is expressed as follows:

$$\text{Operating profit margin} = \frac{\text{Operating profit}}{\text{Sales revenue}} \times 100$$

Operating profit (that is, profit before interest and taxation) is used in this ratio as it represents the profit from trading operations before interest payable is taken into account. It is normally the most appropriate measure of operational performance, when making comparisons. This is because differences arising from the way in which the business is financed will not influence the measure.

For the year ended 31 March 2018, Alexis plc's operating profit margin ratio is:

$$\text{Operating profit margin} = \frac{243}{2,240} \times 100 = 10.8\%$$

This ratio compares one output of the business (operating profit) with another output (sales revenue). The ratio can vary considerably between types of business. Supermarkets, for example, tend to operate on low prices and, therefore, low operating profit margins. This is done in an attempt to stimulate sales and thereby increase the total amount of operating profit generated. Jewellers, on the other hand, tend to have high operating profit margins but have much lower levels of sales volume. Factors such as the degree of competition, the type of customer, the economic climate and industry characteristics (such as the level of risk) will influence the operating profit margin of a business. This point is picked up again later in the chapter.

Activity 7.4

Calculate the operating profit margin for Alexis plc for the year ended 31 March 2019.

The ratio for 2019 is:

$$\text{Operating profit margin} = \frac{47}{2,681} \times 100 = 1.8\%$$

Once again, this indicates a very weak performance compared with that of 2018. In 2018, for every £1 of sales revenue an average of 10.8p (that is, 10.8 per cent) was left as operating profit, after paying the cost of the carpets sold and other expenses of operating the business. By 2019, however, this had fallen to only 1.8p for every £1. The poor ROSF and ROCE ratios appear to have been partially, if not wholly, due to a high level of other expenses relative to sales revenue. The next ratio should provide us with a clue as to how the sharp decline in this ratio occurred.

Before looking at this ratio, however, let us consider **Real World 7.3**. This sets out the target operating profit margins for some well-known car manufacturers.

Real World 7.3

Profit driven

- BMW has a target operating profit margin of between 8 and 10 per cent.
- Volvo has a target operating profit margin of 10 per cent over the business cycle.
- Nissan has a target operating profit margin of 8 per cent.
- Volkswagen has a target operating profit margin of between 6.5 and 7.5 per cent.
- Mercedes-Benz (Car division) has a target profit margin of 8–10 per cent.
- Renault has set a target operating profit margin of 7 per cent by 2022.
- Ford has a long-term target of achieving an operating profit margin target of over 8 per cent.
- Audi has a target operating profit margin of 8–10 per cent.

We can see that, with the exception of Volkswagen and Renault, target operating profit margins fall within the 8 to 10 per cent range.

Sources: BMW Motorcycle Magazine (2018) BMW Earnings and profits hit record high in 2017, bmwmcmag.com, 12 March; Volvo Group website, www.volvogroup.com/investors, accessed 16 November 2018; Banjo, S. (2017) Nissan's moving targets, *Bloomberg*, 8 November, www.bloomberg.com; France24 (2018) Volkswagen profit nearly doubles in 2017, www.france24.com, 23 February; Fitch Ratings (2018) Peer Comparisons: European Auto manufacturers – Fitch ratings, www.fitchratings.com, accessed 16 November 2018; Wadhwa, N. (2018) Daimler targets 9% return on sales across global markets, *Autocar Professional*, 5 April, www.autocarpro.in; Frost, L. and Guillaume, G. (2017) Renault pricing weakness overshadows record first half, europe.autonews.com, 28 July; Colias, M. (2018) Ford profit dented by swings in commodity prices, 24 January; Holloway, H. (2018) Audi records 68% leap in profit as Dieselgate effect fades, www.autocar.uk, 15 March.

Gross profit margin

The **gross profit margin ratio** relates the gross profit of the business to the sales revenue generated for the same period. Gross profit represents the difference between sales revenue and the cost of sales. The ratio is therefore a measure of profitability in buying (or producing) and selling goods or services before any other expenses are taken into account. As cost of sales represents a major expense for many businesses, a change in this ratio can have a significant effect on the 'bottom line' (that is, the profit for the year). The gross profit margin ratio is calculated as follows:

$$\text{Gross profit margin} = \frac{\text{Gross profit}}{\text{Sales revenue}} \times 100$$

For the year ended 31 March 2018, the ratio for Alexis plc is:

$$\text{Gross profit margin} = \frac{495}{2,240} \times 100 = 22.1\%$$

Activity 7.5

Calculate the gross profit margin for Alexis plc for the year ended 31 March 2019.

The ratio for 2019 is:

$$\text{Gross profit margin} = \frac{409}{2,681} \times 100 = 15.3\%$$

The decline in this ratio means that gross profit was lower *relative* to sales revenue in 2019 than it had been in 2018. Bearing in mind that:

> **Gross profit = Sales revenue − Cost of sales (or cost of goods sold)**

this means that cost of sales was higher *relative* to sales revenue in 2019 than in 2018. This could mean that sales prices were lower and/or that the purchase price of carpets had increased. It is possible that both sales prices and purchase prices had reduced, but the former at a greater rate than the latter. Similarly, they may both have increased, but with sales prices having increased at a lesser rate than purchase prices.

Clearly, part of the decline in the operating profit margin ratio is linked to the dramatic decline in the gross profit margin ratio. Whereas, after paying for the carpets sold, for each £1 of sales revenue, 22.1p was left to cover other operating expenses in 2018, this was only 15.3p in 2019.

The profitability ratios for the business over the two years can be set out as follows:

	2018	2019
	%	%
ROSF	33.0	2.0
ROCE	34.7	5.9
Operating profit margin	10.8	1.8
Gross profit margin	22.1	15.3

Activity 7.6

What do you deduce from a comparison of the declines in the operating profit and gross profit margin ratios?

We can see that the difference in the operating profit margin was 9 per cent (that is, 10.8 per cent to 1.8 per cent), whereas that of the gross profit margin was only 6.8 per cent (that is, from 22.1 per cent to 15.3 per cent). This can only mean that operating expenses were greater compared with sales revenue in 2019 than they had been in 2018. The decline in both ROSF and ROCE was caused partly, therefore, by the business incurring higher inventories purchasing costs relative to sales revenue and partly through higher operating expenses compared with sales revenue. We need to compare each of these ratios with their planned levels, however, before we can usefully assess the business's success.

An investigation is needed to discover what caused the increases in both cost of sales and operating expenses, relative to sales revenue, from 2018 to 2019. This will involve checking on what has happened with sales and inventories prices over the two years. Similarly, it will involve looking at each of the individual areas that make up operating expenses to discover which ones were responsible for the increase, relative to sales revenue. Here, further ratios, for example, staff expenses (wages and salaries) to sales revenue, could be calculated in an attempt to isolate the cause of the change from 2018 to 2019. As mentioned earlier, the increase in staffing may well account for most of the increase in operating expenses.

Real World 7.4 discusses how some operating costs can be controlled by unusual means.

Real World 7.4

Having a fly in

McKinsey and Company, the international management consultancy, reports that one of its clients, an airline, saves on operating expenses in an unusual way. Some of the planes operated by the airline have seats that can go flat to make it easier for passengers to sleep on overnight flights. It was the policy of the airline to leave the cabin lights off as late in the morning as possible to avoid passengers demand for – and cost of – breakfast.

Source: Information contained in Dichter, A., Sorensen, A and Saxon, S. (2017) *Buying and Flying: Next Generation Airline Procurement,* McKinsey and Company, www.mckinsey.com, April.

The profitability ratios discussed above are summarised in Figure 7.4.

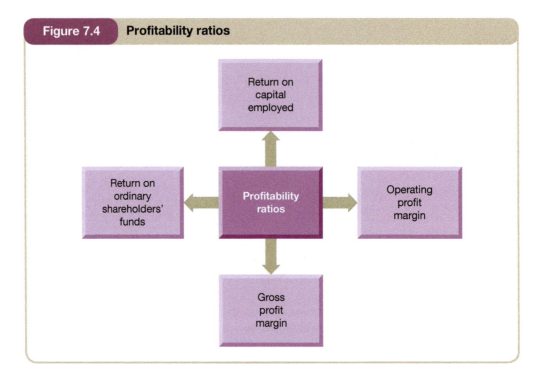

Figure 7.4   **Profitability ratios**

Efficiency

Efficiency ratios are used to try to assess how successfully the various resources of the business are managed. The following ratios focus on some of the more important aspects of resource management:

- average inventories turnover period;
- average settlement period for trade receivables;
- average settlement period for trade payables;
- sales revenue to capital employed; and
- sales revenue per employee.

We shall now look at each of these in turn.

Average inventories turnover period

Inventories often represent a significant investment for a business. For some types of business (for example, manufacturers and certain retailers), inventories may account for a substantial proportion of the total assets held (see Real World 16.1 on page 664). The **average inventories turnover period ratio** measures the average period for which inventories are being held. The ratio is calculated as follows:

$$\text{Average inventories turnover period} = \frac{\text{Average inventories held}}{\text{Cost of sales}} \times 365$$

The average inventories for the period can be calculated as a simple average of the opening and closing inventories levels for the year. In the case of a highly seasonal business, however, where inventories levels vary considerably over the year, a monthly average would be more appropriate. Such information may not, however, be available. This point concerning monthly averaging is equally relevant to any asset or claim that varies over the reporting period and would include trade receivables and trade payables.

In the case of Alexis plc, the inventories turnover period for the year ended 31 March 2018 is:

$$\text{Average inventories turnover period} = \frac{(241 + 300)/2}{1,745} \times 365 = 56.6 \text{ days}$$

(The opening inventories figure was taken from Note 3 to the financial statements.)

This means that, on average, the inventories held are being 'turned over' every 56.6 days. So, a carpet bought by the business on a particular day would, on average, have been sold about eight weeks later. A business will normally prefer a short inventories turnover period to a long one, because holding inventories has costs, for example the opportunity cost of the funds tied up. When judging the amount of inventories to carry, the business must consider such things as the likely demand for them, the possibility of supply shortages, the likelihood of price rises, the amount of storage space available, their perishability and susceptibility to obsolescence.

This ratio is sometimes expressed in terms of weeks or months rather than days: multiplying by 52 or 12, rather than 365, will achieve this.

Activity 7.7

Calculate the average inventories turnover period for Alexis plc for the year ended 31 March 2019.

The ratio for 2019 is:

$$\text{Average inventories turnover period} = \frac{(300 + 406)/2}{2,272} \times 365 = 56.7 \text{ days}$$

The inventories turnover period is virtually the same in both years.

Average settlement period for trade receivables

Selling on credit is the norm for most businesses, except for retailers, and so trade receivables tend to be a necessary evil. A business will naturally be concerned with the amount of funds tied up in trade receivables and try to keep this to a minimum. The speed of payment can have a significant effect on the business's cash flow. The **average settlement period for trade receivables ratio** indicates how long, on average, credit customers take to pay the amounts that they owe to the business. The ratio is as follows:

$$\text{Average settlement period for trade receivables} = \frac{\text{Average trade receivables}}{\text{Credit sales revenue}} \times 365$$

A business will normally prefer a shorter average settlement period to a longer one as, once again, funds are being tied up that may be used for more profitable purposes. Although this ratio can be useful, it is important to remember that it produces an *average* figure for the number of days for which debts are outstanding. This average may be badly distorted by, for example, a few large customers who are very slow or very fast payers.

Since all sales made by Alexis plc are on credit, the average settlement period for trade receivables for the year ended 31 March 2018 is:

$$\text{Average settlement period for trade receivables} = \frac{(223 + 240)/2}{2,240} \times 365 = 37.7 \text{ days}$$

(The opening trade receivables figure was taken from Note 4 to the financial statements.)

Activity 7.8

Calculate the average settlement period for Alexis plc's trade receivables for the year ended 31 March 2019.

The ratio for 2019 is:

$$\text{Average settlement period for trade receivables} = \frac{(240 + 273)/2}{2,681} \times 365 = 34.9 \text{ days}$$

On the face of it, this reduction in the settlement period is welcome. It means that less cash was tied up in trade receivables for each £1 of sales revenue in 2019 than in 2018. Only if the reduction were achieved at the expense of customer goodwill or through high out-of-pocket cost might its desirability be questioned. For example, the reduction may have been due to chasing customers too vigorously or to giving large discounts to customers for prompt payment.

Average settlement period for trade payables

The **average settlement period for trade payables ratio** measures how long, on average, the business takes to pay those who have supplied goods and services on credit. The ratio is calculated as follows:

$$\text{Average settlement period for trade payables} = \frac{\text{Average trade payables}}{\text{Credit purchases}} \times 365$$

This ratio provides an average figure which, like the average settlement period for trade receivables ratio, can be distorted by the payment period for one or two large suppliers.

As trade payables provide a free source of finance for the business, it is perhaps not surprising that some businesses attempt to increase their average settlement period for trade payables. Such a policy can be taken too far, however, and can result in a loss of goodwill of suppliers.

For the year ended 31 March 2018, Alexis plc's average settlement period for trade payables is:

$$\text{Average settlement period for trade payables} = \frac{(183 + 261)/2}{1,804} \times 365 = 44.9 \text{ days}$$

(The opening trade payables figure was taken from Note 4 to the financial statements and the purchases figure from Note 3.)

Activity 7.9

Calculate the average settlement period for trade payables for Alexis plc for the year ended 31 March 2019.

The ratio for 2019 is:

$$\text{Average settlement period for trade payables} = \frac{(261 + 354)/2}{2,378} \times 365 = 47.2 \text{ days}$$

There was an increase between 2018 and 2019 in the average length of time that elapsed between buying goods and services and paying for them. On the face of it, this is beneficial because the business is using free finance provided by suppliers. This may not be so, however, where it results in a loss of supplier goodwill and Alexis plc suffers adverse consequences.

Slow settlement of amounts owed to suppliers is a persistent problem across the world. **Real World 7.5** discusses the results of s survey which reveals that this problem appears to be getting worse.

Real World 7.5

Slow and getting slower

Companies around the world are taking longer to collect payments from customers, leading to a growing risk that they could hit trouble as the global economy slows. Research from trade credit insurer Euler Hermes shows that companies are accepting much longer payment terms from their customers than they were a decade ago. The average global days sales outstanding, or the number of days it takes for suppliers to be paid for their goods or services, has grown by one-tenth since 2008 to 66 days and is likely to increase again this year.

Real World 7.5 *continued*

Ludovic Subran, chief economist at the Euler Hermes, said the trend increases the risk of insolvencies: 'This is one of the dark sides of the recovery. Companies are extending a lot of trust in the way that clients pay them – it is a loosening of discipline.' He added: 'The longer you wait, the more the risk that your clients hit trouble. When there is a cyclical downturn the companies with longer payment terms are those that get hit first.' One in four insolvencies, said Mr Subran, is because of non-payment from customers. The global days' sales outstanding figure increased by 2 days last year, and the increase was widespread. It grew in two out of three countries, and in two out of three sectors. The increases were sharpest in the US, China and the Eurozone, where Spain, Portugal, Greece and the Netherlands stood out as registering particularly large rises in days sales outstanding.

Euler Hermes looked at 25,000 listed companies in 36 countries. The research reveals sharp differences in payment behaviour around the world. Companies in China have to wait an average of 92 days to be paid by their customers while Turkey and Greece also registered high scores. Companies in New Zealand only have to wait for 43 days on average, while South Africa, Denmark and Austria also recorded low numbers. 'Companies are using this "invisible bank" as a way to finance themselves,' said Mr Subran. 'In some sectors, everyone accepts late payments but in others, such as consumer industries, they want shorter payment times because margins are thin and they need the money to buy more supplies.'

In the UK, where days sales outstanding is below average at 53, the government has pledged to tackle what it calls the 'late payment culture'. In his spring statement in March, chancellor Philip Hammond called for evidence 'on how we can eliminate the continuing scourge of late payments – a key ask from small business.'

FT   *Source:* Ralph, O. (2018) Longer customer payment terms spark corporate fears, ft.com, 2 May.

In Chapter 16, we shall look in some detail at the management of the various elements of working capital, including inventories, trade receivables and trade payables. We shall consider the factors that come into play when deciding the appropriate level of each of these elements.

Sales revenue to capital employed

The **sales revenue to capital employed ratio** (or net asset turnover ratio) examines how effectively the assets of the business are being used to generate sales revenue. It is calculated as follows:

$$\text{Sales revenue to capital employed ratio} = \frac{\text{Sales revenue}}{\text{Share capital} + \text{Reserves} + \text{Non-current liabilities}}$$

Normally, a higher sales revenue to capital employed ratio is preferred to a lower one. A higher ratio tends to suggest that assets are being used more productively in the generation of revenue. However, a very high ratio may suggest that the business is 'overtrading' on its assets. In other words, it has insufficient assets to sustain the level of sales revenue achieved. We shall take a closer look at overtrading later in the chapter.

When comparing the sales revenue to capital employed ratio for different businesses, factors such as the age and condition of assets held, the valuation bases for assets and whether assets are leased or owned outright can complicate interpretation.

A variation of this formula is to use the total assets less current liabilities (which is equivalent to long-term capital employed) in the denominator (lower part of the fraction). The same result is obtained.

For the year ended 31 March 2018, this ratio for Alexis plc is:

$$\text{Sales revenue to capital employed} = \frac{2{,}240}{(638 + 763)/2} = 3.20 \text{ times}$$

Activity 7.10

Calculate the sales revenue to capital employed ratio for Alexis plc for the year ended 31 March 2019.

The ratio for 2019 is:

$$\text{Sales revenue to capital employed} = \frac{2{,}681}{(763 + 834)/2} = 3.36 \text{ times}$$

This seems to be an improvement since, in 2019, more sales revenue was being generated for each £1 of capital employed (£3.36) than was the case in 2018 (£3.20). Provided that overtrading is not an issue, and that the additional sales generate an acceptable profit, this is to be welcomed.

Sales revenue per employee

The **sales revenue per employee ratio** relates sales revenue generated during a reporting period to a particular business resource – labour. It provides a measure of the productivity of the workforce. The ratio is:

$$\text{Sales revenue per employee} = \frac{\text{Sales revenue}}{\text{Number of employees}}$$

Generally, businesses would prefer a high value for this ratio, implying that they are deploying their staff efficiently.

For the year ended 31 March 2018, the ratio for Alexis plc is:

$$\text{Sales revenue per employee} = \frac{£2{,}240\text{m}}{13{,}995} = £160{,}057$$

Activity 7.11

Calculate the sales revenue per employee for Alexis plc for the year ended 31 March 2019.

The ratio for 2019 is:

$$\text{Sales revenue per employee} = \frac{£2{,}681\text{m}}{18{,}623} = £143{,}962$$

This represents a fairly significant decline, which merits further investigation. As already mentioned, the number of employees increased quite notably (by about 33 per cent) during 2019. We need to know why this had not generated additional sales revenue sufficient to maintain the ratio at its 2018 level. It may be because the extra employees were not appointed until late in the year ended 31 March 2019.

The efficiency, or activity, ratios may be summarised as follows:

	2018	2019
Average inventories turnover period	56.6 days	56.7 days
Average settlement period for trade receivables	37.7 days	34.9 days
Average settlement period for trade payables	44.9 days	47.2 days
Sales revenue to capital employed (net asset turnover)	3.20 times	3.36 times
Sales revenue per employee	£160,057	£143,962

Activity 7.12

What do you deduce from a comparison of the efficiency ratios over the two years?

Maintaining the inventories turnover period at the 2018 level may be reasonable, although to assess whether this is a satisfactory period we need to know the planned inventories turnover period. The inventories turnover period for other businesses operating in carpet retailing, particularly those regarded as the market leaders, may have been helpful in formulating the plans. On the face of things, a shorter trade receivables settlement period and a longer trade payables settlement period are both desirable. These may, however, have been achieved at the cost of a loss of the goodwill of customers and suppliers, respectively. The increased sales revenue to capital employed ratio seems beneficial, provided the business can manage this increase. The decline in the sales revenue per employee ratio is undesirable but is probably related to the dramatic increase in the number of employees. As with the inventories turnover period, these other ratios need to be compared with planned, or target, ratios.

Figure 7.5 summarises the efficiency ratios that we have discussed.

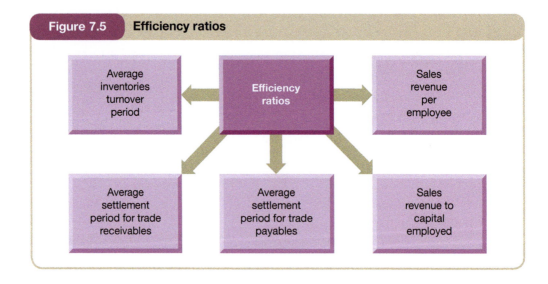

Figure 7.5   Efficiency ratios

Relationship between profitability and efficiency

In our earlier discussions concerning profitability ratios, we saw that return on capital employed (ROCE) is regarded as a key ratio by many businesses. The ratio is:

$$\text{ROCE} = \frac{\text{Operating profit}}{\text{Long-term capital employed}} \times 100$$

where long-term capital comprises share capital plus reserves plus long-term borrowings. This ratio can be broken down into two elements, as shown in Figure 7.6. The first ratio is the operating profit margin ratio and the second is the sales revenue to capital employed (net asset turnover) ratio, both of which we discussed earlier. By breaking down the ROCE ratio in this manner, we highlight the fact that the overall return on funds employed within the business will be determined both by the profitability of sales and by efficiency in the use of capital.

Figure 7.6	The main elements of the ROCE ratio

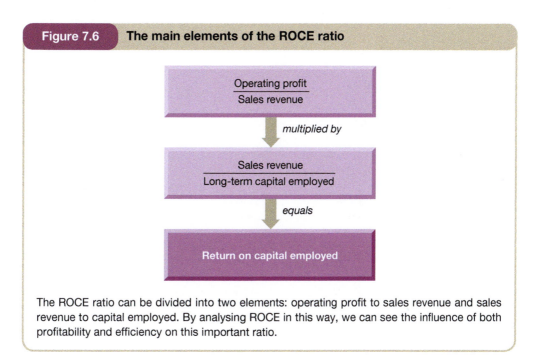

The ROCE ratio can be divided into two elements: operating profit to sales revenue and sales revenue to capital employed. By analysing ROCE in this way, we can see the influence of both profitability and efficiency on this important ratio.

Example 7.2 looks at the return on capital of two different businesses operating in the same industry.

Example 7.2

Consider the following information, for last year, for two different businesses operating in the same industry:

	Antler plc	Baker plc
	£m	£m
Operating profit	20	15
Average long-term capital employed	100	75
Sales revenue	200	300

Example 7.2 *continued*

The ROCE for each business is identical (20 per cent). However, the manner in which that return was achieved by each business is quite different. In the case of Antler plc, the operating profit margin is 10 per cent and the sales revenue to capital employed ratio is 2 times (so, ROCE = 10% × 2 = 20%). In the case of Baker plc, the operating profit margin is 5 per cent and the sales revenue to capital employed ratio is 4 times (and so, ROCE = 5% × 4 = 20%).

Example 7.2 demonstrates that a relatively high sales revenue to capital employed ratio can compensate for a relatively low operating profit margin. Similarly, a relatively low sales revenue to capital employed ratio can be overcome by a relatively high operating profit margin. In many areas of retail and distribution (for example, supermarkets and delivery services), operating profit margins are quite low, but the ROCE can be high, provided that assets are used productively (that is, low margin, high sales revenue to capital employed).

Activity 7.13

Show how the ROCE ratio for Alexis plc can be analysed into the two elements for each of the years 2018 and 2019. What conclusions can you draw from your figures?

ROCE = Operating profit margin × Sales revenue to capital employed

	ROCE	Operating profit margin	Sales revenue to capital employed
2018	34.7%	10.8%	3.20
2019	5.9%	1.8%	3.36

As we can see, the relationship between the three ratios holds for Alexis plc for both years. The small apparent differences arise because the three ratios are stated here only to one or two decimal places.

In the year to 31 March 2019, the business was more effective at generating sales revenue (sales revenue to capital employed ratio increased). However, it fell well below the level needed to compensate for the sharp decline in the profitability of sales (operating profit margin). As a result, the 2019 ROCE was well below the 2018 value.

Liquidity

Liquidity ratios are concerned with the ability of the business to meet its short-term financial obligations. The following ratios are widely used:

- current ratio;
- acid test ratio: and
- cash generated from operations to maturing obligations ratio.

These ratios will now be considered.

Current ratio

The **current ratio** compares the 'liquid' assets (that is, cash and those assets held that will soon be turned into cash) of the business with the current liabilities. The ratio is calculated as follows:

$$\text{Current ratio} = \frac{\text{Current assets}}{\text{Current liabilities}}$$

It seems to be believed by some that there is an 'ideal' current ratio (usually 2 times or 2:1) for all businesses. However, this is not the case. Different types of business require different current ratios. A manufacturing business, for example, will normally have a relatively high current ratio because it will tend to hold inventories of finished goods, raw materials and work in progress. It will also normally sell goods on credit, thereby giving rise to trade receivables. A supermarket chain, on the other hand, will have a relatively low ratio, as it will hold only fast-moving inventories of finished goods and its sales will be for cash rather than on credit (see Real World 16.1 on page 664).

The higher the current ratio, the more liquid the business is considered to be. As liquidity is vital to the survival of a business, a higher current ratio might be thought to be preferable to a lower one. If a business has a very high ratio, however, it may be that excessive funds are tied up in cash or other liquid assets and are not, therefore, being used as productively as they might otherwise be.

As at 31 March 2018, the current ratio of Alexis plc is:

$$\text{Current ratio} = \frac{544}{291} = 1.9 \text{ times (or } 1.9{:}1)$$

Activity 7.14

Calculate the current ratio for Alexis plc as at 31 March 2019.

The ratio for 2019 is:

$$\text{Current ratio} = \frac{679}{432} = 1.6 \text{ times (or } 1.6{:}1)$$

Although this is a decline from 2018 to 2019, it may not be a matter for concern. The next ratio may provide a clue as to whether there seems to be a problem.

Acid test ratio

The **acid test ratio** is similar to the current ratio, but represents a more stringent test of liquidity. For many businesses, inventories cannot be converted into cash quickly. (Note that, in the case of Alexis plc, the inventories turnover period was about 57 days in both years (see page 260).) Once having sold a carpet, the business would have to have waited another five weeks, on average, to receive payment. As a result, there is a good case for excluding this particular asset.

The acid test ratio is calculated as follows:

$$\text{Acid test ratio} = \frac{\text{Current assets (excluding inventories)}}{\text{Current liabilities}}$$

As at 31 March 2018, the acid test ratio for Alexis plc is:

$$\text{Acid test ratio} = \frac{544 - 300}{291} = 0.8 \text{ times (or 0.8:1)}$$

We can see that the 'liquid' current assets do not quite cover the current liabilities, so the business may be experiencing some liquidity problems.

The minimum level for this ratio is often stated as 1.0 times (or 1:1; that is, current assets (excluding inventories) equal current liabilities). However, for many highly successful businesses, it is not unusual for the acid test ratio to be below 1.0 without causing liquidity problems (again, see Real World 16.1 on page 664).

Activity 7.15

Calculate the acid test ratio for Alexis plc as at 31 March 2019.

The ratio for 2019 is:

$$\text{Acid test ratio} = \frac{679 - 406}{432} = 0.6 \text{ times}$$

The 2019 ratio is significantly below that for 2018 and may well be a cause for concern. The underlying reasons for the rapid decline in the ratio should be investigated and, if necessary, steps taken to prevent any further deterioration.

Cash generated from operations to maturing obligations ratio

The **cash generated from operations (CGO) to maturing obligations ratio** compares the cash generated from operations (taken from the statement of cash flows) with the current liabilities of the business. It provides a further indication of the ability of the business to meet its maturing obligations. The ratio is expressed as:

$$\frac{\text{Cash generated from operations}}{\text{to maturing obligations ratio}} = \frac{\text{Cash generated from operations}}{\text{Current liabilities}}$$

The higher this ratio is, the better the liquidity of the business. This ratio has the advantage over the current ratio that the operating cash flows for a period usually provide a more reliable guide to the liquidity of a business than current assets held at the statement of financial position date.

Alexis plc's ratio for the year ended 31 March 2018 is:

$$\text{Cash generated from operations to maturing obligations ratio} = \frac{251}{291} = 0.9 \text{ times}$$

This indicates that the operating cash flows for the year are not quite sufficient to cover the current liabilities at the end of the year.

Activity 7.16

Calculate the cash generated from operations to maturing obligations ratio for Alexis plc for the year ended 31 March 2019.

The ratio for 2019 is:

$$\text{Cash generated from operations to maturing obligations ratio} = \frac{34}{432} = 0.1 \text{ times}$$

This shows an alarming decline in the ability of the business to meet its maturing obligations from its operating cash flows. It confirms that liquidity is a real cause for concern.

The liquidity ratios for the two-year period may be summarised as follows:

	2018	2019
Current ratio	1.9	1.6
Acid test ratio	0.8	0.6
Cash generated from operations to maturing obligations ratio	0.9	0.1

Activity 7.17

What do you deduce from these liquidity ratios?

There has clearly been a decline in liquidity from 2018 to 2019. This is indicated by all three ratios. The most worrying is the decline in the last ratio as it reveals that the ability to generate cash from trading operations has declined significantly in relation to short-term obligations. The apparent liquidity problem may, however, be planned and short term and linked to the increase in non-current assets and number of employees. When the benefits of the expansion come on stream, liquidity may improve. On the other hand, short-term lenders and suppliers may become anxious due to the decline in liquidity. This could lead them to press for payment, which could well cause further problems.

The liquidity ratios that we have discussed are summarised in Figure 7.7.

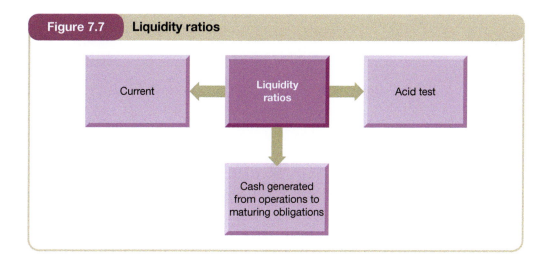

Figure 7.7   Liquidity ratios

Financial gearing

Financial gearing (or financial leverage) occurs when a business is financed, at least in part, by borrowing rather than by owners' equity. The extent to which a business is geared (that is, financed from borrowing) is an important factor in assessing risk. Borrowing involves taking on a commitment to pay interest charges and to make capital repayments. Where the borrowing is heavy, this can be a significant financial burden; it can increase the risk of the business becoming insolvent. Nevertheless, most businesses are geared to some extent.

Given the risks involved, we may wonder why a business would want to take on gearing. One reason is that the owners have insufficient funds, so the only way to finance the business adequately is to borrow. Another reason is that gearing can be used to increase the returns to owners. This is possible provided the returns generated from borrowed funds exceed the cost of paying interest. Example 7.3 illustrates this point.

Example 7.3

The long-term capital structures of two new businesses, Lee Ltd and Nova Ltd, are as follows:

	Lee Ltd £	Nova Ltd £
£1 ordinary shares	100,000	200,000
10% loan notes	200,000	100,000
	300,000	300,000

In their first year of operations, they each make an operating profit (that is, profit before interest and taxation) of £50,000. The tax rate is 20 per cent of the profit before taxation (but after interest).

Lee Ltd would probably be considered relatively highly geared, as it has a high proportion of borrowed funds in its long-term capital structure. Nova Ltd is much lower geared. The profit available to the shareholders of each business in the first year of operations will be:

	Lee Ltd £	Nova Ltd £
Operating profit	50,000	50,000
Interest payable	(20,000)	(10,000)
Profit before taxation	30,000	40,000
Taxation (20%)	(6,000)	(8,000)
Profit for the year (available to ordinary shareholders)	24,000	32,000

The return on ordinary shareholders' funds (ROSF) for each business will be:

Lee Ltd
$$\frac{24,000}{100,000} \times 100 = 24\%$$

Nova Ltd
$$\frac{32,000}{200,000} \times 100 = 16\%$$

We can see that Lee Ltd, the more highly geared business, has generated a higher ROSF than Nova Ltd. This is despite the fact that the ROCE (return on capital employed) is identical for both businesses (that is, (£50,000/£300,000) × 100 = 16.7%)

Note that at the £50,000 level of operating profit, the shareholders of both businesses have generated higher returns as a result of gearing. If both businesses were totally financed by equity, the profit for the year (that is, after taxation) would be £40,000 (that is, £50,000 less 20 per cent taxation), giving an ROSF of 13.3 per cent (that is, £40,000/£300,000).

An effect of gearing is that returns to shareholders become more sensitive to changes in operating profits. For a highly-geared business, a change in operating profits will lead to a proportionately greater change in the ROSF ratio.

Activity 7.18

Assume that the operating profit was £70,000 rather than £50,000. What would be the effect of this on ROSF?

The revised profit available to the shareholders of each business in the first year of operations will be:

	Lee Ltd	Nova Ltd
	£	£
Operating profit	70,000	70,000
Interest payable	(20,000)	(10,000)
Profit before taxation	50,000	60,000
Taxation (20%)	(10,000)	(12,000)
Profit for the year (available to ordinary shareholders)	40,000	48,000

The ROSF for each business will now be:

Lee Ltd

$$\frac{40,000}{100,000} \times 100 = 40\%$$

Nova Ltd

$$\frac{48,000}{200,000} \times 100 = 24\%$$

We can see that for Lee Ltd, the higher-geared business, the returns to shareholders have increased by two thirds (from 24 per cent to 40 per cent), whereas for the lower-geared business, Nova Ltd, the benefits of gearing are less pronounced, increasing by only half (from 16 per cent to 24 per cent). The effect of gearing can, of course, work in both directions. So, for a highly- geared business, a small decline in operating profit will bring about a much greater decline in the returns to shareholders.

The reason that gearing seems to be beneficial to shareholders is that, in practice, interest rates for borrowings tend to be low by comparison with the returns that the typical business can earn. On top of this, interest expenses are tax-deductible, in the way shown in Example 7.3 and Activity 7.18. This makes the apparent cost of borrowing quite cheap. It is debatable, however, whether low interest rates really are beneficial to shareholders. Since borrowing increases the risk to shareholders, there is a hidden cost involved. Many argue that this cost is precisely compensated by the higher returns, giving no net benefit to shareholders. In other words, the apparent benefits of higher returns from gearing are illusory. What are not illusory, however, are the benefits to shareholders from the tax-deductibility of interest payments. We shall discuss this point in a little more detail in Chapter 15.

Activity (7.19)

If shareholders gain from the tax-deductibility of interest on borrowings, who loses?

The losers are the tax authority (ultimately the government) and, therefore, other taxpayers.

The effect of gearing is like that of two intermeshing cogwheels of unequal size (see Figure 7.8). The circular movement in the larger cog (operating profit) causes a more than proportionate movement in the smaller cog (returns to ordinary shareholders).

Figure 7.8   The effect of financial gearing

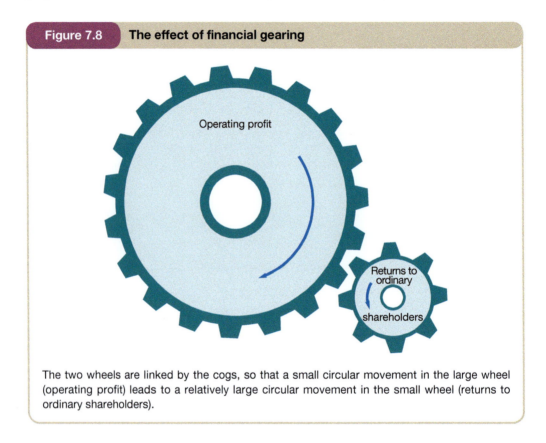

The two wheels are linked by the cogs, so that a small circular movement in the large wheel (operating profit) leads to a relatively large circular movement in the small wheel (returns to ordinary shareholders).

Two ratios are widely used to assess gearing:

- gearing ratio; and
- interest cover ratio.

Gearing ratio

The **gearing ratio** measures the contribution of long-term lenders to the long-term capital structure of a business:

$$\text{Gearing ratio} = \frac{\text{Long-term (non-current) liabilities}}{\text{Share capital + Reserves +}} \times 100$$
$$\text{Long-term (non-current) liabilities}$$

As at 31 March 2018, the gearing ratio for Alexis plc is:

$$\text{Gearing ratio} = \frac{200}{(563 + 200)} \times 100 = 26.2\%$$

This is a level of gearing that would not normally be considered to be very high.

Activity 7.20

Calculate the gearing ratio of Alexis plc as at 31 March 2019.

The ratio for 2019 is:

$$\text{Gearing ratio} = \frac{300}{(534 + 300)} \times 100 = 36.0\%$$

This is a substantial increase in the level of gearing over the year.

Interest cover ratio

The **interest cover ratio** measures the amount of operating profit available to cover interest payable. The ratio may be calculated as follows:

$$\text{Interest cover ratio} = \frac{\text{Operating profit}}{\text{Interest payable}}$$

For the year ended 31 March 2018, the interest cover ratio for Alexis plc is:

$$\text{Interest cover ratio} = \frac{243}{18} = 13.5 \text{ times}$$

This ratio shows that the level of operating profit is considerably higher than the level of interest payable. This means that a large fall in operating profit could occur before operating profit levels failed to cover interest payable. The lower the level of operating profit coverage, the greater the risk to lenders that interest payments will not be met. There will also be a greater risk to the shareholders that the lenders will take action against the business to recover the interest due.

Activity 7.21

Calculate the interest cover ratio of Alexis plc for the year ended 31 March 2019.

The ratio for 2019 is:

$$\text{Interest cover ratio} = \frac{47}{32} = 1.5 \text{ times}$$

Alexis plc's gearing ratios are:

	2018	2019
Gearing ratio	26.2%	36.0%
Interest cover ratio	13.5 times	1.5 times

Activity (7.22)

What do you deduce from a comparison of Alexis plc's gearing ratios over the two years?

The gearing ratio has changed significantly. This is mainly due to the substantial increase in the contribution of long-term lenders to financing the business. The gearing ratio at 31 March 2019 would not be considered very high for a business that is trading successfully. It is the low profitability that is the problem. The interest cover ratio has declined dramatically from 13.5 times in 2018 to 1.5 times in 2019. This was partly caused by the increase in borrowings in 2019, but mainly caused by the dramatic decline in profitability in that year. The situation in 2019 looks hazardous. Only a small decline in future operating profits would result in the profit being unable to cover interest payments.

Without knowledge of the planned ratios, it is not possible to reach a valid conclusion on Alexis plc's gearing.

Figure 7.9 shows the gearing ratios that we considered.

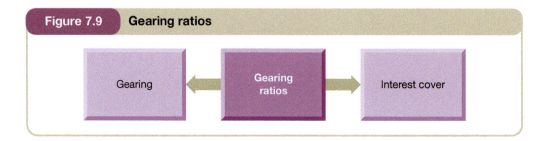

Figure 7.9 **Gearing ratios**

Investment ratios

Various ratios are available that are designed to help shareholders assess the returns on their investment. The following are widely used:

- dividend payout ratio;
- dividend yield ratio;
- earnings per share;
- cash generated from operations per share; and
- price/earnings ratio.

Dividend payout ratio

The **dividend payout ratio** measures the proportion of earnings paid out to shareholders in the form of dividends. The ratio is calculated as follows:

$$\text{Dividend payout ratio} = \frac{\text{Dividends announced for the year}}{\text{Earnings for the year available for dividends}} \times 100$$

In the case of ordinary shares, the earnings available for dividends will normally be the profit for the year (that is, the profit after taxation) less any preference dividends relating to the year. This ratio is normally expressed as a percentage.

For the year ended 31 March 2018, the dividend payout ratio for Alexis plc is:

$$\text{Dividend payout ratio} = \frac{40}{165} \times 100 = 24.2\%$$

Activity 7.23

Calculate the dividend payout ratio of Alexis plc for the year ended 31 March 2019.

The ratio for 2019 is:

$$\text{Dividend payout ratio} = \frac{40}{11} \times 100 = 363.6\%$$

This would normally be regarded as an alarming increase in the ratio over the two years. Paying a dividend of £40 million in 2019 would seem to be very imprudent.

The information provided by the above ratio is often expressed slightly differently as the **dividend cover ratio**. Here, the calculation is:

$$\text{Dividend cover ratio} = \frac{\text{Earnings for the year available for dividend}}{\text{Dividends announced for the year}}$$

For 2018, the ratio for Alexis plc would be 165/40 = 4.1 times. That is to say, the earnings available for dividend cover the actual dividend paid by just over four times. For 2019, the ratio is 11/40 = 0.3 times.

Dividend yield ratio

The **dividend yield ratio** relates the cash return from a share to its current market value. This can help investors to assess the cash return on their investment in the business. The ratio, expressed as a percentage, is:

$$\text{Dividend yield} = \frac{\text{Dividend per share}}{\text{Market value per share}} \times 100$$

For the year ended 31 March 2018, the dividend yield for Alexis plc is:

$$\text{Dividend yield} = \frac{0.067^*}{2.50} \times 100 = 2.7\%$$

The shares' market value is given in Note 1 to Example 7.1 (page 246).

*Dividend proposed/number of shares = 40/(300 × 2) = £0.067 **dividend per share** (the 300 is multiplied by 2 because they are £0.50 shares).

Activity 7.24

Calculate the dividend yield ratio for Alexis plc for the year ended 31 March 2019.

The ratio for 2019 is:

$$\text{Dividend yield} = \frac{0.067^*}{1.50} \times 100 = 4.5\%$$

*$40/(300 \times 2) = £0.067$.

Earnings per share

The **earnings per share (EPS) ratio** relates the earnings generated by the business, and available to shareholders, during a period to the number of shares in issue. For equity (ordinary) shareholders, the amount available will be represented by the profit for the year (profit after taxation) less any preference dividend, where applicable. The ratio for equity shareholders is calculated as follows:

$$\text{Earnings per share} = \frac{\text{Earnings available to ordinary shareholders}}{\text{Number of ordinary shares in issue}}$$

For the year ended 31 March 2018, the EPS for Alexis plc is:

$$\text{EPS} = \frac{£165m}{600m} = 27.5p$$

Many investment analysts regard the EPS ratio as a fundamental measure of share performance. The trend in earnings per share over time is used to help assess the investment potential of a business's shares. Although it is possible to make total profit increase through ordinary shareholders investing more in the business, this will not necessarily lead to an increase in the profitability *per share*.

Real World 7.6 points out the danger of placing too much emphasis on this ratio. The equity fund manager, Terry Smith, argues that, had more attention been paid to ROCE rather than EPS, investors would have spotted that all was not well with Tesco plc, the supermarket giant. He also takes to task, Warren Buffett, the legendary investor, for ignoring his own advice and investing heavily in the business.

Real World 7.6

A trolley load of problems

In his 1979 letter to shareholders, Mr Buffett stated: 'The primary test of managerial economic performance is the achievement of a high earnings rate on equity capital employed (without undue leverage, accounting gimmickry, etc) and not the achievement of consistent gains in earnings per share.'

This makes it all the more surprising to me that both Mr Buffett and the many acolytes who have seemingly followed him to the gates of hell in Tesco, ignored this chart:

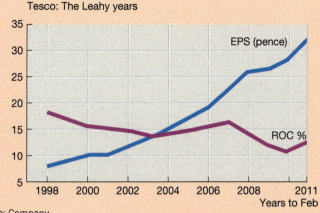

Tesco: The Leahy years

Source: Company

This is not the first such chart that I have come across in which a company reports steadily rising earnings per share (EPS), on which most analysts and 'investors' focus. For them, the rise in EPS seems to have a mesmeric effect like Kaa the snake in The Jungle Book. But they ignore the point that more capital is being employed to generate those earnings at ever lower returns. Add in the fact that Tesco has changed its definition of return on capital employed (ROCE) eight times during those years, and there's more than enough material to send investors running for cover – even those who have less aversion than I do to retailers.

Yet much of the commentary about what has gone wrong at Tesco focuses on Philip Clarke, who took over as chief executive from Sir Terry Leahy in 2011, as if everything was going swimmingly until then. Looking at the ROCE line in the chart it is clear that this was not the case.

Moreover, one thing to bear in mind is that if Tesco's ROCE during the Leahy years fell from a very good 19 per cent to a less than adequate 10 per cent, this is an average of returns on capital employed, which includes both capital invested years ago and more recent commitments. To drag the average ROCE down so dramatically it is likely that returns on new investments in those years were not just inadequate, but in some cases negative – as the ill-starred US expansion proved to be.

Even if return on capital employed does not have the same importance for you as it does for me, or Mr Buffett (at least in 1979), consider this: in 14 of the past 18 years (taking us back to 1997 when Sir Terry became chief executive) Tesco's free cash flow less its dividend (with free cash defined as operating cash flow less gross capital expenditure) was a negative number. In plain English, Tesco was not generating enough cash both to invest and to pay its dividend. In half of those 14 years, the proceeds of fixed asset disposals took the numbers back into the black, but that is not exactly a sustainable source of financing.

So guess what they did instead? Yes, they borrowed it. Tesco's gross debt, which was £894 million when Sir Terry took over, peaked at nearly £15.9 billion in 2009. The company spent much of its free cash on fixed-asset investment and raised debt to help pay the dividend. This is neither healthy nor sustainable, as investors in Tesco have now come to realise.

The concept that this might not be sustainable hardly requires much thought. Neither does charting the ROCE versus the growth in EPS. Yet it is evident that many investors, including it seems Mr Buffett (who has been trimming his Tesco stake in recent years) either didn't do this or ignored the results if they did. It makes me wonder what else they are ignoring.

It is not usually very helpful to compare the EPS of one business with that of another. Differences in financing arrangements (for example, in the nominal value of shares issued) can render any such comparison meaningless. However, it can be useful to monitor changes that occur in this ratio for a particular business over time.

Activity 7.25

Calculate the EPS of Alexis plc for the year ended 31 March 2019.

The ratio for 2019 is:

$$EPS = \frac{£11m}{600m} = 1.8p$$

Cash generated from operations per share

In the short term at least, cash generated from operations (found in the statement of cash flows) can provide a good guide to the ability of a business to pay dividends and to undertake planned expenditures. Many see a cash generation measure as more useful in this context than the earnings per share figure. The **cash generated from operations (CGO) per ordinary share ratio** is calculated as follows:

$$\text{Cash generated from operations per share} = \frac{\text{Cash generated from operations less preference dividend (if any)}}{\text{Number of ordinary shares in issue}}$$

For the year ended 31 March 2018, the ratio for Alexis plc is:

$$\text{CGO per share} = \frac{£251m}{600m} = 41.8p$$

Activity 7.26

Calculate the CGO per ordinary share for Alexis plc for the year ended 31 March 2019.

The ratio for 2019 is:

$$\text{CGO per share} = \frac{£34m}{600m} = 5.7p$$

There has been a dramatic decrease in this ratio over the two-year period.

Note that, for both years, the CGO per share for Alexis plc is higher than the earnings per share. This is not unusual. The effect of adding back depreciation to derive the CGO figures will often ensure that a higher figure is derived.

Price/earnings ratio

The **price/earnings (P/E) ratio** relates the market value of a share to the earnings per share. This ratio can be calculated as follows:

$$\text{P/E ratio} = \frac{\text{Market value per share}}{\text{Earnings per share}}$$

As at 31 March 2018, the P/E ratio for Alexis plc is:

$$\text{P/E ratio} = \frac{£2.50}{27.5p^*} = 9.1 \text{ times}$$

*The EPS figure (27.5p) was calculated on p. 272.

This ratio indicates that the market value of the share is 9.1 times the current level of earnings. It is a measure of market confidence in the future of a business. The higher the P/E ratio, the greater the confidence in the future earning power of the business and, consequently, the more investors are prepared to pay in relation to that current earning power.

Activity 7.27

Calculate the P/E ratio of Alexis plc as at 31 March 2019.

The ratio for 2019 is:

$$\text{P/E ratio} = \frac{£1.50}{1.8p} = 83.3 \text{ times}$$

As P/E ratios provide a useful guide to market confidence about the future, they can be helpful when comparing different businesses. However, differences in accounting policies between businesses can lead to different profit and earnings per share figures. This can distort comparisons.

The investment ratios for Alexis plc over the two-year period are as follows:

	2018	2019
Dividend payout ratio	24.2%	363.6%
Dividend yield ratio	2.7%	4.5%
Earnings per share	27.5p	1.8p
Cash generated from operations per share	41.8p	5.7p
P/E ratio	9.1 times	83.3 times

Activity 7.28

What do you deduce from the investment ratios set out above? Can you offer an explanation why the share price has not fallen as much as it might have done, bearing in mind the much poorer trading performance in 2019?

Activity 7.28 *continued*

Although the EPS has fallen dramatically and the dividend payment for 2019 seems very imprudent, the share price has held up reasonably well (fallen from £2.50 to £1.50). Moreover, the dividend yield and P/E ratios have improved in 2019. This is an anomaly of these two ratios, which stems from using a forward-looking value (the share price) in conjunction with historic data (dividends and earnings). Share prices are based on investors' assessments of the business's future. It seems that the 'market' was less happy with Alexis plc at the end of 2019 than at the end of 2018. This is evidenced by the fact that the share price had fallen by £1 a share. The decline in share price, however, was less dramatic than the decline in profit for the year. This suggests that investors believe the business will perform better in the future. Perhaps they are confident that the large increase in assets and employee numbers occurring during the year to 31 March 2019 will yield benefits in the future; benefits that the business has not yet been able to generate.

Real World 7.7 provides information about the share performance of a selection of large, well-known UK businesses. This type of information is provided on a daily basis by several newspapers, notably the *Financial Times*.

Real World 7.7

Market statistics for some well-known businesses

The following data was extracted from the *Financial Times* of 7 March 2019, relating to the previous day's trading of the shares of some well-known businesses on the London Stock Exchange:

Share	Price (pence)	Chng (pence)	52-week high	52-week low	Yield per cent	P/E	Volume (000s)
Marks and Spencer	279.30	2.50	316.60	240.00	6.70	155.17	8,460.9
Royal Mail	265.60	−2.60	632.60	246.60	9.04	28.87	7,418.0
National Express	433.20	3.00	438.00	356.00	3.12	16.12	535.6
Tesco	232.30	0.40	266.80	187.05	1.29	20.52	18,862.5
Coca Cola HBC AG	2,582.00	−16.00	2,817.00	2,224.00	1.85	23.74	709.0
National Grid	846.30	−3.70	895.10	742.00	5.43	8.61	5,974.5

The column headings are as follows:

Price	Mid-market price in pence (that is, the price midway between buying and selling price) of the shares at the end of trading on 6 March 2019.
Chng	Gain or loss in the mid-market price during 6 March 2019.
High/Low	Highest and lowest prices reached by the share during the 52 weeks ended on 6 March 2019.
Yield	Dividend yield, based on the most recent year's dividend and the current share price.
P/E	Price/earnings ratio, based on the most recent year's (after-tax) profit for the year and the current share price.
Volume	The number of shares (in thousands) that were bought/sold on 6 March 2019.

Let us take as an example National Grid plc, the utility business:

- the shares had a mid-market price of 846.3p each at the close of Stock Exchange trading on 6 March 2019
- the shares had decreased in price by 3.70p during trading on 6 March 2019
- the shares had highest and lowest prices during the previous 52 weeks of 895.10p and 742.00p, respectively
- the shares had a dividend yield, based on the 6 March 2019 price (and the dividend for the most recent year) of 5.43 per cent
- the shares had a P/E ratio, based on the 6 March 2019 price (and the after-taxation earnings per share for the most recent year), of 8.61 times
- during trading on 6 March 2019, 5,974,500 of the business's shares had changed hands between buyers and sellers.

Real World 7.8 shows how investment ratios can vary between different industry sectors.

Real World 7.8

Yielding dividends

Investment ratios can vary significantly between businesses and between industries. To give some indication of the range of variations that occurs, the average dividend yield ratios and average P/E ratios for listed businesses in 12 different industries in Western Europe are shown in Figures 7.10 and 7.11, respectively.

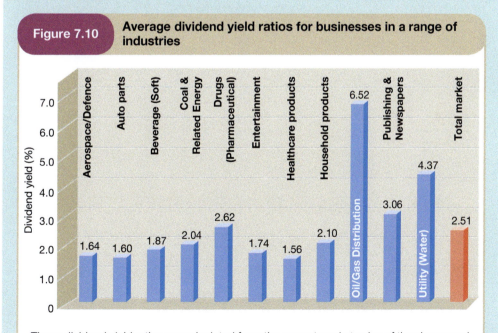

Figure 7.10 Average dividend yield ratios for businesses in a range of industries

These dividend yield ratios are calculated from the current market value of the shares and the most recent year's dividend paid.

Real World 7.8 *continued*

These dividend yield ratios are calculated from the current market value of the shares and the most recent year's dividend paid.

We can see that the average dividend yield for the market as a whole was 2.51 per cent (as shown in Figure 7.10), but there is a wide variation with healthcare products at 1.56 per cent and oil and gas distribution at 6.52 per cent.

Differences in dividend yield can arise for various reasons. Businesses operating in growth industries may be investing heavily in developing new products. This will often mean low, or even no, dividends and low dividend yields. Businesses in mature industries, however, where re-investment opportunities are limited, may pay higher dividends.

Share prices are based on expectations of their future prospects whereas dividends are actual, past, events. Where business within a particular industry have poor prospects, share prices will be lower. These businesses may, however, wish to maintain dividend payments at current levels despite the expected downturn in their fortunes. Thus, a high current dividend and a low share price can also lead to a high dividend yield.

P/E ratios are calculated from the current share price and the most recent year's EPS.

Businesses that have a high share price relative to their recent historic earnings have high P/E ratios. This occurs where their future prospects are considered bright. The average P/E for the market as a whole was 46.52 times but auto parts was as low as 11.39 times and oil and gas distribution as high as 105.67 times.

| Figure 7.11 | Average price/earnings ratios for businesses in a range of industries |

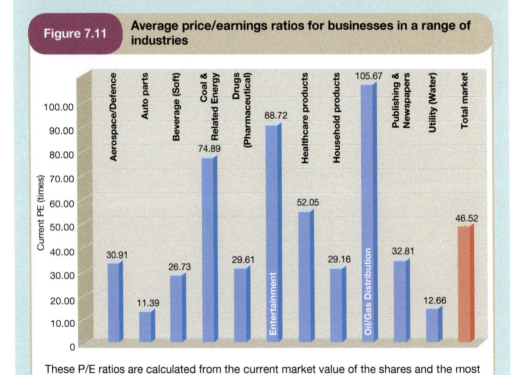

These P/E ratios are calculated from the current market value of the shares and the most recent year's earnings per share (EPS).

Source: Charts compiled from data in Damodaran, A., *Useful Data Sets*, www.stern.nyu.edu/~adamodar/New_Home_Page/data.html, accessed 9 January 2019.

The investment ratios discussed are summarised in Figure 7.12.

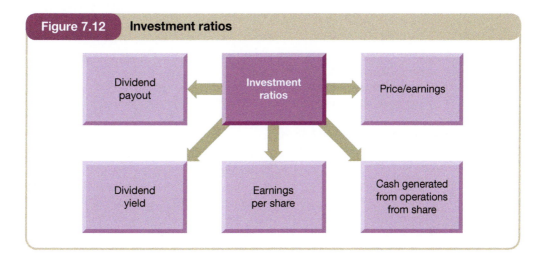

Figure 7.12   Investment ratios

Financial ratios and the problem of overtrading

Overtrading occurs where a business is operating at a level of activity that cannot be supported by the amount of finance that has been committed. This situation is often due to poor financial control over the business by its managers. The underlying reasons for overtrading are varied. It may occur:

- in young, expanding businesses that fail to prepare adequately for the rapid increase in demand for their goods or services, something which often leads to insufficient finance to fund the level of trade receivables and inventories needed to support the level of sales revenue generated;
- in businesses where the managers may have misjudged the level of expected sales demand and, as a result, have underestimated the level of working capital required or have failed to control escalating project costs;
- as a result of a fall in the value of money (inflation), causing more finance to have to be committed to inventories and trade receivables, even where there is no expansion in the real volume of trade; and
- where the owners are unable to inject further funds into the business themselves and/ or they cannot persuade others to invest in the business.

Whatever the reason, the problems that it brings must be dealt with if the business is to survive over the longer term.

Overtrading results in liquidity problems such as exceeding borrowing limits, or slow repayment of borrowings and trade payables. The last of these can result in suppliers withholding supplies, thereby making it difficult to meet customer needs. The managers of the business might be forced to direct all of their efforts to dealing with immediate and pressing problems, such as finding cash to meet interest charges due or paying wages. Longer-term planning becomes difficult as managers spend their time going from crisis to crisis. Ultimately, the business may fail because it cannot meet its maturing obligations – it runs out of cash.

Activity (7.29)

If a business is overtrading, do you think the following ratios would be higher or lower than normally expected?

1 Current ratio
2 Average inventories turnover period
3 Average settlement period for trade receivables
4 Average settlement period for trade payables

Your answer should be as follows:

1 The current ratio would be lower than normally expected. This ratio is a measure of liquidity, and lack of liquidity is a typical symptom of overtrading.
2 The average inventories turnover period would be lower than normally expected. Where a business is overtrading, the level of inventories held will be low because of the problems of financing them. In the short term, sales revenue may not be badly affected by the low inventories levels and, therefore, inventories will be turned over more quickly.
3 The average settlement period for trade receivables may be lower than normally expected. Where a business is suffering from liquidity problems, it may chase credit customers more vigorously in an attempt to improve cash flows.
4 The average settlement period for trade payables may be higher than normally expected. The business may try to delay payments to its suppliers because of the liquidity problems arising.

To deal with the overtrading problem, a business must ensure that the finance available is consistent with the level of operations. Thus, if a business that is overtrading is unable to raise new finance, it should cut back its level of operations in line with the finance available. Although this may mean lost sales and lost profits in the short term, cutting back may be necessary to ensure survival over the longer term.

Trend analysis

It is often helpful to see whether ratios are indicating trends. Key ratios can be plotted on a graph to provide a simple visual display of changes occurring over time. The trends occurring within a business may, for example, be plotted against trends for rival businesses or for the industry as a whole for comparison purposes. An example of trend analysis is shown in **Real World 7.9**.

Real World 7.9

Trend setting

In Figure 7.13, the current ratios of three of the UK's leading supermarket companies are plotted over time.

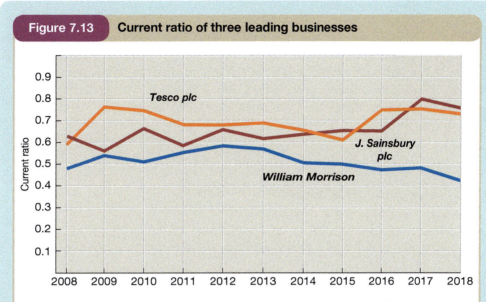

| Figure 7.13 | Current ratio of three leading businesses |

The current ratio for three leading UK supermarket businesses is plotted for the reporting years ended during 2008 to 2018. This enables comparison to be made regarding the ratio, both for each of the three businesses over time and between the businesses.

Source: Ratios calculated from information in the annual reports of the three businesses for each of the years 2008 to 2018.

We can see that the current ratios of the three businesses have tended to move closer. Tesco's ratio was lower than those of its main rivals until 2005; it then overtook Morrison and, in 2009, Sainsbury. Sainsbury's current ratio shows a fairly consistent downward path until 2010. Morrison has tended to maintain the lowest current ratio over time. With well-managed businesses like these, it is highly likely that any changes are the result of deliberate policy.

Source: Annual reports of the three businesses 2008 to 2018.

Using ratios to predict financial failure

Financial ratios, based on current or past performance, are often used to help predict the future. Normally, both the choice of ratios and the interpretation of results are dependent on the judgement and opinion of the analyst. There have been, however, attempts to develop a more rigorous and systematic approach to the use of ratios for prediction purposes. In particular, researchers have investigated the ability of ratios to predict the financial failure of a business.

By financial failure, we mean a business either being forced out of business or being severely adversely affected by its inability to meet its financial obligations. It is often referred to as 'going bust' or 'going bankrupt'. This is, of course, a likely area of concern for all those connected with the business.

Using single ratios

Various ways of using ratios to predict future financial failure have been developed. Early research focused on seeing whether a single ratio was a good or bad predictor of financial failure. It involved tracking a particular ratio (for example, the current ratio) for a business over several years leading up to the date of failure. The purpose was to see whether changes in the ratio revealed a trend that could have been taken as a warning sign.

Beaver (see Reference 1 at the end of the chapter) carried out the first systematic research in this area. He identified 79 businesses that had failed. He then calculated the average (mean) of various ratios for these 79 businesses, going back over the financial statements of each business for each of the 10 years leading up to each business's failure. Beaver then compared these average ratios with similarly derived ratios for a sample of 79 businesses that did not fail over this period. (The research used a matched-pair design, where each failed business was matched with a non-failed business of similar size and industry type.) Beaver found that some ratios exhibited a marked difference between the failed and non-failed businesses for up to five years prior to failure. These ratios were:

- Cash flow/Total debt;
- Net income (profit)/Total assets;
- Total debt/Total assets;
- Working capital/Total assets;
- Current ratio: and
- No credit interval (that is, cash generated from operations to maturing obligations).

To illustrate Beaver's findings, the average current ratio of failed businesses for five years prior to failure, along with the average current ratio of non-failed businesses for the same period, are shown in Figure 7.14.

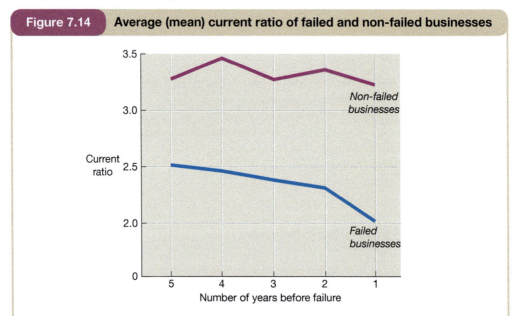

| Figure 7.14 | **Average (mean) current ratio of failed and non-failed businesses** |

The vertical scale of the graph is the average value of the current ratio for each group of businesses (failed and non-failed). The horizontal axis is the number of years before failure. Thus, Year 1 is the most recent year and Year 5 the least recent year. We can see that a clear difference between the average for the failed and non-failed businesses can be detected five years prior to the failure of the former group.

Research by Zmijewski (see Reference 2 at the end of the chapter), using a sample of 72 failed and 3,573 non-failed businesses over a six-year period, found that businesses that ultimately went on to fail were characterised by lower rates of return, higher levels of gearing, lower levels of coverage for their fixed interest payments and more variable returns on shares. While we may not find these results very surprising, it is interesting to note that Zmijewski, like a number of other researchers in this area, did not find liquidity ratios particularly useful in predicting financial failure. Intuition might have led us (wrongly it seems) to believe that the liquidity ratios would have been particularly helpful in this context. As we saw earlier, however, Beaver did find the current ratio to be a useful predictor.

The approach adopted by Beaver and Zmijewski is referred to as **univariate analysis** because it looks at one ratio at a time. Although this approach can produce interesting results, there are practical problems associated with its use.

Activity 7.30

Let us assume that research indicates that a particular ratio is shown to be a good pre-dictor of failure. Can you think of a practical problem that may arise when using this ratio to predict financial failure for a particular business?

Where a particular ratio for a business differs from the average value for that same ratio for non-failed businesses, the analyst must rely on judgement to interpret whether this difference is significant. There is no clear decision rule that can be applied. Different analysts may, there-fore, come to different conclusions about the likelihood of failure.

A further problem arises where more than one ratio is used to predict failure. Let us say, for example, that past research has identified two ratios as being good predictors of finan-cial failure. When applied to a particular business, however, it may be that one ratio pre-dicts financial failure, whereas the other does not. Given these conflicting signals, how should the analyst interpret the results?

Using combinations of ratios

The weaknesses of univariate analysis have led researchers to develop models that com-bine ratios in such a way as to produce a single index that can be interpreted more clearly. One approach to model development, much favoured by researchers, employs **multiple discriminate analysis (MDA)**. This is, in essence, a statistical technique that is similar to regression analysis and which can be used to draw a boundary between those businesses that fail and those businesses that do not. This boundary is referred to as the **discriminate function**. In this context, MDA attempts to identify those factors likely to influence finan-cial failure. However, unlike regression analysis, MDA assumes that the observations come from two different populations (for example, failed and non-failed businesses) rather than from a single population.

To illustrate this approach, let us assume that we wish to test whether two ratios (say, the current ratio and the return on capital employed) can help to predict failure. To do this, we can calculate these ratios, first for a sample of failed businesses and then for a matched sample of non-failed ones. From these two sets of data we can produce a scatter diagram that plots each business according to these two ratios to produce a single co-ordinate. Figure 7.15 illustrates this approach.

Using the observations plotted on the diagram, we try to identify the boundary between the failed and the non-failed businesses. This is the diagonal line in Figure 7.15.

We can see that those businesses that fall below and to the left of the line are predomi-nantly failed and those that fall to the right are predominantly non-failed ones. Note, however, that there is some overlap between the two populations. In practice, the bound-ary produced is unlikely, therefore, to eliminate all errors. Some businesses that ultimately fail may fall on the non-failed businesses side of the boundary. The opposite also happens. However, the analysis will tend to minimise the misclassification errors.

The boundary shown in Figure 7.15 can be expressed in the form

$$Z = a + (b \times \text{Current ratio}) + (c \times \text{ROCE})$$

where *a, b* and *c* are all constants and *b* and *c* are weights to be attached to each ratio. A weighted average or total score (Z) is then derived. By 'constants' we mean that the same values are used for assessing each individual business. The values ascribed to these constants are those that have been found in practice to provide a Z-score that most effectively is able to differentiate between the failed and the non-failed businesses. Using this model to assess a particular business's health, we would deduce the current and ROCE ratios for that business and use them in the equation above. If the resulting Z-score were to come out below a certain value, we should view that business as being at risk.

Note that this example, using the current and ROCE ratios, is purely hypothetical and only intended to illustrate the approach.

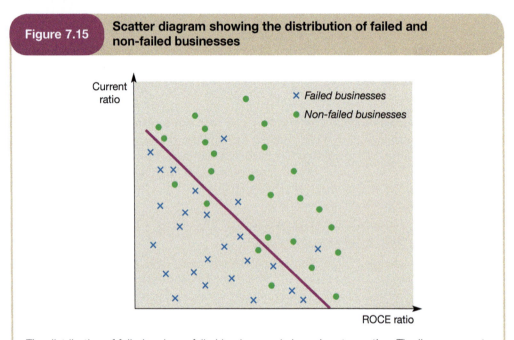

Figure 7.15   **Scatter diagram showing the distribution of failed and non-failed businesses**

The distribution of failed and non-failed businesses is based on two ratios. The line represents a boundary between the samples of failed and non-failed businesses. Although there is some crossing of the boundary, the boundary represents the line that minimises the problem of mis-classifying particular businesses.

Z-score models

Altman was the first to combine financial ratios in a way that successfully predicted financial distress among businesses. The Z-score model that he devised was developed in 1968 and is based on five financial ratios. It is as follows:

$$Z = 1.2a + 1.4b + 3.3c + 0.6d + 1.0e$$

where

a = Working capital (current assets – current liabilities)/Total assets
b = Retained earnings/Total assets
c = Operating profit/Total assets
d = Market value of equity shares/Total liabilities at book (statement of financial position) value
e = Sale revenue/Total assets

The weightings (or coefficients) in the above model are constants that reflect the importance to the Z-score of each of the ratios (*a* to *e*). It is interesting to note that Operating profit/Total assets (a profitability ratio) is given far more weight in the model than Working capital/ Total assets (a liquidity ratio). The five ratios employed were identified by Altman through trial and error, as there is no theory of financial distress to offer guidance as to which ratios should be chosen.

According to Altman, those businesses with a Z-score of less than 1.81 occupy a 'distress zone'. This means that they are unstable and have a high risk of failure within two years. (The lower the score, the greater the risk of failure.) Those with a Z-score greater than 2.99 are considered to be financially stable and occupy a 'safe zone'. Those businesses with a Z-score between 1.81 and 2.99 occupy a 'grey zone' (or zone of uncertainty), where there is some risk of financial distress within two years. The model has demonstrated a high level of predictive ability. In a series of, conducted by Altman, tests over sample periods up to 1999, it had between 80 per cent and 90 per cent accuracy in predicting financial distress one year prior to the event. However, the accuracy of the model diminishes significantly as the lead time increases. (See Reference 3 at the end of the chapter.)

Altman based his original model on US manufacturing businesses but later adapted it to non-manufacturing businesses. (The adapted model excludes the Sales revenue/Total assets ratio as non-manufacturing businesses tend to have a smaller asset base.) Further adaptations were carried out to accommodate private businesses and businesses in emerging markets.

In recent years, other models, using a similar approach, have been developed throughout the world. In the UK, Taffler has developed separate Z-score models for different types of business. (See Reference 4 at the end of the chapter for a discussion of the work of Taffler and others.)

Real World 7.10 is based on an article that shows the distribution of Z-scores among large US companies.

Real World 7.10

From A to Z

A study of the Z-scores of 500 large listed US business was carried out, which revealed the following distribution of scores [see Figure 7.16].

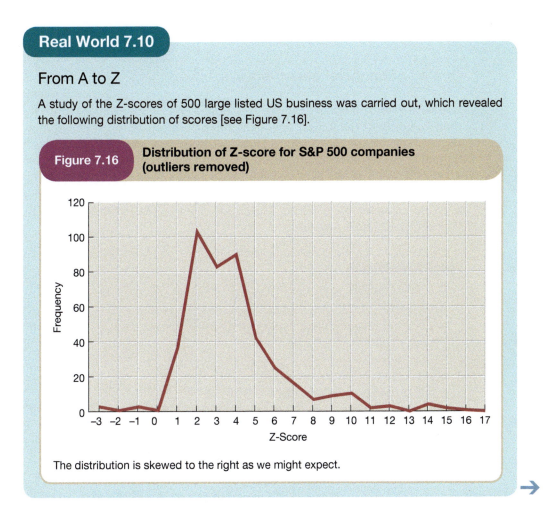

Figure 7.16 Distribution of Z-score for S&P 500 companies (outliers removed)

The distribution is skewed to the right as we might expect.

There has been a great deal of investigation, much of it by academics, into the effectiveness of Altman's Z-score model, or some variation of it. These investigations, which span different economies and industries, overwhelmingly support the model. Further support can be seen through its widespread use among businesses and independent analysts for decision making purpose.

The prediction of financial failure is not the only area where research into the predictive ability of ratios has taken place. Researchers have also developed ratio-based models to assess the vulnerability of a business to takeover by another. This is another area that is of vital importance to all those connected with the business.

Limitations of ratio analysis

Although ratios offer a quick, simple and useful method of analysing the position and performance of a business, they are not without their problems and limitations. We shall now review some of their shortcomings.

Quality of financial statements

It must always be remembered that ratios are based on financial statements. They will, therefore, inherit the limitations of the financial statements on which they are based. In Chapter 2, we saw that one important limitation of financial statements is their failure to include all resources controlled by the business. Internally generated goodwill and brands, for example, are excluded from the statement of financial position because they fail to meet the strict definition of an asset. This means that, even though these resources may be of considerable value, key ratios such as ROSF, ROCE and the gearing ratio will fail to acknowledge their presence.

Activity 7.31

Assume that a business has internally generated goodwill that had been created in earlier years. If this resource were introduced as a non-current asset with an indefinite life in the current statement of financial position, what would be the effect on ROSF, ROCE and the gearing ratio?

The effect of introducing internally generated goodwill will be similar to that of an asset revaluation, which we considered in Chapter 2. Total assets will increase and equity will also increase. An increase in equity will increase the denominator (lower part of the fraction) for all three ratios. This will, in turn, lead to lower ratios than would be the case if the goodwill were not introduced.

The quality of financial statements may also be undermined by deliberate attempts to make them misleading. We discussed this problem of *creative accounting* in Chapter 5.

Inflation

A persistent, albeit recently less severe, problem, in most countries is that the financial results of businesses can be distorted as a result of inflation. One effect of inflation is that the reported value of assets that have been held for any length of time may bear little relation to current values. Generally speaking, the reported value of assets will be understated in current terms during a period of inflation as they are usually reported at their original cost (less any amounts written off for depreciation). This means that comparisons, either between businesses or between periods, will be hindered. A difference in, say, ROCE may simply be due to assets, shown in one of the statements of financial position being compared, having been acquired more recently (ignoring the effect of depreciation on the asset values). Another effect of inflation is to distort the measurement of profit. In the calculation of profit, sales revenue is often matched with costs incurred at an earlier time. This is because there is often a time lag between acquiring a particular resource and using it to help generate sales revenue. For example, inventories may well be acquired several months before they are sold. During a period of inflation, this will mean that the expense may not reflect prices that are current at the time of the sale. The cost of sales figure is usually based on the historic cost of the inventories concerned. As a result, expenses will be understated in the income statement and this, in turn, means that profit will be overstated. One effect of this will be to distort the profitability ratios discussed earlier.

The restricted view given by ratios

It is important not to rely exclusively on ratios, thereby losing sight of information contained in the underlying financial statements. As we saw earlier in this chapter, some items reported in these statements can be vital in assessing position and performance. For example, the total sales revenue, capital employed and profit figures may be useful in assessing changes in absolute size that occur over time, or in assessing differences in scale between businesses. The standard ratios do not provide such information. When comparing one figure with another, ratios measure *relative* performance and position and, therefore, provide only part of the picture. When comparing two businesses, therefore, it will often be useful to assess the absolute size of profits, as well as the relative profitability of each business. For example, Business A may generate £1 million operating profit and have a ROCE of 15 per cent and Business B may generate £100,000 operating profit and have a ROCE of 20 per cent. Although Business B has a higher level of *profitability*, as measured by ROCE, it nevertheless generates lower total operating profits. This fact should not be overlooked.

The basis for comparison

We saw earlier that if ratios are to be useful they require a basis for comparison. Moreover, it is important that we compare like with like. Where the comparison is with another business, there can be difficulties. No two businesses are identical: the greater the differences between the businesses being compared, the greater are the limitations of ratio analysis. Furthermore, any differences in accounting policies, financing methods (gearing levels) and reporting year-ends will add to the problems of making comparisons between businesses.

Statement of financial position ratios

Because the statement of financial position is only a 'snapshot' of the business at a particular moment in time, any ratios based on statement of financial position figures, such as the liquidity ratios, may not be representative of the financial position of the business for the year as a whole. For example, it is common for a seasonal business to have a reporting year-end that coincides with a low point in business activity. As a result, inventories and trade receivables may be low at that time. This means that the liquidity ratios may also be low. A more representative picture of liquidity can only really be gained by taking additional measurements at other points in the year.

Real World 7.11 points out another way in which ratios are limited.

Real World 7.11

Remember, it's people that really count . . .

Lord Weinstock (1924 to 2002) was an influential industrialist whose management style and philosophy helped to shape management practice in many UK businesses. During his long and successful reign at GEC plc, a major engineering business, Lord Weinstock relied heavily on financial ratios to assess performance and to exercise control. In particular, he relied on ratios relating to sales revenue, expenses, trade receivables, profit margins and inventories turnover. However, he was keenly aware of the limitations of ratios and recognised that, ultimately, people produce profits.

In a memo written to GEC managers he pointed out that ratios are an aid to good management rather than a substitute for it. He wrote:

> The operating ratios are of great value as measures of efficiency but they are only the measures and not efficiency itself. Statistics will not design a product better, make it for a lower cost or increase sales. If ill-used, they may so guide action as to diminish resources for the sake of apparent but false signs of improvement.
>
> Management remains a matter of judgement, of knowledge of products and processes and of understanding and skill in dealing with people. The ratios will indicate how well all these things are being done and will show comparison with how they are done elsewhere. But they will tell us nothing about how to do them. That is what you are meant to do.

Source: Extract from Stephen Aris, *Arnold Weinstock and the Making of GEC* (Aurum Press, 1998), published in *The Sunday Times*, 22 February 1998, p. 3.

Self-assessment question 7.1

Both Ali plc and Bhaskar plc operate wholesale electrical stores throughout the UK. The financial statements of each business for the year ended 30 June 2019 are as follows:

Statements of financial position as at 30 June 2019

	Ali plc £m	Bhaskar plc £m
ASSETS		
Non-current assets		
Property, plant and equipment (cost less depreciation):		
Land and buildings	360.0	510.0
Fixtures and fittings	87.0	91.2
	447.0	601.2

	Ali plc £m	Bhaskar plc £m
Current assets		
Inventories	592.0	403.0
Trade receivables	176.4	321.9
Cash at bank	84.6	91.6
	853.0	816.5
Total assets	1,300.0	1,417.7
EQUITY AND LIABILITIES		
Equity		
£1 ordinary shares	320.0	250.0
Retained earnings	367.6	624.6
	687.6	874.6
Non-current liabilities		
Borrowings – loan notes	190.0	250.0
Current liabilities		
Trade payables	406.4	275.7
Taxation	16.0	17.4
	422.4	293.1
Total equity and liabilities	1,300.0	1,417.7

Income statements for the year ended 30 June 2019

	Ali plc £m	Bhaskar plc £m
Revenue	1,478.1	1,790.4
Cost of sales	(1,018.3)	(1,214.9)
Gross profit	459.8	575.5
Operating expenses	(308.5)	(408.6)
Operating profit	151.3	166.9
Interest payable	(19.4)	(27.5)
Profit before taxation	131.9	139.4
Taxation	(32.0)	(34.8)
Profit for the year	99.9	104.6

All purchases and sales were on credit. The market values of a share in Ali plc and Bhaskar plc at the end of the year were £6.50 and £8.20, respectively.

Required:

(a) For each business, calculate two ratios that are concerned with each of the following aspects:
- profitability
- efficiency
- liquidity
- gearing
- investment

(ten ratios in total).

What can you conclude from the ratios that you have calculated?

(b) Calculate the Z-scores for each business using the Altman model. (All workings should be to 2 decimal places.)

(c) Comment on the Z-scores for each business and on the validity of applying the Altman model to these particular businesses.

The solution to this question can be found at the back of the book on pages 756–757.

Summary

The main points of this chapter may be summarised as follows:

Ratio analysis

- Compares two related figures, usually both from the same set of financial statements.
- Is an aid to understanding what the financial statements really mean.
- Is an inexact science so results must be interpreted cautiously.
- Usually requires the performance for past periods, similar businesses and/or planned performance as benchmark ratios.
- Can often benefit from a brief overview of the financial statements to provide insights that may not be revealed by ratios and/or may help in the interpretation of them.

Profitability ratios

- Are concerned with effectiveness at generating profit.
- Most commonly found in practice are the return on ordinary shareholders' funds (ROSF), return on capital employed (ROCE), operating profit margin and gross profit margin.

Efficiency ratios

- Are concerned with efficiency of using assets/resources.
- Most commonly found in practice are the average inventories turnover period, average settlement period for trade receivables, average settlement period for trade payables, sales revenue to capital employed and sales revenue per employee.

Liquidity ratios

- Are concerned with the ability to meet short-term obligations.
- Most commonly found in practice are the current ratio, the acid test ratio and the cash generated to maturing obligations ratio.

Gearing ratios

- Are concerned with relationship between equity and debt financing.
- Most commonly found in practice are the gearing ratio and the interest cover ratio.

Investment ratios

- Are concerned with returns to shareholders.
- Most commonly found in practice are the dividend payout ratio, the dividend yield ratio, earnings per share (EPS), cash generated from operations per share, and the price/earnings (PIE) ratio.

Uses of ratios

- Individual ratios can be tracked to detect trends, for example by plotting them on a graph.
- Ratios can be used to detect signs of overtrading.
- Ratios can be used to predict financial failure.
- Univariate analysis uses a single ratio at a time in an attempt to predict financial failure whereas multiple discriminate analysis (MDA) combines various ratios within a model.

Limitations of ratio analysis

- Ratios are only as reliable as the financial statements from which they derive.
- Inflation can distort the information.
- Ratios give a restricted view.
- It can be difficult to find a suitable benchmark (for example, another business) to compare with.
- Some ratios could mislead due to the 'snapshot' nature of the statement of financial position.

Key terms

For definitions of these terms, see Appendix B.

return on ordinary shareholders' funds ratio (ROSF) *p. 248*
return on capital employed ratio (ROCE) *p. 248*
operating profit margin ratio *p. 251*
gross profit margin ratio *p. 252*
average inventories turnover period ratio *p. 255*
average settlement period for trade receivables ratio *p. 256*
average settlement period for trade payables ratio *p. 256*
sales revenue to capital employed ratio *p. 258*
sales revenue per employee ratio *p. 259*
current ratio *p. 263*
acid test ratio *p. 263*

cash generated from operations (CGO) to maturing obligations ratio *p. 264*
financial gearing *p. 266*
gearing ratio *p. 268*
interest cover ratio *p. 269*
dividend payout ratio *p. 270*
dividend cover ratio *p. 271*
dividend yield ratio *p. 271*
dividend per share *p. 271*
earnings per share (EPS) ratio *p. 272*
cash generated from operations (CGO) per ordinary share ratio *p. 274*
price/earnings (P/E) ratio *p. 275*
overtrading *p. 279*
univariate analysis *p. 283*
multiple discriminate analysis (MDA) *p. 283*
discriminate function *p. 283*

References

1 Beaver, W.H. (1966) Financial ratios as predictors of failure, in *Empirical Research in Accounting: Selected Studies,* pages 71 to 111.

2 Zmijewski, M.E. (1983) Predicting corporate bankruptcy: an empirical comparison of the extent of financial distress models, Research Paper, State University of New York.

3 Altman, E.I. (2000) Predicting financial distress of companies: revisiting the Z-score and Zeta models, New York University Working Paper, June.

4 Neophytou, E., Charitou, A. and Charalambous, C. (2001) Predicting corporate failure: empirical evidence for the UK, University of Southampton Department of Accounting and Management Science Working Paper 01-173.

Further reading

If you would like to explore the topics covered in this chapter in more depth, we recommend the following:

Alexander, D., Britton, A., Jorissen, A. Hoogendoorn, M. and van Mourik, C. (2017) *International Financial Reporting and Analysis,* 7th edn, Cengage Learning EMEA, Chapters 29–31.

Elliott, B. and Elliott, J. (2017) *Financial Accounting and Reporting,* 18th edn, Pearson, Chapters 28 and 29.

Lessambo F. (2019) *Financial Statements: Analysis and Reporting,* Palgrave Macmillan, Chapter 17.

Revsine, L., Collins, D., Johnson, B., Mittelstaedt, F. and Soffer, L. (2017) *Financial Reporting and Analysis,* 7th edn, McGraw-Hill Education, Chapters 5, 8, 9 and 10.

Critical review questions

Solutions to these questions can be found at the back of the book on pages 775–776.

7.1 In the chapter it was mentioned that ratios help to eliminate some of the problems of comparing businesses of different sizes. Does this mean that size is irrelevant when interpreting and analysing the position and performance of different businesses?

7.2 Two businesses operate in the same industry. One has an inventories turnover period that is longer than the industry average. The other has an inventories turnover period that is shorter than the industry average. Give three possible explanations for each business's inventories turnover period ratio.

7.3 Is it responsible to publish Z-scores of businesses that are in financial difficulties? What are the potential problems of doing this?

7.4 Identify and discuss three reasons why the P/E ratios of two businesses operating within the same industry may differ.

Exercises

Solutions to exercises with coloured numbers can be found at the back of the book on pages 797–799.

Basic-level exercises

7.1 Set out below are ratios relating to three different businesses. Each business operates within a different industrial sector.

Ratio	A plc	B plc	C plc
Operating profit margin	3.6%	9.7%	6.8%
Sales to capital employed	2.4 times	3.1 times	1.7 times
Average inventories turnover period	18 days	N/A	44 days
Average settlement period for trade receivables	2 days	12 days	26 days
Current ratio	0.8 times	0.6 times	1.5 times

Required:

State, with reasons, which one of the three businesses is:

(a) a holiday tour operator;

(b) a supermarket chain;

(c) a food manufacturer.

7.2 Amsterdam Ltd and Berlin Ltd are both engaged in retailing, but they seem to take a different approach to it according to the following information:

Ratio	Amsterdam Ltd	Berlin Ltd
Return on capital employed (ROCE)	20%	17%
Return on ordinary shareholders' funds (ROSF)	30%	18%
Average settlement period for trade receivables	63 days	21 days
Average settlement period for trade payables	50 days	45 days
Gross profit margin	40%	15%
Operating profit margin	10%	10%
Average inventories turnover period	52 days	25 days

Required:

Describe what this information indicates about the differences in approach between the two businesses. If one of them prides itself on personal service and one of them on competitive prices, which do you think is which and why?

Intermediate-level exercises

7.3 The directors of Helena Beauty Products Ltd have been presented with the following abridged financial statements:

Helena Beauty Products Ltd
Income statement for the year ended 30 September

	2018		2019	
	£000	£000	£000	£000
Sales revenue		3,600		3,840
Cost of sales				
Opening inventories	320		400	
Purchases	2,240		2,350	
	2,560		2,750	
Closing inventories	(400)	(2,160)	(500)	(2,250)
Gross profit		1,440		1,590
Expenses		(1,360)		(1,500)
Profit		80		90

Statement of financial position as at 30 September

	2018	2019
	£000	£000
ASSETS		
Non-current assets		
Property, plant and equipment	1,900	1,860
Current assets		
Inventories	400	500
Trade receivables	750	960
Cash at bank	8	4
	1,158	1,464
Total assets	3,058	3,324

	2018 £000	2019 £000
EQUITY AND LIABILITIES		
Equity		
£1 ordinary shares	1,650	1,766
Retained earnings	1,018	1,108
	2,668	2,874
Current liabilities	390	450
Total equity and liabilities	3,058	3,324

Required:
Using six ratios, comment on the profitability (three ratios) and efficiency (three ratios) of the business.

7.4 Conday and Co. Ltd has been in operation for three years and produces antique reproduction furniture for the export market. The most recent set of financial statements for the business is set out as follows:

Statement of financial position as at 30 November

	£000
ASSETS	
Non-current assets	
Property, plant and equipment (cost less depreciation)	
Land and buildings	228
Plant and machinery	762
	990
Current assets	
Inventories	600
Trade receivables	820
	1,420
Total assets	2,410
EQUITY AND LIABILITIES	
Equity	
Ordinary shares of £1 each	700
Retained earnings	365
	1,065
Non-current liabilities	
Borrowings – 9% loan notes (Note 1)	200
Current liabilities	
Trade payables	665
Taxation	48
Short-term borrowings (all bank overdraft)	432
	1,145
Total equity and liabilities	2,410

Income statement for the year ended 30 November

	£000
Revenue	2,600
Cost of sales	(1,620)
Gross profit	980
Selling and distribution expenses (Note 2)	(408)
Administration expenses	(194)
Operating profit	378
Finance expenses	(58)
Profit before taxation	320
Taxation	(95)
Profit for the year	225

Notes:
1 The loan notes are secured on the land and buildings.
2 Selling and distribution expenses include £170,000 in respect of bad debts.
3 A dividend of £160,000 was paid on the ordinary shares during the year.
4 The directors have invited an investor to take up a new issue of ordinary shares in the business at £6.40 each making a total investment of £200,000. The directors wish to use the funds to finance a programme of further expansion.

Required:
(a) Analyse the financial position and performance of the business and comment on any features that you consider significant.
(b) State, with reasons, whether or not the investor should invest in the business on the terms outlined.

Advanced-level exercises

7.5 Threads Limited manufactures nuts and bolts, which are sold to industrial users. The abbreviated financial statements for 2018 and 2019 are as follows:

Income statements for the year ended 30 June

	2018	2019
	£000	£000
Revenue	1,180	1,200
Cost of sales	(680)	(750)
Gross profit	500	450
Operating expenses	(200)	(208)
Depreciation	(66)	(75)
Operating profit	234	167
Interest	(–)	(8)
Profit before taxation	234	159
Taxation	(80)	(48)
Profit for the year	154	111

Statements of financial position as at 30 June

	2018	2019
	£000	£000
ASSETS		
Non-current assets		
Property, plant and equipment	702	687
Current assets		
Inventories	148	236
Trade receivables	102	156
Cash	3	4
	253	396
Total assets	955	1,083
EQUITY AND LIABILITIES		
Equity		
Ordinary share capital (£1 shares, fully paid)	500	500
Retained earnings	256	295
	756	795
Non-current liabilities		
Borrowings – bank loan	–	50
Current liabilities		
Trade payables	60	76
Other payables and accruals	18	16
Taxation	40	24
Short-term borrowings (all bank overdraft)	81	122
	199	238
Total equity and liabilities	955	1,083

Dividends were paid on ordinary shares of £70,000 and £72,000 in respect of 2018 and 2019, respectively.

Required:

(a) Calculate the following financial ratios for *both* 2018 and 2019 (using year-end figures for statement of financial position items):

    1 return on capital employed
    2 operating profit margin
    3 gross profit margin
    4 current ratio
    5 acid test ratio
    6 settlement period for trade receivables
    7 settlement period for trade payables
    8 inventories turnover period.

(b) Comment on the performance of Threads Limited from the viewpoint of a business considering supplying a substantial amount of goods to Threads Limited on usual trade credit terms.

7.6 Genesis Ltd was incorporated three years ago and has grown rapidly since then. The rapid rate of growth has created problems for the business, which the directors have found difficult to deal with. Recently, a firm of management consultants has been asked to help the directors to overcome these problems.

In a preliminary report to the board of directors, the management consultants state: 'Most of the difficulties faced by the business are symptoms of an underlying problem of overtrading.'

The most recent financial statements of the business are set out below.

Statement of financial position as at 31 October

	£000	£000
ASSETS		
Non-current assets		
Property, plant and equipment		
Land and buildings at cost	530	
Accumulated depreciation	(88)	442
Fixtures and fittings at cost	168	
Accumulated depreciation	(52)	116
Motor vans at cost	118	
Accumulated depreciation	(54)	64
		622
Current assets		
Inventories		128
Trade receivables		104
		232
Total assets		854
EQUITY AND LIABILITIES		
Equity		
Ordinary £0.50 shares		60
General reserve		50
Retained earnings		74
		184
Non-current liabilities		
Borrowings – 10% loan notes (secured)		120
Current liabilities		
Trade payables		184
Taxation		8
Short-term borrowings (all bank overdraft)		358
		550
Total equity and liabilities		854

Income statement for the year ended 31 October

	£000	£000
Revenue		1,640
Cost of sales:		
Opening inventories	116	
Purchases	1,260	
	1,376	
Closing inventories	(128)	(1,248)
Gross profit		392
Selling and distribution expenses		(204)
Administration expenses		(92)
Operating profit		96
Interest payable		(44)
Profit before taxation		52
Taxation		(16)
Profit for the year		36

All purchases and sales were on credit.
A dividend was paid during the year on ordinary shares of £4,000.

Required:

(a) Calculate and discuss five financial ratios that might be used to establish whether the business is overtrading. Do these five ratios suggest that the business is overtrading?

(b) State the ways in which a business may overcome the problem of overtrading.

7.7 The financial statements for Harridges Ltd are given below for the two years ended 30 June 2018 and 2019. Harridges Limited operates a department store in the centre of a small town.

Income statements for the years ended 30 June

	2018 £000	2019 £000
Sales revenue	2,600	3,500
Cost of sales	(1,560)	(2,350)
Gross profit	1,040	1,150
Wages and salaries	(320)	(350)
Overheads	(260)	(200)
Depreciation	(150)	(250)
Operating profit	310	350
Interest payable	(50)	(50)
Profit before taxation	260	300
Taxation	(105)	(125)
Profit for the year	155	175

Statement of financial position as at 30 June

	2018 £000	2019 £000
ASSETS		
Non-current assets		
Property, plant and equipment	1,265	1,525
Current assets		
Inventories	250	400
Trade receivables	105	145
Cash at bank	380	115
	735	660
Total assets	2,000	2,185
EQUITY AND LIABILITIES		
Equity		
Share capital: £1 shares fully paid	490	490
Share premium	260	260
Retained earnings	350	450
	1,100	1,200
Non-current liabilities		
Borrowings – 10% loan notes	500	500
Current liabilities		
Trade payables	300	375
Other payables	100	110
	400	485
Total equity and liabilities	2,000	2,185

Dividends were paid on ordinary shares of £65,000 and £75,000 in respect of 2018 and 2019, respectively.

Required:

(a) Choose and calculate eight ratios that would be helpful in assessing the performance of Harridges Ltd. Use end-of-year values and calculate ratios for both 2018 and 2019.

(b) Using the ratios calculated in (a) and any others you consider helpful, comment on the business's performance from the viewpoint of a prospective purchaser of a majority of shares.

Supplementary information

Part 4 provides information that is supplementary to the main text.

Appendix A takes the format of a normal textual chapter and describes the way in which financial transactions can be recorded, usually manually, in books of account. Generally, this is by means of the 'double-entry' system, described in basic terms in the appendix.

Appendix B gives definitions of the key terms highlighted throughout the main text and listed at the end of each chapter. The aim of the appendix is to provide a single location to check on the meanings of the major accounting terms used in this book and in the world of finance.

Appendices C, D and E give answers to some of the questions set in the course of the main text. Appendix C gives answers to the self-assessment questions, Appendix D gives the answers to the critical review questions and Appendix E gives answers to those of the exercises that are marked as having their answers provided in the book.

Appendix F is a table of present value factors that can be used to discount future cash flows.

Recording financial transactions

Introduction

In Chapters 2 and 3, we saw how the financial transactions of a business may be recorded by making a series of entries on the statement of financial position and/or the income statement. Each of these entries had its corresponding 'double', meaning that both sides of the transaction were recorded. However, adjusting the financial statements for each transaction, by hand, can be pretty messy and confusing. Where there are many transactions, as there tends to be even for a fairly small business, it is pretty certain to result in mistakes.

For businesses whose accounting systems are on a computer, this problem is overcome because suitable software can deal with a series of 'plus' and 'minus' entries very reliably. Where the accounting system is not computerised, however, it would be helpful to have some more practical way of keeping accounting records. Such a system not only exists but, before the advent of the computer, was the routine way of keeping accounting records. In fact, the system had been in constant use for recording business transactions since medieval times. It is this system that we shall now examine. We should be clear that the system follows exactly the same rules as those that we have already met. Its distinguishing feature is that it provides those keeping accounting records, by hand, with a methodical approach that allows each transaction to be clearly identified and errors to be minimised.

Learning outcomes

When you have completed this appendix, you should be able to:

- explain the basic principles of double-entry bookkeeping;

- write up a series of business transactions and balance the accounts;

- extract a trial balance and explain its purpose; and

- prepare a set of financial statements from the underlying double-entry accounts.

The basics of double-entry bookkeeping

When we record accounting transactions by hand, we use a recording system known as **double-entry bookkeeping**. This system does not use plus and minus entries on the face of a statement of financial position and income statement to record a particular transaction, in the way described in Chapters 2 and 3. Instead, individual transactions are recorded in accounts. An **account** is simply a record of one or more transactions relating to a particular item of asset, claim, revenue or expense, such as:

- cash at bank;
- property, plant and equipment;
- borrowings;
- sales revenue;
- rent payable; and
- equity.

A business may keep few or many accounts, depending on the size and complexity of its operations. Broadly, businesses tend to keep a separate account for each item that appears in either the income statement or the statement of financial position.

An example of an account, in this case the *cash at bank* account, is as follows:

Cash at bank

£	£

We can see that an account, which has a T-shape (and is often known as a *T account*), has three main features:

- a title indicating the item to which it relates;
- a left-hand side, known as the **debit** side; and
- a right-hand side, known as the **credit** side.

One side of an account will record increases in the particular item and the other will record decreases. This, of course, is slightly different from the approach that we used when adjusting the financial statements. When adjusting the statement of financial position, for example, we put a reduction in an asset or claim in the same column as any increases, but with a minus sign against it. However, when T accounts are used, a reduction is shown on the opposite side of the account.

The side on which an increase or decrease is shown will depend on the nature of the item to which the account relates. For example, an account for an asset, such as cash at bank, will show increases on the left-hand (debit) side of the account and decreases on the right-hand (credit) side. However, for claims (that is, equity and liabilities) it is the other way around. An increase in equity or for a liability will be shown on the right-hand (credit) side and a decrease will be shown on the left-hand (debit) side of the relevant account.

To understand why this difference exists, we need to go back to the accounting equation that we first came across in Chapter 2.

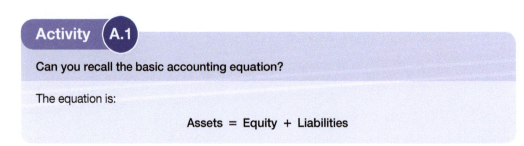

Activity A.1

Can you recall the basic accounting equation?

The equation is:

$$\text{Assets} = \text{Equity} + \text{Liabilities}$$

We can see that assets appear on one side of the equation and equity and liabilities appear on the other. Recording transactions in accounts simply expresses this difference in the recording process. Increases in assets are shown on the debit (left-hand) side of an account and increases in equity and liabilities are shown on the credit (right-hand) side of the account. We should recall the point made in Chapter 2 that each transaction has two aspects. Thus, when we record a particular transaction, two separate accounts will be affected. Recording transactions in this way is known as *double-entry bookkeeping*.

It is worth going through a simple example to see how transactions affecting statement of financial position items would be recorded under the double-entry bookkeeping system. Suppose a new business started on 1 January with the owner introducing initial equity of £5,000 in cash, which was put into a newly-opened business bank account. The cash introduced will appear in a separate *cash at bank* account. It represents an increase in an asset and so will be shown on the debit (left-hand) side of the account as follows:

Cash at bank

	£		£
1 January Equity	5,000		

The corresponding entry, which reflects the introduction of equity by the owner, will appear in a separate *equity* account. It represents an increase in equity and so will be shown on the credit (right-hand) side as follows:

Equity

	£		£
		1 January Cash at bank	5,000

It is usual to show, in each account by way of note, where the other side of the entry can be found. Thus, someone looking at the equity account will know that the £5,000 arose from an introduction of cash. This provides potentially useful information, partly because it establishes a 'trail' that can be followed when checking for errors. By including the date of the transaction, additional information is provided to the reader of these T accounts.

Now suppose that, on 2 January, £600 of the cash in the bank is used to buy inventories. This would affect the *cash at bank* account as follows:

Cash at bank

	£		£
1 January Equity	5,000	2 January Inventories	600

This account, in effect, shows 'positive' cash of £5,000 and 'negative' cash of £600 a net amount of £4,400.

Activity A.2

As you know, we must record the other side of the transaction involving the acquisition of the inventories for £600. See if you can work out what to do in respect of the inventories and then record the transaction.

We must open a separate account for *inventories*. Since inventories are assets, an increase in it will appear on the debit (left-hand) side of the account, as follows:

Inventories

	£		£
2 January Cash at bank	600		

What we have seen so far highlights the key rule of double-entry bookkeeping: each left-hand entry must have a right-hand entry of equal size. Using the jargon, we can say that:

> **Every debit must have a credit.**

It might be helpful at this point to make it absolutely clear that the words 'debit' and 'credit' are no more than accounting jargon for left and right, respectively. When used outside the context of accounting, people tend to use the word 'credit' to imply something good and 'debit' something undesirable. When used in accounting, however, the words 'debit' and 'credit' have no such implication. Each transaction requires both a debit entry and a credit entry. This is true whether the transaction is 'good', like receiving cash from a credit customer, or 'bad', like having to treat a credit customer's balance as worthless because the customer has gone bankrupt.

Recording trading transactions

The rules of double entry also extend to 'trading' transactions, which involve making revenues (sales and so on) and incurring expenses. To understand how these transactions are recorded, we should recall that in Chapter 3 the extended accounting equation was set out as follows:

> **Assets = Equity + (Revenues − Expenses) + Liabilities**

This equation can be rearranged as follows:

> **Assets + Expenses = Equity + Revenues + Liabilities**

We can see that increases in expenses are shown on the same side as assets. This means that they will be dealt with in the same way for recording purposes. Thus, an increase in an expense, such as wages, will be shown on the debit (left-hand) side of the *wages* account and a decrease will be shown on the credit (right-hand) side. Increases in revenues are shown on the same side as equity and liabilities and so will be dealt with in the same way. Thus, an increase in revenues, such as sales, will be shown on the credit (right-hand) side of the *sales revenue* account and a decrease will be shown on the debit (left-hand) side. To summarise, therefore, we can say that:

- Debits (left-hand entries) represent increases in assets and expenses and decreases in equity, liabilities and revenues.
- Credits (right-hand entries) represent increases in equity, liabilities and revenues and decreases in assets and expenses.

Let us continue with our example by assuming that, on 3 January, the business paid £900 to rent business premises for the three months to 31 March. To record this transaction, we should normally open a *rent* account and make entries in this account and in the *cash at bank* account as follows:

Rent			
	£		£
3 January Cash at bank	900		

Cash at bank

	£		£
1 January Equity	5,000	2 January Inventories	600
		3 January Rent	900

The fact that assets and expenses are dealt with in the same way should not be altogether surprising; assets and expenses are closely linked. Most assets transform into expenses as they are 'used up'. Rent, which, as here, is usually paid in advance, is an asset when it is first paid. It represents the value to the business of being entitled to occupy the premises for the forthcoming period (until 31 March in this case). As the three months progress, this asset becomes an expense; it is 'used up'. The debit entry in the rent account does not necessarily represent either an asset or an expense; it could be a mixture of the two. Strictly, by the end of the day on which it was paid (3 January), £30 would have represented an expense for the three days; the remaining £870 would have been an asset. As each day passes, an additional £10 (that is, £900/90 (there are 90 days in January, February and March altogether)) will transform from an asset into an expense. As we have already seen, it is not necessary for us to make any adjustment to the rent account as the days pass. We can, and usually do, separate the expense element from the asset element at the end of the reporting period, as we shall see later in this appendix.

Now let us assume that, on 5 January, the business sold inventories costing £200 for £300 on credit. When we can identify the cost of the inventories sold at the time of sale, we should deal with the sale and the cost of sales separately, with each having its own debits and credits.

First, let us deal with the sale. We need to open separate accounts for both sales revenue and trade receivables – which do not, as yet, exist.

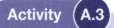 **Activity A.3**

Can you work out what to do in respect of the sale? Show the entries in the relevant accounts.

The sale gives rise to an increase in revenue and so there is a credit entry in the *sales revenue* account. The sale also creates an asset of trade receivables and so there is debit entry in the *trade receivables* account.

The two accounts will, therefore, be as follows:

Sales revenue

	£		£
		5 January Trade receivables	300

Trade receivables

	£		£
5 January Sales revenue	300		

Let us now deal with the inventories sold. Since they have become the expense 'cost of sales', we need to reduce the figure on the inventories account by making a credit entry. We must also make a corresponding debit in a *cost of sales* account, opened for the purpose:

Inventories

	£		£
2 January Cash at bank	600	5 January Cost of sales	200

Cost of sales

	£		£
5 January Inventories	200		

We shall now look at other transactions for our hypothetical business for the remainder of January. They are as follows:

8 January	Bought some inventories on credit costing £800
11 January	Bought some office furniture for £600 cash
15 January	Sold inventories costing £600 for £900, on credit
18 January	Received £800 from trade receivables
21 January	Paid trade payables £500
24 January	Paid wages for the month £400
27 January	Bought inventories on credit for £800
31 January	Borrowed £2,000 from the Commercial Finance Company

We have to open several additional accounts to enable us to record all of these transactions. By the end of January, the set of accounts would appear as follows:

Cash at bank

	£		£
1 January Equity	5,000	2 January Inventories	600
18 January Trade receivables	800	3 January Rent	900
31 January Borrowings	2,000	11 January Office furniture	600
		21 January Trade payables	500
		24 January Wages	400

Equity

	£		£
		1 January Cash at bank	5,000

Inventories

	£		£
2 January Cash at bank	600	5 January Cost of sales	200
8 January Trade payables	800	15 January Cost of sales	600
27 January Trade payables	800		

Rent

	£		£
3 January Cash at bank	900		

Sales revenue

	£		£
		5 January Trade receivables	300
		15 January Trade receivables	900

Trade receivables

	£		£
5 January Sales revenue	300	18 January Cash at bank	800
15 January Sales revenue	900		

Cost of sales

	£		£
5 January Inventories	200		
15 January Inventories	600		

Trade payables

	£		£
21 January Cash at bank	500	8 January Inventories	800
		27 January Inventories	800

Office furniture

	£		£
11 January Cash at bank	600		

Wages

	£		£
24 January Cash at bank	400		

Borrowings

	£		£
		31 January Cash at bank	2,000

All of the transactions from 8 January onwards are similar to those up to that date, which have been discussed in detail. We should, therefore, be able to follow them using the date references as our guide.

Balancing accounts and the trial balance

Businesses keeping their accounts, in the way that we have been following, find it helpful to summarise their individual accounts periodically – perhaps weekly or monthly – for two reasons:

- to see at a glance how much is in each account (for example, to see how much cash the business has left); and
- to check the accuracy of the bookkeeping so far.

Let us look at the *cash at bank* account again:

Cash at bank

	£		£
1 January Equity	5,000	2 January Inventories	600
18 January Trade receivables	800	3 January Rent	900
31 January Borrowings	2,000	11 January Office furniture	600
		21 January Trade payables	500
		24 January Wages	400

Does this account tell us how much cash the business has at 31 January? The answer is partly yes and partly no.

We do not have a single figure showing the cash at bank **balance**, but we can easily deduce this by adding up the debit (receipts) column and deducting the sum of the credit (payments) column. It would be better, however, if the current balance were clearly shown.

To summarise, or *balance,* this account, we simply add up the column with the larger amount (in this case, the debit side) and put this total on both sides of the account. We then record, on the credit side (in this case), the figure that will make that side add up to the total appearing on both sides of the account. We cannot record this balancing figure just once, as that would contravene the double-entry rule. Thus, to preserve the double entry, we must also *carry down* this figure. This involves putting it on the other side of the same account below the totals, as follows:

Cash at bank

	£		£
1 January Equity	5,000	2 January Inventories	600
18 January Trade receivables	800	3 January Rent	900
31 January Borrowings	2,000	11 January Office furniture	600
		21 January Trade payables	500
		24 January Wages	400
		31 January Balance carried down	4,800
	7,800		7,800
1 February Balance brought down	4,800		

Note that the *balance carried down* (usually abbreviated to 'c/d') at the end of one period becomes the *balance brought down* ('b/d') at the beginning of the next. We can now see at a glance what the cash position is, without having to do any mental arithmetic.

Activity A.4

Try balancing the inventories account and then state what we know about the inventories position at the end of January.

The inventories account will be balanced as follows:

Inventories

	£		£
2 January Cash at bank	600	5 January Cost of sales	200
8 January Trade payables	800	15 January Cost of sales	600
27 January Trade payables	800	31 January Balance c/d	1,400
	2,200		2,200
1 February Balance b/d	1,400		

We can see that the business held inventories costing £1,400 at the end of January. We can also see the movements in inventories during January that led to this figure being the inventories balance by the end of the month.

The remaining accounts can be balanced in a similar way. However, we need not balance accounts that have only one entry (for example, the equity account for our business at this point). This is because they are already in as summarised a form as it is possible for them to be. Following the balancing process, the remaining accounts will appear as shown below:

Equity

	£		£
		1 January Cash at bank	5,000

Rent

	£		£
3 January Cash at bank	900		

Sales revenue

	£		£
		5 January Trade receivables	300
31 January Balance c/d	1,200	15 January Trade receivables	900
	1,200		1,200
		1 February Balance b/d	1,200

Trade receivables

	£		£
5 January Sales revenue	300	18 January Cash at bank	800
15 January Sales revenue	900	31 January Balance c/d	400
	1,200		1,200
1 February Balance b/d	400		

Cost of sales

	£		£
5 January Inventories	200	31 January Balance c/d	800
15 January Inventories	600		
	800		800
1 February Balance b/d	800		

Trade payables

	£		£
21 January Cash at bank	500	8 January Inventories	800
31 January Balance c/d	1,100	27 January Inventories	800
	1,600		1,600
		1 February Balance b/d	1,100

Office furniture

	£		£
11 January Cash at bank	600		

Wages

	£		£
24 January Cash at bank	400		

Borrowings

	£		£
		31 January Cash at bank	2,000

Activity A.5

If we now make a list of all the accounts, showing each one's balance, and separately total the debit balances and the credit balances, what should we expect to find and why?

We should expect to find that these two totals are equal. This must, in theory, be true since every debit entry was matched by an opposite and equal-sized credit entry.

Let us see if our expectation in Activity A.5 works in our example, by listing the debit and credit balances in separate columns as follows:

	Debits £	Credits £
Cash at bank	4,800	
Inventories	1,400	
Equity		5,000
Rent	900	
Sales revenue		1,200
Trade receivables	400	
Cost of sales	800	
Trade payables		1,100
Office furniture	600	
Wages	400	
Borrowings		2,000
	9,300	9,300

This listing is known as a **trial balance**. The fact that the totals for each column agree provides *some* indication that we have not made any bookkeeping errors.

We cannot, however, have total confidence that there are no errors. Consider, for example, the transaction that took place on 3 January (paid rent for the month of £900). In each of the following cases, all of which are an incorrect treatment of the transaction, the trial balance would still have agreed:

- The transaction was completely omitted from the accounts, that is, no entries were made at all.
- The amount was misread as £9,000 but then (correctly) debited to the rent account and credited to cash at bank.
- The correct amount of £900 was (incorrectly) debited to cash at bank and credited to rent.

Nevertheless, a trial balance, where the totals agree, provides some assurance that the accounts have been correctly recorded.

Activity A.6

Why do you think the words 'debtor' and 'creditor' are used to describe those who owe money or are owed money by a business?

The answer simply is that debtors have a debit balance (that is, a balance brought down on the debit side) in the books of the business, whereas creditors have a credit balance.

Preparing the financial statements (final accounts)

Providing the trial balance totals agree and we are not aware of any errors in recording, the next stage is to prepare the income statement and statement of financial position. Preparing the income statement is simply a matter of going through the individual accounts, identifying those amounts that represent revenues and expenses of the period, and transferring them to the income statement, which is itself part of the double-entry system.

We shall now do this for the example that we have been using. The situation is complicated slightly for three reasons:

- As we know, the £900 rent paid during January relates to the three months January, February and March.
- The business's owner estimates that the electricity used during January is about £110. There is no bill yet from the electricity supply business because it normally bills customers only at the end of each three-month period.
- The business's owner believes that the office furniture should be depreciated by 20 per cent each year (straight-line).

These complications will require end-of-period adjustments to be made. This is easily handled, however, in the double-entry accounts. Let us see how it is done.

After completing the transfer to the income statement, the rent account will appear as follows:

Rent

	£		£
3 January Cash at bank	900	31 January Income statement	300
		Balance c/d	600
	900		900
1 February Balance b/d	600		

At 31 January, two months' rent is still unused and so £600 will be an asset of the business. This amount, which is carried down as a debit balance, will appear in the 31 January statement of financial position. The remaining £300 (representing January's rent) is an expense for the period. It is credited to the rent account and debited to a newly-opened income statement.

Let us now look at the electricity adjustment. After the transfer to the income statement, the electricity account will be as follows:

Electricity

	£		£
		31 January Income statement	110

As there has been no cash payment or other transaction recorded so far for electricity, an account has not yet been opened. It is, therefore, necessary to open one. We must debit the income statement with the £110 of electricity used during January and credit the electricity account with the same amount. At 31 January, this credit balance reflects the amount owed by this business to the electricity supplier. This balance will, once again, appear on the statement of financial position.

Finally, let us look at the adjustment required regarding the office furniture. The depreciation for the month will be 20% × £600 × $\frac{1}{12}$, that is £10. Normal accounting practice is to charge (debit) this to the income statement, with the corresponding credit appearing in a *Depreciation of office furniture* account. The latter entry will be as follows:

Depreciation of office furniture account

	£		£
		31 January Income statement	10

This £10 balance will be shown in the statement of financial position at 31 January. It is deducted from the office furniture asset, as we shall see shortly.

The balances on the following accounts represent straightforward revenue or expenses for the month of January:

- Sales revenue;
- Cost of sales; and
- Wages.

The balances on these accounts will simply be transferred to the income statement.

To transfer these balances to the income statement, we simply debit or credit the account concerned, such that any balance amount is eliminated, and make the corresponding credit or debit in the income statement. Take sales revenue, for example. The sales revenue account has a credit balance (because the balance represents a revenue). We must debit this account with £1,200 and credit the income statement with the same amount. So a credit balance on the sales revenue account becomes a credit entry in the income statement. For these three accounts, then, we have the following:

Sales revenue

	£		£
31 January Balance c/d	1,200	5 January Trade receivables	300
		15 January Trade receivables	900
	1,200		1,200
31 January Income statement	1,200	1 February Balance b/d	1,200

Cost of sales

	£		£
5 January Inventories	200		
15 January Inventories	600	31 January Balance c/d	800
	800		800
1 February Balance b/d	800	31 January Income statement	800

Wages

	£		£
24 January Cash at bank	400	31 January Income statement	400

The income statement will now be as follows:

Income statement

	£		£
31 January Cost of sales	800	31 January Sales revenue	1,200
31 January Rent	300		
31 January Wages	400		
31 January Electricity	110		
31 January Depreciation	10		

We must now transfer the balance on the income statement (a debit balance of £420).

Activity A.7

What does the balance on the income statement represent and to where should it be transferred?

The balance is either the profit or the loss for the period. In this case it is a loss, as the total expenses exceed the total revenue. This loss must be borne by the owner, and it must therefore be transferred to the equity account.

The two accounts will now appear as follows:

Income statement

	£		£
31 January Cost of sales	800	31 January Sales revenue	1,200
31 January Rent	300		
31 January Wages	400		
31 January Electricity	110		
31 January Depreciation	10	31 January Equity (loss)	420
	1,620		1,620

Equity

	£		£
31 January Income statement (loss)	420	1 January Cash at bank	5,000
31 January Balance c/d	4,580		
	5,000		5,000
		1 February Balance b/d	4,580

The final recording entry was to balance the equity account.

Now all of the balances remaining on accounts represent either assets or claims as at 31 January. These balances can now be used to produce a statement of financial position, as follows:

Statement of financial position as at 31 January

	£
ASSETS	
Non-current assets	
Property, plant and equipment	
Office furniture – cost	600
– depreciation	(10)
	590
Current assets	
Inventories	1,400
Prepaid expense	600
Trade receivables	400
Cash at bank	4,800
	7,200
Total assets	7,790
EQUITY AND LIABILITIES	
Owners' equity	4,580
Non-current liability	
Borrowings	2,000
Current liabilities	
Accrued expense	110
Trade payables	1,100
	1,210
Total equity and liabilities	7,790

The income statement could be written in a more stylish manner, for reporting to users, as follows:

Income statement for the month ended 31 January

	£
Sales revenue	1,200
Cost of sales	(800)
Gross profit	400
Rent	(300)
Wages	(400)
Electricity	(110)
Depreciation	(10)
Loss for the month	(420)

The ledger and its division

The book in which the accounts are traditionally kept is known as the **ledger**, and accounts are sometimes referred to as *ledger accounts*.

The ledger is often divided into separate sections. This is for three main reasons:

- Having all of the accounts in one book means that it is only possible for one person at a time to use the accounts, either to make entries or to extract information.

- It can allow specialisation, thereby allowing individual members of the accounts staff to focus on their own part of the system. This can lead to more accurate and efficient record keeping.
- It can lead to greater security and so reduce the risk of fraud.

Activity A.8

Can you think how dividing the ledger into various sections could reduce the risk of fraud?

A different member of staff can be responsible for writing up each section so that no one has access to the entire set of accounts. It then becomes much more difficult to conceal irregular transactions. A withdrawal of cash, for example, could be recorded in one section with the corresponding entry appearing in another section of the ledger, by a different person.

There are no universally accepted rules on the division of the ledger, but the following division is fairly common:

- *The cash book.* This tends to be all of the accounts relating to cash either loose (notes and coins – often known as *petty cash*) or in the bank.
- *The sales (or trade receivables) ledger.* This contains the accounts of all of the business's individual trade receivables.
- *The purchases (or trade payables) ledger.* This consists of the accounts of all of the business's individual trade payables.
- *The nominal ledger.* These accounts tend to be those of expenses and revenue, for example, sales revenue, purchases, wages, rent, and so on.
- *The general ledger.* This contains the remainder of the business's accounts, mainly those to do with non-current assets and long-term finance.

Summary

The main points in this appendix may be summarised as follows:

Double-entry bookkeeping

- Double-entry bookkeeping is a system for keeping accounting records by hand, such that a relatively large volume of transactions can be handled effectively and accurately.
- There is a separate account for each item of asset, claim, expense and revenue.
- Each account is T-shaped and often known as a 'T account'.
- Left-hand (debit) side of the account records increases in assets and expenses and decreases in revenues, equity and liabilities.
- Right-hand (credit) side records increases in revenues, equity and liabilities and decreases in assets and expenses.
- The words 'debit' and 'credit' have no implication of good or bad in accounting – they are simply jargon for left and right.
- There is an equal credit entry in one account for a debit entry in another.
- Double-entry bookkeeping is used to record day-to-day transactions.

Double-entry bookkeeping and financial statements

- Double-entry bookkeeping can be used to generate the income statement.
- The statement of financial position is a list of the of the accounts on which there is a net figure, or balance, after appropriate transfers have been made to the income statement.

Ledgers

- The accounts are traditionally kept in a *ledger,* a term that persists even with computerised accounting.
- The ledger is often broken down into separate sections, each containing particular types of account.

Key terms

For definitions of these terms, see Appendix B.

double-entry bookkeeping
account

debit
credit
balance
trial balance
ledger

Further reading

If you would like to explore the topics covered in this appendix in more depth, we recommend the following:

Benedict, A. and Elliott, B. (2001) *Practical Accounting,* Financial Times Prentice Hall, 2nd edn, Chapters 2–5.

Fardon, M. (2013) *Computer Accounting Systems Tutorial,* Osborne Books, Chapters 1–12.

Thomas, A. and Ward, A.M. (2015) *Introduction to Financial Accounting,* 8th edn, McGraw-Hill, Chapters 7–10.

Wood, F. and Robinson, S. (2017) *Book-keeping and Accounts,* 9th edn, Pearson, Chapters 2–8.

 ## Exercises

The solutions to all three of these exercises can be found at the back of the book

A.1   In respect of each of the following transactions, state in which two accounts an entry must be made and whether the entry is a debit or a credit. (For example, if the transaction were buying inventories for cash, the answer would be debit the inventories account and credit the cash at bank account.)

(a) Bought inventories on credit.
(b) Owner made cash drawings.
(c) Paid interest on business borrowings.
(d) Bought inventories for cash.
(e) Received cash from a credit customer.
(f) Paid wages to employees.
(g) The owner received some cash from a credit customer, which was taken as drawings rather than being paid into the business's bank account.
(h) Paid a credit supplier.
(i) Paid electricity bill.
(j) Made cash sales.

A.2 (a) Record the following transactions in a set of double-entry accounts:

1 February	Lee (the owner) put £6,000 into a newly-opened business bank account to start a new business
3 February	Bought inventories for £2,600 for cash
5 February	Bought some equipment (non-current asset) for cash for £800
6 February	Bought inventories costing £3,000 on credit
9 February	Paid rent for the month of £250
10 February	Paid fuel and electricity for the month of £240
11 February	Paid general expenses of £200
15 February	Sold inventories for £4,000 in cash; the inventories had cost £2,400
19 February	Sold inventories for £3,800 on credit; the inventories had cost £2,300
21 February	Lee withdrew £1,000 in cash for personal use
25 February	Paid £2,000 to trade payables
28 February	Received £2,500 from trade receivables

(b) Balance the relevant accounts and prepare a trial balance (making sure that it agrees).
(c) Prepare an income statement for the month and a statement of financial position at the month end. Assume that there are no prepaid or accrued expenses at the end of the month and ignore any possible depreciation.

A.3 The following is the statement of financial position of David's business at 1 January of last year:

ASSETS
Non-current assets
Property, plant and equipment

Buildings		25,000
Fittings – cost	10,000	
– depreciation	(2,000)	8,000
		33,000
Current assets		
Inventories of stationery		140
Trading inventories		1,350
Prepaid rent		500
Trade receivables		1,840
Cash at bank		2,180
		6,010
Total assets		39,010

EQUITY AND LIABILITIES

Owners' equity	25,050
Non-current liability	
Borrowings	12,000
Current liabilities	
Trade payables	1,690
Accrued electricity	270
	1,960
Total equity and liabilities	39,010

The following is a summary of the transactions that took place during the year:

1 Inventories were bought on credit for £17,220.
2 Inventories were bought for £3,760 cash.
3 Credit sales revenue amounted to £33,100 (cost £15,220).
4 Cash sales revenue amounted to £10,360 (cost £4,900).
5 Wages of £3,770 were paid.
6 Rent of £3,000 was paid. The annual rental amounts to £3,000.
7 Electricity of £1,070 was paid.
8 General expenses of £580 were paid.
9 Additional fittings were purchased on 1 January for £2,000. The cash for this was raised from additional borrowings of this amount. The interest rate is 10% a year, the same as for the existing borrowings.
10 £1,000 of the borrowing was repaid on 30 June.
11 Cash received from trade receivables amounted to £32,810.
12 Cash paid to trade payables amounted to £18,150.
13 The owner withdrew £10,400 cash and £560 inventories for private use.

At the end of the year:

● The electricity bill for the last quarter of the year for £290 had not been paid.
● Trade receivables amounting to £260 were unlikely to be received.
● The value of stationery remaining was estimated at £150 Stationery is included in general expenses.
● The borrowings carried interest of 10% a year and were unpaid at the year end.
● Depreciation is to be taken at 20% on the cost of the fittings owned at the year end. Buildings are not depreciated.

Required:
(a) Open ledger accounts and bring down all of the balances in the opening statement of financial position.
(b) Make entries to record the transactions 1 to 13 (above), opening any additional accounts as necessary.
(c) Open an income statement (part of the double entry process, remember). Make the necessary entries for the bulleted list above and the appropriate transfers to the income statement.
(d) List the remaining balances in the same form as the opening statement of financial position (above).

Glossary of key terms

ABC system of inventories control A method of applying different levels of inventories control, based on the value of each category of inventories.

Absorption costing (or full costing) Deducing the total direct and indirect (overhead) costs of pursuing some activity or objective, in which an appropriate share of the total manufacturing/service provision overhead cost is included.

Account A section of a double-entry bookkeeping system that deals with one particular asset, claim, expense or revenue.

Accounting The process of identifying, measuring and communicating information to permit informed judgements and decisions by users of the information. *p. 2*

Accounting convention One of the generally accepted rules that accountants tend to follow when preparing financial statements. These have evolved over time to deal with practical problems rather than to reflect some theoretical ideal. *p. 62*

Accounting information system The system used within a business to identify, record, analyse and report accounting information. *p. 12*

Accounting rate of return (ARR) An investment appraisal technique based on the average profit from an investment, expressed as a percentage of the average investment made.

Accruals accounting The system of accounting that follows the accruals convention. This is the system followed in drawing up the statement of financial position and the income statement. *p. 97*

Accruals convention The convention of accounting that asserts that profit is the excess of revenue over expenses, not the excess of cash receipts over cash payments. *p. 97*

Accrued expense An expenses that is outstanding (unpaid) at the end of a reporting period. *p. 93*

Acid test ratio A liquidity ratio that relates the liquid assets (usually defined as current assets less inventories) to the current liabilities. *p. 263*

Activity-based budgeting (ABB) A system of budgeting based on the philosophy of activity-based costing (ABC).

Activity-based costing (ABC) A technique for relating overheads to specific production or provision of a service. It is based on acceptance of the fact that overheads do not just occur but are caused by activities, such as holding products in stores, which 'drive' the costs.

Adverse variance A difference between planned and actual performance, usually where the difference will cause the actual profit to be lower than the budgeted profit.

Ageing schedule of trade receivables A report analysing receivables into categories, according to the length of time outstanding.

Allotted share capital *See* Issued share capital. *p. 140*

Allowance for trade receivables An amount set aside out of profit to provide for anticipated losses arising from debts (trade receivables) that may prove irrecoverable. *p. 114*

Alternative Investment Market (AIM) A stock market for the shares of smaller businesses. AIM is a junior market to the main London Stock Exchange market. It is cheaper for a business to enter and has a lighter regulatory regime.

Amortisation A measure of that portion of the cost (or fair value) of a non-current asset that has been consumed during a reporting period. The word 'amortisation' tends to be used where the particular non-current asset is an intangible one, whereas 'depreciation' is normally used with tangible assets. *p. 98*

Assets Resources held by a business that have certain characteristics, such as the potential to provide economic benefits. *p. 46*

Asset-based finance A form of finance where assets are used as security for cash advances to the business. Factoring and invoice discounting, where the security is trade receivables, are examples of asset-based financing.

Auditors Professionals whose main duty is to make a report to shareholders as to whether, in their opinion, the financial statements of a company show a true and fair view of performance and position and comply with statutory and financial reporting standard requirements. *p. 171*

AVCO *See* Weighted average cost. *p. 108*

Average inventories turnover period ratio An efficiency ratio that measures the average period for which inventories are held by a business. *p. 255*

Average settlement period for trade payables ratio An efficiency ratio that measures the average time taken for a business to pay its trade payables. *pp. 256*

Average settlement period for trade receivables ratio An efficiency ratio that measures the average time taken for trade receivables to pay the amounts owing. *p. 256*

Bad debt An amount owed to the business that is considered to be irrecoverable. *p. 113*

Balance The net of the debit and credit totals in an account in a double-entry bookkeeping system.

Balanced scorecard A framework for translating the aims and objectives of a business into a series of key performance measures and targets.

Bank overdraft A flexible form of borrowing that allows an individual or business to have a negative current account balance.

Batch costing A technique for identifying full cost, where the production of many types of goods and services, particularly goods, involves producing a batch of identical or nearly identical units of output, but where each batch is distinctly different from other batches.

Behavioural aspects of budgetary control The effect on people's behaviour of the various aspects of using budgets as the basis for planning and controlling a business.

Benchmarking Identifying a successful business, or part of a business, and measuring the effectiveness of one's own business by comparison with this standard.

Benefit That outcome, resulting from a course of action, that helps a business to achieve its objectives.

Bond *See* loan note. *pp. 140*

Bonus shares Reserves that are converted into shares and issued 'free' to existing shareholders. *p. 138*

Break-even analysis The activity of deducing the break-even point of some activity by analysing the relationship between cost, volume and revenue.

Break-even chart A graphical representation of the cost and sales revenue of some activity, at various levels, that enables the break-even point to be identified.

Break-even point (BEP) A level of activity where revenue will exactly equal total cost, so there is neither profit nor loss.

Budget A financial plan for the short term, typically one year or less.

Budget committee A group of managers formed to supervise and take responsibility for the budget-setting process.

Budget holder An individual responsible for a particular budget.

Budget officer An individual, often an accountant, appointed to carry out the tasks of the budget committee.

Budgetary control Using the budget as a yardstick against which the effectiveness of actual performance may be assessed.

Business angel An individuals who supplies finance (usually equity finance) to start-up businesses or small businesses wishing to expand. Usually the amount of finance supplied falls between £10,000 and £750,000.

Business cycle The business cycle refers to the contraction and expansion in activity arising within an economy over time.

Business entity convention The convention that holds that, for accounting purposes, the business and its owner(s) are treated as quite separate and distinct. *p. 62*

Called-up share capital That part of a company's share capital for which the shareholders have been asked to pay the agreed amount. It is part of the claim of the owners against the business. *p. 140*

Capital rationing Where the amount of funds committed is insufficient for the investment opportunities available and decisions have to be made concerning the most profitable use of those funds.

Capital reserve A reserve that arise from an unrealised 'capital' profits or gains, or as a result of issuing new shares at a price above their nominal value, rather than from normal realised trading activities. *p. 136*

Carrying amount The difference between the cost (or fair value) of a non-current asset and the accumulated depreciation relating to the asset. The carrying amount is also referred to as the written-down value (WDV) and the net book value (NBV). *pp. 69, 101*

Cash discount A reduction in the amount due for goods or services sold on credit in return for prompt payment.

Cash generated from operations (CGO) per ordinary share ratio An investment ratio that relates the cash generated from operations and available to ordinary shareholders to the number of ordinary shares. *p. 274*

Cash generated from operations (CGO) to maturing obligations ratio A liquidity ratio that compares the cash generated from operations to the current liabilities of the business. *p. 264*

Claims Obligations on the part of a business to provide cash or some other benefit to outside parties. *p. 46*

Committed cost A cost incurred that has not yet been paid, but which must, under some existing contract or obligation, be paid.

Comparability The quality that helps users to identify similarities and differences between items of information. It enhances the usefulness of accounting information. *p. 8*

Compensating variances The situation where two linked variances, one adverse and the other favourable, are of equal size, and therefore cancel each other out.

Conceptual framework The main concepts, or principles, that underpin accounting, which can help in identifying best practice and in developing accounting rules. *p. 169*

Consistency convention The accounting convention that holds that, when a particular method of accounting is selected to deal with a transaction, this method should be applied consistently over time. *p. 113*

Consolidated financial statements *See* Group financial statements. *p. 151*

Consolidating Changing the nominal value of shares to a higher figure (from, say, £0.50 to £1.00) and then reducing the number of shares in issue so that each shareholder has the same total nominal value of shares as before. *p. 135*

Continual budget A budget that is continually being updated so that there is always a budget for a full planning period. (Also known as a 'rolling budget'.)

Contribution margin ratio The contribution from an activity expressed as a percentage of the sales revenue.

Contribution per unit Sales revenue per unit less variable cost per unit.

Control Compelling events to conform to plan.

Convertible loan note A loan note that give investors the right to convert it into ordinary shares at a specified price and a given future date (or range of dates).

Corporate culture The values, attitudes and behaviour displayed towards the company's various stakeholders and to the wider community *p. 191*

Corporate governance Matters concerned with directing and controlling a company. *p. 187*

Corporation tax Taxation that a limited company is liable to pay on its profits. *p. 130*

Cost An amount of resources, usually measured in monetary terms, sacrificed to achieve a particular objective.

Cost allocation Assigning cost to cost centres according to the amount of cost that has been incurred in each centre.

Cost apportionment Dividing cost between cost centres on a basis that is considered to reflect fairly the cost incurred in each centre.

Cost behaviour The manner in which cost alters with changes in the level of activity.

Cost–benefit analysis Methodically weighing the cost of pursuing some objective against the benefits that it likely to generate to enable a decision to be made as to whether to proceed.

Cost centre Some area, object, person or activity for which elements of cost are separately collected.

Cost driver An activity that causes cost in an ABC setting.

Cost of capital The cost to a business of finance needed to fund its investments.

Cost of sales The cost of the goods sold during a period. Cost of sales can be derived by adding the opening inventories held to the inventories purchases for the period and then deducting the closing inventories held. *p. 84*

Cost-plus pricing An approach to pricing output that is based on full cost plus a percentage profit loading.

Cost pool The sum of the overhead costs that are seen as being caused by the same cost driver.

Cost unit The objective for which the cost is being deduced, usually a product or service.

Creative accounting Adopting accounting policies to achieve a particular view of performance and position that preparers would like users to see rather than what is a true and fair view. *p. 192*

Credit An entry made in the right-hand side of an account in double-entry bookkeeping.

Crowdfunding Raising equity funds, typically by small businesses, from a large number of investors often with each investor providing a relatively small sum. A commercial crowdfunding platform usually provides an internet interface between borrower and lenders.

Current asset An asset that is held for the short term. This includes cash itself and other assets that are held for sale or consumption in the normal course of a business's operating cycle. *p. 56*

Current liability A liability that is expected to be settled within the normal course of the business's operating cycle or within twelve months of the statement of financial position date, or which are held primarily for trading purposes, or for which the business does not have the right to defer settlement beyond twelve months of the statement of financial position date. *p. 58*

Current ratio A liquidity ratio that relates the current assets of the business to the current liabilities. *p. 263*

Debenture See Loan note. *p. 140*

Debit An entry made in the left-hand side of an account in double-entry bookkeeping.

Debt factoring A service offered by a financial institution (a factor) that involves the factor taking over the management of the trade receivables of the business. The factor is often prepared to make an advance to the business, based on the amount of trade receivables outstanding.

Deep discount bond A redeemable bond (loan note) offering a rate of interest below the market rate and issued at a discount to its redeemable value.

Depreciation A measure of that portion of the cost (or fair value) of a non-current asset that has been consumed during a reporting period. *p. 98*

Direct cost A cost that can be identified with a specific cost unit, to the extent that the effect of the cost can be measured in respect of that cost unit.

Direct labour efficiency variance The difference between the actual direct labour hours worked and the number of direct labour hours according to the flexed budget (budgeted direct labour hours for the actual output). This figure is multiplied by the budgeted direct labour rate for one hour.

Direct labour rate variance The difference between the actual cost of the direct labour hours worked and the direct labour cost allowed (actual direct labour hours worked at the budgeted labour rate).

Direct materials price variance The difference between the actual cost of the direct material used and the direct materials cost allowed (actual quantity of material used at the budgeted direct material cost).

Direct materials usage variance The difference between the actual quantity of direct materials used and the quantity of direct materials according to the flexed budget (budgeted usage for actual output). This quantity is multiplied by the budgeted direct materials cost for one unit of the direct materials.

Direct method An approach to deducing the cash flows from operating activities, in a statement of cash flows, by analysing the business's cash records. *p. 216*

Director An individual appointed (normally by being elected by the shareholders) to act as part of the most senior level of management of a company (board of directors). *p. 132*

Directors' report A report containing information of a financial and non-financial nature that the directors must produce as part of the annual financial report to shareholders. *p. 184*

Discount factor The rate applied to future cash flows to derive the present value of those cash flows.

Discounting Applying the discount factor to a project's cash flows to take account of the time period involved and the cost of capital. It is, in effect, charging the project with the cost of financing it

Discretionary budget A budgets based on a sum allocated at the discretion of senior management.

Discriminate function (in financial distress assessment) A boundary line, produced by multiple discriminate analysis, which can be used to identify those businesses that are likely to suffer financial distress and those that are not. *p. 283*

Dividend The transfer of assets (usually cash) made by a company to its shareholders. *p. 133*

Dividend cover ratio An investment ratio that relates the earnings available for dividends to the dividend announced, to indicate how many times the former covers the latter. *p. 271*

Dividend payout ratio An investment ratio that relates the dividends announced for the period to the earnings available for dividends that were generated in that period. *p. 270*

Dividend per share An investment ratio that relates the dividends announced for a period to the number of shares in issue. *p. 271*

Dividend yield ratio An investment ratio that relates the cash return from a share to its current market value. *p. 271*

Double-entry bookkeeping A system for recording financial transactions where each transaction is recorded twice, once as a debit and once as a credit.

Dual aspect convention The accounting convention that holds that each transaction has two aspects and that each aspect must be recorded in the financial statements. *p. 65*

Earnings per share (EPS) An investment ratio that relates the earnings generated by the business during a period, and available to shareholders, to the number of shares in issue. *p. 272*

Economic order quantity (EOQ) The quantity of inventories that should be bought with each order so as to minimise the sum of inventories ordering and carrying costs.

Economic value added (EVA®) A measure of business performance that concentrates on wealth generation. It is based on economic profit rather than accounting profit and takes full account of the cost of financing.

Economies of scale Cost savings per unit that result from undertaking a large volume of activities; they are due to factors such as division and specialisation of labour and discounts from bulk buying.

Efficient capital market A capital market (for example, a Stock Exchange) whose prices rapidly and rationally take account of all relevant information.

Enterprise resource planning (ERP) systems An automated and integrated approach to managing a business through a suite of software applications (modules) that record, report, analyse and interpret data for a range of business operations, including production, marketing, human resources, accounting and inventories management.

Equity The owners' claim on the business. In the case of a limited company, it comprises the sum of shares and reserves. *p. 50*

Eurobond A form of long-term borrowing where the finance is raised on an international basis. Eurobonds are issued in a currency that is not that of the country in which the bonds are issued.

Expense A measure of the outflow of assets (or increase in liabilities) incurred in pursuit of generating revenue. *p. 84*

Fair value The value ascribed to an asset as an alternative to historic cost. It is usually the current market values (that is, the exchange values in an arm's-length transaction). *p. 70*

Faithful representation The ability of information to be relied on to represent what it purports to represent. This is regarded as a fundamental quality of useful accounting information. *p. 7*

Favourable variance The difference between planned and actual performance, usually where the difference will cause the actual profit to be higher than the budgeted profit.

Feedback control A form of control where actual performance is compared with planned performance and where action is taken to deal with any future divergences between the two.

Feedforward control A form of control where forecast future performance is compared with planned performance and where action is taken to deal with divergences between the two.

Final accounts The income statement, statement of cash flows and statement of financial position taken together. *p. 45*

Finance The study of how businesses raise funds and select appropriate investments. *p. 2*

Finance lease A financial arrangement where the asset title remains with the owner (the lessor) but the lease agreement transfers virtually all the rewards and risks to the business (the lessee).

Financial accounting The identification, measurement and communication of accounting information for external users (those users other than the managers of the business). *p. 14*

Financial derivative Any form of financial instrument, based on share capital or borrowings, which can be used by investors either to increase their returns or to decrease their exposure to risk.

Financial gearing The existence of fixed-payment-bearing sources of finance (for example, borrowings) in the capital structure of a business. *p. 266*

First in, first out (FIFO) A method of inventories costing that deals with issues of inventories as if the inventories acquired earliest are used (in production or sales) first. *p. 108*

Five Cs of credit A checklist of factors to be taken into account when assessing the creditworthiness of a customer.

Fixed assets *See* Non-current assets. *p. 56*

Fixed charge Where specific assets are pledged as security for a loan.

Fixed cost A cost that stays the same when changes occur to the volume of activity.

Fixed interest rate An interest rate on borrowings that will remain unchanged over the period of the loan, irrespective of rises and falls in market rates of interest.

Fixed overhead spending variance The difference between the actual fixed overhead cost and the fixed overhead cost, according to the flexed (and the original) budget.

Flexible budget A budget that is adjusted to what it would have been had the planned level of output been different, usually to the actual level of output achieved.

Flexing a budget Revising a budget to what it would have been had the planned level of output been different, usually to the actual level of output achieved.

Floating charge Where all a business's assets, rather than specific assets, are pledged as security for a loan. The charge will only fix on specific assets if the business defaults on its obligations.

Floating interest rate An interest rate on borrowings that will rise and fall with market rates of interest.

Forecast A prediction of future outcomes or of the future state of the environment.

Full cost The total amount of resources, usually measured in monetary terms, sacrificed to achieve a particular objective.

Full costing *See* Absorption costing.

Fully paid shares Shares on which the shareholders have paid the full issue price. *p. 140*

Gearing ratio A ratio that relates long-term fixed-return finance (such as borrowings) to the total long-term finance of the business. *p. 268*

Going concern convention The accounting convention that holds that a business is assumed to continue operations for the foreseeable future, unless there is reason to believe otherwise. In other words, it is assumed that there is no intention, or need, to liquidate the business. *p. 65*

Goodwill An intangible, non-current asset that lacks a clear and separate identity. The term is often used to cover various positive attributes such as the quality of products, the skill of employees and the relationship with customers. *p. 67*

Gross profit The amount remaining (if positive) after the cost of sales has been deducted from trading revenue. *p. 86*

Gross profit margin ratio A profitability ratio that expresses the gross profit as a percentage of the sales revenue for a period. *p. 252*

Group financial statements Financial accounting statements that combine the performance, position and cash flows of a group of companies under common control. Also known as 'consolidated financial statements'. *p. 151*

Hire purchase A method of acquiring an asset by paying the purchase price by instalments over a period. Normally, control of the asset will pass as soon as the hire- purchase contract is signed and the first instalment is paid, whereas ownership will pass on payment of the final instalment.

Historic cost What was paid for an asset when it was originally acquired.

Historic cost convention The accounting convention that holds that assets should be recorded at their historic (acquisition) cost. *p. 62*

Holding company *See* Parent company. *p. 150*

Ideal standards Standards that assume perfect operating conditions where there is no inefficiency due to lost production time, defects and so on. The objective of setting ideal standards is to encourage employees to strive towards excellence.

Impairment loss The loss to be reported following an assessment that the value of an asset has been diminished as a result of a change in some fundamental factor relating to the asset, such as the market for the service provided by the asset suddenly collapsing. It should not be confused with depreciation (amortisation), which is concerned with routine loss of value through usage of the asset or passage of time. *p. 72*

Income statement A financial statement (also known as 'profit and loss account') that measures and reports the profit (or loss) the business has generated during a period. It is derived by deducting from total revenue for a period, the total expenses associated with that revenue. *p. 42*

Incremental budgeting Constructing budgets on the basis of what happened in the previous period, with some adjustment for expected changes in the forthcoming budget period.

Indirect cost (or common cost or overheads) The element of production cost (of a product or service) that cannot be directly measured in respect of a particular cost unit – that is, all production cost except direct cost.

Indirect method An approach to deducing the cash flows from operating activities, in a statement of cash flows, by analysing the business's other financial statements. *p. 216*

Inflation An increase in the general price of goods and services resulting in a corresponding decline in the purchasing power of money.

Intangible asset An asset that does not have a physical substance (for example, patents, goodwill and trade receivables). *p. 50*

Interest cover ratio A gearing ratio that divides the operating profit (that is, profit before interest and taxation) by the interest payable for a period. *p. 269*

Internal rate of return (IRR) An investment appraisal technique based on the discount rate for an investment that will have the effect of producing a zero NPV.

International Accounting Standards *See* International Financial Reporting Standards. *p. 166*

International Financial Reporting Standards Transnational accounting rules that have been adopted, or developed, by the International Accounting Standards Board and which should be followed in preparing the published financial statements of listed limited companies *p. 166*

Invoice discounting Where a financial institution provides a loan based on a proportion of the face value of a business's credit sales outstanding.

Irrelevant cost A cost that is not relevant to a particular decision.

Issued share capital That part of the share capital that has been issued to shareholders. Also known as 'allotted share capital'. *p. 140*

Job costing A technique for identifying the full cost per cost unit, where each cost unit is not identical to other cost units produced.

Just-in-time (JIT) inventories management A system of inventories management that aims to have supplies delivered just in time for their required use in production or sales.

Kaizen costing An approach to cost control where an attempt is made to control cost by trying continually to make cost savings, usually only small ones, from one time period to the next during the production stage of the product life cycle.

Last in, first out (LIFO) A method of inventories costing that deals with inventories issues as if the most recently acquired inventories are used (in production or sales) first. *p. 108*

Lead time The time lag between placing an order for goods or services and their delivery to the required location.

Learning curve The curved line on a graph that represents the tendency for people to carry out tasks more quickly as they become more experienced in doing them.

Ledger The book in which accounts are traditionally kept.

Liability A claim of an individual and organisation, apart from the owner(s), that has arisen from past transactions or events, such as supplying goods or lending money to the business. *p. 50*

Limited company A form of business unit that is granted a separate legal existence from that of its owners. The owners of this type of business are liable for debts only up to the amount that they have agreed to invest. *p. 21*

Limited liability The restriction of the legal obligation of shareholders to meet all of the company's debts. *p. 127*

Limiting factor Some aspect of the business (for example, lack of sales demand) that will prevent it achieving its objectives to the maximum extent.

Loan covenant A conditions contained within a loan agreement that are designed to help protect the lenders.

Loan note Long-term borrowings usually made by limited companies. *p. 140*

Loan stock *See* Loan note. *p. 140*

London Stock Exchange A stock exchange located in the City of London that helps larger businesses gain access to new capital and provides a market for investors to buy and sell securities of listed businesses. *p. 131*

Management accounting The identification, measurement and communication of accounting information for the managers of a business. *p. 14*

Management by exception A system of control, based on a comparison of planned and actual performance, that allows managers to focus on areas of poor performance rather than dealing with areas where performance is satisfactory.

Margin of safety The extent to which the planned level of output or sales lies above the break-even point.

Marginal analysis The activity of decision making through analysing variable cost and revenue, ignoring fixed cost.

Marginal cost The additional cost of producing one more unit. This is often the same as the variable cost.

Master budget A summary of individual budgets, usually consisting of a budgeted income statement, a budgeted statement of financial position and a cash budget.

Matching convention The accounting convention that holds that, when measuring income, expenses should be matched to revenue, which they helped generate, in the same reporting period as that in which the revenue was realised. *p. 93*

Materiality The quality of accounting information such that its omission or misrepresentation will alter the decisions that users make. The threshold of materiality will vary from one business to the next. *p. 7*

Materiality convention The accounting convention that states that, where the amounts involved are immaterial, only what is expedient should be considered. *p. 97*

Mortgage A loan secured on property.

Multiple discriminate analysis (MDA) A statistical technique that can be used to predict financial distress; it involves using an index based on a combination of two or more financial ratios. *p. 283*

Net book value *See* Carrying amount. *p. 101*

Net present value (NPV) A method of investment appraisal based on the present value of all relevant cash flows associated with an investment.

Nominal value The face value of a share in a company. Also called par value. *p. 132*

Non-controlling interests That part of the net assets of a subsidiary company that is financed by shareholders other than the parent company. (Formerly known as 'minority interests'.) *p. 151*

Non-current (fixed) asset An asset held that does not meet the criteria of a current asset. They are held for the long-term operations of the business rather than continuously circulating within the business. A non-current asset can be seen as one of the tools of the business. *p. 56*

Non-current liability A liability of the business that is not a current liability. *p. 58*

Non-operating-profit variance A difference between budgeted and actual performance that does not lead directly to a difference between budgeted and actual operating profit. *p. 531*

Offer for sale An issue of shares that involves a public limited company (or its shareholders) selling the shares to a financial institution that will, in turn, sell the shares to the public.

Operating cash cycle (OCC) The period between the outlay of cash to buy supplies and the ultimate receipt of cash from the sale of goods.

Operating gearing (operational gearing) The relationship between the total fixed and the total variable elements of cost for some activity.

Operating lease An arrangement where a business hires an asset, usually for a short time. Hiring an asset under an operating lease tends to be seen as an operating, rather than a financing, decision.

Operating profit The profit achieved during a period after all operating expenses have been deducted from revenues from operations. Financing expenses are deducted after the calculation of operating profit. *p. 86*

Operating profit margin ratio A profitability ratio that expresses the operating profit as a percentage of the sales revenue for the period. *p. 251*

Opportunity cost The cost incurred when one course of action prevents an opportunity to derive some benefit from another course of action.

Ordinary share A portion of ownership of a company owned by those who are due the benefits of the company's activities after all other stakeholders have been satisfied. *p. 133*

Outlay cost A cost that involves the spending of money or some other transfer of assets. *p. 304*

Outsourcing Subcontracting activities to (sourcing goods or services from) organisations outside of the business.

Overhead absorption (recovery) rate The rate at which overheads are charged to cost units (jobs), usually in a job costing system.

Overheads *See* Indirect cost.

Overtrading The situation arising where a business is operating at a level of activity that cannot be supported by the amount of finance that has been committed. *p. 279*

Paid-up share capital That part of the share capital of a company that has been called and paid. *p. 140*

Par value *See* Nominal value. *p. 132*

Parent company A company that has a controlling interest in another company. *p. 150*

Partnership A form of business unit where there are at least two individuals, but usually no more than twenty, carrying on a business with the intention of making a profit. *p. 21*

Past cost A cost that has been incurred in the past.

Payback period (PP) An investment appraisal technique based on the time taken for the initial outlay for an investment to be repaid from its future net cash inflows.

Peer-to-peer lending Lending where a commercial 'platform' acts as the online interface between potential borrowers and potential lenders, where the latter may each provide very small amounts of loan finance.

Periodic budget A budget developed on a one-off basis to cover a particular planning period.

Post-completion audit A review of the performance of an investment project to see whether lessons can be drawn from the way in which the project was appraised and carried out.

Practical standards Standards that do not assume perfect operating conditions. Although they demand a high level of efficiency, account is taken of possible lost production time, defects and so on. They are designed to be challenging yet achievable.

Preference share A share of a company that entitles its owner to the first part of any dividend that the company may pay. *p. 134*

Prepaid expense An expense that has been paid in advance at the end of the reporting period. *p. 96*

Price/earnings (P/E) ratio An investment ratio that relates the market value of a share to the earnings per share. *p. 275*

Private limited company A limited company for which the directors can restrict the ownership of its shares. *p. 128*

Private placing An issue of shares that involves a limited company arranging for the shares to be sold to the clients of particular issuing houses or stockbrokers, rather than to the general investing public.

Process costing A technique for deriving the full cost per unit of output, where the units of output are identical, or it is reasonable to treat them as being so.

Product cost centre Some area, object, person or activity for which cost is separately collected, in which cost units have cost added.

Profit The increase in wealth attributable to the owners of a business that arises through business operations. *p. 83*

Profit before taxation The result when all of the appropriately matched expenses of running a business have been deducted from the revenue for the year, but before the taxation charge is deducted. *p. 147*

Profit for the period The result when all of the appropriately matched expenses of running a business have been deducted from the revenue for the year and then, in the case of a limited company, the taxation charge deducted. *p. 86*

Profit–volume (PV) chart A graphical representation of the contributions (revenue less variable cost) of some activity, at various levels, which enables the break-even point, and the profit at various activity levels, to be identified.

Property, plant and equipment Those non-current assets that have a physical substance (for example, plant and machinery, motor vehicles). *p. 56*

Prudence convention The accounting convention that holds that caution should be exercised when making accounting judgements. *p. 64*

Public issue An issue of shares that involves a public limited company (plc) making a direct invitation to the public to buy shares in the company.

Public limited company A limited company for which the directors cannot restrict the ownership of its shares. *p. 128*

Quality cost The cost of establishing procedures that promote the quality of output, either by preventing quality problems in the first place or by dealing with them when they occur.

Reducing-balance method A method of calculating depreciation that applies a fixed percentage rate of depreciation to the carrying amount of an asset in each period. *p. 101*

Relevance The ability of accounting information to influence decisions. Relevance is regarded as a fundamental characteristic of useful accounting information. *p. 7*

Relevant cost A cost that is relevant to a particular decision.

Relevant range The range of output within which a particular business is expected to operate.

Reporting period The time span for which a business prepares its financial statements. *p. 53*

Reserve Part of the owners' claim (equity) of a limited company that has arisen from profits and gains, to the extent that these have not been distributed to the shareholders or reduced by losses. *p. 132*

Residual value The amount for which a non-current asset is expected to be sold when the business has no further use for it. *p. 100*

Return on capital employed ratio (ROCE) A profitability ratio that expresses the operating profit (that is, profit before interest and taxation) as a percentage of the long-term funds (equity and borrowings) invested in the business. *pp. 248,*

Return on ordinary shareholders' funds ratio (ROSF) A profitability ratio that expresses the profit for the period available to ordinary shareholders as a percentage of the funds that they have invested. *p. 248*

Revenue A measure of the inflow of assets (for example, cash or amounts owed to a business by credit customers), or a reduction in liabilities, arising as a result of trading operations. *p. 83*

Revenue reserve Part of the owners' claim (equity) of a company that arises from realised profits and gains, including after-tax trading profits and gains from disposals of non-current assets. *p. 133*

Rights issue An issue of shares for cash to existing shareholders in proportion to the number of shares already held.

Risk The extent and likelihood that what is projected to occur will not actually occur.

Risk premium The additional return required for investing in a risky project.

Rolling budget *See* Continual budget.

Sale and leaseback An agreement to sell an asset (usually property) to another party and simultaneously to lease the asset back in order to continue using the asset.

Sales price variance The difference between the actual sales revenue figure for the period and the sales revenue figure as shown in the flexed budget.

Sales revenue per employee ratio An efficiency ratio that relates the sales revenue generated during a period to the average number of employees of the business. *p. 259*

Sales revenue to capital employed ratio An efficiency ratio that relates the sales revenue generated during a period to the capital employed. *p. 258*

Sales volume variance The difference between the operating profit as shown in the original budget, and the operating profit as shown in the flexed budget for the period.

Scenario building Creating a model of a business decision, usually on a computer spreadsheet, enabling the decision maker to look at the effect of different assumptions on the decision outcome.

Securitisation Bundling together illiquid physical or financial assets of the same type to provide backing for issuing interest-bearing securities such as bonds.

Security Assets pledged, or guarantees given, to provide lenders with some protection against default.

Segmental financial reports Financial reports that break down the overall results of a business according to its different types of business operations. *p. 180*

Semi-fixed (semi-variable) cost A cost that has an element of both fixed and variable cost.

Sensitivity analysis An examination of the key variables affecting a decision (for example, an investment project) to see how changes in each input might influence the outcome.

Service cost centre Some area, object, person or activity for which cost is collected separately, in which cost units do not have cost added, because service cost centres only render services to product cost centres and to other service cost centres.

Share premium account A capital reserve reflecting any amount, above the nominal value of shares, that is paid for those shares when they are issued by a company. *p. 137*

Shares Portions of the ownership, or equity, of a company. *p. 6*

Sole proprietorship A form of business unit where an individual is operating a business on his or her own account. *p. 20*

Splitting Changing the nominal value of shares to a lower figure (from, say, £1.00 to £0.50) and then issuing sufficient shares so that each shareholder has the same total nominal value of shares as before. *p. 135*

Standard costing Using standard quantities and costs to derive variances, effectively, another name for variance analysis.

Standard quantities and costs Planned quantities and costs (or revenue) for individual units of input or output. Standards are the building blocks used to produce the budget.

Statement of cash flows A statement that shows a business's sources and uses of cash for a period. *p. 42*

Statement of changes in equity A financial statement, required by IAS 1, which shows the effect of gains/losses and capital injections/withdrawals on the equity base of a company. *p. 178*

Statement of comprehensive income A financial statement that extends the conventional income statement to include other gains and losses that affect shareholders' equity. *p. 175*

Statement of financial position A statement that shows the assets of a business and the claims on those assets. It is also known as a 'balance sheet'. *p. 42*

Stepped fixed cost A fixed cost that does not remain fixed over all levels of output but which changes in steps as each new threshold level of output is reached. *p. 332*

Stock Exchange A market where 'second-hand' shares may be bought and sold and new capital raised. *p. 131*

Straight-line method A method of accounting for depreciation that allocates the amount to be depreciated evenly over the useful life of the asset. *p. 100*

Strategic management Setting a course to achieve the business's objectives, taking account of the commercial and economic environment in which the business operates. *p. 26*

Strategic report A report designed to provide a fair review of the company's business. Directors of all but the smallest companies are legally obliged to produce a strategic report, which is required to be a balanced and comprehensive analysis of financial performance for the year and financial position at the end of the year. *p. 185*

Subordinated loan A form of loan where the lender's claim is ranked below those of other loans already in existence.

Sunk cost A cost that has been incurred in the past; the same as a past cost.

Sunk cost fallacy The notion that the decision-maker may feel obliged to pursue a particular course of action because costs have already been committed to it.

Takeover The acquisition of control of one company by another, usually as a result of acquiring a majority of the ordinary shares of the former. *p. 152*

Tangible asset An asset that has a physical substance (for example, plant and machinery, motor vehicles). *p. 50*

Target costing An approach to deriving product costs where the business starts with the projected selling price and from it deduces the target cost per unit that must be met to enable the business to meet its profit objectives.

Tender issue A public issue of shares or loan notes (by a public limited company) where potential investors are invited to state a bid price rather than the company setting the price for the securities.

Term loan Finance provided by financial institutions, for example banks and insurance companies, under a contract with the borrowing business that indicates the interest rate and date of payments of interest and repayment of the loan.

Timeliness The provision of accounting information in time for users to make use of it in their decision making. This quality enhances the usefulness of accounting information. *p. 8*

Total direct labour variance The difference between the actual direct labour cost and the direct labour cost according to the flexed budget (budgeted direct labour hours for the actual output).

Total direct materials variance The difference between the actual direct materials cost and the direct materials cost according to the flexed budget.

Total life-cycle costing An approach to costing that takes account of all the costs that will be incurred during the entire life of a product or service.

Total quality management (TQM) A philosophy concerned with providing products that meet, or exceed, customers' requirements all of the time.

Trade payable An amount owed to a supplier from whom the business has received goods or services on credit. *p. 52*

Trade receivable An amount owed by a customer to whom the business has provided goods or services on credit. *p. 49*

Trade receivable to sales ratio An accounting ratio that relates the end-of-period trade receivables to sales revenue for the period.

Transfer price The price at which goods or services are sold, or transferred, between divisions of the same business. *p. 182*

Trial balance A totalled list of the balances on each of the accounts in a double-entry bookkeeping system.

UK Corporate Governance Code A code of practice for companies that are listed on the London Stock Exchange that deals with corporate governance matters. *p. 189*

Understandability The quality that enables accounting information to be understood by those for whom the information is primarily compiled. This quality enhances the usefulness of accounting information. *p. 8*

Univariate analysis A statistical technique that can be used to help predict financial distress, which involves the use of a single ratio as a predictor. *p. 283*

Value chain analysis Analysing each activity undertaken by a business to identify any that do not add value to the output of goods or services.

Value driver A factor that creates wealth, such as employee satisfaction, customer loyalty and the level of product innovation.

Variable cost A cost that varies according to the volume of activity.

Variable (marginal) costing An approach to costing in which only those costs that vary with the level of output are included in the product cost.

Variance The financial effect, usually on the budgeted profit, of the particular factor under consideration being more or less than budgeted.

Venture capital Finance, usually medium-term equity, provided by certain institutions to small and medium-sized businesses in order to exploit relatively high-risk opportunities.

Verifiability The quality that provides assurance to users that the information provided faithfully represents what it is supposed to represent. It enhances the quality of accounting information. *p. 219*

Weighted average cost (AVCO) An approach to inventories costing, which assumes that inventories entering the business lose their separate identity and any issues of inventories reflect the weighted average cost of the inventories held. *p. 108*

Work in progress Partially completed production of an object or service.

Working capital Current assets less current liabilities. *p. 219*

Written-down value (WDV) *See* Carrying amount. *p. 101*

Zero-base budgeting (ZBB) An approach to budgeting, based on the philosophy that all spending needs to be justified annually and that each budget should start as a clean sheet.

APPENDIX C

Solutions to self-assessment questions

Chapter 2

2.1 **Simonson Engineering**

(a) The statement of financial position should be set out as follows:

Simonson Engineering
Statement of financial position as at 30 September 2019

	£
ASSETS	
Non-current assets	
Property, plant and equipment	
Property	72,000
Plant and machinery	25,000
Fixtures and fittings	9,000
Motor vehicles	15,000
	121,000
Current assets	
Inventories	45,000
Trade receivables	48,000
Cash in hand	1,500
	94,500
Total assets	215,500
EQUITY AND LIABILITIES	
Equity	
Closing balance*	120,500
Non-current liabilities	
Long-term borrowings	51,000
Current liabilities	
Trade payables	18,000
Short-term borrowings	26,000
	44,000
Total equity and liabilities	215,500
*The equity is calculated as follows:	
	£
Opening balance	117,500
Profit	18,000
	135,500
Drawings	(15,000)
Closing balance	120,500

(b) The statement of financial position shows:
- The biggest investment in assets is property, followed by trade receivables and inventories. These combined, account for more than 76 per cent of the value of assets held.
- The investment in current assets accounts for 44 per cent of the total investment in assets.
- The total long-term finance is divided 70 per cent equity and 30 per cent long-term borrowings. There is, therefore, not excessive reliance on long-term borrowings.
- The current assets (which are cash or near cash) cover the current liabilities (which are maturing obligations) by a ratio of more than 2:1.

(c) The revised statement of position will be as follows:

Simonson Engineering
Statement of financial position as at 30 September 2019

	£
ASSETS	
Non-current assets	
Property, plant and equipment	
Property	115,000
Plant and machinery	25,000
Motor vehicles	15,000
Fixtures and fittings	9,000
	164,000
Current assets	
Inventories	38,000
Trade receivables	48,000
Cash in hand	1,500
	87,500
Total assets	251,500
EQUITY AND LIABILITIES	
Equity	
Closing balance	156,500
Non-current liabilities	
Long-term borrowings	51,000
Current liabilities	
Trade payables	18,000
Short-term borrowings	26,000
	44,000
Total equity and liabilities	251,500

Chapter 3

3.1 TT and Co.

Statement of financial position as at 31 December 2018

ASSETS	£
Delivery van (12,000 − 2,500)	9,500
inventories (143,000 + 12,000 − 74,000 − 16,000)	65,000
Trade receivables (152,000 − 132,000 − 400)	19,600
Cash at bank (50,000 − 25,000 −	
500 − 1,200 − 12,000 −	
33,500 − 1,650 − 12,000 +	
35,000 + 132,000 −	
121,000 − 9,400)	750
Prepaid expenses (5,000 + 300)	5,300
Total assets	100,150
EQUITY AND LIABILITIES	
Equity (50,000 + 26,900)	76,900
Trade payables (143,000 − 121,000)	22,000
Accrued expenses (630 + 620)	1,250
Total equity and liabilities	100,150

Income statement for the year ended 31 December 2018

	£
Sales revenue (152,000 + 35,000)	187,000
Cost of goods sold (74,000 + 16,000)	(90,000)
Gross profit	97,000
Rent	(20,000)
Rates (500 + 900)	(1,400)
Wages (33,500 + 630)	(34,130)
Electricity (1,650 + 620)	(2,270)
Bad debts	(400)
Van depreciation ((12,000 − 2,000)/4)	(2,500)
Van expenses	(9,400)
Profit for the year	26,900

The statement of financial position could now be rewritten in a more stylish form as follows:

Statement of financial position as at 31 December 2018

	£
ASSETS	
Non-current assets	
Property, plant and equipment	
Delivery van at cost	12,000
Accumulated depreciation	(2,500)
	9,500
Current assets	
Inventories	65,000
Trade receivables	19,600
Prepaid expenses	5,300
Cash	750
	90,650
Total assets	100,150
EQUITY AND LIABILITIES	
Equity	
Closing balance	76,900
Current liabilities	
Trade payables	22,000
Accrued expenses	1,250
	23,250
Total equity and liabilities	100,150

Chapter 4

4.1 Dev Ltd

(a) The summarised statement of financial position of Dev Ltd, immediately following the rights and bonus issue, is as follows:

Statement of financial position

	£000
Net assets (235 + 40 (cash from the rights issue))	275
Equity	
Share capital: 180,000 shares @ £1 ((100 + 20) + 60)	180
Share premium account (30 + 20 − 50)	–
Revaluation reserve (37 − 10)	27
Retained earnings	68
	275

Note that the bonus issue of £60,000 is taken from capital reserves (reserves unavailable for dividends) as follows:

	£000
Share premium account	50
Revaluation reserve	10
	60

More could have been taken from the revaluation reserve and less from the share premium account without making any difference to dividend payment possibilities.

(b) There may be pressure from a potential lender for the business to limit its ability to pay dividends. This would place lenders in a more secure position because the maximum buffer, or safety margin, between the value of the assets and the amount owed by the business is maintained. It is not unusual for potential lenders to insist on some measure to lock up shareholders' funds in this way as a condition of granting the loan.

(c) The summarised statement of financial position of Dev Ltd, immediately following the rights and bonus issue, assuming a minimum dividend potential objective, is as follows:

Statement of financial position	
	£000
Net assets (235 + 40 (cash from the rights issue))	275
Equity	
Share capital: 180,000 shares @ £1 ((100 + 20) + 60)	180
Share premium account (30 + 20)	50
Revaluation reserve	37
Retained earnings (68 − 60)	8
	275

(d) Before the bonus issue, the maximum dividend was £68,000. Now it is £8,000. Thus, the bonus issue has had the effect of locking up an additional £60,000 of the business's assets in terms of the business's ability to pay dividends.

(e) Before the issues, Lee had 100 shares worth £2.35 (£235,000/100,000) each or £235 in total. Lee would be offered 20 shares in the rights issue at £2 each or £40 in total. After the rights issue, Lee would have 120 shares worth £2.2917 (£275,000/120,000) each or £275 in total.

The bonus issue would give Lee 60 additional shares. After the bonus issue, Lee would have 180 shares worth £1.5278 (£275,000/180,000) each or £275 in total.

None of this affects Lee's wealth. Before the issues, Lee had £235 worth of shares and £40 more in cash. After the issues, Lee has the same total wealth but all £275 is in the value of shares held.

(f) The things that we know about the company are as follows:
- It is a private (as opposed to a public) limited company, for it has 'Ltd' (limited) as part of its name, rather than plc (public limited company).
- It has made an issue of shares at a premium, almost certainly after it had traded successfully for a period. (There is a share premium account. It would be unlikely that the original shares, issued when the company was first formed, would have been issued at a premium.)
- Certain of the assets in the statement of financial position have been upwardly revalued by at least £37,000. (There is a revaluation reserve of £37,000. This, however, may be what is left after a bonus issue took part of the reserve.)
- The company has traded at an aggregate profit (though there could have been losses in some years), net of tax and any dividends paid. (There is a positive balance on retained earnings.)

Chapter 5

5.1   (a) 1 Dividends paid during a reporting period can be shown on the face of that period's statement of changes in equity, but they can equally correctly be shown by way of a note.

2 IAS 1 provides support for three key accounting conventions – accruals, going concern and consistency. It does not specifically support the historic cost convention.

3 IAS 1 does not permit bank overdrafts to be offset against positive bank balances when preparing the statement of financial position. For the sake of relevance they should be shown separately.

(b) **Dali plc**

A striking feature of the segmental reports is that the car parts segment generates the highest revenue – more than the other two segments combined. Nevertheless, it is the aircraft parts segment that generates the highest profit. We can use some simple ratios at this point to help evaluate performance.

We can start by considering the profit generated in relation to the sales revenue for each operating segment. We can see from the table below that the boat parts segment generates the most profit in relation to sales revenue. Around 21 per cent, or £0.21 in every £1, of profit is derived from the sales revenue generated. The total revenue for this segment, however, is much lower than for the other two segments. Although the car parts segment generates the most revenue, less than 6 per cent, or £0.06 in every £1, of profit is derived from the sales revenue generated. It is worth noting that the aircraft parts segment suffered a large impairment charge during the year, which had a significant effect on profits. The reasons for this impairment charge should be investigated.

We can also compare the profit generated with the net assets employed (that is, total assets less total liabilities) for each segment. We can see from the table below that the boat parts segment produces the best return on net assets employed by far: around 82 per cent, that is, £0.82 for every £1 invested. Once again, the car parts segment produces the worst results with a return of less than 24 per cent.

The relatively poor results from the car parts segment may simply reflect the nature of the market in which it operates. Compared with car parts segments of other businesses, it may be doing very well. Nevertheless, the business may still wish to consider whether future investment would not be better directed to those areas where greater profits can be found.

The investment in non-current assets during the period in relation to the total assets held is much higher for the boat parts segment. This may reflect the faith of the directors in the potential of this segment.

The depreciation charge as a percentage of segment assets seems to be high for all of the operating segments – but particularly for the car parts division. This should be investigated as it may suggest poor buying decisions.

Table of key results

	Car parts	Aircraft parts	Boat parts
Total revenue	£360m	£210m	£85m
Segment profit	£20m	£24m	£18m
Net assets (assets less liabilities)	£85m	£58m	£22m
Segment profit as a percentage of sales revenue	5.6%	11.4%	21.2%
Segment profit as a percentage of net assets employed	23.5%	41.4%	81.8%
Total assets	£170m	£125m	£44m
Expenditure on non-current assets	£28m	£23m	£26m
Depreciation	£80m	£55m	£15m
Depreciation as a percentage of segment assets	47.1%	44.0%	34.1%

Chapter 6

6.1 **Touchstone plc**

Statement of cash flows for the year ended 31 December 2018

	£m
Cash flows from operating activities	
Profit before taxation (after interest) (see Note 1 below)	60
Adjustments for:	
Depreciation	16
Interest expense (Note 2)	4
	80
Increase in trade receivables (26 − 16)	(10)
Decrease in trade payables (38 − 37)	(1)
Decrease in inventories (25 − 24)	1
Cash generated from operations	70
Interest paid	(4)
Taxation paid (Note 3)	(12)
Dividend paid	(18)
Net cash from operating activities	36
Cash flows from investing activities	
Payments to acquire tangible non-current assets (Note 4)	(41)
Net cash used in investing activities	(41)
Cash flows from financing activities	
Issue of loan notes (40 − 20)	20
Net cash used in financing activities	20
Net increase in cash and cash equivalents	15
Cash and cash equivalents at 1 January 2018	
Cash	4
Cash and cash equivalents at 31 December 2018	
Cash	4
Treasury bills	15
	19

Notes:

1 This is simply taken from the income statement for the year.
2 Interest payable expense must be taken out, by adding it back to the profit before taxation figure. We subsequently deduct the cash paid for interest payable during the year. In this case, the two figures are identical.
3 Companies pay 50 per cent of their tax during their accounting year and the other 50 per cent in the following year. Thus the 2018 payment would have been half the tax on the 2017 profit (that is, the figure that would have appeared in the current liabilities at the end of 2017), plus half of the 2018 tax charge (that is, $4 + (^1/_2 \times 16) = 12$).
4 Since there were no disposals, the depreciation charges must be the difference between the start and end of the year's non-current asset values, adjusted by the cost of any additions:

	£m
Carrying amount at 1 January 2018	147
Additions (balancing figure)	41
	188
Depreciation (6 + 10)	(16)
Carrying amount at 31 December 2018	172

Chapter 7

7.1 **Ali plc and Bhaskar plc**

(a) To answer this question, you may have used the following ratios:

	Ali plc	Bhaskar plc
Return on ordinary shareholders' funds ratio	$\dfrac{99.9}{687.6} \times 100 = 14.5\%$	$\dfrac{104.6}{874.6} \times 100 = 12.0\%$
Operating profit margin ratio	$\dfrac{151.3}{1{,}478.1} \times 100 = 10.2\%$	$\dfrac{166.9}{1{,}790.4} \times 100 = 9.3\%$
Inventories turnover period ratio	$\dfrac{592.0}{1{,}018.3} \times 12 = 7.0$ months	$\dfrac{403.0}{1{,}214.9} \times 12 = 4.0$ months
Settlement period for trade receivables ratio	$\dfrac{176.4}{1{,}478.1} \times 12 = 1.4$ months	$\dfrac{321.9}{1{,}790.4} \times 12 = 2.2$ months
Current ratio	$\dfrac{853.0}{422.4} = 2.0$	$\dfrac{816.5}{293.1} = 2.8$
Acid test ratio	$\dfrac{(853.0 - 592.0)}{422.4} = 0.6$	$\dfrac{(816.5 - 403.0)}{293.1} = 1.4$
Gearing ratio	$\dfrac{190}{(687.6 + 190)} \times 100 = 21.6\%$	$\dfrac{250}{(874.6 + 250)} \times 100 = 22.2\%$
Interest cover ratio	$\dfrac{151.3}{19.4} = 7.8$ times	$\dfrac{166.9}{27.5} = 6.1$ times
Earnings per share	$\dfrac{99.9}{320} = 31.2$p	$\dfrac{104.6}{250} = 41.8$p
Price/earnings ratio	$\dfrac{650}{31.2} = 20.8$ times	$\dfrac{820}{41.8} = 19.6$ times

(*Note*: It is not possible to use any average ratios because only the end-of-year figures are provided for each business.)

Ali plc seems more effective than Bhaskar plc at generating returns for shareholders, as indicated by the higher ROSF ratio. This may be partly caused by Ali plc's higher operating profit margin.

Both businesses have a very high inventories turnover period; this probably needs to be investigated. This ratio is particularly high for Ali plc. Both may suffer from poor inventories management.

Ali plc has a lower settlement period for trade receivables than Bhaskar plc. This may suggest that Bhaskar plc needs to exert greater control over trade receivables.

Ali plc has a much lower current ratio and acid test ratio than Bhaskar plc. The acid test ratio of Ali plc is substantially below 1.0: this may suggest a liquidity problem.

The gearing ratio of each business is quite similar. Neither business seems to have excessive borrowing. The interest cover ratio for each business is also similar. The ratios indicate that both businesses have good profit coverage for their interest charges.

Earnings per share is significantly higher for Bhaskar plc than for Ali plc. However, the P/E ratio for Bhaskar plc is slightly lower. This latter ratio suggests that the market considers Ali plc has slightly better prospects than Bhaskar plc.

To draw better comparisons between the two businesses, it would be useful to calculate other ratios from the financial statements. It would also be helpful to calculate ratios for both businesses over (say) five years as well as key ratios of other businesses operating in the same industry.

(b) The Altman Z-score model is as follows:

$$Z = 0.717a + 0.847b + 3.107c + 0.420d + 0.998e$$

where

a = Working capital/Total assets
b = Accumulated retained profits/Total assets
c = Operating profit/Total assets
d = Book (statement of financial position) value of ordinary and preference shares/
    Total liabilities at book (statement of financial position) value
e = Sales revenue/Total asets

For Ali plc, the Z-score is:

$$0.717[(853.0 - 422.4)/1{,}300.0] + 0.847(367.6/1{,}300.0) + 3.107(151.3/1{,}300.0)$$

$$+0.420[320.0/(190.0 + 422.4)] + 0.998(1{,}478.1/1{,}300.0) = \underline{2.193}$$

For Bhaskar plc, the Z-score is:

$$0.717[(816.5 - 293.1)/1{,}417.7] + 0.847(624.6/1{,}417.7) + 3.107(166.9/1{,}417.7)$$

$$+0.420[250.0/(250.0 + 293.1)] + 0.998(1{,}790.4/1{,}417.7) = \underline{2.457}$$

(c) The Z-scores for these two businesses are quite close, with Bhaskar looking slightly safer. They are both in the 'zone of ignorance' category of businesses and, therefore, difficult to classify (a Z-score between 1.23 and 4.14). This is quite unusual since the Altman model is able confidently to classify 91 per cent of businesses. Clearly, these two businesses fall into the remaining 9 per cent.

It is questionable whether the Altman model is strictly applicable to UK businesses, since it was derived from data relating to US businesses that had failed. On the other hand, it probably provides a useful insight.

Solutions to critical review questions

Chapter 1

1.1 The economic cost of providing accounting information should be less than the expected economic benefit from having the information available. In other words, there should be a net economic benefit from producing it. If this is not the case, it should not be produced. There are obvious problems, however, in determining the precise value of the benefit. There are also problems in determining the costs involved. Hence, making a judgement about whether to provide additional accounting information is far from straightforward.

Economics is not the only issue to consider, particularly in the context of financial accounting. Social and other factors may well be involved. It can be argued, for example, that society has a right to certain information about a large business, even though this information may not have any direct economic value to society.

1.2 The main users of financial information for a university and the way in which they are likely to use this information may be summed up as follows:

Students	Whether to enrol on a course of study. This would probably involve an assessment of the university's ability to continue to operate and to provide the resources that fulfil students' needs.
Other universities and colleges	How best to compete against the university. This might involve using the university's performance in various aspects as 'benchmarks' when evaluating their own performance. These aspects may include costs incurred, student fee income generated and new investments made in facilities.
Employees	Whether to take up or to continue in employment with the university. Employees might assess this by considering the ability of the university to continue to provide employment and to reward employees adequately for their labour.
Government/ funding authority	How efficient and effective the university is in undertaking its various activities. What additional funding the university may need.
Local community representatives	Whether to allow/encourage the university to expand its premises. To assess this, the university's ability to continue to provide employment for the community, to use community resources and to help fund environmental improvements may be considered.
Suppliers	Whether to continue to supply the university at all; also whether to supply on credit. This would involve an assessment of the university's ability to pay for any goods and services supplied.

Lenders	Whether to lend money to the university and/or whether to require repayment of any existing loans. To assess this, the university's ability to meet its obligations to pay interest and to repay the principal would be considered.
Board of governors and managers (faculty deans and so on)	Whether the performance of the university requires improvement. Performance to date would be compared with earlier plans or some other 'benchmark' to decide whether action needs to be taken. Whether there should be a change in the university's future direction. In making such decisions, management will need to look at the university's ability to perform, its resources and at the opportunities available to it.

We can see that the users of accounting information and their needs are similar to those of a private-sector business.

1.3 Accounting, like a spoken language, is a form of communication. It provides those with an interest in a business with a common means of understanding its financial health and performance. However, while a spoken language is general purpose in nature and can cover a wide range of different issues, the language of accounting is restricted to financial issues. It does not, therefore, have the same breadth of 'vocabulary' as a spoken language.

1.4 Since we can never be sure what is going to happen in the future, the best that we can often do is to make judgements on the basis of past experience. Thus, information concerning performance in the recent past may well be a useful source on which to base judgements about possible future performance.

Chapter 2

2.1 The owner seems unaware of the business entity convention in accounting. This convention requires a separation of the business from the owner(s) of the business for accounting purposes. The business is regarded as a separate entity and the statement of financial position is prepared from the perspective of the business rather than that of the owner. As a result, funds invested in the business by the owner are regarded as a claim that the owner has on the business. In the standard layout of the statement of financial position, this claim will be shown alongside other claims on the business from outsiders.

2.2 A statement of financial position does not show what a business is worth, for two major reasons:

1 Only those items that can be measured reliably in monetary terms are shown on the statement of financial position. Thus, things of value such as the reputation for product quality, skills of employees and so on will not normally appear in the statement of financial position.
2 The historic cost convention results in assets often being recorded at their outlay (acquisition) cost rather than their current value. For certain assets, the difference between historic cost and current value may be significant.

2.3 The statement of financial position is a static financial statement, showing only the situation at a single moment in time, whereas the other two major statements – the income statement and statement of cash flows – are dynamic, showing flows of wealth and cash over time. We saw in Chapter 1 that a business exists in order to generate wealth for its owners. The amount of wealth (profit) generated for a particular period is revealed in the income statements. As a result, this statement tends to be the main focus of attention for many users. The statement of cash flows is also of critical importance. In order to survive over time, a business must have an uninterrupted capacity to pay its debts when they fall due. This means that there must be sufficient cash available when needed.

Apart from its static nature, we saw in the chapter, that the statement of financial position provides only a restricted view of financial health. Nevertheless, the statement of financial position still offers important insights and should not be regarded as of secondary importance. To understand the financial health of a business all three major financial statements must be examined.

2.4 Some object to the idea of humans being treated as assets for inclusion on the statement of financial position. It is seen as demeaning for humans to be listed alongside inventories, plant and machinery and other assets. Others argue, however, that humans are often the most valuable resource of a business and that placing a value on this resource will help bring to the attention of managers the importance of nurturing and developing this 'asset'.

Humans are likely to meet the criterion of an asset relating to the right to potential economic benefits, otherwise there would be little point in employing them. The criterion relating to control is, however, more problematic. A business cannot control humans in the same way as most other assets, but it can control the rights to their employment services. This makes it possible to argue that this criterion can be met.

The criterion concerning whether the value of humans (or their services) can be measured with any degree of certainty poses the major difficulty. Apart from the unusual circumstances relating to professional footballers mentioned in the chapter, humans tend to defy reliable measurement.

Chapter 3

3.1 When preparing the income statement, it is not always possible to determine accurately the expenses that need to be matched to the sales revenue for the period. It is perhaps only at some later point that the true position becomes clear. Nevertheless, we must try to include all relevant expenses and so estimates of the future have to be made. These estimates may include accrued expenses, depreciation charges and bad debts incurred. The income statement would lose much of its usefulness if we were to wait for all uncertainties to become clear.

3.2 Depreciation attempts to allocate the cost or fair value, less any residual value, of an asset over its useful life. Depreciation does not attempt to measure the fall in value of the asset during a particular accounting period. Thus, the carrying amount of the asset appearing on the statement of financial position normally represents the unexpired part of its cost, or fair value, rather than its current market value.

3.3 The convention of consistency aims to provide some uniformity in the application of accounting policies. In certain areas, there may be more than one method of accounting for an item, for example inventories. The convention of consistency states that, having decided on a particular accounting policy, a business should continue to apply the policy in successive periods. While this helps to ensure more valid comparisons can be made of business performance *over time,* it does not ensure that valid comparisons can be made *between businesses.* Different businesses may still consistently apply different accounting policies.

3.4 An expense is that element of the cost incurred used up during the reporting period. An asset is that element of cost carried forward on the statement of financial position that will normally be used up in future periods. Thus, both assets and expenses arise from costs being incurred. The major difference between the two is the period over which the benefits (arising from the costs incurred) accrue.

Chapter 4

4.1 A private limited company would seem to be more appropriate. The principal advantage of a company being public is its ability to offer issues of new shares to the general public. This seems not to be a consideration for this particular business, since you and your friend feel that you can finance the start up and planned expansion from your own resources. Being a private company means that neither you nor your friend could sell her, or his, shares to a third party without both agreeing to it. This may well be something that you would both prefer at this stage.

4.2 Some businesses arrange, at considerable economic cost, to have their shares listed on the London Stock Exchange (LSE). They do this because they see the need for their shareholders to have an easy means of selling their shares whenever they choose. Unless investors have the opportunity to sell their shares through the LSE, they will be reluctant to take up shares issued by a business. This would make it more difficult and, probably, more costly for a business to raise equity finance. Thus, the LSE barring a business's shares from being traded could present serious problems for the business.

4.3 It can be argued that all debts should be paid in full and this should be the cornerstone of a civilised society. Business owners should, therefore accept their debt obligations and should not expect to be released from any part of these when things go wrong. Where debt obligations are limited, it diminishes personal responsibility. It means that a portion of the losses incurred by the business owners will be transferred to others. This, in turn, may encourage very risky, or undesirable, behaviour by the owners. They are placed in a position where the 'downside' risk from a perilous venture will be limited but the 'upside' potential will not.

4.4 It is normally only the holders of ordinary shares who have voting rights and, as a result, exercise control over the company. By issuing preference shares their voting rights and therefore their control over the company, will not be diluted. Existing holders of ordinary shares may not wish to participate in a new share issue but, equally, may not wish to see their control over the company diluted. A preference share issue may, therefore, be more acceptable to them.

Preference shares are a less risky form of share than ordinary shares as they confer the right to the first slice of any dividends declared by the company. In an economic environment where investors are wary of taking on too much risk, preference shares may have greater appeal. A preference share issue may, therefore, offer the company a better chance of raising the funds required.

Chapter 5

5.1 Accounting is an evolving subject. It is not static and so the conceptual framework that is laid down at any particular point in time may become obsolete as a result of changes in our understanding of the nature of accounting information and its impact on users and changes in the economic and social environment within which accounting is used. We must accept, therefore, that accounting principles will continue to evolve and that existing ones must be frequently reviewed.

5.2 Managers may shy away from an open and meaningful evaluation of the performance and position of a business because of the risk of litigation. If legal action may result from making statements in good faith or making predictions that prove to be inaccurate, managers will be advised by their lawyers to be very guarded and to stick to making only bland statements. To avoid this risk, managers acting in good faith could be awarded some sort of legal protection (safe harbour). This should help to improve the quality of their commentaries. In the UK, the directors' liability for the strategic report is protected by a 'safe harbour' provision.

5.3 Accounting rules impose an important discipline on managers. They help to ensure that unscrupulous directors do not exploit their position and portray an unrealistic view of financial health. They are also important for the purpose of comparability, both over time and between businesses.

Harmonisation may lead to sovereignty-related problems. Each country has its own tax laws, banking laws, financial regulations and stock exchange rules. International accounting rules may well conflict with these national rules. Furthermore, international rules may not fit well with the local business culture and the way in which businesses operate.

Harmonisation may also lead to some businesses, which operate solely within the confines of its own country, having to comply with international rules.

5.4 The main methods of creative accounting are misstating revenues, massaging expenses, misstating assets, concealing 'bad news' and inadequate disclosure.

Harmonisation of accounting rules will often draw on best practice occurring in highly-developed countries. Other countries may well have weaker rules in place, leading to poor quality financial reporting. By harmonising accounting rules, businesses operating within those countries will need to comply with more demanding rules for financial reporting.

Chapter 6

6.1 Cash is normally required in the settlement of claims. Employees, contractors, lenders and suppliers expect to be paid in cash. When businesses fail, it is their inability to find the cash to pay claimants that actually drives them under. These factors lead to cash being the pre-eminent business asset. It is studied carefully to assess the ability of a business to survive and/or to take advantage of commercial opportunities.

6.2 With the direct method, the business's cash records are analysed for the period concerned. The analysis reveals the amounts of cash, in total, that have been paid and received in respect of trading operations. This is not difficult in principle, or in practice if it is done by computer, as a matter of routine.

The indirect method takes the approach that, while the profit (loss) for the reporting period is not equal to the net inflow (outflow) of cash from operations, they are fairly closely linked to the extent that appropriate adjustment of the profit (loss) for the period figure will produce the correct cash flow one. The adjustment is concerned with interest payable during, the depreciation charge for, and movements in relevant working capital items over, the period.

The indirect method may help to shed light on the quality of reported profits by reconciling profit with the net cash from operating activities for a period. A business must demonstrate an ability to convert profits into cash. Revealing the link between profits and cash is, therefore, very helpful.

6.3 One reason for tightly defining cash is simply to promote comparability between different businesses or, perhaps, between different time periods for the same business. The more tightly a factor is defined, the greater the possibility of producing comparable financial statements.

A second reason is to attempt to avoid the possibility that managers produce a statement of cash flows that could mislead users of the statement, perhaps deliberately. For example, some ordinary shares in another business would not fall within the definition of a cash equivalent because the apparent value of those shares, in terms of cash receivable for them is uncertain. Also, a failure to define cash tightly opens the door to all sorts of assets being treated as a cash equivalent. A business might, for example, claim that trade receivables are a cash equivalent, on the grounds that the next step in the business cycle is for the customer to pay. Including receivables in this way simply defeats the whole idea of the statement as one that is concerned strictly with liquid cash.

6.4 During a particular reporting period, profit and net cash inflows may well diverge significantly. There are several possible reasons for this, including the following:

- Changes in inventories, trade receivables and trade payables. For example, an increase in trade receivables during a reporting period would mean that the cash received from credit sales would be less than the credit sales revenue for the same period.
- Cash may have been spent on new non-current assets or received from disposals of old ones; these would not directly affect profit.
- Cash may have been spent to redeem or repay a financial claim or received as a result of the creation or the increase of a claim. These would not directly affect profit.
- Tax charged in the income statement is not normally the same as the tax paid during the same reporting period.
- Where the period covers the whole life of the business, the timing differences mentioned would become irrelevant and the profit and net cash flows figures would move together.

Chapter 7

7.1 Size may well be an important factor when comparing businesses:

- Larger businesses may be able to generate economies of scale in production and distribution to an extent not available to smaller businesses.
- Larger businesses may be able to raise finance more cheaply, partly through economies of scale (for example, borrowing larger amounts) and partly through being seen as less of a risk to the lender.
- Smaller businesses may be able to be more flexible and 'lighter on their feet' than can the typical larger business.

These and other possible factors may lead to differences in performance and position between larger and smaller businesses.

7.2 Three possible reasons for a long inventories turnover period are:

- poor inventories controls, leading to excessive investment in inventories;
- inventories hoarding in anticipation of price rises, shortages or increased future sales;
- to be able to offer customers a wide range of products or to be able to supply promptly at all times.

A short inventories turnover period may be due to:

- tight inventories controls, reducing excessive investment in inventories and/or the amount of obsolete and slow-moving inventories;
- an inability to finance the required amount of inventories to meet sales demand;
- a difference in the mix of inventories carried by similar businesses (for example, greater investment in perishable goods which are held for a short period only).

These are not exhaustive lists; you may have thought of other reasons.

7.3　In view of the fact that Z-scores are derived from information that is published by the businesses themselves, it is difficult to argue that Z-scores should not be made publicly available. Indeed, many of those connected with a business – shareholders, lenders, employees and so on – may find this information extremely valuable for decision making. Nevertheless, there is a risk that a poor Z-score will lead to a loss of confidence in the business among investors and suppliers which may, in turn, prevent the business from taking corrective action as lines of credit and investment will be withdrawn.

7.4　The P/E ratio may vary between businesses within the same industry for the following reasons:

- *Accounting policies.* Differences in the methods used to compute profit (for example, inventories valuation and depreciation) can lead to different profit figures and, therefore, different P/E ratios.
- *Different prospects.* One business may be regarded as having a much brighter future due to factors such as the quality of management, the quality of products, or location. This will affect the market price investors are prepared to pay for the share and hence will also affect the P/E ratio.
- *Different asset structure.* The business's underlying asset base may be much higher and this may affect the market price of the shares.

Solutions to selected exercises

Chapter 2

2.1 Paul

Statement of cash flows for Thursday

	£
Opening balance (from Wednesday)	59
Cash from sale of wrapping paper	47
Cash paid to purchase wrapping paper	(53)
Closing balance	53

Income statement for Thursday

	£
Sales revenue	47
Cost of goods sold	(33)
Profit	14

Statement of financial position as at Thursday evening

	£
Cash	53
Inventories of goods for resale (23 + 53 − 33)	43
Total assets	96
Equity	96

2.2 Paul (*continued*)

Equity

	£
Cash introduced by Paul on Monday	40
Profit for Monday	15
Profit for Tuesday	18
Profit for Wednesday	9
Profit for Thursday	14
Total business wealth (total assets)	96

Thus, the equity, all of which belongs to Paul as sole owner, consists of the cash he put in to start the business plus the profit earned each day.

2.3 **Helen**

Income statement for day 1

	£
Sales revenue (70 × £0.80)	56
Cost of sales (70 × £0.50)	(35)
Profit	21

Statement of cash flows for day 1

	£
Cash introduced by Helen	40
Cash from sales	56
Cash for purchases (80 × £0.50)	(40)
Closing balance	56

Statement of financial position as at end of day 1

	£
Cash balance	56
Inventories of unsold goods (10 × £0.50)	5
Total assets	61
Equity	61

Income statement for day 2

	£
Sales revenue (65 × £0.80)	52.0
Cost of sales (65 × £0.50)	(32.5)
Profit	19.5

Statement of cash flows for day 2

	£
Opening balance	56.0
Cash from sales	52.0
Cash for purchases (60 × £0.50)	(30.0)
Closing balance	78.0

Statement of financial position as at end of day 2

	£
Cash balance	78.0
Inventories of unsold goods (5 × £0.50)	2.5
Total assets	80.5
Equity	80.5

Income statement for day 3

	£
Sales revenue ((20 × £0.80) + (45 × £0.40))	34.0
Cost of sales (65 × £0.50)	(32.5)
Profit	1.5

Statement of cash flows for day 3

	£
Opening balance	78.0
Cash from sales	34.0
Cash for purchases (60 × £0.50)	(30.0)
Closing balance	82.0

Statement of financial position as at end of day 3

	£
Cash balance	82.0
Inventories of unsold goods	–
Total assets	82.0
Equity	82.0

2.6 Crafty Engineering

(a)
Statement of financial position as at 30 June last year

	£000
ASSETS	
Non-current assets	
Property, plant and equipment	
Property	320
Equipment and tools	207
Motor vehicles	38
	565
Current assets	
Inventories	153
Trade receivables	185
	338
Total assets	903
EQUITY AND LIABILITIES	
Equity (which is the missing figure)	441
Non-current liabilities	
Long-term borrowings (loan from Industrial Finance Company)	260
Current liabilities	
Trade payables	86
Short-term borrowings	116
	202
Total equity and liabilities	903

(b) The statement of financial position reveals a large investment in non-current assets. It represents more than 60 per cent of the total investment in assets (565/903). The nature of the business may require a heavy investment in non-current assets. The current assets exceed the current liabilities by a large amount (approximately 1.7 times). Hence, there is no obvious sign of a liquidity problem. However, the statement of financial position reveals that the business has no cash balance and is therefore dependent on the continuing support of short-term borrowing to meet maturing obligations.

When considering the long-term financing of the business, we can see that about 37 per cent (that is, 260/(260 + 441)) of total long-term finance is supplied by borrowings and about 63 per cent (that is, 441/(260 + 441)) by the owners. This level of long-term borrowing seems high but not excessive. However, we need to know more about the ability of the business to service the borrowing (that is, make interest payments and repayments of the amount borrowed) before a full assessment can be made.

Chapter 3

3.1   Comments

(a) Equity does increase as a result of the owners introducing more cash into the business, but it will also increase as a result of the owners introducing other assets (for example, a motor car) and by the business generating revenue by trading. Similarly, equity decreases not only as a result of withdrawals of cash by owners but also by withdrawals of other assets (for example, inventories for the owners' personal use) and through the business incurring trading expenses. Generally speaking, equity will alter more as a result of trading activities than for any other reason.

(b) An accrued expense is not one that relates to next year. It is one that needs to be matched with the revenue of the reporting period under review, but that has yet to be met in terms of cash payment. As such, it will appear on the statement of financial position as a current liability.

(c) The purpose of depreciation is not to provide for asset replacement. It is an attempt to allocate the cost, or fair value, of the asset (less any residual value) over its useful life. Depreciation provides a measure of the amount of a non-current asset that has been consumed during a period. This amount is then charged as an expense for the period. Depreciation is a book entry (the outlay of cash occurs when the asset is purchased) and does not normally entail setting aside a separate amount of cash for asset replacement. Even if this were done, there would be no guarantee that sufficient funds would be available at the end of the asset's life for its replacement. Factors such as inflation and technological change may mean that the replacement cost is higher than the original cost of the asset.

(d) In the short term, the current value of a non-current asset may exceed its original cost. However, nearly all non-current assets wear out over time through being used to generate wealth. This will be the case for buildings. Thus, some measure of depreciation is needed to reflect the fact that the asset is being consumed. Some businesses revalue their buildings upwards where the current value is significantly higher than the original cost. Where this occurs, the depreciation charge should be based on the revalued amount, which will result in higher depreciation charges.

3.3   The generation of profit combined with downward movement in cash may arise for various reasons, including the following:

- the purchase for cash during the period of assets (for example, motor cars and inventories) which were not all consumed during the period and so will not affect expenses as much as cash;
- the payment of an outstanding liability (for example, borrowings), which will have an effect on cash but not on expenses in the income statement;
- the withdrawal of cash by the owners from the equity invested, which will not affect the expenses in the income statement; and
- the generation of revenue on credit where the cash has yet to be received. This will increase the sales revenue for the period but will not increase the cash balance until a later time.

3.4   Missing values

(a) Rent payable – expense for period	£9,000
(b) Rates and insurance – expense for period	£6,000
(c) General expenses – paid in period	£7,000
(d) Interest (on borrowings) payable – prepaid	£500
(e) Salaries – paid in period	£6,000
(f) Rent receivable – received during period	£3,000

3.7   Nikov and Co.

An examination of the income statements for the two years reveals a number of interesting points, which include:

- an increase in sales revenue and gross profit of 9.9 per cent in 2018;
- the gross profit expressed as a percentage of sales revenue remaining at 70 per cent;
- an increase in salaries of 7.2 per cent;
- an increase in selling and distribution costs of 31.2 per cent;
- an increase in bad debts of 392.5 per cent;
- a decline in profit for the year of 39.3 per cent; and
- a decline in the profit for the year as a percentage of sales revenue from 13.3 per cent to 7.4 per cent.

We can see that the business has enjoyed an increase in sales revenue and gross profits, but this has failed to translate to an increase in profit for the year because of the significant rise in overheads. The increase in selling costs during 2018 suggests that the increase in sales revenue was achieved by greater marketing effort, and the huge increase in bad debts suggests that the increase in sales revenue may be attributable to selling to less creditworthy customers, or to a weak debt-collection policy. There appears to have been a change of policy in 2018 towards sales, which has not been successful overall as there has been a dramatic decline in profit for the year.

Chapter 4

4.1

Limited companies can no more set a limit on the amount of debts they will meet than can individuals. They must meet their debts up to the limit of their assets, just as we as individuals must. In the context of owners' claim, 'reserves' mean part of the owners' claim against the assets of the company. These assets may or may not include cash. The legal ability of the company to pay dividends is not related to the amount of cash held.

Preference shares do not carry a guaranteed dividend. They simply guarantee that the preference shareholders have a right to the first slice of any dividend that is paid. Shares of many companies can, in effect, be bought by one investor from another through the Stock Exchange. Such a transaction has no direct effect on the company, however. These are not new shares being offered by the company, but 'second-hand' (that is, existing) shares that are being sold between investors.

4.2

(a) The first part of the quote is incorrect. Bonus shares should not, of themselves, increase the value of the shareholders' wealth. This is because reserves, which belong to the shareholders, are used to create bonus shares. Thus, each shareholder's stake in the company has not changed.

(b) This statement is incorrect. Shares can be issued at any price, provided that it is not below the nominal value of the shares. Once the company has been trading profitably for a period, the shares are likely to be worth more than their nominal value: that is, the amount at which they were issued when the company was first formed. In such circumstances, issuing shares at above their nominal value would not only be legal, but essential to preserve the wealth of existing shareholders relative to new shareholders.

(c) This statement is incorrect. From a legal perspective, the maximum dividend payable is based on the amount of a company's revenue reserves. This amount represents any after-tax profits or gains realised that have not been eroded through, for example, payments of previous dividends. From a legal perspective, cash availability is not an issue. It would be perfectly legal for a company to borrow funds in order to pay a dividend – although whether this would be commercially prudent is another question.

(d) This statement is partly incorrect. Companies do indeed have to pay tax on their profits. Depending on their circumstances, shareholders might also have to pay tax on their dividends.

4.4 Iqbal Ltd

Year	Maximum dividend £	
2015	0	No profit exists out of which to pay a dividend.
2016	0	There remains a cumulative loss of £7,000. Since the revaluation represents a gain that has not been realised, it cannot be used to justify a dividend.
2017	13,000	The cumulative net realised gains are derived as (−£15,000 + £8,000 + £15,000 + £5,000).
2018	14,000	The realised profits and gains for the year.
2019	22,000	The realised profits and gains for the year.

4.6 Pear Limited

Statement of financial position as at 30 September 2019

	£000
ASSETS	
Non-current assets	
Property, plant and equipment	
Cost (1,570 + 30)	1,600
Depreciation (690 + 12)	(702)
	898
Current assets	
Inventories	207
Trade receivables (182 + 18 − 4)	196
Cash at bank	21
	424
Total assets	1,322
EQUITY AND LIABILITIES	
Equity	
Share capital	300
Share premium account	300
Retained earnings (104 + 41 − 25)	120
	720
Non-current liabilities	
Borrowings – 10% loan (repayable 2025)	300
Current liabilities	
Trade payables	88
Other payables (20 + 30 + 15 + 2)	67
Taxation	17
Dividend approved	25
Borrowings – bank overdraft	105
	302
Total equity and liabilities	1,322

Income statement for the year ended 30 September 2019

	£000
Revenue (1,456 + 18)	1,474
Cost of sales	(768)
Gross profit	706
Salaries	(220)
Depreciation (249 + 12)	(261)
Other operating costs (131 + (2% × 200) + 2)	(137)
Operating profit	88
Interest payable (15 + 15)	(30)
Profit before taxation	58
Taxation (58 × 30%)	(17)
Profit for the year	41

Chapter 5

5.3 I. Ching (Booksellers) plc

Statement of comprehensive income for the year ended 31 May 2019

	£000
Revenue	943
Cost of sales	(460)
Gross profit	483
Distribution expenses	(110)
Administrative expenses	(212)
Other expenses	(25)
Operating profit	136
Finance charges	(40)
Profit before tax	96
Taxation	(24)
Profit for the year	72
Other comprehensive income	
Revaluation of property, plant and equipment	20
Foreign currency translation differences for foreign operations	(15)
Tax on other comprehensive income	(1)
Other comprehensive income for the year, net of tax	4
Total comprehensive income for the year	76

5.4 Manet plc

Statement of changes in equity for the year ended 31 May 2019

	Share capital £m	Share premium £m	Revaluation reserve £m	Translation reserve £m	Retained earnings £m	Total £m
Balance as at 1 June 2018	250	50	120	15	380	815
Changes in equity for the year						
Dividends (Note 1)					(80)	(80)
Total comprehensive income for the year (Note 2)	–	–	30	(5)	160	185
Balance at 31 May 2019	250	50	150	10	460	920

Notes:

1 Dividends have been shown in the statement rather than in the notes. Either approach is acceptable.

2 The effect of each component of comprehensive income on each component of shareholder equity must be shown. The revaluation gain and loss on exchange translation are each transferred to a specific reserve and the profit for the year is transferred to retained earnings.

5.5 (a) The 'comply or explain' approach means that companies listed on the London Stock Exchange are expected to comply with the requirements of the UK Corporate Governance Code or the directors must give the shareholders good reason why they do not. Failure to do one or the other can lead to the company's shares being suspended from listing.

An advantage of this approach is that it provides a company with a degree of flexibility over its governance procedures. Where, for example, a company is dealing with a crisis situation, the board of directors may feel that a single, strong leader is required. It may, therefore, be decided that one person will occupy the roles of both chairman and chief executive. Although this is contrary to the UK Code, shareholders may agree, given the particular circumstances, to merging the two roles.

A disadvantage is that, when applying the UK Code, an element of subjectivity is involved. The UK Code requires, for example, that the directors establish a satisfactory dialogue with shareholders. This may, however, be interpreted in different ways and so it may be difficult to establish whether compliance has really occurred. It may also be difficult to make comparisons between companies.

(b) Preparing a strategic report may present a problem for accountants. For information to be credible to all interested parties, accountants should be as neutral as possible in measuring and reporting the financial performance and position of the business. The strategic report requires some interpretation of results and there is always a risk of bias, or at least the perception of bias among some users, in what items are reported and how they reflect on business performance. The board of directors is charged with running the business and it is logical that the directors accept full responsibility for preparing the report. This should be made clear to users.

5.7 **Turner plc**

We can see from the table below that the software segment generates the highest revenue, but also generates the lowest profit. We can use some simple ratios at this point to help evaluate segmental performance. We can start by considering the profit generated in relation to the sales revenue for each operating segment. We can see from the table below that the engineering segment generates the most profit in relation to sales revenue. Around 23 per cent, or £0.23 in every £1, of profit is derived from the sales revenue generated. However, for the software segment, only 4 per cent, or £0.04 in every £1, of profit is derived from the sales revenue generated.

We can also compare the profit generated with the net assets employed (that is, total assets less total liabilities) for each segment. We can see from the table below that the electronics segment produces the best return on net assets employed: around £0.65 for every £1 invested. Once again, the software segment produces the worst results.

The reasons for the relatively poor results from the software segment need further investigation. There may be valid reasons; for example, it may be experiencing severe competitive pressures. The results for this segment, however, are not disastrous: it is making a profit. Nevertheless, the business may wish to re-evaluate its long-term presence in this market.

It is interesting to note that the software segment had the highest new investment in non-current assets during the period – as much as the other two segments combined. The reason for such a large investment in such a relatively poorly performing segment needs to be justified. It is possible that the business will reap rewards for the investment in the future; however, we do not have enough information to understand the reasons for the investment decision.

Depreciation charges in the software segment are significantly higher than for the other operating segments. This may be because the segment has more non-current assets, although we do not have a figure for the non-current assets held. The depreciation charge as a percentage of segment assets is also higher and the reasons for this should be investigated.

Table of key results

	Software	Electronics	Engineering
Total revenue	£250m	£230m	£52m
Segment profit	£10m	£34m	£12m
Net assets (assets less liabilities)	£85m	£52m	£30m
Segment profit as a percentage of sales revenue	4.0%	14.8%	23.1%
Segment profit as a percentage of net assets employed	11.8%	65.4%	40.0%
Expenditure on non-current assets	£22m	£12m	£10m
Total assets	£140m	£90m	£34m
Depreciation	£60m	£35m	£10m
Depreciation as a percentage of segment assets	42.9%	38.9%	29.4%

Chapter 6

6.1 (a) An increase in the level of inventories would, ultimately, have an adverse effect on cash.

(b) A rights issue of ordinary shares will give rise to a positive cash flow, which will be included in the 'financing' section of the statement of cash flows.

(c) A bonus issue of ordinary shares has no cash flow effect.

(d) Writing off some of the value of the inventories has no cash flow effect.

(e) A disposal for cash of a large number of shares by a major shareholder has no cash flow effect as far as the business is concerned.

(f) Depreciation does not involve cash at all. Using the indirect method of deducing cash flows from operating activities involves the depreciation expense in the calculation, but this is simply because we are trying to find out, from the profit before taxation (after depreciation) figure, what the profit before taxation *and* depreciation must have been.

6.3   **Torrent plc**

Statement of cash flows for the year ended 31 December 2018

	£m
Cash flows from operating activities	
Profit before taxation (after interest) (see Note 1 below)	170
Adjustments for:	
Depreciation (Note 2)	78
Interest expense (Note 3)	26
	274
Decrease in inventories (41 − 35)	6
Increase in trade receivables (145 − 139)	(6)
Decrease in trade payables (54 − 41)	(13)
Cash generated from operations	261
Interest paid	(26)
Taxation paid (Note 4)	(41)
Dividend paid	(60)
Net cash from operating activities	134
Cash flows from investing activities	
Payments to acquire plant and machinery	(67)
Net cash used in investing activities	(67)
Cash flows from financing activities	
Redemption of loan notes (250 − 150) (Note 5)	(100)
Net cash used in financing activities	(100)
Net decrease in cash and cash equivalents	(33)
Cash and cash equivalents at 1 January 2018	
Bank overdraft	(56)
Cash and cash equivalents at 31 December 2018	
Bank overdraft	(89)

Notes:

1   This is simply taken from the income statement for the year.
2   Since there were no disposals, the depreciation charges must be the difference between the start and end of the year's plant and machinery values, adjusted by the cost of any additions.

	£m
Carrying amount at 1 January 2018	325
Additions	67
Depreciation (balancing figure)	(78)
Carrying amount at 31 December 2018	314

3   Interest payable expense must be taken out, by adding it back to the profit before taxation figure. We subsequently deduct the cash paid for interest payable during the year. In this case, the two figures are identical.
4   Companies pay 50 per cent of their tax during their accounting year and 50 per cent in the following year. Thus the 2018 payment would have been half the tax on the 2017 profit (that is, the figure that would have appeared in the current liabilities at the end of 2017), plus half of the 2018 tax charge (that is, $23 + (\frac{1}{2} \times 36) = 41$).
5   It is assumed that the cash payment to redeem the loan notes was simply the difference between the two statement of financial position figures.
6   It seems that there was a bonus issue of ordinary shares during the year. These increased by £100m. At the same time, the share premium account balance reduced by £40m (to zero) and the revaluation reserve balance fell by £60m.

6.6 **Blackstone plc**

Statement of cash flows for the year ended 31 March 2019

	£m
Cash flows from operating activities	
Profit before taxation (after interest) (see Note 1)	1,853
Adjustments for:	
Depreciation (Note 2)	1,289
Interest expense (Note 3)	456
	3,598
Increase in inventories (2,410 − 1,209)	(1,201)
Increase in trade receivables (1,173 − 641)	(532)
Increase in trade payables (1,507 − 931)	576
Cash generated from operations	2,441
Interest paid	(456)
Taxation paid (Note 4)	(300)
Dividend paid	(400)
Net cash from operating activities	1,285
Cash flows from investing activities	
Proceeds of disposals	54
Payment to acquire intangible non-current asset	(700)
Payments to acquire property, plant and equipment	(4,578)
Net cash used in investing activities	(5,224)
Cash flows from financing activities	
Bank borrowings	2,000
Net cash from financing activities	2,000
Net decrease in cash and cash equivalents	(1,939)
Cash and cash equivalents at 1 April 2018	
Cash at bank	123
Cash and cash equivalents at 31 March 2019	
Bank overdraft	(1,816)

Notes:
1 This is simply taken from the income statement for the year.
2 The full depreciation charge was that stated in Note 2 to the question (£1,251m), plus the deficit on disposal of the non-current assets. According to Note 2, these non-current assets had originally cost £581m and had been depreciated by £489m, giving a net carrying amount of £92m. They were sold for £54m, leading to a deficit on disposal of £38m. Thus, the full depreciation expense for the year was £1,289m (that is, £1,251m + £38m).
3 Interest payable expense must be taken out, by adding it back to the profit before taxation figure. We subsequently deduct the cash paid for interest payable during the year. In this case, the two figures are identical.
4 Companies pay tax at 50 per cent during their accounting year and the other 50 per cent in the following year. Thus the 2019 payment would have been half the tax on the 2018 profit (that is, the figure that would have appeared in the current liabilities at 31 March 2018), plus half of the 2019 tax charge (that is, $105 + (^1/_2 \times 390) = 300$).

6.7   **York plc**

Statement of cash flows for the year ended 30 September 2019

	£m
Cash flows from operating activities	
Profit before taxation (after interest) (see Note 1)	10.0
Adjustments for:	
Depreciation (Note 2)	9.8
Interest expense (Note 3)	3.0
	22.8
Increase in inventories and trade receivables (122.1 − 119.8)	(2.3)
Increase in trade payables (82.5 − 80.0)	2.5
Cash generated from operations	23.0
Interest paid	(3.0)
Taxation paid (Note 4)	(2.3)
Dividend paid	(3.5)
Net cash from operating activities	14.2
Cash flows from investing activities	
Proceeds of disposals (Note 2)	5.2
Payments to acquire non-current assets	(20.0)
Net cash used in investing activities	(14.8)
Cash flows from financing activities	
Increase in long-term borrowings	3.0
Share issue (Note 5)	5.0
Net cash from financing activities	8.0
Net increase in cash and cash equivalents	7.4
Cash and cash equivalents at 1 October 2018	
Cash at bank	9.2
Cash and cash equivalents at 30 September 2019	
Cash at bank	16.6

Notes:

1   This is simply taken from the income statement for the year.

2   The full depreciation charge was the £13.0m, less the surplus on disposal (£3.2m), both stated in Note 1 to the question. (According to the table in Note 4 to the question, the non-current assets disposed of had a net carrying value of £2.0m. To produce a surplus of £3.2m, they must have been sold for £5.2m.)

3   Interest payable expense must be taken out, by adding it back to the profit before taxation figure. We subsequently deduct the cash paid for interest payable during the year. In this case, the two figures are identical.

4   Companies pay 50 per cent of their tax during their accounting year and the other 50 per cent in the following year. Thus the 2019 payment would have been half the tax on the 2018 profit (that is, the figure that would have appeared in the current liabilities at 30 September 2018), plus half of the 2019 tax charge (that is, $1.0 + (^1/_2 \times 2.6) = 2.3$).

5   This issue must have been for cash since it could not have been a bonus issue – the share premium is untouched and 'Reserves' had altered over the year only by the amount of the 2019 retained earnings (profit for the year, less the dividend). The shares seem to have been issued at their nominal value (par). This is a little surprising since the business has assets that seem to be above that value. On the other hand, if this was a rights issue, the low issue price would not have disadvantaged the existing shareholders since they were also the beneficiaries of the advantage of the low issue price.

Chapter 7

7.1   Three businesses

A plc operates a supermarket chain. The grocery business is highly competitive and, in order to generate high sales volumes, it is usually necessary to accept low operating profit margins. Thus, we can see that the operating profit margin of A plc is the lowest of the three businesses. The inventories turnover period of supermarket chains also tend to be quite low. They are often efficient in managing inventories, and most supermarket chains have invested heavily in inventories control and logistical systems over the years. The average settlement period for receivables is very low as most sales are for cash, although, when a customer pays by credit card, there is usually a small delay before the supermarket receives the amount due. A low inventories turnover period and a low average settlement period for receivables usually mean that the investment in current assets is low. Hence, the current ratio (current assets/current liabilities) is also low.

B plc is the holiday tour operator. We can see that the sales to capital employed ratio is the highest of the three. This is because tour operators do not usually require a large investment of capital: they do not need a large asset base in order to conduct their operations. The inventories turnover period ratio does not apply to B plc. It is a service business, which does not hold inventories for resale. We can see that the average settlement period for receivables is low. This may be because customers are invoiced near to the holiday date for any amounts outstanding and must pay before going on holiday. The lack of inventories held and low average settlement period for receivables leads to a very low current ratio.

C plc is the food manufacturing business. We can see that the sales to capital employed ratio is the lowest of the three. This is because manufacturers tend to invest heavily in both current and non-current assets. The inventories turnover period is the highest of the three. Three different kinds of inventories – raw materials, work in progress and finished goods – are held by manufacturers. The average receivables settlement period is also the highest of the three. Manufacturers tend to sell to other businesses rather than to the public and their customers will normally demand credit. A one-month credit period for customers is fairly common for manufacturing businesses, although customers may receive a discount for prompt payment. The relatively high investment in inventories and receivables usually results in a high current ratio.

7.2   Amsterdam Ltd and Berlin Ltd

The ratios for Amsterdam Ltd and Berlin Ltd reveal that the average settlement period for trade receivables for Amsterdam Ltd is three times that for Berlin Ltd. Berlin Ltd is therefore much quicker in collecting amounts outstanding from customers. On the other hand, there is not much difference between the two businesses in the time taken to pay trade payables.

It is interesting to compare the difference in the trade receivables and payables settlement periods for each business. As Amsterdam Ltd allows an average of 63 days' credit to its customers, yet pays suppliers within 50 days, it will require greater investment in working capital than Berlin Ltd, which allows an average of only 21 days to its customers but takes 45 days to pay its suppliers.

Amsterdam Ltd has a much higher gross profit margin than Berlin Ltd. However, the operating profit margin for the two businesses is identical. This suggests that Amsterdam Ltd has much higher overheads (as a percentage of sales revenue) than Berlin Ltd. The average inventories turnover period for Amsterdam Ltd is more than twice that of Berlin Ltd. This may be due to the fact that Amsterdam Ltd maintains a wider range of inventories in an attempt to meet customer requirements. The evidence therefore suggests that Amsterdam Ltd is the business that prides itself on personal service. The higher average settlement period for trade receivables is consistent with a more relaxed attitude to credit collection (thereby maintaining customer goodwill) and the high overheads are consistent with incurring the additional costs of satisfying customers' requirements. Amsterdam Ltd's high inventories levels are consistent with maintaining a wide range of inventories, with the aim of satisfying a range of customer needs.

Berlin Ltd has the characteristics of a more price-competitive business. Its gross profit margin is much lower than that of Amsterdam Ltd, that is, a much lower gross profit for each £1 of sales revenue. However, overheads have been kept low, the effect being that the operating profit margin is the same as Amsterdam Ltd's. The low average inventories turnover period and average settlement period for trade receivables are consistent with a business that wishes to minimise investment in current assets, thereby reducing costs.

7.6   **Genesis Ltd**

(a)
$$\text{Current ratio} = \frac{232}{550} = 0.42 : 1$$

$$\text{Acid test ratio} = \frac{104}{550} = 0.19 : 1$$

$$\text{Inventories turnover period} = \frac{128}{1,248} \times 365 = 37 \text{ days}$$

$$\text{Average settlement period for trade receivables} = \frac{104}{1,640} \times 365 = 23 \text{ days}$$

$$\text{Average settlement period for trade payables} = \frac{184}{1,260} \times 365 = 53 \text{ days}$$

It is difficult to make a judgement in the absence of any basis for comparison, but there is some suggestion that the business is overtrading. Both of the liquidity ratios look weak. The acid test ratio should probably be around 1:1. Customers are paying more than twice as quickly as suppliers are being paid. This suggests that pressure may be being applied to the former to pay quickly, perhaps with adverse results. It may also imply that payments to suppliers are being delayed because of a lack of available finance.

(b) Overtrading must be dealt with either by increasing the level of funding to match the level of activity, or by reducing the level of activity to match the funds available. The latter option may result in a reduction in operating profit in the short term but may be necessary to ensure long-term survival.

7.7 **Harridges Ltd**

(a)

	2018	2019
ROCE	$\dfrac{310}{1,600} = 19.4\%$	$\dfrac{350}{1,700} = 20.6\%$
ROSF	$\dfrac{155}{1,100} = 14.1\%$	$\dfrac{175}{1,200} = 14.6\%$
Gross profit margin	$\dfrac{1,040}{2,600} = 40\%$	$\dfrac{1,150}{3,500} = 32.9\%$
Operating profit margin	$\dfrac{310}{2,600} = 11.9\%$	$\dfrac{350}{3,500} = 10\%$
Current ratio	$\dfrac{735}{400} = 1.8$	$\dfrac{660}{485} = 1.4$
Acid test ratio	$\dfrac{485}{400} = 1.2$	$\dfrac{260}{485} = 0.5$
Trade receivables settlement period	$\dfrac{105}{2,600} \times 365 = 15$ days	$\dfrac{145}{3,500} \times 365 = 15$ days
Trade payables settlement period	$\dfrac{300}{1,560*} \times 365 = 70$ days	$\dfrac{375}{2,350*} \times 365 = 58$ days
Inventories turnover period	$\dfrac{250}{1,560} \times 365 = 58$ days	$\dfrac{400}{2,350} \times 365 = 62$ days
Gearing ratio	$\dfrac{500}{1,600} = 31.3\%$	$\dfrac{500}{1,700} = 29.4\%$

* Used because the credit purchases figure is not available.

(b) There has been a considerable decline in the gross profit margin during 2019. This fact, combined with the increase in sales revenue by more than a third, suggests that a price-cutting policy has been adopted in an attempt to stimulate sales. The resulting increase in sales revenue, however, has led to only a small improvement in ROCE and ROSF.

Despite a large cut in the gross profit margin, the operating profit margin has fallen by less than 2 per cent. This suggests that overheads may have been more tightly controlled during 2019. Certainly, overheads have not risen in proportion to sales revenue.

The current ratio has fallen a little and the acid test ratio has fallen by more than half. Although liquidity ratios tend to be lower in retailing than in manufacturing, the liquidity of the business should now be a cause for concern. However, this may be a passing problem. The business is investing heavily in non-current assets and is relying on internal funds to finance this growth. When this investment ends, the liquidity position may improve quickly.

The trade receivables period has remained unchanged over the two years, and there has been no significant change in the inventories turnover period in 2019. The gearing ratio seems quite low and provides no cause for concern given the profitability of the business.

Overall, the business appears to be financially sound. Although there has been rapid growth during 2019, there is no real cause for alarm provided the liquidity of the business can be improved in the near future. In the absence of information concerning share price, it is not possible to say whether an investment should be made.

Present value table

Present value of £1, that is, $1/(1 + r)^n$

where r = discount rate
n = number of periods until payment

Periods	Discount rates (r)										
(n)	1%	2%	3%	4%	5%	6%	7%	8%	9%	10%	
1	0.990	0.980	0.971	0.962	0.952	0.943	0.935	0.926	0.917	0.909	1
2	0.980	0.961	0.943	0.925	0.907	0.890	0.873	0.857	0.842	0.826	2
3	0.971	0.942	0.915	0.889	0.864	0.840	0.816	0.794	0.772	0.751	3
4	0.961	0.924	0.888	0.855	0.823	0.792	0.763	0.735	0.708	0.683	4
5	0.951	0.906	0.863	0.822	0.784	0.747	0.713	0.681	0.650	0.621	5
6	0.942	0.888	0.837	0.790	0.746	0.705	0.666	0.630	0.596	0.564	6
7	0.933	0.871	0.813	0.760	0.711	0.665	0.623	0.583	0.547	0.513	7
8	0.923	0.853	0.789	0.731	0.677	0.627	0.582	0.540	0.502	0.467	8
9	0.914	0.837	0.766	0.703	0.645	0.592	0.544	0.500	0.460	0.424	9
10	0.905	0.820	0.744	0.676	0.614	0.558	0.508	0.463	0.422	0.386	10
11	0.896	0.804	0.722	0.650	0.585	0.527	0.475	0.429	0.388	0.350	11
12	0.887	0.788	0.701	0.625	0.557	0.497	0.444	0.397	0.356	0.319	12
13	0.879	0.773	0.681	0.601	0.530	0.469	0.415	0.368	0.326	0.290	13
14	0.870	0.758	0.661	0.577	0.505	0.442	0.388	0.340	0.299	0.263	14
15	0.861	0.743	0.642	0.555	0.481	0.417	0.362	0.315	0.276	0.239	15

Periods (n)		Discount rates (r)										
	11%	12%	13%	14%	15%	16%	17%	18%	19%	20%		
1	0.901	0.893	0.885	0.877	0.870	0.862	0.855	0.847	0.840	0.833	1	
2	0.812	0.797	0.783	0.769	0.756	0.743	0.731	0.718	0.706	0.694	2	
3	0.731	0.712	0.693	0.675	0.658	0.641	0.624	0.609	0.593	0.579	3	
4	0.659	0.636	0.613	0.592	0.572	0.552	0.534	0.516	0.499	0.482	4	
5	0.593	0.567	0.543	0.519	0.497	0.476	0.456	0.437	0.419	0.402	5	
6	0.535	0.507	0.480	0.456	0.432	0.410	0.390	0.370	0.352	0.335	6	
7	0.482	0.452	0.425	0.400	0.376	0.354	0.333	0.314	0.296	0.279	7	
8	0.434	0.404	0.376	0.351	0.327	0.305	0.285	0.266	0.249	0.233	8	
9	0.391	0.361	0.333	0.308	0.284	0.263	0.243	0.225	0.209	0.194	9	
10	0.352	0.322	0.295	0.270	0.247	0.227	0.208	0.191	0.176	0.162	10	
11	0.317	0.287	0.261	0.237	0.215	0.195	0.178	0.162	0.148	0.135	11	
12	0.286	0.257	0.231	0.208	0.187	0.168	0.152	0.137	0.124	0.112	12	
13	0.258	0.229	0.204	0.182	0.163	0.145	0.130	0.116	0.104	0.093	13	
14	0.232	0.205	0.181	0.160	0.141	0.125	0.111	0.099	0.088	0.078	14	
15	0.209	0.183	0.160	0.140	0.123	0.108	0.095	0.084	0.074	0.065	15	

Periods (n)		Discount rates (r)										
	21%	22%	23%	24%	25%	26%	27%	28%	29%	30%		
1	0.826	0.820	0.813	0.806	0.800	0.794	0.787	0.781	0.775	0.769	1	
2	0.683	0.672	0.661	0.650	0.640	0.630	0.620	0.610	0.601	0.592	2	
3	0.564	0.551	0.537	0.524	0.512	0.500	0.488	0.477	0.466	0.455	3	
4	0.467	0.451	0.437	0.423	0.410	0.397	0.384	0.373	0.361	0.350	4	
5	0.386	0.370	0.355	0.341	0.328	0.315	0.303	0.291	0.280	0.269	5	
6	0.319	0.303	0.289	0.275	0.262	0.250	0.238	0.277	0.217	0.207	6	
7	0.263	0.249	0.235	0.222	0.210	0.198	0.188	0.178	0.168	0.159	7	
8	0.218	0.204	0.191	0.179	0.168	0.157	0.148	0.139	0.130	0.123	8	
9	0.180	0.167	0.155	0.144	0.134	0.125	0.116	0.108	0.101	0.094	9	
10	0.149	0.137	0.126	0.116	0.107	0.099	0.092	0.085	0.078	0.073	10	
11	0.123	0.112	0.103	0.094	0.086	0.079	0.072	0.066	0.061	0.056	11	
12	0.102	0.092	0.083	0.076	0.069	0.062	0.057	0.052	0.047	0.043	12	
13	0.084	0.075	0.068	0.061	0.055	0.050	0.045	0.040	0.037	0.033	13	
14	0.069	0.062	0.055	0.049	0.044	0.039	0.035	0.032	0.028	0.025	14	
15	0.057	0.051	0.045	0.040	0.035	0.031	0.028	0.025	0.022	0.020	15	

Index

Page entries in **bold** refer to terms defined in the Glossary